The Full Package

LOU POWERS

Also by Lou Powers

Discreet Rear Entrance Volume I
Discreet Rear Entrance Volume II

jimmyeyebrow.com

DEDICATION

To you, the reader. Thank you for taking the time to read this latest adventure of Jimmy Eyebrow – Budget Hitman. I hope you have as much enjoyment reading it as I did writing it for you.

My promise to you is that I will always deliver you stories that are an enjoyable, and at times idiotic, escape from the bleak modern world in which we live. No agendas, no moral messages, and no pearl-clutching – just a fun story.

All I ask in return is that if you enjoy the book, tell someone about Jimmy Eyebrow and his crazy band of companions and help spread the word.

Thank you again for your support of Jimmy Eyebrow – it means a lot.

PROLOGUE

The word "hate" does not adequately capture the depth to which Annabelle Longchamp detested her husband, Gabriel. Forty-four years Monsieur Longchamp's junior, Annabelle initially tolerated the pomposity and arrogance that accompanied his traditional Parisian heritage, but it was certainly not love that drove her to him – indeed far from it. In a strategic play as old as time itself, Annabelle had taken up residence in the bedchamber of a much older husband of convenience for one simple reason. One motivating factor above all others. Money. Lots of it.

Gabriel Longchamp was an extraordinarily talented banker who had connections through all levels of society in Europe. However it was in Latin America where his true fortune was ultimately found. To be sure, the contacts throughout the European financial fraternity that he had spent a lifetime cultivating played a significant role in his ultimate success, and it was through these contacts that he was able to parlay his network into a well-oiled money-laundering operation the likes of which the world was unlikely to see again. Among all the money men in the shadowy world of high volume currency movement, Longchamp had no peer, and for his skills he was rewarded very generously by his longtime employer, the Ortiz family.

The Ortiz family oversaw an enormous drug operation in Colombia, and such was Longchamp's longevity that he had served three successive patriarchs of the clan. And it was precisely this longevity that eventually drove Annabelle Longchamp to do what she did. When she had first married

1

Gabriel, he was already a man of advanced years, and she figured that the ultimate payoff upon his inevitable passing would be reward enough for the handful of years spent debasing herself in his cadaverous embrace. But there was one significant flaw in her plan – a problem of significant magnitude given her desired outcome. The problem was that the man simply would not die of his own accord. As such, it fell to Annabelle to try and rectify the issue. A problem it may be, but not insurmountable.

It all seemed quite simple at first – a heart attack during a vigorous lovemaking session would be an easy enough task surely, especially for a man of his age. But regrettably for Annabelle, she was soon to find that her elderly husband had the stamina of a thoroughbred and the libido to match. How a man of his years managed to accomplish what he did, she could not understand. But as the days of being led to the tomb-like bedroom and being unwelcomely ravished by the crypt-keeper began to accumulate, she knew that this course of action was not going to have the intended outcome. Indeed, so repellant was he that there were times when she considered abandoning her long-term plan altogether.

But stick it out she did, by encouraging him to take up all manner of risky sports, including motorcycle racing, cross-country horse riding, and even downhill skiing for a short period. But much to Annabelle's dismay and disgust, not only did Gabriel continuously avoid being zipped into a body bag, but he excelled at all the pursuits that had been suggested to him. The net result of Annabelle's efforts in this regard was eleven trophies, one sprained ankle, a split fingernail, and one episode of Gabriel accidentally soiling himself during a clean-and-jerk in the home gymnasium after Annabelle had changed the labels on his weights. And through it all, including the soiling incident, the unilateral lovemaking continued unabated.

She had tried dropping a gargoyle on his head from atop their château with no success. She had seduced a local criminal to murder Gabriel but was left disappointed when instead, he quite unsurprisingly disappeared with the five thousand Euros that she had provided him as a down payment. In the end, she fell back on the time-honored method of husband-dispatch that had served women since the world's first unhappy marriage, which coincidentally corresponded closely to the advent of marriage itself. Poison – tried and true. Poison would be her mechanism of choice.

History is filled with tales of aggrieved women exacting their revenge via clandestine means, be it insecticide in a drink, or death cap mushrooms in a beef wellington, and Annabelle had now suffered enough – she was going to join the sisterhood and finish the issue once and for all.

But as with everything in this tragic saga, even poisoning did not come without its challenges. First and foremost was the fact that she was going to have to make Gabriel's death appear natural, lest she be identified as the underlying cause of his mortality and subsequently excluded from his estate. The money was, after all, the ultimate goal so it was essential that she keep her eyes on the prize. As such, a slow and steady approach that would mimic a natural death was required. And in situations such as that, women throughout history have turned to one constant – arsenic.

And so began the long and winding path toward arrhythmia, hypotension and Gabriel Longchamp being found on the floor of his bathroom surrounded by copious amounts of vomit. Except, as always, it did not play out like that. Instead, the process dragged on, and on… and on. Despite Annabelle's diligent efforts, Gabriel's demise continued to remain as elusive as ever. Until one day when the two of them boarded a plane bound for a meeting with Alejandro Ortiz, the latest head of the Ortiz empire.

Gabriel was clearly unwell upon taking his seat, but Annabelle assured the first-class concierge that he was simply tired and the rest he would get on the journey to Colombia would be all that was needed to rejuvenate. The time ticked by and then, as the flight entered its ninth hour, it finally happened – years of effort were about to come to fruition. Annabelle had noticed Gabriel's breathing change markedly an hour earlier, but she had said nothing and instead ordered a glass of champagne in anticipation of events to come. As Gabriel now began convulsing, Annabelle nudged him out into the aisle where he slumped to the floor of the cabin.

"Oh no! Won't someone help my husband!" she wailed.

Quick as a flash, a gentleman leapt from a nearby seat and made his way toward the scene. "I'm a doctor," he announced. "Give me some space please."

Jesus, you have GOT to be kidding me, thought Annabelle to herself. *Seriously? Hopefully he's a podiatrist or something, and not a real doctor.*

After a brief examination, the doctor summoned the Purser. "We need to get this man emergency assistance. Please inform the Captain that I recommend we make an emergency landing."

They were still hours from Colombia and Annabelle had no idea where they would choose to make their unscheduled landing to offload her now critically ill husband. She could only hope that if he somehow managed to survive until touchdown, their destination was somewhere where medical incompetence was rife and could play right into her long game that was now nearing its soul-sapping conclusion, many more years later than she had originally anticipated.

CHAPTER 1

The Stinking Benjamins

There is a place in the forest, not far from Coffee Pond, where the red trillium flowers bloom with vigor. A wildflower with a deep crimson coloring, the red trillium also goes by the somewhat unappealing name of Stinking Benjamins, due to their propensity to smell like rotting flesh – a very distinct smell that is the primary means by which the flower attracts an abundance of insects to assist the pollination process. A further, and rather unintended benefit of the aroma is the increase in probability that any historical nefarious activity that may have occurred in the area is duly concealed from the hyper-sensitive nasal receptors of cadaver dogs.

And it was there among the trees, in one heavily fertilized patch of soil, where the remains of Simon Fitzgerald had been disposed, much to the appreciation of the surrounding flora. Fitzgerald was a disreputable investment fund manager who, as time went by, was found to be not so much incompetent or unlucky, but rather a full-blown conman who ripped off his clients while exhibiting the same degree of empathy as an Orca circling a seal on a rapidly disintegrating ice floe. The destruction wrought by Fitzgerald on what are colloquially termed "mum and dad investors" was vast and led to financial ruin for dozens of families who could ill-afford to see their life savings burn on Fitzgerald's altar of narcissistic and obscene personal excess.

One such investor was Jim, a customer at one of Jimmy Eyebrow and Joe Purple's favorite eating establishments - *The Sundancer Inn*. Unbeknown to his wife Jeannie, Jim had invested, and lost, their entire nest-egg with Fitzgerald. And it was precisely Jim's predicament that had sparked Eyebrow's interest in becoming a private-enterprise gun-for-hire, over Joe Purple's violent objections. Hearing of Jim's plight, Eyebrow had approached him with a proposition that was quickly rebuffed, with Jim noting that his desire for a budget hitman was little more than a tongue-in-cheek joke.

But Jim still had not disclosed the gravity of the situation to Jeannie, and once apprised of the magnitude of their loss, along with the means by which their money had been siphoned away, Jeannie took the initiative and demanded that Jim again reach out to the strange man at *The Sundancer*. And so it was that Eyebrow received his first private-enterprise engagement – Jim and Jeannie's last five thousand dollars in exchange for the dispatch of conman supreme, Mr. Simon Fitzgerald.

To think that only one of Fitzgerald's aggrieved clients would be gunning for him though would be folly of the highest order, and even as Eyebrow was discussing the finer points of the contract, Fitzgerald had already been tracked down by another disgruntled client and fed through a wood-chipper in the forest, subsequently providing the local population of Stinking Benjamins with ample sustenance for the looming spring. The perpetrator of this deed either evaporated into the ether or simply chose never to exhibit any outward behavior that would betray their involvement – the result of which led to Jimmy Eyebrow being erroneously credited with the hit, as seemed to happen remarkably frequently in Eyebrow's world.

Eyebrow's moral compass wasn't always adequately calibrated, and on this occasion, he genuinely wrestled with the ethics of taking Jim and Jeannie's money without delivering a service. But on the other hand, he was trying to establish a business. So, in the end, he split the difference – he claimed credit for the purposes of building a reputation for quality service, while at the same time telling Jim and Jeannie to keep their hard-earned money. Ultimately, the money was inconsequential thanks to his poker windfall in Las Vegas. Or if one felt it necessary to split hairs, Conrad St. Claire's poker winnings. But beginning to develop a body of work that he could use as validation was more important at that stage of his enterprise's evolution.

Another aspect of Eyebrow's budding business empire was exactly the reason why Joe Purple now sat directly across from him with a bemused look on his face, struggling to find the right words to express his bewilderment at the development sitting in front of him. Several moments of awkward silence went by before Purple spoke.

"You've outdone yourself this time Eyebrow. Every time I think you can't possibly descend further into retardation, you somehow manage to reset the bar. Business cards? Are you fucking serious Eyebrow? You decided to get business cards printed?"

"It's essential for a new business Joe," replied Eyebrow.

Purple caressed the card that read *Max Von Steel – Budget Hitman* and shook his head gently. "Look, first things first Eyebrow, and I'll give credit where it's due because I'm not a complete arsehole – the pearl finish and spot varnish is a quality piece of work. *But*, and it's a big but in this case… in your line of business I would have thought other things might trump advertising. I don't know, maybe things like… and this is just a suggestion Eyebrow… staying fucking anonymous!"

"I'm not sure what the big deal is here Joe," said Eyebrow mournfully.

"Look, far be it from me to interfere with your business activities, but I think it's a ridiculous idea. Beyond ridiculous in fact. It's like, put ridiculous on a scale and when you get to the end, add another few new spaces." Purple paused in thought, seeking another metaphor to ram the point home. "Somewhere in the world Eyebrow, is the biggest library on the planet. Fuck knows where it is… maybe the Library of Congress, could be one of those university ones… who fucking cares. Point being that in there would be a book about ridiculousness that has the records of the most idiotic things ever done. When you're finished with this idea, they're going to have to put out a new edition because you'll blow everything before you away."

"You don't have to be mean about it Joe," added Eyebrow as he quickly pivoted the conversation to Purple's own business venture that was born after lamenting the lack of quality pizza in the area. "It can't be more ridiculous than you deciding to open a pizza restaurant named Turd's."

"Hey, I can't fucking help that," snapped Purple. "We're fugitives, just in case you'd forgotten, and I can't exactly put my actual name up in neon lights. I didn't ask for that fucking idiotic name, and I'm still pissed about how all of that went down. They screwed me over. You know it and I know it."

"Regardless Joe, it's not a very good name."

"Well, smartarse, as it happens, I might be expanding my workforce soon," said Purple smugly. "Trying out a new young guy tomorrow actually. Maybe you could come by and sit in seeing as you're suddenly the fucking expert on running a pizza shop."

"Jesus Joe, you sound more like Marco every day."

Purple was indeed trying out a new potential employee the following day. But it wasn't due to the success of his shop, which was barely staying afloat week by week. Instead, Purple and an attractive forty-something single mother had fallen into the same orbit around town, most likely not by coincidence on Purple's part, and he was trying to impress her by offering her son a job. Apparently, he had a disability that had impacted his previous job situation but in Purple's experience, disability was certainly no impediment to working in a pizza shop.

Purple examined Eyebrow's business card once more, sliding his fingers along the edges as he did so. "You need to think this through Eyebrow. Can't you just find a job in a fucking shop or something like that? I've got a normal job, why can't you?"

"My skill-set is different Joe," replied Eyebrow.

"Jesus Christ, what fucking skill set?" snapped Purple. "When are you going to get it through that brick you call a skull that you're not a real fucking hitman?"

"We've all got to start somewhere Joe," replied Eyebrow as he stood. "And anyway, you've never been a pizza shop owner before, but you're willing to give it a try. I'm just doing the same."

"Difference being Eyebrow, I'm not planning on killing anyone. Which reminds me… I've left the chicken defrosting on the bench." Purple also stood and began making his way to the door. "Might have to pack this show up and get back to the shop because it's been sitting out since about eight last night. You coming Eyebrow?"

"Sure thing Joe," replied Eyebrow as he followed Purple out the door, destined for Coffee Pond's newest eating establishment – *Turd's Pizza*. As far as everyone in town knew, *Turd's* was run by an unremarkable out-of-towner, with his unusual friend a constant presence in the shop. Minus the mobility scooter, Eyebrow had essentially become Coffee Pond's slimmed down version of Lou the Whale. There was nothing in plain sight to indicate that the two newcomers in the area were a former federal agent who went rogue and a catastrophically inept hitman. And that's how Eyebrow and Purple liked it – off the radar. Because for so long as their blip stayed off the screen, they had barely a care in the world.

CHAPTER 2

Chicken Apocalypse

It was ten the following morning and the undesirably named *Turd's Pizza* was still several hours from opening. But true to his word, Joe Purple, or technically Turd Ferguson, was allowing his lady friend's son to prepare a few pizzas as a trial ahead of potentially securing a job there. Jimmy Eyebrow was also in attendance – after all, it's not like he had much else to do. Coffee Pond was a peaceful and relaxing vacation destination, but once the lure of water activities and nature walks subsided, the place didn't really exude excitement. But it was safe, and far from the public gaze, so it suited Eyebrow and Purple's needs well.

As it turned out, the boy's mother was on point when she highlighted her son's disability. The problem was, Purple had not really enquired further and was therefore unprepared for the actual nature of his affliction.

"*Giant tits!*" came the cry from the preparation area.

Purple sidled up to Eyebrow and leant in to speak. "Jesus Christ, she didn't mention he had fucking Tourette's."

"He's tossing those ingredients around a fair bit too, Joe."

"Fuck, this is going to be a challenge," said Purple before turning toward his young visitor. "How are you finding it Sam?"

"Yeah, I really like it. It's enjoyable… *arsehole!* Sorry Turd - *a turd's a shit!* - that just happens sometimes."

"It's OK buddy, don't worry about it," replied Purple.

"You're surprisingly tolerant today," Eyebrow noted skeptically.

"Means to an end pal, means to an end."

Eyebrow pivoted the conversation to some business he wished to discuss. "Have you got a moment Joe? I wanted to talk to you about something."

"Sure, just a second." Purple turned back to Sam. "You OK to put that in the oven when you're done?"

"Yep. How long for?"

"Do it by sight. Just put it in for now and then give me a few moments here with this defective. I'll come and show you how to check it shortly."

Purple and Eyebrow walked over to the table next to the window. "What do you want to talk about Eyebrow? Another brilliant business plan? Sex doll rental maybe? A chain of female fitness gyms in Afghanistan? International ivory trading perhaps?"

"No, not a new idea Joe. I was just letting you know that I have a meeting tomorrow with a potential client."

"How the fuck did that happen?" snorted Purple.

"I think I came recommended after the crooked investment guy situation," replied Eyebrow.

"*Jizz in a cup!*"

Purple glanced over his shoulder toward the prep area. "Jesus, this is going to take some getting used to. You know what it's like Eyebrow? It's like getting to see what used to be going on inside Rick's brain all the time, except out here in the real world. Anyway, back to the matter at hand – how did you possibly get recommended based on a job you never did?"

"You and I know that Joe, but others think that I did it."

Purple leant back in his chair, tapped out a cigarette and lit it. He inhaled deeply, drawing down what looked like at least a third of the shaft in one go. Pausing, and then exhaling a plume of smoke only marginally less voluminous than a low-yield nuclear weapon, he stared directly at Eyebrow, with a firm look in his eyes. "Can I fucking remind you how that scenario played out last time? Do you actually appreciate the number of times you almost ended up dead because of what people *thought* you did?"

"But I didn't Joe. That's just the nature of the business. Gotta accept the risks."

"Yeah, but I got dragged, against my will might I add, into accepting the risks too you idiot – risks that I never fucking signed on for. Can we please remember that *I'm* the one who ended up on the ground in the fucking desert with a shotgun being emptied into me?"

"*Chicken apocalypse!*"

Purple closed his eyes and muttered to himself. "Jesus, what the fuck is a chicken apocalypse?"

"Probably what you'll end up making with that chicken you left out Joe," replied Eyebrow.

"I should have really tossed that, shouldn't I," noted Purple before breathing deeply and, after a few seconds, returning to the previous matter of discussion. "You know what I am in this relationship Eyebrow? I'm the silent investor. You go off and do whatever the fuck you want, while I somehow end up accepting a disproportionate amount of the risk." Purple dragged on his cigarette again. "What's this job anyway?"

"A woman wants me to take care of her stepbrother. From what it sounds like, there's an estate that needs to be divided up and he's being a prick about it."

"How do you know she's not the one being a prick?" observed Purple.

"I guess I don't," replied Eyebrow. "I'm going to meet her tomorrow morning so maybe I'll get more of an idea then."

"Well, you do that Eyebrow, but as I've told you before, keep me out of it. I might not be a federal agent anymore, but I do have *some* morals. Me just shutting up and letting you go on your merry way is even pushing that boundary. Yet… here we are."

Purple butted out his cigarette, stood and made his way to the preparation area to check on Sam's progress. Opening the oven door, he gazed inside to perform a quality assessment on Sam's work. "What do you think Turd?" asked Sam.

"Tell you the truth buddy, that looks pretty fucking good," replied Purple, reaching for the pizza peel. "Inside the oven, believe it or not, you'll have some spots that are hotter than others." Purple now slipped the peel under the pizza and spun it around. "You need to make sure that you try to give it a spin along the way to get a nice even cook on it." Purple pointed to the pizza's crust. "See that char starting to come up there? Nice job pal… nice job. I might be able to use you around here."

Purple returned to where Eyebrow was sitting and slumped down across from him. "You're really gonna let him cook Joe?" asked Eyebrow.

"*Fart in a handbag!*"

"Jesus no. Can you imagine turning that loose on customers? I'd be bankrupt in a fucking week. But he can do the dough and the cheese for me." Purple twisted a key off his tag and tossed it to Sam. "Heads up buddy!"

"What's this?" asked Sam.

"Key to the place. I'll need you to start turning up at eleven each morning to prep everything for the day. You interested in working here?"

"Fucking fuck fuck yes!" shouted Sam joyously.

Purple wasn't too sure about Sam's response. "Was that an actual answer, or one of those weird fucking things you do?"

"A tic?" replied Sam. "No, it wasn't a tic. I was just excited. *Diarrhea dogshit!* ...OK, that one... yeah, that one was a tic though."

"Can you take some medicine for it or something?" asked Purple.

"Nah, but it's not as bad if I can really concentrate on doing something. It's when my brain activity slows down that it happens the most."

"Jesus, not sure how you'll cope in a fucking pizza shop then," muttered Purple quietly before he turned to Eyebrow. "So, Eyebrow... to this upcoming job of yours. I'm not going to talk you out of it am I?"

"It could be my big break Joe," said Eyebrow.

"Or it could be your fucking downfall."

"I'll stay alert Joe, but I'm OK rolling the dice on it."

Purple tapped out yet another cigarette. "Yeah, well just remember that I want no part of it. Don't be dragging me into your shit-filled blow-up swimming pool again." Purple flicked his cigarette lighter closed and inhaled deeply. "Just promise me one thing Eyebrow."

"What's that Joe?"

"Just... be fucking careful."

CHAPTER 3

Roaring Jack

Jimmy Eyebrow sat alone at a small table outside a café in town, awaiting the meeting with his potential new client. Sipping his hot chocolate, he was soon joined by a well-dressed woman who appeared to be in her early to mid-fifties. Her clothing and jewelry indicated that she was either a woman of financial means, or could at least present a credible façade of being one. "Mister Von Steel I presume," she said as she offered her hand.

Eyebrow stood and reached towards her. "Yes, that's me." Even though the public-facing transition from Jimmy Eyebrow to Max Von Steel had been undertaken some time ago now, Eyebrow still sometimes had trouble fully embracing his new government-issued persona. Not once though did it cross his mind about the displeasure his sponsors would have if they ever found out that he was running a clandestine murder for hire business using the credentials that they had provided him.

"We should go somewhere else," said the woman. "The park across the street. Let's take a walk." This was a sound move on her part – far better to discuss the logistics of murdering someone while on the move than to be sitting within earshot of every other customer at the café. As the two of them crossed the road, Eyebrow remained silent, preferring to allow his potential client to take the lead, which she did momentarily. "You've come highly recommended Mister Von Steel. You did a job for a friend of mine a little while back I believe."

"The investment guy?"

The woman simply nodded her head and continued walking. "I'd like you to consider taking on another job if you have the capacity."

"I'm pretty free at the moment. What are the details?"

"My stepbrother Claudius," she replied dryly before stopping and turning to look directly at Eyebrow. "Such a pathetically grandiose name isn't it. His mummy built him up to be so perfect." The woman held her hands up mockingly. "Oh, my Claudius can do no wrong… God how I had to suffer through that from the moment she and my late father married." The two of them resumed their stroll. "And now, with my father's estate being divided up like a damn birthday cake, I find that darling little Claudius has somehow managed to shoehorn his way in there and virtually cut my sister and I out completely. I trust you understand my frustration here Mister Von Steel?"

"Absolutely," replied Eyebrow. "Would this fix your problem?"

"If by 'fix my problem', you mean getting that pissant out of my life, then yes, my immediate issue will be resolved."

"And you and your sister will be back in the will?"

"That's a bit more complicated, but it would be a good start," the woman replied.

Before they could discuss the situation further, Eyebrow noticed that a derelict had risen from the park bench a little further along the path and was now approaching them with intent. Up until that moment, Eyebrow had not seen any derelicts, bums… vagrants, call them what you will, during his time around the area. But this guy looked disturbingly aggressive, so Eyebrow placed a hand on his companion's arm and suggested that they avoid any confrontation. But as they turned, they ran headlong into two men walking directly behind them.

Momentarily taken aback, Eyebrow was relieved when one of the men produced a badge. "Police," he said succinctly.

"Thank God," replied Eyebrow. "There's a bum just behind us that looks like trouble. Can you help us?"

The police officer looked over Eyebrow's shoulder at the approaching man. "You happy Danny?" he surprisingly asked the bum.

"Yep, I think we're OK," he replied.

Eyebrow was confused about what was going on, but what happened next certainly set the matter straight. "You two are both under arrest for conspiracy to commit murder."

The woman shot a disgusted look directly at Eyebrow. "You set me up?" she bellowed. "You're a goddamn cop?"

"No, I'm not a cop," replied Eyebrow. "You've set *me* up."

"No, I didn't set you up," she retorted before assessing the situation and turning to the officer. "I'm saying nothing until I consult with my lawyer."

"Fine with me," the officer replied. "You're both coming back to the station to be processed, after which you're welcome to call someone. Turn around please, both of you, and put your hands behind your backs." Eyebrow and his companion did as they were told while their rights were being dutifully recited to them, his companion wincing as the handcuffs were applied to her wrists.

As they were both being marched towards separate vehicles, Eyebrow's mind raced. This was not good – in fact this was the very embodiment of the concept of "not good," even bordering on "catastrophic". As they made their way to the police station, Eyebrow pondered how he could get out of the situation. Maybe their case was flimsy? Maybe it would fall apart under the lack of credible evidence? That idea was dashed within minutes of initial processing commencing.

With his pockets emptied, the duty sergeant summoned the detective who had confronted Eyebrow in the park. A brief discussion ensued before the detective made his way to Eyebrow. "Care to explain this?" he said, never taking his eyes off Eyebrow as he slid a business card across the table. Eyebrow glanced down to see *Max Von Steel – Budget Hitman* staring directly back at him. His heart sank – Joe Purple had been correct about it being a ridiculous idea. And now Eyebrow was going to have to pay the price.

"Can I call someone please?" asked Eyebrow meekly.

"When we're finished processing you, yes," replied the detective.

A short time later, with the initial administration complete and his ill-fitting jail issue footwear causing him to walk with little more than a shuffle, Eyebrow made his way to the telephone to dial the number for *Turd's Pizza*. Naturally he wasn't ordering a meal – that was the furthest thing from his mind at that point in time. But Joe Purple was his only friend, so it was in Purple where Eyebrow sought salvation.

The first time Eyebrow dialed, the call rang out. "Can I try again?" he asked the officer next to him.

"Sure, go ahead."

Eyebrow dialed again and waited. After what seemed an eternity, the call was answered. "We're not open yet," came Purple's voice abruptly from the other end.

"Joe, it's me," said Eyebrow frantically. "I'm in trouble."

"Are you locked in a fucking toilet cubicle again Eyebrow?"

"No, Joe. It's serious. I'm in jail."

"What the fuck! How did that happen?"

"My meeting this morning didn't end well."

"Ahh, Jesus Christ Eyebrow. Question here – what did you end up doing with your business cards? Tell me you didn't have them on you. Please, for the love of God tell me that you weren't carrying them."

"I had one on me Joe. It was a business meeting," replied Eyebrow.

"I'm not sure I'm gonna be able to help you here pal."

"Can you come and get me out?" pleaded Eyebrow.

"How the fuck do you suggest I do that? What are you being charged with?"

"Conspiracy to commit murder, or something like that."

"Fuck me Eyebrow. I can't help you here, I'm sorry. You're gonna need a big-ticket lawyer to get yourself out of this one. And when I say big-ticket, I mean... like... OJ Simpson's fucking lawyer or something."

"So, you can't help me, Joe?" replied Eyebrow mournfully.

Eyebrow could hear Purple draw breath on the other end of the line. "Jesus... leave it with me Eyebrow. I can't get you out, but I'll call around and see if I can find you a good lawyer. It's gonna fucking cost you though, you know that right?"

"That's OK Joe, I can cover it. Thanks for your help."

"Remember when I said that no matter how hard I try not to get involved, you always seem to drag me along into the chaos you create? Well... here we are again, aren't we. Fuck me Eyebrow. Word of advice here – you say nothing more to anyone until I find you a lawyer, got it?"

"Got it Joe. Thanks."

As Eyebrow was being escorted back to his holding cell, a tall, sharply dressed man strode purposefully into the station and made a beeline directly for the duty sergeant. "I'm here to see my client," he announced firmly.

Jesus Joe, that was quick, thought Eyebrow to himself. "Over here," said Eyebrow, waving at the man.

The man looked at Eyebrow dismissively while the officer at Eyebrow's side placed a hand on his back and directed him toward his cell. "He's not your lawyer you fucking moron." The officer motioned towards Eyebrow's once potential client who was sitting in a neighboring holding cell. "He's hers." The officer ushered Eyebrow into the cell he was sharing with a sleeping drunk. "You can cool your heels in here."

"Do I have to be in here with this guy?" asked Eyebrow pleadingly. "I think he's shit himself."

The officer smirked. "Let me check with the concierge sir. Maybe we can find you a suite that's available."

The suite life – how Eyebrow now yearned for the days where he was lounging in luxury at the *Imperial Palace*, or the *Bellagio*. What he'd give for a nice seafood buffet at that point. He closed his eyes and bemoaned his life choices. He'd been handed a golden opportunity for a new life in the idyllic surrounds of Coffee Pond and he'd completely blown it. He had been offered the keys to the kingdom, and he'd slapped them away with his fateful decision to enter private enterprise.

Joe Purple's advice to forego his idiotic idea now held a lot more weight than Eyebrow had originally given it, and he wished that he had heeded Purple's guidance. Like a man facing the gallows who suddenly becomes born-again, Eyebrow vowed that if he could get out of this situation, he'd turn over a new leaf and commit to it.

Eyebrow was wondering how long it might take Joe Purple to secure legal representation for him, when he noticed some activity around the duty sergeant's desk. The detectives who had arrested Eyebrow had been summoned to the desk and several of them now huddled around a computer monitor. The senior detective pointed to something on the monitor, at which point they all raised their eyes and looked directly at Eyebrow. *What the fuck's happening?* thought Eyebrow as he watched on.

The detective stalked towards Eyebrow's holding cell and opened the door. He made to speak before clamping his hand over his nose, his voice muffled beneath his hand. "Jesus, what's happened in here?"

Eyebrow pointed at his cellmate. "That guy's shit himself, I'm pretty sure of it."

"Fuck me," replied the detective as he grabbed Eyebrow by the arm. "Come out into the office with me. I can't talk to you in here, it fucking stinks." He turned to his uniformed colleagues and pointed to the cell. "Can we get that guy cleaned up in there? Someone? Anyone? Like, now!"

He then directed his attention back to Eyebrow, stooping slightly to look him directly in the eye. At least that's what Eyebrow suspected the intention was, but the ultimate result was somewhat comical given that the detective had a lazy eye of reasonably significant note. As he stood there, one eye was definitely pointed toward him, but Eyebrow had no idea whether that was the eye under control, or its wandering counterpart.

"Who the fuck are you?" he asked firmly.

Eyebrow quickly glanced to the side to ensure that he was the only one there. Satisfied that the detective was in fact speaking to him, he offered a simple response. "You have my details."

"Yeah, I have the name you've given me. But the question I want answered is, *who are you*, really?" The detective stared angrily at Eyebrow awaiting an answer.

"I'm not sure what you mean," said Eyebrow meekly.

The detective straightened and drew breath. "We're playing that game, are we? OK then, let me tell you what happened when we pumped your details into the system, and we'll see if that jogs your memory." Eyebrow now had a sneaking suspicion that he might know where this conversation was headed. "So, we punch your name into the database over there, and suddenly, we have a bunch of noises and flashing lights going off. It looks like a fucking rave over there at the moment."

Eyebrow sensed that he might be able to leverage the situation to his advantage. "Does that mean I can go?" he asked, optimistically. His glimmer of hope, however, was soon to be dashed.

"Oh, absolutely not sunshine," said the detective with a chuckle. "You're staying right here for now. Apparently, we have to babysit you while we get in touch with some emergency contact that's listed on your file."

"I don't know what you mean," replied Eyebrow.

"Whatever pal," the detective retorted. "Something's up with you. I've never seen a goddamn record like yours before. We've even got a code phrase that we have to give to whoever the fuck answers the number we've gotta call. That's not normal. Something's going on here."

Eyebrow was understandably curious. "What's the code phrase?"

The detective stared at him sternly, or at least as sternly as his affliction would allow. "Roaring Jack."

CHAPTER 4

Emergency Contact No. 2

The crime stats told the story – the homicide rate in the city was significantly lower since Jimmy Eyebrow had been taken off the streets. And even though the two variables were most likely unrelated and nothing more than pure coincidence, it didn't stop Detective Leo Bishop from ensuring that the point was adequately hammered home when discussing his recent body of work during his annual pay review.

However, with no murders reported in excess of eight weeks now, and most every open investigation cleared from the books, the question that the department now grappled with was what to do with their idle squad of homicide detectives. Which is why, after their adrenaline-fueled escapade in Las Vegas, Leo Bishop and Ike McFadden, now bereft of meaningful duties, found themselves assigned to mopping up the multitude of petty crimes that were still at a high-water mark – the decline in murders not being replicated across other forms of lawbreaking.

Sitting across the table from them on this day was a middle-aged birthday party performer, reeking of cigarette smoke and alcohol, and dressed in a bedraggled clown outfit. He had been arrested for exposing himself at a birthday party earlier in the day, and given that Bishop and McFadden were currently assigned to the cases that were either the most unremarkable or least desirable, it had fallen to them, under protest, to conduct the interview.

From leading a multi-jurisdictional taskforce that brought down a *Who's Who* of international crime, to now questioning inebriated sexual degenerates – how fortunes can turn on the head of a pin. Bishop, visibly frustrated, was leading the questioning. "I'm just having a little trouble here Klaus, in understanding how it accidently popped out, as you're claiming."

"I swear detective, it was an accident. Look, I need to show you something," said Krazy Klaus the clown as he stood. "These fucking pants, look at the size of 'em. There's a gap that's supposed to be on the back because I do this gag where I bend over, and it looks like I've ripped my pants, and everyone can see my jocks. But I put the fucking things on backwards today." Klaus pointed towards his crotch. "See?"

"Jesus Christ, Klaus, I don't need to see that," replied Bishop. "I could probably buy that excuse, if you were actually wearing underwear. I'm just having a tough time believing that not only did you manage to put your pants on backwards, but you also forgot to put on your underwear as well."

McFadden added an observation. "AND, it's the third time that it's happened in the past six weeks apparently."

Klaus sat down again and threw his hands up. "Look, I admit that maybe I like a drink from time to time."

"I wouldn't have guessed that," remarked Bishop snidely before Klaus continued.

"And maybe my judgement was a bit clouded when I was getting ready to perform."

"But *three* times, Klaus," said Bishop. "If you can't dress yourself properly then you need to get into a different line of business. Flopping the tackle out at birthday parties is completely unacceptable."

"You can't be doing that shit," added McFadden.

"I'll be fucking ruined if I'm not allowed to do parties," pleaded Klaus. "It's my livelihood."

"Well, maybe you should have considered that before embarking on this perverted journey of exhibitionism," replied Bishop. "You're a menace."

Klaus was preparing to continue pleading his case for leniency when Dennis Burnett knocked on the door and made his way into the interview room. "Gentlemen, can I see you outside for a moment? Leave the clown in here for the time being."

Bishop and McFadden made their way into the hallway outside the office. "What's up Dennis?" asked Bishop.

"We've got a situation that's arisen," replied Burnett.

"Don't tell me there's a goddamn magician as well," said Bishop. "Have we uncovered a clandestine ring of performing perverts?"

"Leo, please. This is serious," replied Burnett.

Bishop sensed that Burnett was indeed carrying news of some magnitude. "Sorry Dennis. What's the situation?"

"It's Eyebrow."

"Ahh, fuck me. There's a name I was hoping to never hear again. What's happened?"

"You know how when you fill out a form for HR, you need to list some emergency contacts? Well, it was the same when Eyebrow and Purple went into the relocation program. The feds were the primary contact point if something went awry, but because of our involvement, we were listed as the emergency contact if the feds couldn't be contacted. There's a code phrase and all – real James Bond shit."

Bishop sensed where the conversation was headed. "Jesus Christ, what's going on?"

McFadden likewise had by now also formed a reasonably sound hypothesis as to what was transpiring. "You've been contacted, haven't you Dennis."

"That I have. It would seem that Eyebrow's been arrested, and when they punched his name into the booking system, apparently the screen lit up like the fucking nuke scene in Oppenheimer. The first point of contact was Black and Dekker, but neither of them are available. The feds wouldn't give the local police any further information, just that they weren't available. Away on secret government business by the sound of it. So, the next port of call was… us."

"Fuck me, what's he done?" asked Bishop.

"Apparently, he's set up his own murder-for-hire business. They nabbed him negotiating a job with a potential client."

"Are you fucking kidding me! I thought it'd be something in the same general category as that fucking clown in the interview room, but not a full-blown felony."

"What the fuck was he thinking?" added McFadden.

"No clue whatsoever," replied Burnett. "But according to the agreement that the department signed with the feds, we now have to render whatever assistance we can in the matter."

"What exactly does that entail, Dennis?" asked Bishop skeptically.

Burnett paused momentarily and inhaled deeply as he considered what he knew the next course of action needed to be, as well as the associated grief that would undoubtedly come with it. "It means that you two need to go home and pack your bags again, because you're off on another road trip."

CHAPTER 5

The Nine Cent Nightmare

Leo Bishop and Ike McFadden's hastily organized trip back to Coffee Pond was not without its teething problems. Having already annihilated the annual budget thanks to the Las Vegas experience, Dennis Burnett's approach to the Finance branch for another out-of-town trip was met with disdain at the perceived extravagance of the Homicide operations. The Finance branch after all was staffed by civilians, not serving officers, and as such, dealt in pure numbers at the expense of operational reality. The chief antagonist for Burnett was the head of the branch, Keith Neville, who had long been held in contempt by Burnett by virtue of the fact that not only was he named Keith, but also that he had a first name as a surname – something that had always irked Burnett.

Neville was his usual abrasive self on this day. "I can't approve this Dennis. You're already significantly over-budget after that Las Vegas holiday your two detectives went on."

Burnett fired back. "Well first of all *Keith*, it wasn't a fucking holiday."

Neville cut Burnett short. "There's no need for profanity detective. I have an important job to do here, and I don't appreciate your tone."

Burnett continued, undeterred. "And secondly, it isn't up to you to decide whether something's approved or not. It's already been approved by Bernie so I just need you to free up the funds for me to access."

"By 'Bernie', I presume you mean Captain Bernard. And yes, I have the requisition here. But the R26 form that he submitted doesn't have sufficient detail as to the intended purpose of the funds."

"That's not an operational matter you need to know," replied Burnett.

"Well, be that as it may…" began Neville, before being cut off abruptly by Burnett.

"Keith, I don't have fucking time for this. I need that money released today, or so help me God, I'm going to deliberately fuck up every month-end reconciliation that I do by nine cents, from now until I retire. And I will then leave you to have to find out where I made the mistake."

Neville shifted uncomfortably. "We can write off nine cents."

"You can, I know that. But you wouldn't, would you Keith… it'd burn away inside you like a coal seam fire that you just can't put out. You'd wake up with night sweats trying to work out where the error is. Is that what you want your future to be Keith? Every month? The same recurring nightmare?"

"I'd prefer not," replied Neville succinctly.

"So, what's going to happen here?"

"Look, under the circumstances, I can accept 'operational matters' as the purpose, even though it's rather vague. I will however be recommending that you attend the next fiscal responsibility training course that's being run."

"If that's what it takes to get the money released Keith, then I will be there with great enthusiasm."

"The mockery of a highly valuable training initiative is unnecessary detective," replied Neville as he began keying in the necessary codes that would allow Burnett access to the contingency funds he needed for the unexpected Jimmy Eyebrow development.

And now, with the administrative aspect tied off back home, Bishop and McFadden found themselves seated across the desk from Detective William Egan who had first alerted Burnett to the unfolding situation that was contained, for now at least, within holding cell number two. Bishop and McFadden were both weary from their travel but had made their way to the small police station as a matter of priority after their arrival in town, their roll-along luggage stowed for now at the edge of Egan's desk.

After formalities were completed, Egan cut to the chase, enquiring as to what was going on with his star resident. Silence ensued as neither Bishop nor McFadden were aware of which one of the two of them Egan had directed the question to, as he had one eye trained on each man – a situation that was as unusual as it was unnerving. Bishop eventually plucked up the courage to begin the briefing, which resulted in Egan shifting his head slightly in his direction, although McFadden still remained marginally, and disconcertingly, within Egan's peripheral gaze.

"The man you're holding at the moment, Mister Von Steel, is, shall we say, a friend of the department. And we're under an obligation to assist him should he find himself in a situation, such as the one he's stumbled into here."

"This guy didn't stumble into jack shit," retorted Egan. "We've got him dead to rights. He was even carrying these." Egan slid one of Eyebrow's business cards across the desk to Bishop.

Bishop looked at the card and muttered to himself. "Fuck me…" He handed the card to McFadden before addressing Egan once more. "I'm sure there's a logical explanation for this. Maybe the cards are just a gag or something?"

"Even if they were, we have him discussing the business of a hit with a client, so he's not getting out of this."

"So are you still holding the other guy as well?" asked Bishop.

"It was a woman," replied Egan. "And no, her lawyer sprung her not long after we brought them both in. I couldn't let your guy go though."

"Well you can let him go now that we're here."

"Oh, I know that I can let him go, detective. Your boss and I have already spoken briefly."

"Excellent then. We'll go and have a chat with him and then we'll be on our way."

Egan smiled – the type of grin that, from history, both Bishop and McFadden knew meant that they were about to receive news that neither man expected. "I'm sorry to say gentlemen, but you won't be on your way anywhere. At least not anywhere out of town. We'll be releasing Mister Von Steel, but it'll be into your custody until his trial."

"His trial?" replied Bishop, surprised.

Egan leant back in his chair, increasing the already pronounced angle between his divergent lines of sight. "You don't think he's just being released without charge, do you? This is a criminal we're talking about. He's *going* to be standing trial. And you two are going to be babysitting him until then."

"I'm sorry?" said Bishop.

"Oh, Burnett didn't tell you?"

Bishop and McFadden exchanged bemused glances with one other. "Tell us what?" asked Bishop.

"You two are staying right here in town to look after him. There's some heavy shit going on in the background, I can tell. So, if he's being released at your request, then you're responsible for making sure that he doesn't vanish ahead of his trial. This guy has precisely zero roots in this town – it's like he just appeared out of thin air. If ever there was a walking definition of flight risk, this guy is it. So… you're going to make sure that doesn't happen."

Bishop shot a look at McFadden. "Did Dennis mention anything about this to you, Mac?"

"Nothing Leo." McFadden turned to Egan. "Are you sure there hasn't been a mistake?"

"Absolutely certain. You can check with your boss if you want, but we've already got you a couple of rooms at a nice local motel, so you may as well make yourselves comfortable."

"I can't fucking believe this," sighed Bishop. "I'll talk to Dennis shortly. In the meantime, we need to speak with Eye…" Bishop quickly corrected himself. "…Von Steel."

"Be my guest," said Egan as he tossed the holding cell keys to Bishop. "I'll get the paperwork ready while you're doing that."

Bishop and McFadden took the short walk to where Eyebrow was being held. As they approached, Eyebrow looked up, his face breaking out into a huge smile once he saw them. "Detective Bishop!" he exclaimed with glee while bounding toward them. "What are you doing here?"

Bishop opened the cell door. "Well might we ask you the same question, Eyebrow. What the fuck have you done here?"

"I made a mistake detective. A terrible, terrible mistake. I'm sorry."

"Well, sorry isn't going to be enough for this one. What the fuck were you thinking?"

"I wasn't thinking. I understand that now."

"Too right you weren't thinking." Bishop produced the card that Egan had given him earlier. "Business cards? Are you fucking serious?"

"That's what Joe said too," replied Eyebrow sadly. "He thought it was a bad idea as well."

"Wait, he knew about this?" asked McFadden.

"He didn't play a part in any of it," replied Eyebrow defensively. "He told me that he wasn't going to support what I was doing, so this is all on me. Joe's clean."

"Where is he now?" asked Bishop.

Eyebrow glanced at the clock in the booking area. "Probably at his pizza shop."

Bishop paused in silence momentarily before gesturing to McFadden. "Can I see you out here for a moment Mac?" Bishop made his way out into the office, while at the same time advising Eyebrow to remain where he was until called for. "Can you believe this shit Mac? How the fuck did we end up with this job? Where the hell's Black… or Dekker?"

"Couldn't tell you, Leo. But it looks like we're stuck here. What's our plan of attack do you think?"

"We don't have a lot of choice by the sound of it. I guess we'll just have to spring Eyebrow, go and grab Purple as well, and then take them back out to the lake for a briefing. We'll have to speak with Dennis to get the whole picture. Jesus, I can't believe he just dropped us in the shit like this."

"Would you have made a scene if he'd told us before we came out here?" asked McFadden.

"Chances are high."

McFadden raised his eyebrows and shrugged in response. "I'd say he probably made a wise business decision then."

Bishop rubbed his eyes, the realization now dawning that Eyebrow was back in his life. He walked back to Eyebrow's cell – slowly, subconsciously hoping to prolong the inevitable, even if it was just by a few seconds. He looked at Eyebrow and breathed heavily – not once, but two deep sighs. "Get up, you're coming with us."

Eyebrow leapt to his feet and hastily made his way to the door. "Yes!" he exclaimed. "We're getting the band back together."

Bishop groaned at the thought. If Eyebrow insisted on using a band analogy though, Bishop hoped that maybe, possibly, there would be some cohesion, stability and professionalism to their forthcoming time together, much like U2 had maintained for their entire career. But deep down inside, he feared, with justification, that things may end up much more like an Oasis tour.

CHAPTER 6
Old Glory

To complete the quartet, Bishop and McFadden, with Eyebrow in the back seat, had swung by *Turd's Pizza* for a surprise visit to Joe Purple. He was prepping the shop for opening at the time of their arrival and was, as expected, aggrieved that Bishop and McFadden were demanding that he abandon the day's plans and instead accompany them, along with Eyebrow, back to Coffee Pond for a briefing on the current situation.

Bishop, McFadden and Purple now sat on the deck of Purple's cottage while Eyebrow, seemingly oblivious to the gravity of the matter at hand, had opted for a quick dip in the lake. Bishop took the opportunity to discuss the Eyebrow situation directly with Purple. "Why didn't you do something?" he asked.

"What the fuck was I supposed to do?" replied Purple. "I'm not his fucking keeper. I told him that he shouldn't be doing that shit, but he wouldn't listen. What did you want me to do? Lock him up in a fucking basement somewhere? He's his own man – I can only offer guidance."

"You're supposedly the responsible one though," pushed Bishop.

"Yeah, I *am* fucking responsible. That's why I've got myself a job and started my own business. I might be responsible, but not for him. In case you hadn't noticed, I'm not on the payroll anymore. That fucking moron is NOT my responsibility. Nowhere did I sign up for that."

"But as his friend…" started Bishop, before Purple quickly cut him short.

"Whoa, hold up there buddy! We're not *friends*. We're very loose acquaintances who happen to be in the witness relocation program together and living in neighboring houses. That's all. I hold my standards a bit fucking higher than that."

"I don't know, Leo," added McFadden with a smile. "I detect a distinct Bert and Ernie thing going on here."

"I agree Mac. Best buds I'd say."

"Fuck off," replied Purple sharply. "I admit, I may have the tiniest soft spot for him after what we've been through together, but he's hardly best man material."

"Well regardless, we're going to need your assistance," said Bishop before pausing in disbelief as Eyebrow climbed from the water and sauntered toward them like a Sean Connery-era James Bond. "Jesus Christ Eyebrow!" he exclaimed, pointing at the crotch-hugging swimmers that Eyebrow was sporting – swimmers that looked like they were made from an American flag. "What the fuck are those?"

"These? I got them from a shop that was having a Fourth of July promotion. They're awesome right?" Eyebrow accompanied his words with a quick twirl, revealing that the stars and stripes encircled the entire outfit – what there was of it at least.

Bishop looked less than impressed. "Not sure 'awesome' is the correct word usage there, Eyebrow."

"I almost poked my eyes out with a fucking fork the first time I looked out the window and saw him prancing around in those," added Purple. He turned his attention to Eyebrow. "I fucking told you Eyebrow that they were too over the top."

Bishop threw Eyebrow a towel. "For Christ sake, cover up and come sit with us for a few minutes. We need to discuss business." Bishop waited until Eyebrow was seated before addressing both he and Purple. "I need to impress on you the seriousness of this situation Eyebrow. I've managed to get hold of Black and he's not happy."

"Great," muttered Purple with a sigh. "Is he coming here to lecture us?"

"I wish he was," replied Bishop. "But unfortunately, because Mac and I are already here, everyone further up the food chain feels that it's best for us to stay here babysitting the two of you while they try to work out how to resolve the matter."

"Hey, I didn't do a fucking thing here!" argued Purple.

"Exactly. You didn't do anything to nip this in the bud before it could escalate, even though you saw it coming from a mile away."

Purple was clearly annoyed at his vicarious involvement in something that was entirely Eyebrow's doing. "When did that become my job? If I lived next to an asylum, you wouldn't expect me to be responsible for the lunatics inside. So how come this Bedlamite's actions blow back onto me?"

"I'm afraid, given the unusual circumstances of what happened, you two are joined at the hip."

Purple winced at this analogy, triggered by the memory of an almost identical conversation all that time ago at Honest Dom's estate following the Ray DeVecchio fiasco. He sighed and closed his eyes. *Fuck me, how did we get back to this point.* "So, what's next?" he asked Bishop. "Are we relocating again?"

"No, exactly the opposite. You'll be parking yourselves right here, keeping your heads down, and staying away from any sort of activity that's likely to get you thrown into jail again."

"Can I still work in the shop?"

"Yes, that's fine. But the two of you aren't to leave town. As much as it irks me, you're now our responsibility, God help us."

"Where are you staying?" asked Eyebrow. "I can fix up the guest room if you'd like."

"There won't be any need for that," replied Bishop. "We're staying at a motel in town." Bishop slid a flyer that Egan had given him across the table to Purple. "That's the place there. So, what's going to happen from this point is that each day at ten am, the two of you are going to report in with us at this motel. You'll physically present yourselves – both of you. No phone-ins or sick notes. Each day, at ten am, you will be there so we can ensure that you're still in town."

"Do we have to come together?" asked Purple.

"Couldn't care less about how each of you gets there. Together… alone… at the head of a fucking marching band, I really don't give a shit. The only thing that matters is that you both show your faces at ten o'clock each day."

"Do you know how long it'll be before we know what's happening with me?" asked Eyebrow.

"No idea," replied Bishop.

"I'm trying to get him a lawyer," added Purple.

"No need for that," said Bishop. "The feds are trying to work something out on that front."

Purple looked relieved. "Good, because the only one I could find in this town was a fucking probate lawyer. Don't know how much use he'd be."

Bishop stood and adopted a serious tone. "I need to know something. I need to know, honestly, if either of you are planning on running." He shifted his gaze to settle on Purple. "Because there's history here."

"Hey, I've got nothing to run from," snapped Purple. "I've done precisely zero illegal shit here."

Bishop looked at Eyebrow. "What about you?"

"I'm not going anywhere. I'm very happy, right here."

"Well, short of handcuffing the two of you to us, which is something that I find remarkably unappealing, I guess we're going to have to accept those rock-solid guarantees of yours." Bishop turned to McFadden. "Anything to add Mac?"

"All good here Leo," he replied as he stood, taking the cue that the day's formalities were at a close.

"OK then. Mac and I will retire to our two-star resort next to the carwash, while you two delinquents can just stay here in your nice little taxpayer funded accommodation right on the waterfront. That sounds fair, right Mac?"

"Yeah, sounds equitable," replied McFadden sarcastically.

"We'd better be seeing both of you tomorrow," said Bishop firmly. "Ten am… got it?"

"Yes," replied Purple.

"Got it," added Eyebrow.

Bishop and McFadden's formal duties for the day were now complete and they could make their way back into town, grab some dinner and settle in for the night at *Lucky's Motel*. From the time that the arrest of Max Von Steel triggered the alarm bells that led to their hastily organized journey to Coffee Pond, they hadn't had much time to decompress. As such, the idea of a hot shower and a soft bed certainly had its appeal, even if the motel had little else to offer.

But as was often the case when it came to anything concerning Jimmy Eyebrow, trouble was looming. Because at the same time as Von Steel's arrest had notified Bishop and McFadden of Eyebrow's predicament, it had also alerted someone else to his location.

CHAPTER 7

Ten am

Lucky's Motel – Bishop and McFadden's new home away from home – was a classic drive-up configuration, with a double-level layout bracketing the large central parking area. The motel was designed with a transient clientele in mind and as such, there was little in the way of meeting facilities, save for a small sitting area off the side of the reception desk where the lobby's arrangement of brochures advertised the area's range of tourist attractions. After a surprisingly comfortable night of rest, Bishop now begrudgingly gazed periodically at his watch, waiting for the ten am hour to approach. Given that his pending meeting with Jimmy Eyebrow and Joe Purple that morning had minimal formality associated with it, he chose simply to wait outside his room, coffee in hand, for the first of their daily check-ins.

On this day, Eyebrow and Purple arrived together, not at the scheduled ten am, but at nine forty-five. As they entered the carpark, Bishop raised his coffee mug and beckoned them over toward his room. "You're early, well done," he said as they emerged from their vehicle.

"Let's get this over and done with," said Joe Purple. "Let us sign whatever we have to, and we'll be on our way."

"Oh, there's nothing to sign," replied Bishop. "No formalities. I've seen you now so you're free to go."

"Are you shitting me?" snapped Purple. "That's all there is to it?"

"Just need to ensure that you're still in town."

Purple remained displeased at being tarred with the same brush as Eyebrow. "I still don't know why I need to be here. I haven't done a fucking thing wrong. Why do I have to check in along with him?"

Bishop took a sip of coffee before answering. "I'm just following orders. Apparently, you two are a package deal."

"Well next time you speak with Harry, let him know that I think it's bullshit."

"Hey, I don't like it any more than you do. You think I want to be here doing this entry-level task? You know what jobs we have to do from the moment you drive out of here today until you come back at ten tomorrow morning? Nothing... not a fucking thing. We are here solely to make sure, each morning, that you two haven't skipped town. We have precisely five minutes of work each day, and then we'll just watch daytime TV and read a magazine. Maybe do a bit of sightseeing, but that'll be on our own dime because the department's blown the budget thanks to your Vegas extravaganza. Guess how much we get for meal allowance each day... care to have a stab?" Bishop looked toward Purple, awaiting a response.

"I have no idea," replied Purple.

"No, please... just have a guess," pushed Bishop.

"I don't know... a hundred bucks?"

"A hundred bucks!" Bishop laughed heartily at Purple's estimate. "We get thirty bucks, that's it. You know what I had for breakfast this morning? A fucking two-day-old, glazed donut from the lobby. That's the limit of the breakfast buffet here." Purple now understood that he was playing the role of sounding board for Bishop's frustrations, and there was more to come. "You know what the worst part is? That we don't even know how fucking long we're going to be doing this for. We could be here for a few days, or it could be months... no-one can tell us. The local police and the feds need to work this out, and all the while, we're stuck in the middle of it."

"Months?" enquired Eyebrow.

"Yes," said Bishop. "It's still early days so we have no idea what's happening. This is all being dealt with higher up the totem pole, and Mac and I are just the pawns at the bottom. So, we might be doing this for a while. Anyway, I've fulfilled my obligation for today, as have you, so you can be on your way. I'll see you here again tomorrow." Bishop turned, walked back into his room, and closed the door behind him, leaving Eyebrow and Purple to begin their day.

Like most days, Eyebrow had no commitments, so he accompanied Purple along to *Turd's* to help him set up. Purple directed Eyebrow to the kitchen area. "You know how to make dough, right Eyebrow?"

"Sure thing Joe," he replied.

"Marco never used sugar, but I put it in mine. Make sure you add sugar."

"You got it," said Eyebrow.

The two of them hadn't been underway for long before a knock at the front door demanded their attention. Purple turned to see a small wiry man beckoning him towards the door. "We're not open yet!" yelled Purple. The man was persistent, continuing to wave Purple towards him. "Fuck me," muttered Purple. "This better not be the fucking health inspector. I don't have time for that shit today."

Purple walked to the front of the store and eased the door slightly ajar, repeating his earlier advice to the man. "We're not open yet pal."

The man forced his way through the door and came directly to the point. "I'm looking for Max Von Steel. Is he here?"

"No idea who that is…" began Purple, before Eyebrow interrupted the conversation from behind the counter.

"I'm Max Von Steel," he announced enthusiastically. Purple turned and shot Eyebrow an angry glare – something from the "shut the fuck up" category.

With Purple's gaze directed elsewhere, the man barged forward and reached inside his jacket. "Then that means that you're Jimmy Eyebrow," he said as he made a beeline towards him.

"Get the fuck down Eyebrow!" yelled Purple as he rushed towards the man, bringing him down to the wooden floor with a relatively well-executed crash tackle. Purple quickly sunk his knee into the man's back and secured his arms, drawing an angry retort from below.

"For Christ sake, get off me!" he yelled. "I'm just trying to deliver a message." The man motioned with his eyes towards his hand. It was not brandishing a gun, as Purple had expected, but rather a plain white envelope.

"How the fuck did you know about Eyebrow?" snarled Purple, still maintaining his tight grip on the man's arms.

"Just read the letter," he answered.

"You're not a debt collector, are you?" asked Eyebrow. "Because if you are, you're the most relentless one I've ever met."

"No, I'm not a fucking debt collector," the frustrated man replied. "Just… read the letter."

Purple snatched the letter from the man's hand and passed it to Eyebrow, never allowing the man the opportunity to rise. Eyebrow moved to a booth, tore open the envelope and read.

My Dearest Jimmy,

Please excuse this unorthodox method of communication. I expect that the gentleman who delivered this note to you is currently being held at gunpoint or similar – rest assured, he means you no harm. His name is Carl by the way.

Jimmy, I have a request of you, if you would entertain an old man's thoughts. I have a task that I would like you to consider, although I understand if you have chosen to leave this life behind. I trust you Jimmy Eyebrow, hence my outreach. I would not ask you if I had anyone else available to me who was half as trustworthy.

Carl has all the details if you wish to know more. If not, please send Carl on his way and we will consider our relationship closed. If that is the path you wish to take, I will look back on our brief friendship with great fondness.

Your old friend.

Esteban.

Eyebrow's face was beaming as he finished the letter. "It's from Esteban! Joe, let this guy up. He's a friend of Esteban."

Purple didn't respond, instead barking at the man. "How the fuck did Gutierrez know where to find Eyebrow?"

"No idea. I just know that he knows a lot of stuff. He has people everywhere. He can find shit out when he needs to."

Purple glared at Eyebrow. "It's that fucking arrest of yours. I bet it set alarms bells ringing everywhere. For fuck sake, if you've been tracked then I probably have too."

Eyebrow directed his attention to the man on the floor. "What's your name?"

"Carl," replied the man.

"That's what Esteban says in the letter, Joe. This guy's legit. Let him up."

"You sure about this Eyebrow?" asked Purple.

"It's all good Joe, let him up."

Purple looked at Eyebrow with a hint of skepticism. "OK, then, but it's on your head." Purple directed his attention to Carl as he stood. "I'll be watching you pal."

"Let's sit," said Carl as he walked over to a booth, shaking his arms and stretching out his back along the way. Once the two of them were seated, with Purple hovering close by, Carl expanded upon Esteban Gutierrez's brief note. "Mister Gutierrez has a job that he wants you to consider doing."

"He mentioned that in the letter," said Eyebrow. "What's the job?"

Purple swiftly interjected. "You're not actually considering this, are you Eyebrow? Seriously? You're on fucking bail for a murder conspiracy charge and you haven't snuffed this request out in the first two seconds of it being mentioned? For Christ sake, think Eyebrow… think."

Carl turned to Purple. "This is a low-risk proposition. No guns, no killing." Carl looked back toward Eyebrow. "Are you two a partnership? Why am I talking to him anyway?"

The implications of recently failing, on multiple occasions, to heed Joe Purple's advice still resonated strongly with Eyebrow, and he was determined not to freeze Purple out this time. "I trust Joe's advice, Carl. If it's not a hit job, then what sort of job is it?"

"It's more of an investigation job… information gathering, that's it. Mister Gutierrez has a close associate who needs help, and he suggested that you're someone he trusts to do the job. Mister Gutierrez's associate has been moving money to a business partner on a regular basis, but it seems that the money's gone missing. I'm only the messenger so I don't know much more, other than the fact that it sounded like it was a lot of money."

"What is it that you want me to do?"

"Mister Gutierrez and his friend want you to try and find the money, that's all. The cash was being managed by some low-level accountant, and he never said where he was keeping it. By the time alarm bells started ringing, the guy had disappeared."

"Dead?" enquired Eyebrow.

"No idea," replied Carl. "I know that after the accountant disappeared, Mister Gutierrez's friend had some men pull the accountant's place apart trying to find the cash. Cut their way into the safe, checked the roof space, punched holes in the wall, even ripped up the floorboards looking for it – nothing."

"Why me?" asked Eyebrow. "This seems outside my range."

"Mister Gutierrez says that he trusts you, that's why. Apparently, your loyalty and discretion are second to none. His associate asked for the help of someone trustworthy, and apparently you fit the job description."

"I don't know about this," said Eyebrow.

"You don't need to make a decision right now. I'm just bringing you the initial information. You'll have to meet with Mister Gutierrez and his associate to discuss the actual details of the job, because I'm not really over the detail myself… just the high-level stuff."

"Ahhh, there's where the problem's going to come," said Purple from the side. "Eyebrow can't leave town."

"Is that true?" Carl asked Eyebrow.

"What, you think I'm lying?" snapped Purple. "Tell him, Eyebrow."

"He's right," said Eyebrow. "Joe and I have to stay here in town." Eyebrow paused in thought momentarily before turning to Joe Purple. "Actually, that's not entirely true though Joe."

"Jesus, what you thinking Eyebrow?" sighed Purple.

"We only need to actually be in town at ten each morning. We've got nearly twenty-four hours each day to do whatever we want."

"I don't like where this is going Eyebrow."

"Could we meet Esteban nearby? Somewhere that we could get to and back within twenty-four hours?" Eyebrow asked Carl.

"I could enquire."

Purple interjected. "You'd better drop the 'we' aspect of this thing Eyebrow. I'm playing no part in it."

"Come on Joe, I'd need your help," pleaded Eyebrow.

Purple pushed back. "So far, I'm clean in all this shit. They've tried to corral me for not stopping your last fucking escapade so I'm not giving them any ammo to come back at me with."

Eyebrow turned to Carl. "Esteban's been good to me, and I owe him. Try to set something up. And please remember that wherever we meet, I need to be back here by ten the next day."

CHAPTER 8
David

Marcus Bloom and David Gallagher met when they were both twelve years old, long before Bloom would be consumed by Joe Purple. And given that neither had a particularly broad circle of friends at the time, they immediately formed a tight bond with one another. As twelve-year olds they spent a lot of time exploring the tree-lined stream in their hometown and playing football together on the road, always vacating for the occasional vehicle of course. Eventually they graduated from street football to play the real game and spent their teenage years on the same team.

Oftentimes when a girl comes along, friendships can be fickle, but Marcus and David remained loyal friends, even when one, or both, began enjoying the company of any of the eligible young ladies in town. Indeed, during those times when both were in the company of another, many double dates were arranged at the local movie theatre and, as they got older, they even organized several couples' weekends away.

Marcus and David knew each other's families so well that they were effectively interchangeable at times, rarely needing little more than to simply announce their attendance at each other's house as they strolled through the door. Such was the brotherly bond that existed between Marcus and David that even other family members saw each as part of their own family circle. David's younger sister Claire once famously asked Marcus to accompany her to an important ball in town – one that required extensive practice beforehand to ensure that the dance portion of the evening was flawless. Her rationale in asking Marcus to be her partner, which she explained in no uncertain terms to him, was because she wanted to ensure that she partnered with someone who she had absolutely no interest whatsoever entering into a relationship with.

As they got older, their activities, like most kids, evolved from football and exploring, to partying and experimenting with exactly how much liquor a human body can process at any given time. On one occasion at an otherwise benign house party at the Gallagher residence, Marcus pushed his metabolism's blood to alcohol ratio within an inch of its limit, waking up the following morning in Claire's bed, clad only in his underwear.

Frantic about what events had transpired the previous evening and what repercussions were awaiting him in the living room, he slinked out sheepishly and was relieved to be reminded by Mrs. Gallagher that Claire wasn't even there the night before, instead having a sleepover of her own at a friend's house. Mrs. Gallagher then advised that it was in fact her that had carried a highly intoxicated and incapacitated Marcus into the bedroom, stripped his clothes and laid him to rest, periodically checking on him throughout the night to ensure that she hadn't laid him to rest in the colloquial sense of the phrase.

After they finished their formal schooling, both of them bummed around in menial jobs for a few years – Marcus in a department store and David selling furniture. And then, at age twenty-two, Marcus raised the prospect of joining the police force, and he found a willing accomplice in David. In short order, both were progressing through the selection process on their way to being accepted into the same recruitment intake. Upon graduation they were assigned to the same city, though not the same station, thus eliminating any chance of them continuing their friendship as partners.

But on-the-job partners or not, it didn't interfere with Marcus and David maintaining their near-lifelong friendship out of hours, subject of course to opposing shift requirements. Having long since concluded their alcohol retention thesis, they both now understood, within a broad margin of error at least, where their limits could be found. And it was armed with this knowledge they were able to burn through the local nightclub scene with a swagger that only the bullet-proof exuberance of youth can manifest. For nearly three years their stars burned brightly. But as with all things, the end loomed. The nightclubs changed – some closing permanently and others morphing to the point where the old establishment became unrecognizable. The people they ran with started settling down and going out less frequently. More and more, Marcus and David began feeling out of place.

Coupled with this, Marcus had slowed down the booze intake, preferring instead to enjoy his Sundays going for a walk in summer, or watching football in winter, as opposed to popping half a box of aspirin while hugging the toilet for a large portion of the day. The thought of hitting the town until the wee hours was becoming less appealing, which led to the events of October second – a day, or more accurately a *night*, that was doomed to hang over Marcus Bloom like a dark cloud for all time.

It was four in the afternoon when David called, enquiring as to whether Bloom felt like hitting the town that night. Bloom did not. He tried to find the motivation, but he simply wasn't feeling it. David concluded the call by noting that he would be at *The Mustang Club* if Bloom changed his mind. Around ten pm, Bloom received another call from David who had now made his way to *Pablo's* – a bar in the seedier part of town. Again, David asked Bloom to come out to meet him, and again Bloom declined, due in part to the fact that the unexpectedly long movie he had settled in with that evening was nearing its climax. As the call ended, both men agreed to meet up the following day for a BBQ.

It was to be the last time Marcus and David spoke.

As the clock ticked past two in the morning, Bloom's phone again buzzed. Rubbing his eyes, he saw that it was David's mother calling him. A wave of foreboding rolled over him - he'd been a police officer for several years by that point and he knew that phone calls coming at that time of night were rarely good. He sat up on the edge of the bed, preparing to get himself dressed for what was likely to be a trip to the hospital. It was his hope at least that whatever had befallen David wasn't too serious.

But it was.

David's mother was distraught, and Marcus was the first person beyond immediate family whom she had called. Bloom's phone hit the floor within moments of Mrs. Gallagher informing him that David had been murdered, less than half a block from *Pablo's*. Bloom wasn't interested in detail at that stage – his grief was immediate. His soul was instantaneously ripped in two and a part of him died at that very moment – it may as well have been lying in a chalk outline right next to his best friend.

Eighty-two days. That was how long it took to eventually locate and arrest the perpetrator – a petty criminal who had stabbed David three times in the chest for the sake of the nine dollars in his wallet. As if David's death wasn't already enough for his family to bear, to learn that in the eyes of his attacker his life was worth less than ten bucks was gut-wrenching. But worse was to come.

The prosecutor overseeing the case had long felt that it was his obligation to give greater weight to ensuring the civil liberties of those whom he referred to as "society's most vulnerable," over the actual pursuit of justice. Despite the vehement objections of David's family, the prosecution did not oppose bail, instead trusting David's killer to comply with a community supervision order ahead of his trial. That the man was a transient recidivist with no fixed abode did not seem to register with the prosecutor's office, and it came as little surprise when the man swiftly disappeared, never to set foot in the courtroom again.

Marcus struggled mightily to move on from David's death, especially the never-ending guilt that weighed upon him about not being there on the night in question. He constantly replayed the same questions. If he had been there as David had asked him to be, would he still be alive? Would all the variables that led to David crossing paths with his eventual murderer be different? Bloom hated *Pablo's*, so would they have even been in that neighbourhood?

Bloom needed to redirect his life, and a year to the day after David's murder, he resolved to apply to transition his law enforcement career from a local focus to federal. He could no longer cope with the day-to-day operational aspects of street duty. He'd become broody and over time withdrew further and further from his colleagues.

And while the topic was masterfully avoided during his federal interview screening process, there was no question that Bloom had been deeply affected by the outcome of David's incident. The grief that was left in its wake and the efforts put in by local police to finally apprehend the suspect, only for the guy to be cut loose, had left Bloom now entirely devoid of any attachment to outcomes. He would do what he needed to do, and he legitimately didn't care what came out the other end. He wasn't going to get himself emotionally invested when he knew that one stroke of a bureaucrat's pen could undo all his work.

In the end, his "don't give a shit" method served as both a blessing and a curse when it came to ultimately going undercover as a federal agent. A blessing because Agent Marcus Bloom was able to slip seamlessly into his role like a chameleon, devoid of any emotional baggage. But the flip side of that coin was the danger that went hand in hand with that ability – the potential to be consumed by the adopted persona and go native. And it was precisely that inherent danger that had manifested and led to Marcus Bloom, now two name changes down the track, sitting alone in *Turd's Pizza*, cigarette smoke encircling his head, contemplating how he had ended up where he now was – in the middle of nowhere, alone and anonymous.

But – and this was what was on his mind that day – he wasn't entirely alone. He had Eyebrow. Hours after Carl and Eyebrow had departed following the delivery of Esteban Gutierrez's request for assistance, Purple sat and pondered deeply. Try as he may to deny it, Eyebrow was the closest thing to a friend that he had. The task that Gutierrez had proposed sounded benign, but Purple knew that it was not without danger.

All those years ago, a young Marcus Bloom, with his whole life ahead of him, let his friend down by not being there when he needed him the most, and the consequences were catastrophic. But that version of Marcus Bloom was long gone – nothing more than a memory now. Where Marcus Bloom once resided, Joe Purple now stood. And it was Joe Purple who resolved at that moment that history would not be repeated.

CHAPTER 9

Señor Turd

Jimmy Eyebrow and Joe Purple were two hundred miles from home as they eased into the parking lot of the *Diamond Oaks Country Club* where they had arranged to meet Rafael Santiago, the friend of Esteban Gutierrez who Carl had mentioned a couple of days earlier during his visit to Coffee Pond. Purple's presence in the car with Eyebrow, despite his previous assertion that he and Eyebrow were not a package deal, was driven almost exclusively by his moment of reflection two days earlier while sitting alone at *Turd's*. He'd let a friend down once before, and he wasn't going to do it again.

So, against all better judgement, here he was once more – off on another escapade with Jimmy Eyebrow. It was his hope that this time it would be significantly less anxiety-inducing than the last adventure that resulted in him lying face down in the dirt of Dry Lake Valley, his life balancing on the knife edge that was his and Eyebrow's acting ability. First indications, albeit with limited background offered, were that this current job should fall a little lower on the idiocy spectrum. But Purple also knew all too well that when it came to Jimmy Eyebrow, even the most mundane tasks had a habit of spiraling into a vortex of calamity.

Waiting to meet them in the lobby was Carl, who greeted them warmly, even though the three of them had only met once before, and under tense circumstances. "Gentlemen, welcome," he said as he reached in and hugged Eyebrow, much to his surprise.

Carl then turned to Purple who swiftly stopped him. "I'm OK pal. Not into the hugging thing."

"As you wish," replied Carl, beckoning Eyebrow and Purple outside toward the manicured garden. "This way if you will."

"Is Esteban here?" asked Eyebrow as they strode through the lobby.

"No, but he'll be joining us on the phone," replied Carl, who then stopped and faced them just before exiting the doorway into the gardens. "I do need to advise you of something before we begin. Mister Gutierrez is aware of your current status as protectees, but Mister Santiago is not. We must be mindful to use your assumed names during this meeting, as that is what Santiago has been told."

"I'm fine with that," said Eyebrow before Purple added his predictable response from the flip side of that coin.

"Fuck me, seriously? Do we really have to do that? Can't I just make some shit up? Like... Chuck Atlas or something? It's not like the guy knows me."

"I'm sorry Mister Ferguson, he's already been made aware of who his visitors are."

"Jesus... OK, let's get on with it then," replied Purple with a begrudging sigh. Carl ushered Eyebrow and Purple outside and through the lush shrubbery toward a cabana where three men sat. One stood as they approached – most likely Santiago, Eyebrow surmised. Eyebrow also noticed that he was much smaller than he'd envisaged – possibly only five-five, maybe five-six at a pinch.

"Señor Von Steel?" he enquired as he extended his hand toward Eyebrow. "I am Rafael Santiago. It is a pleasure to meet one of Esteban's trusted friends."

"Nice to meet you sir," replied Eyebrow before being waved off by Santiago.

"Please, Rafael is perfectly fine." Santiago then turned his attention to Purple and extended his hand in greeting toward him. "And you must be Señor Turd, Max's assistant."

Purple shot an immediate death-stare in Eyebrow's direction but understanding the situation at hand, bit his tongue... for now at least. Purple turned back to Santiago and spoke while shaking his hand. "Ferguson actually. And if I could clear something up, I'm not his assistant. I'm his..." Purple paused as the words were stuck in his throat. "...I'm his partner."

"Ahh, that's very progressive of you," replied Santiago with a smile. "Lovely to see a family, even an unorthodox one, this close."

"Whoa hold up!" snapped Purple. "His *business* partner."

"Sorry, my mistake," replied a contrite Santiago. "I haven't made the best of starts here have I Señor Ferguson. Please, sit, both of you," he said, directing Eyebrow and Purple toward two vacant seats. Santiago then spoke towards a phone that was sitting in the middle of the table. "Esteban, can you hear us OK?"

"Yes, I can hear you perfectly," came the reply. "Max, thank you for making the time to meet with us," said Gutierrez, eliciting a smile from Eyebrow, knowing that Gutierrez was playing his part in the Max Von Steel pantomime.

"Esteban, it's great to hear from you," replied Eyebrow. "Have you been well?"

"Exceptionally," replied Gutierrez. "I am in first-rate health and enjoying life to the fullest. I'm sorry that I could not be there in person, but we must make a time to catch up soon."

"I'd like that. What are we here for today?"

"I'll leave the details to Rafael. But you personally are here because I trust you. Your unwavering loyalty throughout our journey has always been appreciated, and when Rafael came to me asking if I had someone who could help him, I knew that I could trust you unconditionally."

"Thank you Esteban, that means a lot."

"I'll let Rafael brief you on the matter before us, but I'll remain on the line here if I'm needed," said Gutierrez, handing stewardship of the meeting back to Santiago.

"Thank you, Esteban," said Santiago. "Before we go any further, would either of you like a drink? We have juice or iced tea."

"I'd like a juice please," said Eyebrow.

"I'm OK," added Purple.

Santiago poured a glass of juice and passed it to Eyebrow before sitting and acknowledging the other two men at the table for the first time. "Gentlemen, these are my associates who will be assisting you on this task, if you choose to accept it of course." Santiago pointed toward a tall bald man on his left – unlikely to be native to whatever Santiago's country of origin was. "This is Yuri."

Santiago now shifted his gaze to the right where a shorter, stockier man sat. "And this is Pasquale." As all four men rose and exchanged greetings, both Eyebrow and Purple noted that Pasquale, or "PQ" as he had introduced himself, was quite rotund. The word "stocky" may have been the politically correct means by which to describe him, but in reality, shuffling along the fine line of obesity may have been more apt.

Formalities complete, Santiago began laying out the issue at hand. "Max... may I call you Max?" Eyebrow nodded in reply. "Max, in a nutshell, the issue I have is that I have had some money go missing. And, if I may add, it is a considerable amount." Santiago leant forward and lowered his voice. "For some time, my business has been channeling funds to a business partner in South America, but in recent times, the flow of money has dried up. Ceased in fact. As you can imagine, my business partners are anxious to find out what has happened."

Yuri now entered the conversation. "I hold myself partly responsible here because I set Mister Santiago up with a man named Julian Cooper – an accountant. He's been managing the money transfers and I've been his handler, but now the money has gone completely missing."

"When Carl came to see us, he said that the accountant's gone missing," said Purple. "You found him yet?"

Yuri leant back in his chair. "No. Under normal circumstances he'd be my first port of call. But I can't interrogate him if I can't find him."

"So what do you want from us?" asked Eyebrow.

Santiago again took the lead in the conversation. "What I need is a second set of eyes and a different viewpoint Max. Esteban speaks very highly of you, and I need you to try and find out what's happened to my missing money."

"And Cooper?" enquired Eyebrow.

Santiago waved his hand in response. "He is irrelevant to what I'm asking you to do. I am just hoping that you can help us find the missing money. That's all. We have looked for where he's hidden this money, but to no avail."

"How much are we talking about?" asked Eyebrow.

"Not pertinent Max, suffice to say, it would take up a significant space wherever it is hidden. We've already checked his house where his office is located, and it wasn't in his safe. Not in his roof space, that we could see, nor in any other location that's obvious. It must have been hidden in a secret spot in his house or moved off-site somewhere. All I need is your help, that's all I ask. You may have no further success than we have had, but I just need a fresh set of eyes and Esteban assured me that you will keep this somewhat delicate matter completely confidential."

"Can I talk to my colleague here for a moment?" asked Eyebrow.

"Of course," replied Santiago. "Completely understandable."

Eyebrow and Purple rose and ambled across the manicured lawn, away from where Santiago and his entourage sat. Eyebrow made to speak but was cut off by Purple. "Your fucking assistant??? Where the fuck did he get that idea?"

"I swear Joe, it wasn't from me," replied Eyebrow defensively. "It must have been from that other guy, Carl."

"Yeah, well don't be thinking that you can run with it," snapped Purple. "Anyway, let's talk about this fucking proposal. I want to go on record and say that I'm picking up a weird vibe from Laurel and Hardy there. I think there's more than meets the eye to this whole situation. Something's off."

"It seems pretty safe to me Joe. We just have to find the money, that's all. And if we can't, then nothing bad happens. He just wants us to try our best."

"It can't be that simple. And besides, he wants *you* to try and find the money. The jury's still out on whether I'll join you... I'm not sure yet. Every fucking thing that you touch goes to hell in a handbasket and I end up being dragged along behind you." Purple paused before continuing. "If I'm being honest though, I'm struggling to see where this could go off the rails. It seems straightforward, on the surface at least, but it never fucking is Eyebrow... it never is. I'm skeptical, and fucking rightly so, but..."

Eyebrow's anticipation grew while Purple pondered. "So... are we in?"

Purple gazed off in thought for a few moments before screwing up his face and forcing out his reply. "Against my better instincts, I think that maybe we could do this." Eyebrow was visibly excited at the development. "But there's two big conditions here, Eyebrow," cautioned Purple.

"Sure thing Joe. What's that?"

"Firstly, we need to work strictly within our twenty-three-hour window. I am absolutely NOT fucking things up by failing to check in with Bishop. Whatever we do, even if we need to do it over a couple of days, we need to be back at Coffee Pond by ten each morning. That's non-negotiable Eyebrow. And secondly, something's off with Santiago's guys. The fat one doesn't say shit, and the Russian's balls-deep in the whole missing money thing. The money man was *his* guy for Christ sake. You do what you need to do, but I'll be staying alert around those two pricks."

"So, I'll tell Santiago that we'll do it?" asked Eyebrow, confirming the essence of Purple's position on the matter.

"It's a reluctant yes Eyebrow. But if I so much as sniff trouble, I'm pulling both of us out. Got it?"

"Got it Joe," replied Eyebrow as he made his way enthusiastically back toward Santiago.

"OK, we're in," was Eyebrow's simple response

"Wonderful," replied Santiago.

Gutierrez's voice joined them from the phone on the table. "That is fantastic to hear. Thank you, Max."

"We do have an issue though," said Purple, interrupting the positivity. "We can't be gone for more than twenty-four hours, or we'll be missed. We have a hard deadline of ten o'clock each morning, so how far away is this job?"

Gutierrez spoke. "Yes, Carl mentioned that matter, Mister Ferguson. It's a two-hour flight from your nearest airport, but quite achievable. We could have you outbound before lunch and then back home in the evening, with plenty of time for your commitment the following morning."

"You'd be on the ground for eight or nine hours at the most," added Yuri from the sideline.

Eyebrow looked at Purple. "Eight or nine hours," he said with a satisfied look on his face. "Not much could go wrong in the space of eight or nine hours, right?"

CHAPTER 10
Middle Seat

Jimmy Eyebrow had two check-ins to attend to on this morning. The first had already been completed – his daily presentation to detective Leo Bishop at *Lucky's Motel*. That one had gone off without a hitch, as expected. But now it was time for the second, and this one was far more anxiety-inducing. As he stood at the airline check-in counter in preparation for his flight to the job that Santiago had tasked him with, he could feel a bead of sweat forming on his brow. He had handed over his identification as requested and now, as every elapsed second felt like half a lifetime, he hoped that the name "Max Von Steel" wasn't going to trigger flashing neon signs and a disco ball to fall from the ceiling as it had in the police station previously.

Much to his surprise, it was exactly the opposite as the check-in officer handed him his boarding pass. "Thank you Mister Von Steel. You'll see that we've upgraded you to business class for today's flight. You're welcome to use the lounge while you wait."

Eyebrow was stunned. "How much extra do I need to pay for that?"

"It's complimentary Mister Von Steel," replied the check-in officer.

Eyebrow turned to Joe Purple, who was at the neighboring check-in desk, alongside Yuri and PQ. Eyebrow waved his boarding pass to Purple. "Our lucky day!" he said with a huge smile. Joe Purple had lived his life in the Eyebrow era constantly on-edge, but this development brought a little joy to his otherwise dour demeanor.

"I've never travelled business class before," Purple said excitedly to the check-in officer who sported a name badge reading *Noelene*.

"The three of you are travelling together?" she replied blandly.

"Yes, we're together," said Purple before pointing toward Eyebrow at the next desk. "We're with that guy."

"Uh-huh," was Noelene's only response, delivered without raising her gaze from the screen in front of her. The whir of the printer signaled the production of their boarding passes, and they were soon passed across the countertop. "There you go gentlemen. Seats thirty D, E and F. You'll be entering via the rear stairs on the tarmac."

Purple was taken aback. "Wait... so we're not upgraded like our other guy over there?" Purple nodded in Eyebrow's direction.

Noelene briefly glanced where Purple had indicated before replying. "I'm sorry Mister Ferguson, but complimentary upgrades are entirely random."

Purple digested the "entirely random" aspect, certain that the airline viewed Max Von Steel as far worthier of an upgrade than Turd Ferguson. "Where are *our* seats then?" he asked.

"Back row," replied Noelene.

"Jesus..." muttered Purple. "Do we get any extra legroom or anything? Look at the height of this guy," he added, pointing to Yuri.

"I'm sorry sir, those are the seats that the system has allocated you. I must note too, that as they're in the last row, the seats don't recline, though you probably wouldn't need that on a flight of this length anyway."

Purple could do little but simply stare back. "Is there anything redeeming about our seats at all?"

Noelene paused in thought momentarily. "They're right next to the toilet, so you won't have far to walk if you need to go." Any further conversation with Purple was swiftly terminated as Noelene shifted her gaze back to the queue and raised her hand. "Next in line please!" she bellowed.

Eyebrow was waiting to the side, but Purple brushed past gruffly, palm raised toward him. "Not talkin' to you at the moment you prick," he snarled. Reneging on his position immediately, Purple stopped, turned and addressed Eyebrow. "How the fuck is it that everything always works out for you?"

"What happened?" asked Eyebrow, oblivious to the upgrade situation, or lack thereof as the case may be.

"Don't worry about it," replied Purple dismissively. "Just... don't worry about it. Enjoy your fucking lounge access, priority boarding and extra luggage allowance. Don't worry about us peasants."

While the prospect of complimentary business class lounge access was appealing to Eyebrow, he nonetheless forewent the luxury in order to stay with his colleagues in the general waiting area. With Purple sulking like a kid refused a chocolate bar at the supermarket, and PQ being a man of no words, Eyebrow spent the bulk of his time chatting with Yuri. "How long is the flight?" he asked.

"An hour and fifty minutes," replied Yuri. "Call it two hours I guess."

"Do we get a meal?"

Yuri glanced toward a sullen Joe Purple before lowering his voice. "I expect you will, but we won't."

"I'd better not mention it then."

"Probably wise."

The conversation was interrupted by an announcement.

Ladies and gentlemen, general boarding for flight 1213 will commence shortly. In the meantime, we would now like to invite our business class passengers and those passengers with special needs to make their way to the gate for priority boarding.

Joe Purple leant forward and passed a snide remark to Eyebrow. "Well, will you look at that. You fit both fucking categories. Off you go then. Do you need me to carry your luggage for you sir?"

Eyebrow rose and began to make his way toward the gate. "I'll see you on the plane," he said to Purple as he passed him. But that would not be the case, which was probably a good thing for Eyebrow, given Purple's already disagreeable state. While Eyebrow was ushered along the air bridge to his seat at the front, Purple, Yuri and PQ were consigned to walking through the engine exhaust and heavy aroma of jet fuel to their stairs at the rear of the plane. And as Eyebrow was comfortably settled in enjoying his welcome drink, the three men in row thirty now began the process of organizing their carry-on luggage and seating arrangements.

Purple looked down at the seat number on his boarding pass – 30E. *Great, the fucking middle, right in between these two freaks.* Purple glanced at PQ whose ample girth was now exaggerated inside the cramped confines of the plane. "Which seat do you have PQ," asked Purple.

PQ glanced at his boarding pass. "Window," was his simple reply.

"Would you consider swapping?" asked Purple.

"I'd prefer to stay in our assigned seats. It's probably the rules."

"Bullshit. They wouldn't care."

"I think I'll stay where I'm assigned," said PQ.

Purple now turned to Yuri. "How about you? Would you consider swapping?" Yuri towered over Purple so he knew that likelihood of Yuri willingly parting with a seat that offered him marginally more legroom was non-existent, which was confirmed within moments.

"I'm happy with the aisle."

"Fuck it," muttered Purple under his breath. Middle seat it would have to be. He eased himself in gently, uncomfortably bracketed on each side by this odd couple that he had only known for twenty-four hours. His discomfort was exacerbated soon after takeoff when, moments after the seatbelt sign was extinguished, PQ unbuckled his belt and began to rise.

"That's what I was waiting for," he said. "Move out of the way, I need to hit the can."

"Jesus Christ," muttered Purple before he turned to Yuri. "Up you get, we've gotta let him out." PQ wasn't wasting any time though and had already began trying to squeeze past Purple, releasing a fart in the process. "Fuck me!" snapped Purple. "Just wait for a second will you. We're trying to get out of your way."

Yuri was attempting to stand but the man across the aisle in seat 30C had already decided that now was the time to enter the aisle and rummage through his carry-on luggage in the overhead bin. Purple barked at the man clogging the aisle. "Come on pal, this guy's about to shit himself. Can we get out of here please?"

"I'm almost done," replied the man.

"Buddy, just move to the side so that we can get out, I beg of you." The man conceded and moved rearward toward the toilet. Purple sighed and rubbed his eyes. "Seriously? You're going to literally move into the one place where you know he needs access to?" PQ farted once again, leading Purple to now frantically wave his arms up the aisle. "That way pal... move up THAT way for Christ sake. This guy's seconds away from a complete fucking prolapse by the sound of it... we need to get him out."

With some realignment of bodies that really shouldn't have been that complicated, PQ was ultimately able to extract himself from the seats and make his way to the tiny restroom, and not a moment too soon judging by the subsequent sounds that were soon echoing from within.

Purple sat down again with a small amount of free space now available due to PQ's temporary absence and closed his eyes in thought. *Fuck me, this is going to be the longest two hours of my life.* He then groaned audibly, knowing too that he still had that evening's return flight to come.

CHAPTER 11

Eight or Nine Hours

Thanks to his priority disembarkation privileges, Jimmy Eyebrow was already awaiting his trio of companions inside the airport after they had finally clambered up the stairs from the tarmac. Eyebrow was fed, refreshed and relaxed, and made a beeline directly for Joe Purple before Yuri subtly waved him off and silently mouthed "no" as a precautionary measure. Purple's face looked like he'd just taken first prize in the annual international lemon-sucking competition and Eyebrow now understood Yuri's preemptive warning to him. Eyebrow knew from history that the appropriate course of action would be to allow silence to prevail until such time as Purple felt up to any interaction.

When this day job was first discussed at the *Diamond Oaks*, it was estimated that they would be on the ground for around eight or nine hours. That back-of-the-envelope estimation now proved to be remarkably accurate as Eyebrow glanced at the clock in the arrivals hall – the period between that moment and the time they would need to present themselves back at the check-in desk that evening, coming in at precisely eight and a half hours. Barring any unforeseen occurrences, that would be ample time for at least a first pass at the task.

Yuri had arranged for a hire car to be waiting for them and in less than an hour after leaving the airport, they were pulling into the driveway of Julian Cooper's house that doubled as the office for his accountancy business.

Walking inside, Eyebrow and Purple noted that the place was in a state of disarray, thanks to earlier efforts by Yuri, PQ, and whoever else, to locate Santiago's missing stash of cash. "What are we actually looking for here?" asked Eyebrow, trying to get a handle on what the official brief was.

"We're not really all that sure," replied Yuri. "We're looking for either the cash itself, or something that will give us an indication about where it could be. A secret void somewhere in the house, a key to an off-site storage facility... anything that can help piece together what's happened."

"And you've already searched the place yourselves?" Eyebrow asked.

"Yes. But this is why Mister Santiago asked for you to assist – so that we can get a fresh perspective. There has to be something here that we're missing." Yuri made his way to the staircase. "I'm going to check upstairs again with PQ, so be sure to call out if you need me for anything. Be methodical. Try to think of things that we may have overlooked."

"Sure thing," replied Eyebrow as he turned to see Joe Purple inspecting the large loungeroom in silence. Eyebrow sidled up beside him and lowered his voice. "I don't know what I'm looking for here Joe. I'm not qualified for this stuff."

"No shit," replied Purple snidely. "What you need to look for Eyebrow is anything that doesn't seem quite right. Things that are out of place... odd. I'm not talking about just mess, but things that just don't make sense. Kind of like if I walked into your place and found a woman there. First thing I'd be doing is watching her eyelids for a fucking morse code distress signal."

Eyebrow followed along as Purple swept through the loungeroom. The room was carpeted, and Purple inspected the edges, all the way around the room. "Carpet's securely stapled down and looks like it has been for a while. It doesn't appear that there's anything under it." He lifted the corner of a large mirror that hung over the fireplace and peered behind it. "Nothing behind here," he remarked. He then turned his attention to the fireplace itself. "Get down there Eyebrow and stick your head up the chimney. Tell me what you see."

Eyebrow, obedient as always, did what was asked of him. "I can't see much Joe," he said, his voice muffled from within the chimney.

"Can you see the sky?"

"Yes."

"So there's no bag or anything inside the chimney?"

"Doesn't look like it."

The two men then made their way through the loungeroom's French doors, onto the patio and into the garden. A thorough investigation outside yielded no indication that any earth had been disturbed or that there were any new or unusual structures present.

"What do you think Joe?" asked Eyebrow.

"Not seeing anything yet Eyebrow. Let's try the garage." Both men spent the better part of half an hour assessing the garage and while no useful intelligence was gathered with regards to the missing money, Purple's interest was however piqued by the presence of two vehicles that were securely garaged within. "That's interesting," he muttered.

"What's interesting Joe?" asked Eyebrow, who had to that point offered minimal benefit to the process as Joe Purple's formal investigative training began to leech through, resulting in him taking a lead role in proceedings.

"Just a thought at the moment," replied Purple. "Come with me upstairs." The two returned inside the house and ascended the stairs, Purple calling out to their two associates. "Yuri? PQ? Are you two up here?"

"Yeah, up here," came Yuri's response from the upstairs hallway. "Everything OK?"

"We're not having much luck here," said Purple. "How about you?"

"Nothing here," replied Yuri.

"Where's the master bedroom?" asked Purple.

"Right down the end," said Yuri, pointing along the hallway. "You got a hunch about something?"

"No, nothing in particular. Just checking something." Purple beckoned for Eyebrow to join him in the bedroom.

"What's up Joe?" whispered Eyebrow.

"Just bear with me for a bit," said Purple as they entered the room. "Check the drawers in the dresser." Eyebrow opened the drawers while Purple delved into the closet. "Anything out of the ordinary?" asked Purple.

"No, everything seems to be here," replied Eyebrow.

"Exactly. Same here. Look." Purple stepped aside and presented Eyebrow with a complete closet full of suits, sports coats, casual jackets, pants and shoes.

Eyebrow wasn't sure about the purpose of Purple's point. "I'm not following Joe."

Purple edged closer to Eyebrow and lowered his voice. "Everything's here Eyebrow. His cars, his clothes, his shoes… it's all here. They said that he disappeared somewhere but there's nothing here that looks like he packed up and left. Whatever happened to him, it wasn't by his own choice."

At that moment, Yuri entered the room. "Everything OK in here?"

Purple was evasive, not yet wishing to discuss his observation with anyone other than Eyebrow. "Yeah, just checking the back of the closet for hidden panels or anything like that. We should check his office. I guess you've gone over that pretty heavily?"

"That was the area we hit first the other day. Like everywhere else… nothing. But you two have a look, because you might see something that we didn't."

"Is it downstairs?" asked Purple.

"Next room over from the loungeroom," replied Yuri.

Entering the office space, Eyebrow and Purple could see that Yuri wasn't exaggerating – the room had been turned over far more thoroughly than the others they'd seen to that point. Set into the wall on the left as they entered was a medium sized reinforced safe that was flung open with nothing but a few bits of paperwork inside – clearly the first port of call for Santiago's initial recovery crew. Purple investigated the rear of the safe for any indication that it may have a false wall, but it, and the side walls, appeared to be solid.

"Look around for anything that might be out of place Eyebrow," said Purple as he began thumbing through the various papers in the safe. There wasn't much of interest contained in the pile of paperwork – a large stack of bank statements and some small invoices that clearly didn't come close to the amounts that Santiago was alluding to.

Eyebrow in the meantime was perusing Cooper's desk, his eye falling upon a plain sticky note that was attached to a pen caddy. "Looks like we have a phone number over here Joe." Eyebrow waved the small square of yellow paper in Purple's direction.

"Show me," said Purple as he walked closer. Eyebrow flipped the note around, revealing the details. "That's not a phone number," said Purple after briefly checking the note. "It's too long, and it's got letters in it. I'd say that's a password, Eyebrow."

Eyebrow looked around the room to try and identify a computer. "A password to what?" Any further investigation though was quickly cut short by the crunch of a vehicle making its way up the driveway at the front of the house, after which a loud shriek emanated from upstairs. This was followed not long after by the low rumble of PQ running down the stairs.

PQ stuck his head through the office door in a panic. "Cops!" he screeched. "Shut the fuck up, both of you. Hide somewhere."

"Ahh, Jesus fucking Christ Eyebrow, this is bad," wailed Purple.

The two men crouched behind Cooper's desk. Eyebrow was frantic. "What do we do Joe?"

"We stay still, and very fucking quiet is what we do," replied Purple as a voice came from the front door.

"Mister Cooper, it's the police! We've had a report from your neighbor of some suspicious activity. Are you OK in there?" Silence ensued, which elicited a further announcement from the officer. "Mister Cooper, are you there? We're coming inside. If there's anyone in here, make yourself known now."

"Should we just let them know we're here Joe?" whispered Eyebrow.

"Are you fucking insane?" whispered Purple in response. "We're fucked if we do. You're currently on bail for conspiracy to commit murder, remember?" Purple quickly assessed the situation. "We need to get out Eyebrow. The door to the garden in the next room... we need to get there. Stay down." Purple crouched and made his way to the doorway that separated the office from the loungeroom, cognizant of the fact that he was bringing them one room closer to the front of the house where an unknown number of police were congregating. It could have been a single officer, or it could have been several, he couldn't tell. But he knew that the longer they stayed, the worse it would get for them.

As Purple and Eyebrow edged into the loungeroom, a voice barked. "YOU! Stop where you are!"

"Ahh, fuck it," sighed Purple, turning in defeat.

"You at the top of the stairs! Show yourself now!"

"Thank Christ," said a jubilant Purple, now knowing that it wasn't he or Eyebrow who had been spotted. "He hasn't seen us. Quick Eyebrow, into the yard." Purple could now hear the officer at the front door call to his partner. *Fuck... two of them at least*, thought Purple to himself before turning to Eyebrow. "There'll be more coming soon. We gotta go." Sure enough, Purple soon heard one of the officers speak into his radio.

"Bravo-two-two requesting immediate backup to our location. Unknown number of intruders. Possibly armed."

"Go Eyebrow, go!" whispered Purple as they made their way through the French door and across the yard.

"What about the others?" asked Eyebrow.

"Not our fucking problem," snapped Purple. "We need to think about us and us alone. They're old enough to look after themselves."

Eyebrow and Purple cut through the bushes, leapt the fence and sped across the neighboring yard at full pace – destination unknown at that point. There were a lot of moving parts in play at that moment, not the least of which was their need to be back at the airport that evening for their flight home. But for now, that concern was secondary, with immediate short-term survival taking priority. They needed to put as much distance between themselves and Cooper's house before police reinforcements arrived.

What was to become of Yuri and PQ, they didn't know. But both Eyebrow and Purple knew that escaping the current red-hot predicament was paramount, so they did what they were both accomplished at – they ran.

And run they did – frenetically. But this town was alien to them, so run they may, but to where, they had not a clue.

CHAPTER 12

The Cold Wallet

Jimmy Eyebrow stood outside the small convenience store, or more accurately, stooped – his hands resting on his thighs and sweat cascading from his forehead. He was soon joined by Joe Purple who exited the store holding two large bottles of water. Without a word, Purple handed one bottle to Eyebrow and then cracked the lid off his own, ingesting the ice-cold contents with great vigor. He stood and wiped his forehead. "We're in big fucking trouble here Eyebrow. This has gone sideways rapidly."

"What do you think happened to the others?" asked Eyebrow.

"No fucking idea. But I think this expedition has come to a swift end. We're going to have to go home and tell your buddy that there's nothing else we can help with."

"I think you might be right Joe. What do we do now?"

Purple glanced around the area. "First things first, I need a piss, desperately." Purple pointed up the road. "Let's go this way and see if we can find a restroom."

They had sufficiently distanced themselves from whatever was playing out back at Cooper's house and as such, both men agreed that running had now become redundant. Instead, they ambled up the road, allowing their bodies time to reset and their legs to begin the process of de-jellification. They were soon upon what appeared to be a small shopping strip, and Eyebrow spotted a bar not far ahead.

"Up there Joe, they'd have a toilet for sure," he said, pointing in the general direction of the small single level building.

Once inside, Purple made a beeline directly for the men's room at the rear, while Eyebrow shuffled over to the side wall and perused the place. For that time of the day, it was remarkably busy inside with groups of patrons milling around the floorspace, and five out of the six tables occupied.

The atmosphere was filled with the cacophony that comes with everyone in an enclosed space speaking simultaneously, while at the same time no individual voice being distinguishable from another. It was just a constant, nonsensical chatter. Eyebrow looked around, a sense of claustrophobia beginning to overwhelm him. The babbling of what sounded like a thousand voices, the clinking of glasses – Eyebrow could feel his chest beginning to strain under the pressure.

And then he saw something at the other end of the room that chilled his blood. The coiffed silver hair, the suit – it couldn't be... Lucky Vic. Eyebrow's heart didn't skip just one beat, it skipped multiple. How could this be? Vic was dead, Eyebrow was sure of it. He'd been there at St. Margaret's on the night he died and had seen him with his own two eyes. All logic told him that this could not possibly be Vic, yet there he was.

The man turned, carrying a tray of drinks to his friends at a nearby table. A wave of euphoric relief washed over Eyebrow – it was clearly not Lucky Vic. Logic had thankfully prevailed on this day. On the verge of hyperventilating, Eyebrow rubbed his eyes and tried to compose himself.

This task was complicated as another man snuck up on Eyebrow from the side, startling him in his already heightened state. Eyebrow spun quickly and assessed the man, noting that he was wearing a Salvation Army uniform. Eyebrow pivoted his gaze back toward the de facto Vic, but he no longer bore any resemblance – the mind-bending moment evaporating, as hallucinations are prone to do.

The Salvation Army man spoke, a tinge of concern in his voice. "Are you OK my friend?"

Eyebrow rubbed his eyes. "Yeah, I'm OK. Just... thought I saw someone I knew."

Eyebrow reached inside his jacket and fumbled for some money for the collection tin that the man held. Before departing earlier that morning, Eyebrow had grabbed a stack of cash from his bag of ill-gotten poker winnings. At that point though, he hadn't had a chance to break any of the notes, much to the

Salvation Army's benefit, as he folded a crisp hundred-dollar bill and slid it into the tin. "There you go pal," he said to the appreciative officer.

Spotting Joe Purple returning from the men's room, Eyebrow quickly made his way toward him. "We gotta go Joe," he said frantically. "I'm starting to see shit. I might be going mad."

"Calm down Eyebrow," replied Purple. "What do you mean?"

Eyebrow lowered his voice for no particular reason, other than to maybe assuage his own embarrassment. "I saw Vic."

"Where the fuck did you see him?"

"Here. Right here. I was a hundred percent certain that it was him. But... it ended up not being him. It was just some random guy."

"So... it *wasn't* Vic?"

"Not in the end. But up until then it WAS him. Do you get what I mean?"

"Not a fucking clue Eyebrow. While I'm pretty sure that I support your theory about mental illness playing a significant part in this, maybe you just need something to eat." Purple glanced towards the bar. "Should we get something here?"

"Not here Joe. I've got to get out of this place. It's doing my head in."

"As you wish," replied Purple as he guided Eyebrow toward the door and out onto the sidewalk. He looked around, assessing their location. Fortunately, he didn't have to look far, identifying a small diner up and across the road. "Over there Eyebrow."

Much to Eyebrow's relief, the diner was far less crowded than the bar they'd just left and thankfully, much quieter. Upon sitting down, only one other booth was occupied, but that was vacated soon thereafter, leaving Eyebrow and Purple as the only customers. As both men replenished their fuel stocks with a full breakfast, even though it was afternoon, they discussed the situation at hand in more depth.

"Something's not right with all this Eyebrow," said Purple. "The money guy, he didn't take off anywhere. Something's happened to him, and those other pricks know what, I'm sure of it."

"They seem OK to me Joe," replied Eyebrow.

"Bullshit," snapped Purple. "Something's up, but I can't work out if it's both, or only one. Both of them are fucking weird in their own way. But whichever way you look at it, shit's not adding up here. I don't even know if we were actually looking for money, or if they had us trying to find something else that they weren't letting on about."

As the diner attendant sidled up alongside their table to replenish their coffee, Eyebrow reached into his hip pocket and produced the folded Post-It note that he'd hastily stashed prior to their emergency departure from Cooper's office. "Do you think this password might have been what they were looking for?"

Purple examined the characters written on the note, shaking his head. "No idea. We're assuming that this is a password, but a password to what?"

"If it isn't a password, then what is it?"

"Haven't got a fucking clue."

The diner attendant, whose name was Jed according to his name tag, finished filling Eyebrow's coffee mug. "I can tell you what that is."

Purple flashed a glare in Jed's direction. "I don't recall inviting you to this fucking conversation."

"Hold up Joe," added Eyebrow, before directing his attention to Jed. "What do you think it is?"

Jed reached for the note. "May I?"

"Go ahead," replied Purple, glaring toward Eyebrow as he spoke. "Looks like we're trusting anyone these days."

Jed flipped the paper around and analyzed it momentarily. "It's a key."

"What the fuck's a key?" asked Purple.

"For crypto," replied Jed. "It's a crypto key."

Eyebrow shrugged his shoulders – a gesture reciprocated by Purple. Clearly neither had a clue what Jed was talking about. Purple turned to Jed. "You're going to have to speak to us like we're retarded, which he actually is." He accompanied his words with a nod in Eyebrow's direction. "What the fuck is a crypto key and how does it work?"

"Can I sit?" asked Jed.

"Be our guest," replied Purple as he shuffled further into the booth.

Jed sat and began to explain to Eyebrow and Purple exactly what it was that they had in front of them. "This is a key for a crypto wallet." He examined their response for any indication that they understood what he was referring to, but there was none as they simply sat motionless, staring blankly back at him. It was as if he was holidaying on Easter Island. "Crypto – money that's stored in cyberspace. Entirely virtual."

"If it's virtual then why is it written on a piece of paper?" asked Eyebrow.

"Crypto is stored in one huge, big pool in the virtual world," said Jed. "Everyone's money is in the same bucket. But your wallet is what gives you access to your part of the bucket. There's lots of different types of wallets. Accounts managed by a third party, or wallets on a hard drive, that sort of stuff. But what you have here is what's called a cold wallet. It's called cold because it's not connected to anything. No-one can hack it."

"Because it's written down on paper?" asked Eyebrow.

"Precisely," replied Jed.

It all now began to make sense to Eyebrow. "It was never cash Joe. Everyone's been looking for a bag of cash, but it's not there. He's turned it into computer money."

"Computer money… I like that," said Jed with a smile.

Purple entered the discussion. "So this number here is our access to the bucket that you're talking about? We can get in and look around?"

"That all depends on what sort of key it is. If it's a private key then you have access to whatever's in there. But if it's just the public key then it only shows you the part of the bucket where the money is, but not what's in there. It's like a street address – anyone can drive by and see the outside of the house, but you need a key to get inside. The private key is the critical thing to have."

Purple pushed the slip of paper toward Jed. "Then which one is it? Private or public?"

"Beyond my skill set."

Purple gruffly snatched the note back. "Then why the fuck are we talking?"

"It's beyond *my* skill set," repeated Jed. "But I have some friends who could probably help. I finish here at six if you wanted to meet up again and I can hook you up with them."

Purple looked across the table forlornly. "You know what I'd say Eyebrow, so let's just skip to the part where you do exactly the opposite."

"We might have found the money we were looking for Joe," said Eyebrow with a smile. "Let's meet his friends."

CHAPTER 13

I Might Know a Guy

Jimmy Eyebrow and Joe Purple were exhausted, and both wanted nothing more than to sink into their own beds back in Coffee Pond. But as the clock approached six in the evening, they were far from home and potential rest was still a long time into the future. This day had been taxing, and they still had more to do – namely meet with Jed's associates in order to determine exactly what it was that Eyebrow had retrieved from Cooper's office. As promised, Jed emerged from the diner only minutes after six o'clock and joined Eyebrow and Purple who had been waiting outside.

"How far do we have to go?" asked Purple.

"About three minutes away," replied Jed as they began to walk. "We only need to go about a block." Sure enough, a block to the east, the three of them stopped outside an establishment named *Zander's* – a pizza shop.

"Fuck me, always a pizza shop," muttered Purple. He turned to Eyebrow. "Why do our lives seem to revolve around fucking pizza shops?"

"Don't know Joe," replied Eyebrow. "Just how the universe works I guess."

"Well, let's do this," said Purple as they opened the door and walked inside. Purple suddenly stopped dead in his tracks and immediately placed a hand on Eyebrow's arm. "Don't move, Eyebrow," he cautioned fearfully.

"What is it, Joe?" asked Eyebrow, concerned.

Purple stood rock solid, assessing the interior of the shop. There was a pushbike attached to the wall and the tables looked as though they'd been sourced from a deceased estate sale. His gaze shifted to the pizza cook who was wearing braces, black rimmed glasses and sported a dark green flat cap. Purple was frozen in place as he whispered to Eyebrow. "I think we might be in trouble here Eyebrow."

Eyebrow scanned frantically from side to side. "What's up Joe?"

"This isn't a normal pizza shop."

"What do you mean?"

Purple's whispered reply was tinged with a sense of dread. "I think this is a fucking hipster pizza shop."

"You want to grab something to eat?" asked Jed.

"I'm fucking hesitant," replied Purple dryly.

"I wouldn't mind something Joe," said Eyebrow. "We've still got a long night ahead of us."

Purple looked at his watch and turned to Jed. "We have to be back at the airport by nine-thirty so let's get something to eat and then meet your friends." Purple glanced toward a table in the back corner where two guys about the same age as Jed were seated. "Is that them?"

"Yeah, that's them," said Jed as he walked over to the counter. Eyebrow and Purple followed to where the braces-wearing cook was waiting. Purple glanced at the name embroidered onto his apron – *Alixzander*.

"Evening Alex," said Purple politely.

Purple was met with a response that was laced with offence taken. "It's not Alex. I'm Alixzander, per the name that you can see written right here." Alixzander pointed obnoxiously toward his apron.

"Easy up there pronouns. That's not how you spell Alexander. I saw that but thought that you'd bought it from some fucking Chinese knockoff website or something."

"Oh my God, could you be any more offensive?" whined Alixzander.

"He probably could Alex," said Eyebrow without skipping a beat. "Please don't give him a challenge."

Purple simply shook his head. "Look, just give me a pepperoni."

"We don't do pepperoni here," replied Alixzander.

"What the fuck do you mean you don't do pepperoni!" Purple turned toward Eyebrow, incredulous. "Can you believe this shit Eyebrow? No pepperoni?"

Eyebrow joined in Purple's dismay. "Yeah, come on. You've gotta have pepperoni in a pizza shop pal."

"Not here," replied Alixzander, gesturing to the stand of menus on the countertop to Purple's left. "You can peruse our menu if you'd like."

Purple and Eyebrow each grabbed a menu and began scanning it. Eyebrow turned to Purple and whispered. "They put corn on the pizza, Joe."

"Jesus Christ," muttered Purple. "What the fuck is this shit? Chickpeas? And fucking eggplant? No pizza has eggplant on it."

"It's popular here," replied Alixzander.

"Ugh... tell you what, just give me a Margherita," sighed Purple.

"I'm not familiar with that one," replied Alixzander.

"The fuck!" snapped Purple. "You run a pizza shop and you don't know what a fucking Margherita is? Do you have sauce?"

"Six different kinds," replied Alixzander.

"I'm not interested in your hipster sauces. Do you have stock-standard pizza sauce?"

"We have wood-pressed tomato sauce."

"Close enough. Do you have basil?"

"Yes. It's hand foraged."

"I don't give a shit if it's picked by a nine-year-old in some fucking Cambodian prison farm. If you've got it, then we're almost there. Now, surprise me by telling me that you have cheese."

"What kind?"

Purple closed his eyes and tapped his head against the counter in frustration. He then stood silently for a moment before stalking around the counter into the preparation area. "Out of my way. You want to cook proper pizza, then watch and learn."

"You're not allowed back here," said Alixzander meekly, perhaps sensing that his protestation was moot – an observation that proved to be entirely correct as Purple ignored the direction and barged his way toward the ingredients.

With the efficiency of a surgeon, Purple began the process of introducing Alixzander to the joys of the simple Margherita pizza. "Base?"

"Over here," replied Alixzander, pointing to the pre-prepared balls of dough.

Purple grabbed a ball and began forming it into a base. "Not sure about the consistency here pal, but we'll make do. Sauce? And by sauce, I mean tomato, not some weird artichoke-based shit."

"Third sauce tray along," said Alixzander, directing Purple to an array of sauce trays.

Purple gazed into the tray neighboring the one containing Alixzander's wood-pressed creation. "What the hell is that?"

"Chipotle and pumpkin sauce," replied Alixzander.

"Jesus Christ," muttered Purple as he gave that tray a wide berth, before spooning out a generous amount of tomato sauce and spreading it across the base. "Now, stick with me Alex, because here's where I'm getting nervous – the cheese... you're gonna tell me that you have multiple types of cheese, aren't you?"

"Yes."

"Just reel 'em off and I'll tell you when to stop."

"Gorgonzola."

"Nope."

"Humboldt Fog goat's cheese..."

"Jesus... keep going."

"Mozzarella."

"Boom! There it is Alex! Where's the mozzarella?" Alixzander shuffled alongside Joe Purple and opened a drawer, revealing a selection of mozzarella balls. "Oh wow," noted Purple with genuine appreciation. "Actual mozzarella. I'm impressed Alex." Purple proceeded to place several balls of cheese atop the pizza before reaching for the basil and sprinkling a small handful across the top. "And there you have it Alex – the basic, yet deceptively tasty Margherita." Purple carried the pizza toward the oven. "Now all we have to do is....." Purple stopped and stared at the oven. "What the fuck is that?"

"What?" asked Alixzander.

Purple pointed to the temperature gauge on the oven. "That! What the fuck is going on there? One-seventy-five? Jesus, tell me that's broken."

"That's what we cook at, low and slow," replied Alixzander.

Purple was bewildered at this development. "Fuck me, you're not baking a cake pal. You've gotta crank that thing up to four hundred at least. How long does it take you to churn out a pizza at that temperature?"

"About thirty-five to forty minutes."

"For the love of all things holy, turn that up now!" barked Purple. "Pump it up, wait a few minutes and then stick this thing in for me." Purple placed his hand on Alixzander's shoulder. "Trust me on this Alex... trust me."

Purple turned and looked at Eyebrow with a satisfied look on his face. He said nothing, but Eyebrow knew that his friend felt supremely accomplished with his hastily convened culinary demonstration. It remained to be seen how the pizza would come out the other end, but for now it was time to get down to the actual business at hand as Jed ushered them toward the table where his two associates had been observing the lesson.

The first of the two leant forward and introduced himself. "I'm Ryan. And we've been telling him since he opened that the crusts need to be crispier. It's like bread sometimes. Thanks for doing that."

"No problem," said Purple before gesturing toward Eyebrow. "This is the guy you're dealing with now."

Eyebrow shook hands with Ryan, as well as the second young man who introduced himself as Ethan. Eyebrow knew that he and Purple were racing against the clock, so he got straight to the point of the meeting. He slid the slip of paper across the table. "Jed tells us that this thing here is a key of some sort."

Ryan looked at it and slid it across to Ethan who spoke. "I agree. This is a crypto key."

"What type?" asked Eyebrow. "Jed said that there's like... what was it?"

Jed jumped in to assist. "Public and private."

Ryan flipped open his laptop, reached for the slip of paper and typed the characters into whatever program he had open. "Give me a moment." After a short time, he swung the laptop around for Eyebrow, Purple and Jed to view the screen. "See that on the screen? I was able to find the wallet using that character set, so it's the public key."

"What does that mean?" asked Eyebrow.

Ethan offered his assessment. "It means that all you have is a publicly available account number."

"So we can't get into the account?" said Eyebrow.

"Correct. You can see it but can't access it," said Ethan.

"You need the corresponding private key to get into it," added Ryan.

Jed joined the conversation. "Remember when I told you that it's easy to have an address, but you also need the key to get inside? That's what you have here – the address, that's all. You don't have the key to get inside and look around."

Joe Purple leant forward to enter the discussion. "So how do we get the key? That's why we've come to you guys. You're the experts here."

"You can't," replied Ethan. "That's the beauty of crypto. It's virtually impenetrable."

"You say *virtually* impenetrable," said Purple with a tinge of curiosity sprinkled into his comment. "Does that mean it's possible?"

Ethan and Ryan looked at one another with raised eyebrows. Ryan rubbed his chin before speaking. "Mathematically yes, but realistically it's not possible." He pointed to the string of characters on the paper. "What you have here, the public key, is actually derived from the private key, so they're related. But the process used to turn the private key into a public one is so complex that it'd take the lifetime of the Earth to reverse-engineer it."

"So you guys can't do it for us?" asked Eyebrow.

"Hell no," said Ryan. "This is way beyond our ability. Probably way beyond anyone's ability."

"It's designed to be impenetrable," added Ethan. "You could try to brute-force your way in, but you'd be dead from old age before you'd barely left the gate. I'm not saying that there isn't some way to do it, but if there is, it's top-secret, high-end stuff."

Silence ensued – silence that drove Joe Purple to make an observation to Eyebrow. "You're awfully quiet there. What are you thinking about?"

Eyebrow didn't respond immediately, appearing to be deep in thought. Eventually he spoke, but not to Purple. He instead directed his question to Ryan. "You say that if there was anyone who could break these codes, they'd need to be, like, a professional?"

"Absolutely," replied Ryan. "And I mean high-end."

Eyebrow sat in continued silence, the cogs of thought clearly ticking over. Everyone, even Joe Purple by that point, suspected that something was evolving and as such remained silent in anticipation of what was to come. Eventually Eyebrow turned to Purple and uttered a simple phrase.

"I think I might know a guy."

CHAPTER 14

Pivot

Thanks to Joe Purple's expert guidance, the consensus among the assembled crew at *Zander's* was that Alixzander had turned out a half-decent Margherita pizza. Fine-tuning would be required, mostly around the dough composition, but in time and with appropriate mentoring, it was possible that *Zander's* could potentially meet Joe Purple's lofty standards at some point in the future. Even if Alixzander's appetite for change was limited, Purple at least hoped that the oven temperature issue would be given appropriate consideration moving forward.

Beyond the pizza matter though, Eyebrow and Purple's quest to uncover the secret of the mystery note retrieved from Cooper's desk had brought about mixed results. On one hand, they now knew that their sequence of mystery characters was a public key for a cryptocurrency wallet. But that was where their success came to a grinding halt, as it was also determined that the contents of the associated wallet was no more accessible with that key than it was without it. But Eyebrow had also given Joe Purple a somewhat ambiguous observation that he may possibly have a solution for that problem. However, he needed to return to Coffee Pond if he was to pursue that plan any further.

The afternoon had progressed into the early evening and after bidding farewell to the *Zander's* crew, Eyebrow and Purple made their way back to the airport for their late evening flight home. They were still unaware as to the fate of either Yuri or PQ after the incident earlier in the day, and they pondered the possibilities, including the prospect of one, or even both, currently being in custody. Then again, they could also be already waiting at the airport, all four of them preparing to reconvene after a hectic day. Maybe they would soon all be enjoying a drink together at the airport bar and laughing at the remarkably close call they'd just had.

But there would be no drinks, and no joyous back slapping that night. With their alert level elevated, Eyebrow and Purple alighted from the taxi at the airport and cautiously made their way toward the check-in area. Within moments, trouble was apparent. Discreetly reconnoitering the check-in desk for their airline, they quickly identified no fewer than five uniformed police officers milling around the area, with an additional two more formally attired men discussing something behind the desk with an airline manager.

As the two watched the officers stroll up and down the assembled passengers, Purple sensed danger. "They're looking for us, and the other two," he whispered.

"How can you be sure?" asked Eyebrow.

"There's no other logical explanation for it – not that I can think of anyway."

"What do we do now Joe?" asked Eyebrow. "We've got to get back before ten tomorrow."

"Fuck, I don't know Eyebrow. Let's get out of here so I can think." Purple ushered Eyebrow out the door and along the concrete concourse at the front of the airport. It only took a couple of minutes to be far enough away from the clamour of the passengers, taxis, and roll-along luggage that they could stop and secrete themselves in the shadows to discuss the current state of play.

"How can we get home in time Joe?" asked Eyebrow mournfully. "Is there a train or something?"

"Not that I know of," replied Purple. "Not from here to where we need to go anyway."

"What about a car? Could we hire a car?"

Purple did some quick mental calculations. "There's no way we'd make it in time, even if we drove at top speed and didn't stop. I'm not up to driving all night after the day we've had. What about you?"

"Fair point Joe. What can we do then?"

Purple paced for a few moments, looking toward the evening sky as a light plane went overhead on its approach to somewhere other than the main airport behind them. He turned to Eyebrow. "We need a significant pivot here Eyebrow. You've got a wad of cash on you, right?"

"Sure thing Joe. What are you thinking?"

Purple began walking, dragging Eyebrow back to the taxi rank with him. "There's another airport. It's a small one for private planes. We passed it on the way here. We could go back there and pay someone to fly us home."

"How do you know someone will be there who can take us?"

"I don't, but what other option do we have?"

"You're right, we don't have one," replied Eyebrow. "Let's go."

The two slid into the back seat of a waiting taxi, gave their directions to the driver and disappeared into the night, leaving the assembled law enforcement contingent waiting helplessly for two suspects who would never arrive. The nearby airport, or "aerodrome" as it was noted on the gate, was only a ten-minute drive away and after paying their driver, Eyebrow and Purple began the process of trying to secure a private plane to get them back home. There was no office, at least not one open at that time of night, and very little activity in general occurring around the facility.

Beginning to despair, the two of them finally located a man tending to a mid-size Gulfstream – its polished ruby-red livery glistening in the artificial light being cast from the hangar bay. The plane was spotless and clearly a well-maintained, modern piece of equipment. Eyebrow and Purple walked over and announced their presence so as not to startle the man. "Hello sir," said Purple.

The man spun around. "Hey fellas. What can I do for you?"

From his vantage point, Purple could peer inside the plane's open forward door and see the plush leather interior. "Beautiful plane," he said.

"Isn't it just," replied the man proudly. "It was only delivered six months ago, so it's still a baby by plane standards."

Eyebrow too was mesmerized by the luxurious aircraft. By his reckoning, if they were going to travel on a private plane, then they may as well do it in style. "Are you a pilot?" Eyebrow asked the man.

"I am indeed," he said as he greeted them with a firm, calloused handshake. "The name's Lester."

"Max," replied Eyebrow. "And this is…"

Purple was quick to interject. "Ferguson."

"What can I help you two gentlemen with tonight?" asked Lester.

"We need to get back to Coffee Pond tonight, as a matter of urgency," said Purple. "Could we hire you and your plane? We have cash." Purple turned to Eyebrow. "Show him."

Eyebrow pulled a block of hundred-dollar bills from his jacket pocket, one hundred and change less than ten thousand dollars, due to his earlier donation to the Salvation Army and the meal at the diner. "Payment isn't a problem."

Lester's eyes appeared ready to burst free from their sockets at the sight of Eyebrow's cash. "I can see that. Does it have to be tonight? I wouldn't normally fly this late. We could go in the morning, and I'd have you there before lunchtime."

Eyebrow pulled Purple aside and lowered his voice. "That's probably a bit tight isn't it?"

"Absolutely," replied Purple. "Lunchtime won't cut it." Purple turned to Lester. "If we left first thing in the morning, would we be where we have to be by around nine? It only took us two hours to fly here so it should only be two hours back, right?"

"If you flew here commercial then we're going to be slower going back. I don't think my plane could get you there by nine if we waited until tomorrow."

Purple turned back to Eyebrow. "It's gotta be tonight then. It's our only chance. Pay the man whatever he needs. This sort of private plane probably costs a fortune to hire but we're over a fucking barrel here."

Eyebrow handed his wad of cash to Lester. "Here take what you need. We need to leave tonight."

Lester took the cash and stuffed it into his jacket pocket. "Fair warning, it might be a wild ride."

Eyebrow glanced again at the Gulfstream, picturing the luxurious leather interior where he and Joe Purple would be transported home. They might even catch a much-needed nap along the way. "I'm sure it'll be fine," he said.

Lester gave the Gulfstream one last ceremonial wipe with the rag he was holding and then reached under the fuselage and pressed the button that retracted the steps and sealed the door.

"OK then, let's go," he said as he began to walk toward one of the other hangars.

"Where are we going?" asked Eyebrow, somewhat confused.

"Down to where my plane is," replied Lester without breaking stride.

"Wait, this isn't your plane?"

Lester turned and looked at Eyebrow with a puzzled look on his face. "Hell no. I couldn't afford something like that. That plane belongs to Mister DuBois. I'm just the cleaner. My plane's down here."

"Ahh, fuck me," muttered Joe Purple. "What have we gotten ourselves into Eyebrow?"

"I'm sure it's OK Joe. The guy's a pilot, and he has a plane so it can't be that bad."

Lester yanked open the door on the old hangar to reveal a single propellor Cessna. "There it is. She's a beauty isn't she!" he said proudly. "Bought her in '79 and haven't needed to change a part yet. I service her myself."

Purple pulled Eyebrow abruptly to the side. "Are you fucking kidding me Eyebrow? This has fucking Buddy Holly written all over it. I'm not getting in that thing. I don't even trust it to get off the ground."

"Yeah, not what I was expecting either Joe," replied Eyebrow. "If we don't do this, do we have any other options?"

Purple turned and walked a few steps out onto the tarmac, arms folded across his chest. He paused and gazed toward the night sky for a few seconds before turning back to Eyebrow. "It's a coin flip Eyebrow. If we don't do this, then I can't see any way that we're back before ten tomorrow. So, it's a choice – do we do this, or do we fuck up everything back home? I probably end up coming out clean either way because it'll be you getting locked up, not me. I haven't been accused of jack shit, other than failing to guard the door of the asylum. I'll probably get yelled at yet again, but that'll be it for me. What do you want to do? Get in that flying death trap or go to jail? In the end, it'll be your choice."

Eyebrow alternated his gaze three or four times between Purple and Lester's plane before answering. "I don't want to go to jail Joe. Let's trust him."

Eyebrow and Purple walked back over toward Lester who was crouched underneath the plane brandishing a two-inch long bolt. "Come and help me find where this goes. It was on the ground here, but I can't see where it's come from."

Purple sighed deeply. "You sure you can't take the hit on this one Eyebrow? Jail might not be *that* bad."

After a few minutes of searching, the three of them had been unable to locate where the suspect bolt had originated. "To hell with it," said Lester brusquely. "Maybe it fell out my pocket. We'll be OK. Let's get going." Lester tapped the fuel tank, analysing the tone of the returned sound. "We should have enough in there I'd say. Might borrow a bit from the reserve but we should be right."

"Ahh, don't you have to do, like, pre-flight checks for that sort of shit before you leave?" asked Purple.

Lester laughed in response. "HA! Not with this baby. That *was* my pre-flight check. I've been flyin' for so long that I can sense exactly how much I'm holding. I guess that's how I have to do it these days though, because the fuel gauge don't work anyway. Been flyin' on gut feel for over twenty years now. Three people… we'll fly around ten thousand feet at a bit over half power… we should be right on the mark."

Both Eyebrow and Purple were hoping for a little more redundancy than "right on the mark," but they had made their decision, and in the end, they were out of any viable alternative options anyway. And even though subsequent developments had made their initial gamble seem a little riskier, they were committed to strapping in and riding out whatever sphincter-puckering experience lay ahead of them.

CHAPTER 15

PAN

Lester's small plane and its three occupants droned through the night sky on its way to whatever hobby airfield was nearest to Coffee Pond. The plane was listed as being designed for four people, but even three was a stretch – the reference subjects back in the time when the plane was designed must have been of much smaller stature. With Lester in command of the controls, Joe Purple was squashed next to him in the co-pilot's seat, while Eyebrow was hunched over in the rear compartment.

Without the pressurization of a commercial airliner, not only did the Cessna fly at a much lower altitude, but the interior comfort was also far less controlled than its commercial cousin. Even though Lester had the heater pumping out warm air, Eyebrow still sat uncomfortably, his arms hugging his jacket tight across his chest.

"How do you know where you're going Lester?" asked Purple.

"Just experience mainly." Lester tapped the instrument panel. "I know where I'm going on the map and I've got my way-finder here, so I just follow it until I hit the city I'm headed to. I tend to know where the airport is at most of the places I can fly to, so I just line up and take her in."

"Do you have to talk to a tower or anything?"

"Not at the strips where I land. It's all self-regulated. You just keep your eyes open and take care. Everyone looks out for everyone else. You do need to talk to a tower sometimes when you're in shared airspace, just so that you don't get sucked into the engine of an Airbus or something. But usually we're pretty much trusted to do the right thing." Lester proceeded to take his hands off the controls. "Here, have a go at flying her."

Purple was shocked. "What? No way! I haven't got a fucking clue what I'm doing here."

"It's easy," said Lester. He tapped the artificial horizon gauge on the instrument panel. "See this? It shows you how the plane's sitting. When we're cruising like this, just keep the lines straight and we'll stay nice and level."

Purple hesitantly tried what Lester advised. "Like this?"

"Just like that. Good job. Now, turn it just a little and you'll see the plane on the gauge move and show you how far you're over."

"I don't know about this," replied Purple nervously.

"Just be gentle," said Lester.

Purple turned the controls in a manner that he classified as "gentle," but in aviation terms was rather abrupt, causing the plane to lurch suddenly over onto its left-hand side. "Holy fuck!" he yelled before Lester brought the plane back to its original position.

"That's OK," said Lester. "Give it another try. Be really gentle. Just bring it over a fraction." Purple did as instructed and found that this time, the movement was far smoother. Lester continued his instruction. "Now, bring it back just as gently and line your plane up on the horizon again." Again, Purple did as he was told and with a few recalibrations under Lester's watchful eye, was able to re-centre the plane on a stable track once more.

"Holy shit, I did it!" yelled Purple. "Did you see that Eyebrow?" Purple turned and looked into the rear compartment. That action, coupled with his hands still being on the controls, led to the plane jerking sharply to the left, forcing Lester to recorrect again.

"Don't forget that your hands are on the controls," he counselled. "If you turn around, your hands want to turn with you. You need to compensate. You'll have to keep that in mind if you want to be a pilot."

"I don't want to be a pilot though," replied Purple.

"Well bad luck," said Lester as he eased himself out of his seat. "You're a pilot now, because I need a piss."

"Whoa, hang on pal!" yelled Purple. "I can't fly this thing alone."

"You'll be fine. Just keep it steady and it'll fly itself. It's simple aerodynamics, like a huge glider. All you need to do is make sure that nothing interrupts the flying bit. I'm just going to be back here. You're not alone."

"Where the fuck are you going for a piss? There's no toilet on here."

"I'm not gonna make it to the next stop. I'll need to do it out the door. I really shoulda gone before we left."

"Are you fucking insane?" screeched Purple. "What do you mean you'll do it out the door?"

"I'll just slide the door open and take a piss outside." Lester turned to Eyebrow. "Just hold my belt for me while I'm standing there." Eyebrow hesitantly reached over and grabbed Lester's belt while Lester slid the side door open, the thunderous rush of two-hundred kilometre an hour wind immediately slamming into the passenger compartment. "Hold on!" yelled Lester, turning to Eyebrow as he unbuttoned the front of his pants.

Lester began urinating into the void but the relentless maelstrom outside picked everything up and flung it every which way. The contents of Lester's bladder were soon being splattered to all points of the cabin, with a disproportionate amount finding its way onto Eyebrow due to his proximity to the source. Lester turned to Eyebrow and spoke with confidence, yelling above the roar. "I think most of it's going outside!"

Joe Purple was aware of the chaos behind him and turned to yell in Eyebrow's direction. "What the fuck's going on back there, Eyebrow? I can smell piss!" In doing so, Purple neglected the earlier piloting advice from Lester and again lurched the plane over to the left, but this time was able to correct it himself without Lester's intervention.

"Joe!" yelled Eyebrow from the rear.

"Hang on a moment Eyebrow," replied Purple. "I'm just trying to steady this thing."

"Joe!" repeated Eyebrow.

"For fuck sake, wait!"

Eyebrow was undeterred. "Joe, we've got a problem."

"Jesus Christ, what is it?" Purple angrily looked over his shoulder before staring in disbelief at the situation presenting itself in the cabin. "Ahhh, Eyebrow, where the fuck's Lester?"

"That's what I was trying to tell you Joe. He's gone."

A wave, or more accurately a tsunami, of fear suddenly enveloped Purple. "What the fuck do you mean he's gone, Eyebrow? Where the fuck is he?"

Eyebrow's face had instantly lost its colour as he pointed to the open door, the cold night air still howling through the cabin. "I swear Joe, one moment he was here and the next he was gone."

"Are you telling me, that our fucking pilot… fell out of the plane?" The desperation in Purple's voice was unmistakable.

Eyebrow nodded his head softly. "It wasn't my fault, Joe."

Purple now had to work overtime to keep his emotions in check, otherwise the plane he now had solo command of would surely plummet to the ground with he and Eyebrow screaming hysterically inside. "FUCK! FUCK! FUUUUUCK!" was the best he could muster as a response. On the verge of hyperventilation, he yelled to Eyebrow. "Shut the fucking door!"

Eyebrow, still dripping with Lester's urine, did as he was told and then scurried toward the cockpit where an ashen-faced Joe Purple was gripping the controls like a python, trying to keep the plane steady. "What do we do now Joe?"

The panic was evident across Purple's face, and it was very real. "I don't know Eyebrow. I literally don't know. I know enough to keep this thing going straight and that's it."

"Do you think you could land it?"

"Did you see us do any fucking landing instruction earlier, Eyebrow? I've had precisely three minutes of training and I'm keeping the thing straight, which is the full extent of my knowledge."

"Do you think you could work it out?"

"No, I don't think I could fucking work it out!" snapped a clearly stressed Purple. "We're screwed Eyebrow. I'm just gonna fly this thing in a straight line until we run out of fuel and die, and even then, I have no idea when that'll happen because the fucking fuel gauge on this piece of shit isn't working."

The two men sat in stunned silence for a few moments before Eyebrow pulled out his phone. "I need you to get lower Joe. Can you do that?"

"Why do we need me to go lower?"

"Trust me Joe, just get lower if you can."

"Ahh, fuck me," said Purple in full knowledge that doing nothing was not a viable option. Placing trust in Eyebrow had a checkered history, but desperate times called for desperate measures, and right about now was as desperate as it could get. Lester had shown Purple the basics of left/right and up/down so, pushing the controls forward ever so gently, Purple began to descend. As his air speed increased in concert with his descent, Purple eased back on the controls to level out again, heeding Lester's lesson by using the artificial horizon as his guide.

"Is this far enough Eyebrow?" asked Purple.

Eyebrow looked at his phone. "No, we need to go lower."

"What the fuck is your plan here Eyebrow? Are you calling a taxi for us?"

"Just go lower Joe, trust me."

Now was not the time to argue, so once more Purple descended further before levelling out again. "How about now?"

Eyebrow looked at his phone again. "This might be OK."

"Are you going to tell me what you're doing?"

"Just a moment," said Eyebrow as he began keying something onto his phone screen. After a few moments, he squeezed into Lester's now vacant pilot's seat and flipped the screen around so that Purple could see it. "You can watch a video about how to land a plane, Joe."

"Jesus fucking Christ Eyebrow!" snapped Purple. "Tell me you're joking?"

"No, I'm not. You can find all sorts of useful stuff on here. What have we got to lose?" Eyebrow scrolled through the screen and showed Purple. "Here, see?"

Purple glanced at Eyebrow's screen. "That's a fucking 747 you idiot. As we both know, I'm no fucking pilot, but I'm pretty sure there's a couple of differences between that and what we're flying now."

"Well, what are we flying now?" asked Eyebrow.

"A Cessna," replied Purple, tapping the name on the control panel.

Eyebrow deftly keyed his phone and waited a few moments. "Here we go."

A few moments of silence ensued before Purple spoke. "Well? Are you going to show me or not?"

"I'm just waiting for an ad to finish Joe. I can't skip it. Just give me another ten seconds."

Purple perused the night sky in front of the plane as it cruised through the darkness, identifying the glow of city lights far off to his eleven o'clock position. "I'm gonna go that way Eyebrow," he announced before executing an adjustment to his flight path that was remarkably smooth given the current panic-inducing circumstances.

"OK, the video's starting Joe," said Eyebrow.

"Well, I've got to find somewhere to land first Eyebrow, so just cool the jets for a while. I haven't got a fucking clue what I'm looking for, so we'll need to get closer to the city over there. I'm sure if we fly around long enough then we'll find the airport. Should be lit up like a Christmas tree at this time of night."

Eyebrow let the video play so that the two of them could get a first pass of the process of landing their plane – successfully they hoped. Eventually the video reached the point where air speed was discussed. "Where's the speedo on this thing Joe?"

The two of them explored the console before Purple settled on the air speed gauge. "I think this is it."

"How fast are we going?" asked Eyebrow.

"Looking at this, about one-twenty-five or so," replied Purple.

"OK, well you need to be at about sixty when you're trying to land. You'll need to slow down a bit when you find the airport."

"How the fuck do I do that?" Purple looked under the console to where his feet were. "There are pedals, but I haven't got a clue what they do. It's just been flying by itself, so it doesn't look like there's an accelerator down there. Is one of them a brake?"

"Try one," said Eyebrow.

Filled with uncertainty, Purple gingerly eased his foot ever so lightly onto one of the pedals, causing the plane to move to the right. "Holy shit Eyebrow! What the fuck was that?" Purple pressed the other pedal, and the plane gently swung to the left. "These fucking things move the plane. Where's the brake?"

Eyebrow keyed something else into his phone. He looked at the phone, then to the controls, and back to the phone again before pointing to the throttle knob on the console. "I think this is it. This thing here makes us go faster or slower. Give it a push."

"Fuck, I don't know about this Eyebrow." Purple's finger hovered over the throttle before he tapped it as if being kissed by a butterfly. Nothing.

"You might need to push it a bit harder," observed Eyebrow.

"I know... I know," replied Purple. "If I'm being honest, I'm shitting myself here and I'm trying not to hit it too hard. Just give me a moment." Purple took a deep breath and adjusted the throttle gently, causing the tone of the engine to increase, accompanied, surprisingly, by an uptick in the air speed. "Fuck! That made it go faster Eyebrow!"

"Maybe you don't push it Joe. Maybe you need to pull it."

"Jesus Christ Eyebrow, I just did what you fucking told me to!" Purple now eased the throttle knob toward him this time, which thankfully seemed to have the desired effect. Most importantly though, there was no noticeable reduction in altitude. Purple looked at the airspeed gauge. "One-fifteen. We slowed down. I think that's it Eyebrow."

With the basics of turning, descending and slowing now understood, Purple began to feel that his chances of pulling off a landing were increasing. The broader odds still swung in favour of Purple and Eyebrow ultimately being smeared along the ground somewhere, but at least it was no longer the virtual certainty that it had been not too long ago. The next order of business was to find a place to land, and as the lights of the city began to spread beneath them, both men set about the task of identifying where the airport was.

"There!" said Purple, identifying what was almost certainly the airport off to his right. Banking the plane accordingly, he set off for a fly-by to determine exactly what he was dealing with and which direction he needed to line himself up on. Approaching the airport, a voice came across the radio.

Aircraft approaching on heading two-two-zero, identify.

Purple and Eyebrow looked at each other, unsure of what to do. "Is he talking to us Joe?" asked Eyebrow. The radio crackled again.

I say again. Aircraft approaching on heading two-two-zero, you are entering restricted air space. Identify.

Purple picked up the radio handset. "Are you talking to us pal?"

This is air traffic control. Are you the pilot of the small plane approaching HJG on heading two-two-zero?

"I haven't got a clue buddy. I'm in a small plane, and I'm approaching the airport. But I'm no fucking pilot and I've got no idea about my direction."

Sir, you are about to enter the commercial airspace of Henry J. Gatling Airport. Please turn to heading three-three-zero immediately.

"Sorry, pal. No idea what you're talking about. Just so you know, me and my friend here are in a fucking shitful situation at the moment, and I've got no intention of dying. So the only place I'm turning is towards your airport where I'm going to have a crack at landing this piece of shit. So if anyone's on that runway, I'd suggest that you get 'em off quickly."

Several moments of silence passed before the voice on the radio responded. *Unidentified aircraft, are you declaring an emergency?*

"Well, our pilot fell out of the plane, and I'm learning how to land from a fucking internet video, so yeah... we're a bit fucked up." There was further silence. "Hello?" added Purple.

Unidentified aircraft, say again. It sounded like you said that your pilot fell out of the plane.

"That's exactly what I said. Fell out when he was taking a piss. Now can you help me get this fucking thing on the ground or not? Preferably in one piece."

Campbellfield Sky Port is ten miles to your two o'clock. Turn to heading three-one-zero and await further instructions.

By that point, Purple had successfully navigated the plane to a point where he could line up with the main airport runway. "Not happening pal. I'm coming in on this big runway, so you'd better make room."

A flurry of further radio communications followed, advising other air traffic in the vicinity to hold their positions or go around, which cleared the path for Purple to make his way, heart pounding, towards the runway. "How's that video going Eyebrow? I need to hear the bit about actually landing."

"Remember you have to slow down Joe."

Purple adjusted the throttle and reduced the speed below one hundred knots as he eased the plane slowly downward. "I'm worried I might miss it Eyebrow," he said, his voice wavering.

"It's a huge runway Joe," said Eyebrow reassuringly. "Ten times bigger than what this size plane would normally need. You'll be fine." Eyebrow continued watching the video. "It says to put the flaps out a bit."

"Where are the flaps? You never said anything about fucking flaps!" Eyebrow didn't respond immediately. "Eyebrow? Where's the controller for the fucking flaps?"

"Hang on Joe, it's buffering."

"Are you fucking kidding me? Hurry up!"

"OK, here it is." Eyebrow pointed to the console. "That's the flaps. Put them to twenty."

Purple flicked the switch to twenty as instructed, causing the plane to abruptly slow and lose altitude. "Fuck!" exclaimed Purple as he lifted the nose and applied a little more throttle. "What do I do now Eyebrow?"

"Just keep slowing until you get to about sixty and keep going down. Try to line it up and fly low over the runway. Once we're over it, just level it and fly about ten feet above the ground for a bit."

"And then what?"

"You just slow it right down, lift the nose of the plane a bit and it says we'll just fall onto the runway. Just make sure we don't do it from too high up."

"Jesus, OK Eyebrow. Here we go. Fuck me, I've never been this shit scared in my life. You might want to put your head between your legs and kiss your arse goodbye here. Whatever happens, I've done my best OK?"

"I trust you Joe, just do the best you can," said Eyebrow as he braced himself for impact.

Purple cycled through Eyebrow's instructions in his head. He was now over the runway. He eased the plane lower while at the same time throttling back on the power. He levelled off... not sure if he was ten feet above the runway or higher. By now he was halfway along the tarmac – he needed to act soon. Purple throttled right back and lifted the nose gently. As foretold by Eyebrow, the plane sunk for what seemed an eternity, until a massive thud signalled their arrival on *terra firma*. The landing was far from textbook, and both men knew that their spines were going to revisit this moment for several days afterwards. But they were down, and thus far still alive. But they were not slowing.

"Nose Joe! Put the nose down!" yelled Eyebrow.

"How the fuck do I slow down Eyebrow?" barked Purple. Eyebrow looked at his phone while Purple waited for a reply. "I'm running out of room here Eyebrow, hurry up!"

"The pedals!" yelled Eyebrow again. "They turn into brakes when we're on the ground!"

Purple applied his full weight to the pedals and the plane thankfully began slowing. They had used nearly all of the 3,122 metres of runway available to them and when they finally came to a halt, the two men erupted in raucous celebration. This had been a death-defying feat for the ages and was a defining moment in both their lives. All the tension of the night was jettisoned amid an avalanche of yelling and high-fives in the midst of a comradery that would have been inconceivable not too long ago.

But any popping of the champagne would need to be put on hold because an unscheduled landing such as theirs at a major airport was not something that would simply be waved off. A kaleidoscope of red, blue and orange lights now barreled towards them in a procession that must have numbered at least a dozen vehicles.

"Shit! What do we do now Joe?" asked a now panicked Jimmy Eyebrow. They'd done everything they could to get back for their ten o-clock deadline and it was all about to come to nothing within the next few minutes if they couldn't somehow extract themselves from the circus that was about to roll up to their stationary plane.

Purple looked around the area. "Hold on tight Eyebrow," he said as he throttled up and began rolling past the end of the runway and onto the grass.

"What are you doing Joe?" asked Eyebrow.

"Getting us the fuck out of here," replied Purple sharply. The plane hurtled through the grassed area abutting the runway, bouncing across a culvert along the way. Purple had turned Lester's pride and joy into a race car, and they thundered away from the pursuing vehicles toward the perimeter fence. Purple didn't slow down as the fence approached with ferocious speed and the plane crashed straight through it, ripping the propellor from its housing and shearing the starboard wing off.

As the plane came to a halt, Purple unbuckled his seat belt, opened the door and beckoned for Eyebrow to do likewise. "Let's go Eyebrow! We need to get the fuck out of here now!" The two of them leapt from the aircraft and absconded into the dark – Eyebrow with a slight nod of appreciation to the now mortally damaged Cessna that had performed so admirably right when they needed it the most.

They were on the ground, and they were alive – that was the overriding aspect of their current situation. Whatever happened from that point, the fact that they'd survived against the odds trumped any negative outcomes. But that didn't mean that they weren't now committed to avoiding those negative outcomes, primarily the cavalcade of law enforcement and security behind them who were all desperate to identify the two mystery men who had absconded into the night after crash landing a light plane at the city's main airport.

CHAPTER 16

Trooping the Colour

The air was heavy with the smell of sweat, urine and general grime, but this was neither the New York City subway, nor the streets of Paris. Rather, it was the interior of the taxi that Jimmy Eyebrow and Joe Purple were in, rushing to their ten o'clock deadline at *Lucky's Motel*. Neither of them had slept for close to thirty hours as their escape and evade activities at the airport had consumed almost every minute up until that point.

It took Eyebrow and Purple several hours to successfully elude their pursuers to the stage where they both felt comfortable that the immediate threat was mitigated, and they could both take a moment to rest. But rest would be brief because as the sun rose, they still needed to get back to their meeting location – a location that at that moment, remained a considerable distance away.

And now, as the over-worked meter in the taxi ticked past two hundred dollars, and with the clock reading 9:55am, Eyebrow and Purple rolled into the parking lot at *Lucky's* with a full five minutes to spare. They spotted Leo Bishop standing atop the first-floor landing, coffee in hand, and as the taxi slowly eased past him with Eyebrow and Purple making themselves known through the window, he offered a simple wave, as if he were the King inspecting Trooping the Colour.

Over a day without rest, multiple encounters that could have seen them locked up, defying death at ten thousand feet and running through the night – all for a brief drive-by and cursory acknowledgment. After the frenetic previous thirty hours, it was finally time to return, exhausted, to their lakeside sanctuary.

The taxi pulled up outside Purple's cabin and with Eyebrow attending to the payment, both men trudged wearily inside. "I'm fucking spent Eyebrow," said Purple as he slumped into a chair. "Whatever we're doing today, it's gonna have to wait because I need sleep. I can't function."

"Agree Joe," replied Eyebrow softly. "I'm going to change my clothes, have a quick shower and go to bed."

Purple rose and began moving toward his own bedroom. "I'm skipping the shower part. But then again, I'm not the one covered in someone else's piss. I'll catch up with you later tonight." Purple then stopped, paused for a moment and spoke without turning. "Thanks for your help in the plane Eyebrow. I'm not sure I would have been able to do it by myself." As Purple continued into the bedroom, shutting the door behind him, Eyebrow smiled at Purple's simple recognition of his efforts.

Purple was likely already asleep before Eyebrow had even walked into his own cabin next door. Eyebrow knew that his own slumber wouldn't be far behind but before closing his eyes, a shower was essential. He peeled off his clothes and deposited them into a plastic bag – not the first time that a job had gone considerably off the rails, resulting in him being covered in human excrement. Showered and feeling fresh, Eyebrow was so exhausted that he didn't even bother re-dressing, instead falling into bed completely naked and drifting off within moments of his head hitting the pillow.

Sleeping the sleep of the dead, neither man rose before the orange glow of the setting sun began to take hold. A little later, with the last sliver of light dimming across the horizon, Eyebrow and Purple sat on the deck with drinks in hand, preparing to debrief on the previous day's activities.

"I wonder what happened to Yuri and PQ?" asked Eyebrow.

"No idea," replied Purple. "But I tell you what, even though we managed to scrape ourselves out of that shitshow yesterday, we're not home free so long as those two are still in the wind. We don't even know if they're in jail or in the same situation we were in, trying to get back home. They wouldn't have to rush like we did though, so they could take their time."

"Should I call Esteban?" asked Eyebrow.

"Not yet. We need to work out what the fuck we're dealing with, especially with that crypto key. Didn't you say that you know someone who can help?"

"I might have a guy," replied Eyebrow. "I don't know for sure, but I could ask him." Eyebrow rose and beckoned Purple to follow him. "Come on over to my place."

The two made their way to the neighbouring cabin and walked inside, where Eyebrow opened the cupboard in his sitting room, retrieved his duffel bag of cash and began rummaging through it. A noise outside suddenly put Joe Purple on high alert. "Did you hear that?" he asked Eyebrow.

"No, what was it?"

Purple stood rock solid in complete silence, scanning the area. "It sounded like someone was outside." He held his finger up and moved closer to the window. The noise was there again. Footsteps – definitely footsteps. "Are you expecting a visitor Eyebrow?"

"No," whispered Eyebrow.

Purple looked around the room for a weapon, but nothing presented itself immediately. The closest thing he could find was a lump of wood from the fireplace, but that would have to do. Purple could hear footsteps warily approaching the front door and as they halted directly outside, Purple flung the door open and swung the lump of wood at the unknown person who had snuck up on them. Striking the man to the side of the head, he immediately fell to the ground clutching his scalp.

"Jesus!" he yelled, the pain evident in his voice. "What the hell!"

Purple moved over to the man and prepared to strike once more when he looked down and identified PQ writhing on the ground. "What the fuck are you doing here? And why are you lurking around here like that?"

"I wasn't fucking lurking," replied PQ as he rose from the ground, a small trickle of blood rolling down the side of his face. "I was coming to find you."

"Where's Yuri?" asked Eyebrow.

"You haven't seen him?" said PQ.

"No."

"Have you talked to him before I got here?"

"No."

"Good. Because he's the one who set us up at Cooper's place. He's up to his eyeballs in this shit."

"I fucking knew it!" said Purple triumphantly. "I told you something wasn't right, didn't I Eyebrow?"

"You sniffed it out Joe, that's for sure," replied Eyebrow before turning to PQ. "Where's Yuri now?"

"No idea. I was able to high-tail it out of there just in time, but I don't know what happened to him. Could be in jail for all I know."

Purple wasn't pleased about the situation and glared at Eyebrow. "This had better not have any fucking blowback onto me. I started out completely clean here, but I seem to be getting dragged into more and more shit that I never intended to get involved in."

"We'll be OK Joe, I'm sure of it," replied Eyebrow confidently. "We've managed to get ourselves out of every other bit of trouble, haven't we?"

"Yesterday, and last night in particular, wasn't what I'd call a 'bit of trouble' Eyebrow," snapped Purple. "We've been fucking lucky up to this point, and my worry is that the luck's going to run out, probably in spectacular fashion."

PQ now re-entered the conversation. "So now we have to go back to Mister Santiago and tell him that we didn't find the money?"

"Not necessarily," replied Eyebrow. "We found a crypto key." Before Eyebrow could go any further though, Purple quickly interjected.

"But it was a false alarm. Nothing. Not even a real crypto key. Just random numbers and shit." Purple placed his hand on Eyebrow's arm and turned to speak to him. "Can I talk to you over here for a moment please?" Purple guided Eyebrow toward the far end of the sitting room and lowered his voice. "Just slow down a bit on giving too much information away Eyebrow. We need to be careful here. We don't really know if we're fully out of danger yet."

Eyebrow glanced toward PQ who was mopping his lacerated head with some hand towel near the kitchen. "You think he's playing some sort of game Joe?"

"I can't tell. I'm just saying, let's stay alert." Purple now returned the conversation to the point where they had been prior to PQ's reappearance. "What was it that you wanted to show me? You said you had a guy?"

"Yes," whispered Eyebrow as he produced a business card that he had retrieved from his duffel bag earlier. "I remembered this, and I was hoping that I'd kept it. This might be our guy, Joe."

Purple took the card from Eyebrow's hand and assessed it. "You think this guy might be able to help?"

"Can't hurt to ask."

"How do you know him?"

"Long story Joe."

Purple massaged the card in his hand as he read the name again. *Stuart Spaulding – Iron Key Consulting.*

CHAPTER 17

The Sherpa and the Banker

The following day, Eyebrow, Purple and PQ sat on the deck of Purple's cabin taking breakfast – the morning sun beaming from a cloudless sky and bouncing off the shimmering lake. The long, warm days of summer were rapidly approaching, and this one was already giving every indication that a comfortably warm, short-sleeved kind of day was looming. It was Purple's hope though that it was not so warm as to entice Eyebrow and his star-spangled jocks into the water.

PQ's arrival the night before meant that lodging had to be found for him, and he had bunked in Joe Purple's cabin for the evening. Purple nonetheless maintained reservations not only about PQ, but also his now absent associate Yuri. It had been a restless night for Purple as his sleep state lurked barely below the consciousness level, his brain remaining on high alert for any untoward nocturnal activity from PQ. In the end, there was none, and PQ had thus far offered no indication that his visit to Coffee Pond was anything other than a professional engagement.

Purple looked at his watch and stood. "We have to get going PQ. Gotta make our daily appointment."

"I'll come with you," said PQ as he too stood.

"No, not on this one," replied Purple. "We can't be turning up with you. Bishop will know something's not right. No… this is just me and Eyebrow. The place is yours while we're gone. There are spare towels in the bathroom if you feel like having a swim."

Purple was correct that it would be toying with danger to arrive at their daily check-in with PQ in tow, but there was also another element at play – Purple needed to discuss the current state of play with Eyebrow, and he wanted to do so without the ever-present PQ lurking in the background.

Leaving PQ on house-sitting duties, Eyebrow and Purple weaved their way down the short dirt road leading from their cabins and after hitting the main road, cruised into town with plenty of time to spare – a starker contrast to the previous day could not be crafted if one were to try. This day though, as they entered the motel car park, there would be no royal inspection from the balcony. Bishop instead waved them in and beckoned to them to join him at the tiny table outside his room.

Bishop was seated, coffee mug in one hand and his newspaper in the other. "Please, sit down," he said as Eyebrow and Purple approached.

"There's only one other chair," observed Purple.

"Yes, I know," replied Bishop dismissively as he took a sip of coffee and folded his newspaper onto the table. Without any consideration for his companion, Purple quickly lowered himself onto the chair, leaving Eyebrow to lean against the railing. Purple glanced toward Bishop's newspaper that had two headlines prominently visible on the front page – *Man Falls from Sky* and *Airport Drama*. He felt his heart rate increase, worried that this was the reason why Bishop had summoned them that morning. Had the pieces been put together and in turn led directly back to he and Eyebrow? Had the local police in Cooper's hometown identified them and contacted Bishop?

Ultimately, the actual purpose of their audience with Bishop was far more benign. "Just giving you an update on the current situation," Bishop said to Eyebrow. "I'm sorry to say, but we're at least a few weeks away from any movement. There are a few moving parts here apparently, so we all have to sit tight."

"Does that mean we need to keep doing this every day for the next few weeks?" asked Eyebrow.

"Interesting you should ask that," replied Bishop, who turned and called to an adjacent room. "Mac! Can you come here please?" While waiting for McFadden to appear, Bishop returned to Eyebrow's question. "Firstly, yes. But secondly, I need to know something. Can I trust you two?"

"How do you mean?" asked Eyebrow.

"I mean, can I trust the two of you to not abscond? Is there any chance whatsoever that you're going to leave town?"

Eyebrow gulped and glanced toward Purple who in turn responded on Eyebrow's behalf. "Absolutely not."

"You'll both stay right here?" reiterated Bishop.

Purple was concerned that Bishop might be setting them up for something but nonetheless reinforced his initial answer. "Right here. We are not going anywhere detective."

Bishop paused for a few seconds before continuing, McFadden having now joined them. "OK then. Mac, they've given their assurance that they'll be good citizens and stay where they're told."

"Good to hear," replied McFadden.

Bishop continued. "Now, given that we've found out that we need to keep doing this for God knows how long, I'm not ashamed to say that both detective McFadden and I are on the verge of going insane here."

"That much is true," said McFadden with a slow nod of agreement.

Bishop now laid out what the next few days would bring. "So, we're going to put our trust in you. Detective McFadden is going to go and do something interesting for the weekend. No idea what he's planning, but I'm willing to bet that it sure as hell won't involve this place."

"Sound hypothesis there Leo," noted McFadden.

"And as for me – I have something that I need to take care of this weekend as well. So, here's where I get really nervous because…" Bishop drew breath. "I'm willing to forego the check-ins this weekend IF you give me your rock-solid guarantee that you'll stay right here and keep out of trouble."

This development pleased Joe Purple on a number of fronts, not the least of which was that it was now clear that even though the details of he and Eyebrow's recent path of destruction were sitting right in front of Bishop, there had been no connection made. "We will most definitely stay right here, and we won't even jaywalk." Purple looked at Eyebrow. "Isn't that right Eyebrow?"

"Absolutely Joe."

Silence ensued, Bishop clearly weighing up the reward to risk ratio of his proposition. Eventually he nodded silently and then spoke. "OK, this weekend you are both off the clock. But come Monday, it's business as usual. And no trouble, got it? So help me God, if I hear that you've so much as walked away from a toilet without flushing it, I will plant my foot so far up your arse that they'll need that fucking cave rescue team from Thailand to extract it. Do I make myself clear?"

"Absolutely," replied Purple.

Bishop turned to Eyebrow. "And you?"

"No trouble. Got it."

Bishop now waved them away. "Alright, that's enough for today. We'll see you back here tomorrow and then you have the weekend off." Eyebrow and Purple didn't need any further encouragement, and they were both bounding down the steps within moments of the final words falling from Bishop's mouth. Bishop leant over the railing and called to them once more. "You're still required back here tomorrow! Don't forget that."

After the two had departed, Bishop turned and sat back at his tiny table. "You going to be OK this weekend, Leo?" asked McFadden.

"I'll be fine thanks Mac. Just not the best time to be baby-sitting those two fuck ups."

"Well, if you need me, you've got my number. I'll have my phone on all weekend."

"Thanks Mac, I appreciate it."

A short distance away, Eyebrow and Purple were making haste back home. Once they were out of sight of the motel, they pulled off to the side of the road, at which point Eyebrow retrieved both his phone and Spaulding's business card from his pocket. "Should we call him?" Eyebrow asked Purple.

"Yes, do it while we're stopped here. I don't want that other prick to know what we're up to yet." Eyebrow obediently dialed Spaulding's number. "Put it on speaker," directed Purple.

A few moments elapsed before a voice on the other end answered. *Good afternoon, Iron Key Consulting, this is Louise.*

"Hello. May I speak to Mister Spaulding please," said Eyebrow.

Who's speaking please?

"Tell him it's Conrad St. Claire. He should remember me." A look of bewilderment spread across Joe Purple's face, to which Eyebrow covered the phone with his hand and whispered back. "Trust me."

I'm sorry, but Mister Spaulding doesn't do phone consultations, came the reply.

"I'm not after a consultation. I just want to ask if he's able to help us with something."

I'm sorry Mister St. Claire, but as I noted, Mister Spaulding doesn't consult on the phone. Are you in the London area?

Eyebrow looked at Purple forlornly before answering. "No, I'm not in London. Could you please just tell him that Conrad St. Claire's on the phone?"

Mister Spaulding isn't in the office at the moment Mister St. Claire. Would you like me to check and see when he's available for you to meet with him?

"I can't meet with him face to face. Can you call him and let him know that I'm trying to get in contact with him? Maybe you could ask him if this one time he could meet with me on the phone?"

I don't expect he'll make an exception Mister St. Claire, but I'll certainly contact him and ask. Will you be on this same number for the next hour?

"Yes, I will. Will he call me back?"

No, I'll call you back Mister St. Claire. Please leave it with me and I'll return your call as soon as possible.

"Thank you," said Eyebrow, after which the call terminated, leaving both he and Purple sitting on the side of the road in silence.

That silence was broken by Joe Purple. "What the fuck is this Conrad St. Claire shit? That's the guy they thought you murdered in Vegas. Why are you using his name?"

"That's who Spaulding thinks I am. We played in that poker tournament together and everyone thought I was St. Claire. That's the only way he'll remember me."

Purple rolled his eyes at the revelation. "Jesus Christ. Every time I think that I might have some sort of understanding about you, something else comes along. You're a man with a lot of fucking layers, Eyebrow."

"I'm not really that complex Joe," replied Eyebrow. "The whole St. Claire situation was just one of those things I guess."

"Well, be that as it may..." Purple started to respond, but was cut off by the sound of Eyebrow's phone ringing. "Fuck me, that was quick."

Eyebrow answered and was greeted again by Louise from the other end. *Mister St. Claire?*

"Yes," replied Eyebrow.

Mister St. Claire, I've spoked to Mister Spaulding, and he remembers you well. He asked me to pass on his regards.

"That's very nice to hear, thank you," replied Eyebrow.

As to a meeting, I'm sorry to say but as I expected, he'll be unable to do a phone consultation. It's his policy I'm afraid. He asked me to let you know that he would be more than happy to receive you if you happen to be in London.

Eyebrow leant towards Purple and whispered. "What does 'receive you' mean Joe?"

Purple spoke equally as softly in reply. "It's fancy way of saying that he'll have you as a guest, or some shit like that."

"Ahh, that's good, because it sounded like some sort of kinky sexual shit." Eyebrow turned his attention back to the phone call. "I don't think I'll be able to do that. I might have to get back to you."

Very well Mister St. Claire. Feel free to consider your options and get back to us at your convenience. I'll advise Mister Spaulding accordingly.

"Thank you. I'll be in touch," said Eyebrow as he hung up the call. He stayed silent and gazed toward the floor of the car. "Looks like we won't be able to do anything else Joe. We may as well just go home."

Purple could sense that Eyebrow was deflated, and the tone of his voice was lathered in disappointment. Purple considered saying something and initially squeaked out the slightest of sounds before he caught himself and slipped into contemplation about what he was about to suggest. He played out the pros and cons in his head and the scale certainly came down quite noticeably on the con side. Purple had nothing to lose from this setback – he could easily slip straight back into his adopted life as a local restauranteur and put all the events of the past few days behind him. It was, after all, Eyebrow who carried all the legal baggage.

But even though Eyebrow was the sherpa, Purple was, as he'd noted previously, the silent investor. And just like the rich banker and the local guide hauling his baggage up the slopes of Mount Everest, the reality was that if disaster struck, they'd likely meet their doom together – their vastly different backgrounds having precisely zero influence on their ultimate shared fate. As Eyebrow's disappointment became evident, Joe Purple stared directly ahead before closing his eyes, letting out an audible sigh and speaking. "We don't have to check in for this entire weekend Eyebrow. If you think about it, if we time everything right, it doesn't take *that* long to get to London and back."

CHAPTER 18

The Men of Many Names

The weather on the previous day at Coffee Pond had been spectacular, with the prospect of summer firmly at the top of everyone's thoughts. But not so on this day. In a stunning change of fortune, the rain had arrived with vengeance, along with the wind and an accompanying drop in temperature. As such, it was a slow and careful drive for Eyebrow and Purple as they made their way to *Lucky's Motel* for the day's check-in, after which they would have a brief window of freedom – freedom that they intended to exploit to its fullest.

Swinging the car into the car park in a now well-practiced manner, they peered through the wipers that were vigorously slapping water from the windscreen. It was their hope that Bishop would not summon them out of their dry shelter and thankfully, Bishop appeared to have as much interest in venturing out as they did. Standing snugly in his doorway, he firstly waved to them in acknowledgement, after which he gestured with his hands that he expected the two of them to stay right there in town for the duration of his time away. He concluded by alternating two fingers between his eyes and the two men in the car, the universal signal for "I'll be watching".

But both Eyebrow and Purple suspected that Bishop's gesture was little more than symbolism, and that he would *not* be watching them. At least that was their hope, because as they waved and turned the trunk of the car towards Bishop, the two travel cases within remained unseen, as did the airline tickets to London that Eyebrow and Purple had in their jacket pockets – or more accurately, inside the pockets of Max Von Steel and Turd Ferguson, alongside the passports bearing the same names.

Following their call to the offices of *Iron Key Consulting* the previous day, Eyebrow and Purple had done the math and determined that with the entire weekend free from obligation, they would have ample time for a flying visit to London to meet with Stuart Spaulding, Eyebrow's friend from the poker tournament in Las Vegas. But adding to the complexity of the operation, while Jimmy Eyebrow would be travelling under the name Max Von Steel, he would also be masquerading as Conrad St. Claire for their meeting with Spaulding.

Jimmy Eyebrow – reinvented as Max Von Streel, while impersonating the late Conrad St. Claire. And Joe Purple – formerly federal agent Marcus Bloom, but now living life as Turd Ferguson. Two men, six names – they would have to stay on top of their game to ensure that no slip-ups were made. Simmering below the surface also for Purple from the moment they booked their tickets was the concern that their situation from several days prior had still not been resolved. There remained the very real probability that their names had been flagged following the abortive mission to investigate Cooper's residence and as such, it would not be until he heard the sound of the landing gear being retracted on his outbound flight that he might, just possibly, permit himself to relax a little.

It was at Purple's insistence that they had only booked two tickets to London, with PQ left behind at Coffee Pond, hopefully oblivious to their departure until they were well on their way early in the evening. Purple still could not decipher any cues from PQ and he remained skeptical about his motives, hence why he felt far more comfortable travelling with Eyebrow alone, rather than having the spectre of PQ looming over them the entire time. Arriving at the airport, both men scanned the check-in hall for any signs of danger, and unlike their most recent airport experience, there was nothing apparent. No armed police officers assessing the passengers, and no suited agents patrolling the check-in counters – nothing out of the ordinary.

Sliding into the check-in queue, it therefore came as a surprise when a voice came from behind them. "What the fuck are you two doing here?"

Startled, Eyebrow and Purple quickly spun around to find PQ standing directly behind them. Purple clutched at his chest. "Jesus Christ! What the fuck are YOU doing here?"

"I'm keeping tabs on the two of you. You don't think that I just sit around watching daytime TV when you go out do you? What the fuck are you up to? Where are you two going?"

"We've got a lead on Santiago's money if you must know," said Purple snidely. "But we've got this under control so you can go back to the lake and wait for us to get home. Eyebrow's probably got some suspect DVDs under the floorboards that you could watch to pass the time."

"Not a chance," replied PQ as he retrieved his phone and started dialing. "Don't you fucking go anywhere without me." Eyebrow and Purple had no intention of complying and shuffled along with the line as it slowly snaked its way to the check-in counter. PQ pointed and cautioned them to stay where they were. "Mister Santiago said that I have to go with you," he announced.

"We don't need you," snapped Purple.

PQ pushed the phone in Purple's direction. "Do you want to speak with him yourself?"

Eyebrow leant in close and whispered to Purple. "We might have to let him come with us Joe."

Purple closed his eyes, sighed and looked at PQ. "Jesus Christ, OK. I don't need to speak with him. But we're not waiting for you. We're about to check in so you've got to get your own ticket. If we leave without you then, bad luck pal."

PQ quickly ended his call, shoved the phone back in his pocket and hurried toward the service desk. "Maybe the flight's full and they don't have space for him," noted Eyebrow.

"That'd be the ideal fucking scenario," replied Purple, annoyed at this turn of events that had seen them pick up a chaperone when it was something that they neither wanted, nor needed.

Annoyance now made way for anxiety as Eyebrow and Purple reached the front of the queue and were summoned to the check-in desk by a tall bespectacled customer service agent named George. Eyebrow, like Purple beside him, could feel a bead of sweat forming on his forehead, knowing that this could be the moment when the terminal in front of George would light up like the Baghdad skyline circa-1991. The passports of Max Von Steel and Turd Ferguson, while genuine, nonetheless could trigger some form of alert. And then there was also the possibility of blowback from their previous travel episode.

There was a lot that could go wrong, and Eyebrow steeled himself for what the next couple of minutes had in store as he and Purple slid their tickets and passports across the smooth countertop.

"Traveling together today gentlemen?" asked George as he retrieved their travel documents. There was no turning back now. Whatever the fates had in store would now need to be played out.

"Yes," replied Eyebrow, hoping that his simple monosyllabic response contained no hint of his growing nervousness.

George continued the formalities of the process without shifting his gaze from the monitor in front of him. "And where are you flying to today?"

"London," replied Eyebrow.

George began scanning their passports. Eyebrow could sense that Joe Purple was experiencing the same inner fear as he was while they waited. Eventually George lifted his gaze and spoke directly to them. *This is it*, thought Eyebrow to himself. *We're fucked.*

"How many pieces of baggage today?" asked George with a smile.

Purple exhaled, hoping that it wasn't overtly noticeable. "Just one each," he said, the relief washing over him. He placed his small bag onto the belt and after it was tagged and dispatched, Eyebrow did likewise. Given the overnight flight, they were only staying in London briefly, returning on Sunday evening in plenty of time for their Monday check-in with Bishop. As such, they had both been able to pack relatively light, each toting little more than a couple of changes of clothes and associated essentials. "Can I ask a favor please?" said Purple.

"Certainly sir," replied George. "I'll see what I can do for you. What is it I can help you with?"

Purple glanced in the direction of PQ who was at the service desk enquiring about purchasing a ticket on the flight. "Can you give us seats next to a passenger who's already checked in? We don't want an empty seat next to us."

"Of course, Mister Ferguson. That's easy." George keyed the necessary details into the check-in system, which in turn spat out two boarding passes. George slid the documents across the counter. "Thirty-two A and C, enjoy your flight."

Purple perused the boarding passes before replying to George. "A and C. Those seats aren't side-by-side, are they? Is there someone sitting between us?"

George smirked. "There is at the moment, but I suspect he won't stay for long. It says that he booked the middle seat alone, and people usually do that to try and secure the whole row for themselves. I guess they assume that people will just leave that row alone when they're booking a seat. It's the whole social media 'travel hack' thing that everyone seems to be doing these days." George leant over the counter and lowered his voice, his face now exploding in a mischievous grin. "But if I see that on the system, I'll always surround them and teach them that it's a dangerous game to play."

Purple nodded and smiled back in appreciation before turning to Eyebrow. "I like this guy," he said with a chuckle. "We should hit the Indian food before we leave."

"He won't want to stay in the middle seat once you've arrived," advised George. "I'd bet my house that he'll offer to move to one of your seats… he'll make it sound like he's doing you a favor by letting you sit together."

Purple tapped his boarding pass on the counter and thanked George for his insight. "We'll keep that in mind when the time comes."

Thankful that their names did not appear to have raised any red flags in the travel database, Eyebrow and Purple made their way toward the departure gates to identify somewhere to get something to eat. It was still over an hour and a half until their flight would start boarding so they had plenty of time to relax and subsequently amble to their departure gate. It was Eyebrow and Purple's hope however that their surplus of available time was not reciprocated for PQ and that time was his enemy. It would make things much easier for both of them if PQ were to be left at the gate staring dejectedly at their flight as it lifted off, bound for London.

CHAPTER 19

Remembering the Addis Ababa Incident

Despite living on the shores of an idyllic lake, Jimmy Eyebrow and Joe Purple hadn't had a lot of time to relax in recent times, due almost exclusively to the chaos that perpetually followed in Eyebrow's wake – chaos that also always seemed to drag the unwilling Joe Purple along with it. But for now, as they shuffled down the aisle toward the seats on their flight to London, they looked forward to at least a few hours of respite, even if it was going to be in a semi-reclined position, and in the company of a complete stranger.

As they approached their seats, they identified the mystery passenger that George had alluded to during the check-in process. As Eyebrow and Purple gazed directly at him, the man's face fell as he realized that his ambitious plan to secure not only his own, but the neighboring seats as well, was about to come to nought. One thing that struck Eyebrow immediately as he stared at their new seatmate was the size of the man's head. He turned and nudged Joe Purple. "Hey Joe, is it just me, or is that guy's head really big?"

"Yeah, I noticed it too Eyebrow. Fuck me, that guy's a sniper's dream."

"Is it his entire head, or just the forehead do you think?"

"It's the whole thing. Christ, that head's so massive that I bet he can remember tomorrow."

Arriving at row thirty-two, Eyebrow and Purple were keen to see if George's earlier hypothesis would hold true. They were not disappointed.

"Oh, hi guys," said the man as he began to stand. "I'm not sure how I got this seat but if you two are travelling together then I'd be happy to swap out so that you can sit with each other."

Eyebrow and Purple glanced at one another and smiled devilishly. "No, we'll be fine," said Purple. "You keep your seat."

The man was taken aback and gulped at the thought that his original strategy was not only about to fail, but it would do so in a spectacular manner, leaving him as the holder of the dreaded middle seat, on a long-haul flight of all things. "Are you sure?" he said with a hint of desperation in his voice. "I really don't mind, especially if the two of you want to sit together."

Purple now realized that their in-flight entertainment that evening could transcend the video screen in the seatback, and he set in motion what would become several hours of torment for their hapless associate who was going to be sandwiched between them for the duration of the journey. "No, it's all good," said Purple. "I'd prefer not to sit next to him anyway. He has a weird skin infection that he refuses to get treatment for."

Eyebrow was readying to rebut Purple's blatantly false statement when he picked up a cue in Purple's eyes and, with the penny dropping about what he was up to, understood that the game was now afoot. "I tried, remember? But the doctor said it's incurable." A mortified look spread across the man's face as Eyebrow continued. "Anyway, I'm happy not to be sitting next to you after the Addis Ababa incident."

"What was the Addis Ababa incident?" asked the man, the concern resonating through his voice.

Purple glared in Eyebrow's direction. "We don't talk about Addis Ababa." By that point, Purple was lowering himself into his seat and, relaxing his tone, added one final observation. "Anyway, it wouldn't have happened if that guy hadn't invaded my personal space."

Their large-craniumed seatmate now sat, ashen-faced and silent. This was no doubt the genesis of his resolution to never again try the seat hack suggestion. Indeed, not long after that flight – within days in fact – he was destined to upload a video to social media titled: "*I tried this seat hack. See how it turned out.*"

With both men now seated, Eyebrow gazed toward the front of the plane, noting that the flow of onboarding passengers had slowed. He spoke to Purple, with no regard for their reluctant associate wedged between them. "I haven't seen PQ yet Joe. Do you think he made it?"

"I'm hoping not," replied Purple. "How long until we leave?"

"No idea," said Eyebrow. "Twenty minutes or so I guess."

"Ugh… this is painful. I'm getting a migraine thinking about it. I need a fucking headache tablet." Purple turned to their seatmate. "You'd have a few boxes in your bag wouldn't you pal?"

"Sure, I think I've got something," he replied as he began rummaging through his carry-on under the seat rest. "Here you go," he said, flourishing a box. "How many do you need?"

"Whatever you'd take, halve it," replied Purple. The man passed two tablets to Purple who in turn tossed them into his mouth, washed them down and settled back into the waiting game, hoping that PQ would not make an appearance. As the departure time approached, the flow of incoming passengers had long since ceased and both Eyebrow and Purple now wondered if their luck was in fact holding. An announcement from the Purser cast doubt on that hope.

Good evening everyone. As we're nearing our departure time, we'd like to ask that you ensure all hand luggage is now stowed securely in the overhead lockers, with smaller items under the seat in front of you. We're just waiting on our final passenger to make their way to the gate, after which we should have you on your way.

Purple groaned and looked toward Eyebrow. "Fuck me, that's him isn't it. The prick's holding up the entire plane."

"Might be someone else Joe," replied Eyebrow. However, with the words barely out of his mouth, a sweaty and very radiant PQ appeared at the front of the cabin and began his exhausted shuffle down the aisle, all the while scanning the interior of the plane for Eyebrow and Purple. Ultimately spotting them, PQ signaled questioningly as to whether there was space for him to sit with them. Purple very quickly waved him off, noting that both he and Eyebrow were already in the company of another passenger.

Eyebrow and Purple's companion noted the exchange and offered his contribution. "If he's with you, I can swap seats if you'd like. I'm sure the flight attendants could organize it."

"Don't even fucking think about it pal," snarled Purple. "You're staying right here in your assigned seat."

A look of concern flashed across the man's face. "Is there something going on here? Am I… am I being taken hostage?"

"What the fuck? No! Jesus, you're not being taken hostage," snapped Purple. "We just don't want anything to do with that prick while we're on the plane. We need a break from him. Don't overthink things, which I understand in your case might be difficult."

The man though remained in a heightened state. "I don't know anything that would be of value if you *are* planning to take me hostage. I swear."

"Jesus Christ, relax pal," said Purple. "You're in no danger. I mean… my associate here did once kill a guy in an easy chair by ramming a dildo down his throat, but he's off the clock today so you've got nothing to worry about. Don't bother him, and he won't bother you." The man glanced at Eyebrow who simply shrugged his shoulders in response. Purple reassuringly patted his neighbour on the leg. "Once we're in the air, grab a drink, recline and rest up buddy. It'll all be over before you know it."

"What will all be over?" replied the man, his voice wavering. "You mean the flight, right? That's what you mean?"

"Yeah… the flight, of course," whispered Purple as he shifted his gaze wistfully out the window.

Needless to say, relaxation did not come to Eyebrow and Purple's cerebrally enhanced seating companion over the following hours. The announcement that the time was approaching to prepare for descent was met with a slight uptick in the man's demeanor, although he remained guarded, even as the flaps were extended and the thud of the landing gear locking into place signaled that landing was imminent. But while his disposition picked up as each minute passed, Eyebrow's was soon to be dealt a mighty blow.

As the plane slowed and exited the runway to commence its journey to the gate, the obligatory welcome message began being relayed to all passengers. *Ladies and gentlemen, welcome to London where the local time is seven twenty-five am on Saturday…*

"Fuck!" screeched Eyebrow, possibly a little louder than he should have, prompting a stern glare from Purple. "What did she just say Joe?"

Purple wasn't sure what Eyebrow was referring to. "She said welcome to London. Where else did you think we'd end up if we booked a ticket to London? Fucking Berlin?"

"No Joe, I mean the day and time."

"It's about half past seven Saturday morning," replied Purple before realising that something seemed amiss. "What exactly is the problem here Eyebrow?"

"It's Saturday Joe, that's the problem."

"Yeah… the day after we left Eyebrow. What's the issue?"

"I thought time went backwards on a long flight," stammered Eyebrow. "I thought we'd get there on the same day we left."

"Uhh, no," replied Purple. "London was already ahead of us when we left so why the fuck would it be behind us when we arrive?"

"He's thinking about the date line," added their seatmate, who then turned to Eyebrow. "We don't cross the date line on this flight. We don't gain or lose days."

"And this is a problem, *why* Eyebrow?" asked Purple skeptically.

"I thought we were arriving on Friday. I booked our hotel for two nights, but now it's already Saturday."

Purple sighed and closed his eyes momentarily. "For fuck sake Eyebrow."

"It was a mistake Joe." Eyebrow paused as another realization dawned on him. "Oh, shit! That means we're meeting Spaulding *today*!"

"Jesus Christ Eyebrow," muttered Purple. "Well, I haven't slept, I stink, and my mouth tastes like I've licked an ashtray, so hopefully we have a few minutes to freshen up before we hit the road. Let's not fuck around when we get off the plane Eyebrow. Save the duty free shopping for the trip home." Purple paused for a moment before continuing. "You've booked the return ticket for Sunday, right? Tomorrow?"

"Yes, I did that bit right Joe. I just thought we'd have another day in London and we wouldn't be rushed."

Eyebrow's gross misunderstanding of world time had created an issue for the two men, though it wasn't insurmountable. While an open-topped double-decker bus tour might now be off the cards, the meeting with Spaulding was still in play and Eyebrow was thankful that despite his miscalculation, he at least hadn't messed that part up. All that remained now as the plane eased up against the air bridge was to be as efficient as possible in making their way through the sprawling complex that is Heathrow Airport. And as anyone who has been there will tell you, the words "Heathrow" and "efficient" are rarely seen in a sentence together.

CHAPTER 20

Memoriam Interruptus

Leo Bishop had just alighted from the well-worn sandstone step outside the florist when he felt the mobile phone in his pocket buzz. He fumbled with the two bouquets of flowers he was cradling as he struggled to extract the vibrating device from his pocket, turning the screen towards himself and seeing that the caller was Dennis Burnett. "Fuck me Dennis, not today," he muttered to himself before lifting the phone to his ear. "Dennis, what can I do for you."

Burnett was immediately apologetic on the other end of the call. "Leo, I'm really sorry to be bothering you today. You know that I wouldn't call you unless absolutely necessary."

"What's up?" replied Bishop, neither acknowledging nor dismissing Burnett's apology.

"Leo…" began Burnett before pausing to draw breath. "It's Eyebrow. When was the last time you saw him?"

Bishop grimaced – why, on today of all days, was Eyebrow a necessary topic of discussion? Bishop rubbed his eyes in frustration as he prepared to respond. "He checked in with me yesterday, as required. That was the last time I saw him. Do I dare to ask why, Dennis?"

"We may have a situation. I got a call from Black who advised me that Max Von Steel – *our* Max Von Steel, departed the country, bound for the UK last night. Did you know about this Leo?"

Bishop began pacing up and down the sidewalk in front of the florist. "Ahh, fuck me. No, I didn't know about it Dennis. What the fuck is he up to?"

"I've got no idea. Obviously he's involved in something that we don't know about. We were hoping that maybe he'd given you some sort of clue about what that might be."

"Nothing at all. Both he and Purple have been nothing but their usual annoying selves."

"That's another thing," added Burnett. "It looks like Purple's gone with him, and according to the seating arrangements supplied by the airline, they appear to be travelling with someone else – a guy named Charles Dunk. Black ran a check on this Dunk character, and he came back clean – a few traffic tickets… nothing major. But, and here's the interesting thing, Black did a full background, and the guy works as a low-level engineer for a defense contractor named Triochron Industries."

An all-too familiar wave of dread began to wash over Bishop. "Jesus Dennis. What's going on here? Why the fuck would Eyebrow and Purple be travelling to England with someone who works for a defense contractor? Are we certain that the three of them are travelling together?"

"No, we don't know with certainty," replied Burnett. "All we know is that the three of them are sitting together. Nothing more, nothing less."

"Something's not right though Dennis, I can feel it. What's in play here?"

"No clue whatsoever Leo. But what I do know is that by skipping the country, his goose is going to be cooked if and when he returns. He's back behind bars the moment he steps off that return flight. It took a lot of diplomacy to get him sprung the first time so if he's going to shit on the goodwill like this, I'm moving the risk off the books."

"Do we know if he's booked to come back?" asked Bishop.

"Apparently he'll be back Sunday night. So whatever they're up to, it's a flying visit."

"Leave it with me Dennis," said Bishop. "I'm about to drive out to Oakwood and then I'll make some calls."

"I'm really sorry to do this to you today," said Burnett, the empathy in his voice resonating from the phone.

"Don't worry about it Dennis. I'll get onto it, just give me a little bit, OK?"

"Of course Leo. Keep me updated, that's all I ask."

"Will do," said Bishop as the two men farewelled each other, after which Bishop stowed the phone back into his pocket, composed himself and strode towards his car for the short drive to his destination. Whatever it was that Eyebrow was up to, it could wait an hour before demanding Bishop's attention.

A few thousand miles away, Jimmy Eyebrow and Joe Purple had successfully, and very anxiously, cleared UK immigration, reinforcing that the passports of their new identities were indeed the real deal. Within moments of exiting the plane, Charles Dunk, their large-headed seatmate of the past seven hours had stridden through the immigration gates, finally free from torment, although oblivious to the fact that he had now been flagged as a person of interest. Meanwhile, PQ had been consumed by the departing passengers from his section, leaving Eyebrow and Purple with just the final task of clearing customs before their arrival in London was formalised.

As they walked, Purple offered some thoughts. "I have to say Eyebrow, I was impressed with your improv skills on the plane with seven-heads. Where the fuck did you pull that Addis Ababa line from? That sounded way too fucking intellectual for you."

"I watched a documentary about the place Joe," replied Eyebrow. "I guess the name just stuck with me. Do you know that they use a different calendar there?"

"I did not know that Eyebrow. Can you believe that shit? I just learnt something from you."

With little more than a small suitcase each for a couple of nights away from home, Eyebrow and Purple were strolling through the "nothing to declare" lane when a uniformed man stepped in front of Eyebrow and directed him to step to the side. "If you could come over this way please sir," said the officer as he ushered Eyebrow toward a large table. Purple began to accompany Eyebrow before the man spoke again. "There's no requirement for you to join us sir. You're free to continue."

Purple knew that what was happening was problematic, so he made his case to remain by Eyebrow's side. "He's legally retarded and I'm his carer."

"Very well sir," said the man. "If the two of you could step over to the table and place your bags on top."

Purple leant close to Eyebrow and whispered. "What the fuck have you done this time Eyebrow?"

"I don't think I've done anything Joe, I swear," whispered Eyebrow in return.

"Please tell me you haven't brought your fucking business cards," snarled Purple softly.

"No. I didn't bring any. I've learnt my lesson there." Eyebrow placed his bag atop the table and turned his attention to the man. "Is there a problem here?"

"Just a routine check," replied the man, although Eyebrow couldn't shake the feeling that there was nothing routine about it. "Did you pack your bag yourself sir?" asked the officer.

"Yes," replied Eyebrow.

"And do you mind if I open the case?"

"No, go ahead."

"How long are you intending to stay in the UK?" asked the officer as he unzipped Eyebrow's small suitcase.

"Two nights," replied Eyebrow before being corrected by Joe Purple who glared at him.

"Well, just one night now. It was supposed to be two, but someone couldn't work out dates and times."

The officer suddenly stopped rummaging through Eyebrow's luggage, a look of horror spreading across his face. "Bloody hell, what on earth is this?" he exclaimed, never lifting his eyes from the contents of Eyebrow's case. "What *is* this?" he repeated before turning to a colleague and beckoning him over. "Gareth! Could you come and look at this please."

"Fuck me, what have you got in there Eyebrow?" asked a now very concerned Joe Purple. "Did you bring your entire porn collection with you?"

"I don't know what it is that he's looking at Joe," replied Eyebrow.

By this point, the officer's colleague, who they presumed was Gareth, had arrived and was similarly horrified by what he saw in Eyebrow's suitcase. He looked up and stared directly at Eyebrow. "You know that this sort of thing can get you thrown into jail here?"

Both Eyebrow and Purple were now overcome with worry. Clearly something had gone awry with Eyebrow's luggage and all that remained to be seen was what the actual nature of the transgression was. The first officer reached into the case and held up Eyebrow's tiny pair of star-spangled swimming trunks. "What on earth am I looking at here? Where the bloody hell do you think you're going to be wearing these in the UK?" A broad grin now broke out over his face, accompanied by a raucous laugh from Gareth as both officers revelled in the fact that their quintessential British sense of humor had reeled their visibly flustered international visitors in – hook, line and sinker.

Joe Purple had breathed many sighs of relief during his time with Eyebrow, few larger than this one. The thought of being incarcerated in a foreign prison was not appealing and now that he knew that the officers' concerns were little more than an elaborate gag, he made his case for absolution. "I've told him multiple times that those things are a fucking disgrace. I have to see him in that fucking atrocity a couple of times a week. I'm sorry you had to experience this."

The officer returned the trunks to the suitcase and continued his search. "They are rather appalling," he said to Eyebrow before Gareth added his observation.

"You weren't planning on wearing those in public, were you?"

Purple joined the conversation. "That's what I was wondering too. Where the fuck did you plan on unleashing those things in London?"

"The hotel has a pool," replied Eyebrow. "I just thought I might have a swim while we're here."

The officer completed his search, closed Eyebrow's suitcase and slid it across the table. "Please exercise caution with those sir. They're maybe one step away from being classified as a dangerous weapon. You're free to continue."

"So, there was no problem?" asked Eyebrow.

"No, just a routine check sir, that's all. We'll pull people from the line randomly through the day for spot checks. Usually the contraband we find is food or weapons, but I have to admit, I've never seen anything quite like those swimmers before." He turned to his associate. "Gareth? You ever seen anything like that?"

"Never," replied Gareth. "That's certainly one I didn't have pegged as a possibility today."

The first officer now directed Eyebrow and Purple toward the exit. "Anyway, you're free to go straight through now. Enjoy your visit to the UK."

"Thank you," replied Eyebrow as he and Purple popped the handles on their small suitcases and wheeled them toward the exit and onward to the madness of the arrivals terminal and the associated confusion as to how they would make their way into the city. Waiting outside was PQ, the men now reconvening as a trio, much to Joe Purple's annoyance.

"What was going on in there?" he probed.

Eyebrow made to answer, but Purple pre-empted him. "Nothing for you to concern yourself with." Purple now turned to Eyebrow. "What time are we meeting with your guy?"

Eyebrow glanced at his watch. "Ten o'clock, so we don't have much time. Have either of you been to London before? Do you know where we're going?"

"Not me," replied Purple.

"No, never," added PQ.

Purple jumped in again. "Can I just point out Eyebrow that there seems to be a remarkable lack of preparation on your part in relation to this entire trip."

"I've tried my best Joe," said Eyebrow. "I'm not a travel agent."

Purple looked around the chaotic terminal. "I haven't got a fucking clue about how we catch a train or a bus from this place, so it might have to be a taxi."

"I agree Joe," replied Eyebrow. "Let's just get a cab to take us straight to Spaulding's office."

And with that, the three men strode outside and onward to the taxi rank – destination, Canary Wharf. Eyebrow was hoping that the meeting with his old poker buddy Stuart Spaulding would yield results with regards to the hunt for Santiago's missing money. And while that outcome was a possibility, Jimmy Eyebrow had no inkling, at that point at least, as to the magnitude of the domino that was about to be pushed over.

CHAPTER 21

No Secrets

Half a mile, that's all it was. But it was half a mile too far for Joe Purple, who was primed to explode in the back of the taxi that he, Eyebrow and PQ had procured at the airport for what they all thought would be a quick dash into London. Now, as their time crawling through the traffic ticked past an hour, Purple could no longer contain his frustration. "Jesus fucking Christ! How far was that fucking airport from the city? How much further do we have to go?"

"You can see Canary Wharf through there," said the taxi driver, pointing towards the conglomeration of high-rise buildings that loomed through the window. "It shouldn't be long now."

Purple leant forward and glanced at the meter. "Holy shit!" he exclaimed as he pivoted towards Eyebrow. "It's already a hundred and twenty-five pounds!"

"How much is that in our money Joe?" asked Eyebrow.

Purple paused for a moment before responding. "I don't know, but it's a fucking lot." He sighed at the sight of the traffic still sitting between them and their destination. "Come on, we're getting out of here and we'll walk the rest of the way. Pay the man Eyebrow."

"Are you sure?" asked Eyebrow. But Purple had already grabbed his bag and was exiting the vehicle. As PQ prepared to follow, Eyebrow quickly counted out the required fare, plus a small tip, handed it to the driver and joined his colleagues as they wove through the stationary traffic toward the sidewalk.

"Fuck me, that was ridiculous," moaned Purple as they began to amble toward the heart of Canary Wharf where Spaulding's office was located.

"You have to admit though Joe, we got to see a lot of stuff on the way in," noted Eyebrow.

"Yeah, I'll give you that, but we were crammed into the back of a fucking cab, so I didn't get a lot of enjoyment out of it. I was about to go stir crazy." Purple turned toward PQ. "And you – fuck me, do you think it's possible to breathe any louder? It's been like sitting with fucking Darth Vader for the past hour. I feel sorry for the poor guy who sat next to you on the plane."

"Hey, I can't help that you prick!" snapped PQ. "I've got a problem with my fucking epiglottis."

"What the fuck is an epiglottis?"

"A thing in your throat. Mine doesn't work as well as everyone else's, that's all."

"Well, be that as it may, I'm glad I don't have to put up with it overnight. I don't know where you're staying, but Eyebrow and I have already organised our hotel, so it won't be with us. Maybe you could find somewhere near the train station where your breathing can just blend into the background noise."

"Hey, fuck you pal," said an agitated PQ as a horn sounded from beside them. Glancing to the right they saw their taxi driver give them a wave as he passed them, the traffic now frustratingly free flowing. Thankfully, the remaining walk was incident-free, and it wasn't long before they arrived at the offices of *Iron Key Consulting* and, despite their tediously slow trip from the airport, almost right on time.

Before they went inside, Eyebrow spoke to both Purple and PQ. "Remember guys, for this meeting, I'm Conrad St. Claire. That's who Spaulding thinks I am. Try to play along with that please."

"You got it, *St. Claire*," replied Purple.

"No problem," added PQ.

Eyebrow composed himself and walked into the office where he was greeted pleasantly by a receptionist, most likely the person he had spoken to on the phone a few days prior. "Good morning sir. Do you have an appointment?"

"Yes, I do. The name's St. Claire. Conrad St. Claire."

Purple leant over to PQ and whispered in his ear. "Here we go. He's about to start the whole fucking James Bond thing now that he's in London."

"Of course, Mister St. Claire," replied the receptionist. "So nice to finally meet you. Please, take a seat and I'll let Mister Spaulding know that you're here. Your associates are welcome to make a coffee and wait in the lounge area while you meet with Mister Spaulding."

"They can't come in with me?"

"No, that won't be possible I'm afraid. Mister Spaulding wasn't aware that you were bringing your staff with you, so he's only prepared for you." Joe Purple grimaced at the notion that he was again perceived as Eyebrow's subordinate – the second time it had happened in a short space of time.

"OK then," replied Eyebrow meekly before he turned and walked toward Purple and PQ. "Looks like you two need to wait out here."

"That's OK my Lord," sneered Purple. "We'll go and wait for you in the servants' quarters."

"It's not my fault Joe…" Eyebrow began before the receptionist emerged from an office and beckoned him in.

"Mister Spaulding will see you now Mister St. Claire. Can I bring you a drink? Coffee? Tea?"

"Could I have an orange juice?"

"Certainly Mister St. Claire. Make your way in and I'll be with you shortly."

Eyebrow turned to the others. "I'll be back soon. Wish me luck." Turning again, he stepped into the office where Spaulding, who was seated behind a desk, stood and made his way across the room to give his guest a hearty welcome.

"St. Claire, lovely to see you again."

"Same here," replied Eyebrow.

Spaulding directed Eyebrow towards a large sitting area that had a spectacular view along the Thames, with the Tower Bridge visible off in the distance. "Please, have a seat." The receptionist arrived in quick time with Eyebrow's orange juice and placed it on the glass table in front of him, alongside a coffee for Spaulding.

"If there's anything else you'd like Mister St. Claire, don't hesitate to ask," she said as she turned on her heels and departed.

"Thank you, Louise," said Spaulding.

Eyebrow also conveyed his appreciation. "Thank you."

Spaulding opened proceedings informally. "So, St. Claire… final table hey? I'm sorry I couldn't be there the following day. Once I'd been eliminated myself, I didn't see the need to hang around."

"You didn't miss much. I was out pretty early. Had a great hand but the other guy had a better one. Still, it was a lot of fun."

"Good to hear." Spaulding now leant forward a little and took a sip of his coffee before continuing. "So, tell me, what brings you here to my office today?"

"I'm hoping you might be able to help me with something," replied Eyebrow, digging in his pocket for the slip of paper that had been retrieved from Julian Cooper's office. He slid the small Post-It note across the glass toward Spaulding. "I was told that this was a crypto key, or something like that. Is that correct?"

"Certainly would appear to be," replied Spaulding as he massaged the slip of paper between his fingers. "What do you need my help with?"

"I need to get into it. I was told that getting access to it just by using that number is impossible. Is that right?"

"Who told you that?"

"We met a guy who helped us after we found this, and he introduced us to some other guys who seemed like they were computer experts or something. They had a look at it and told us all about crypto and how it's basically impossible to hack into it if you don't have the right passwords, or codes, or whatever the hell it is that you need."

"Well, they're pretty much correct St. Claire. That's the appeal of crypto currency – when done the right way, it's very secure. The flip side of that of course is that with such a high level of security comes the risk that your funds could be locked in the nether for all time if you lose the record of your credentials. Which brings me to my next, and very important question St. Claire – who does this belong to? I'm guessing it doesn't belong to you. I mean, why would you need my help accessing something that was already yours?"

Eyebrow pondered the wisdom of disclosing either his task, or his employer, preferring instead to keep the matter vague. "I'm just trying to help out a friend, that's all."

Spaulding stood and walked over to the window. As he stared across the vastness of the city, he spoke without turning to Eyebrow. "You have to understand St. Claire, that this isn't some two-bit operation that I run here. There are certain aspects of the security game that I specialise in, and a very particular skill set that I offer my clients. I'm meeting with you here today as a continuation of our all too brief friendship from Las Vegas. But my services are not cheap and in order to do my job, I cannot deal with vagaries and obfuscation."

Spaulding turned to Eyebrow. "The confidential nature of anything that is discussed within these walls is paramount to my business model." Spaulding now walked slowly toward Eyebrow as he spoke. "There can be no secrets here. I do not care what the circumstances are that led to you having this key St. Claire. My business is helping those who cannot find help elsewhere. So, in order for me to help *you*, I will ask you again – who does the key belong to, and what is the context behind your call for assistance?"

Eyebrow felt overwhelmed by the situation. Spaulding was clearly a high-level professional and yet again, Eyebrow now found himself on the threshold of crossing into a world that was far beyond his capability. He now faced a fork in the road – the first option being that he could thank Spaulding for his time, go home apologetically and empty-handed to Gutierrez and Santiago, and just resume his day-to-day life.

Or... he could step up, disclose all to Spaulding and work on resolving Santiago's situation, even if it led him down a path that was as unfamiliar as it was dangerous. Given that his current legal situation back home wasn't particularly appealing, Eyebrow decided that moving forward was the preferable option over simply giving up. His only hope was that Joe Purple would concur with his judgement.

Spaulding sat as he sensed that Eyebrow was readying to speak. "I have a friend... a very powerful friend. A colleague of his asked for his help and so he called me to assist."

"Go on," said Spaulding, intrigued by this new layer to the man he knew as Conrad St. Claire that was being revealed.

"His friend..." began Eyebrow before being cut off.

"Does this friend have a name?"

"Santiago. Mister Santiago thought that his accountant had been stealing money from him." Spaulding made to speak but Eyebrow suspected what he was going to ask and pre-empted him. "I don't know how much exactly, but from what I understand, it's a *lot*. The problem is that this accountant has disappeared and we were sent to check out his house to try and find where he's hidden the money."

"Who is, 'we'?" asked Spaulding.

"Me, the two guys out in the waiting room, and one other guy that we lost along the way."

"Lost, as in, he was killed?"

"No. The cops turned up while we were there, and we all split. We don't know what happened to him."

"Is that where you found this?" asked Spaulding, pointing to the Post-It note.

"Yeah, it was in his office."

"An office at his house, or a different office?"

"He worked from his house by the look of it. At first, I thought this was a password to something, but the guy at the diner told us it was a crypto key."

"Who's the guy at the diner?"

"Just the guy who was working there. He saw Joe and I talking about how we didn't know what it was, and he told us that it looked like a crypto key."

"And you said that some other guys checked it out for you?"

"Yeah. They were at a pizza shop near the diner."

"Do you remember the name of the place?"

"No, I can't remember."

Spaulding sunk into thought for a brief period, leaving a long silence hanging in the air that Eyebrow dared not interrupt. Eventually he leant back in his chair and crossed his legs. "What you have here is what's called a cold wallet."

"Yeah, that's what the pizza guys called it," said Eyebrow quickly.

"Then they seem to know what they're talking about," continued Spaulding. "And, they were also correct in that having only this key presents significant difficulties in accessing what's within."

"They said it's impossible," added Eyebrow.

"And they'd be close to the mark there St. Claire. Close, but not entirely accurate. Just trying to brute force your way in would indeed be a futile effort. You'd need a thousand years to even get close, unless you got extraordinarily lucky. But if one were to have a more, shall we say… *sophisticated* method at one's disposal, then while the difficulty remains high, it's not entirely beyond the realm of possibility." Spaulding let his words linger, waiting for a response.

Eyebrow took a moment to pick up the cue but eventually responded. "And, do you have a method to do that?"

"I may St. Claire… I may. But it's not something I can do without considerable effort and, I suspect, time." Eyebrow made to speak but Spaulding raised a finger to halt him. "Now I need to know something St. Claire – are you operating in a dangerous space with this affair? Is it possible that your life could be in peril?"

"Jesus, my life always seems to be in peril these days, so yes, I'd say that this has potential to dump me in the shit again."

Spaulding leant over the table, flourishing the Post-It note between his fingers. "Then you need to be smart here. This little thing is your insurance policy. For so long as this key remains out of the hands of anyone who may be after you, then you'll be safe... to a degree of course. Now, that being said, I'm going to need you to leave the key with me so that I can do my investigation." Eyebrow appeared concerned at this request, but Spaulding elaborated. "We'll write something up on an identical note with some variation to the actual key. If anyone asks if you've got it, then you can show them that you still have it safely tucked away. I'll keep the original and work on it for you." Spaulding stood, made his way to the door and opened it. "Louise, can you come in here please?"

"What can I do for you Mister Spaulding?" she asked.

Spaulding turned to Eyebrow. "Do you have your phone on you St. Claire?"

Eyebrow eased the phone from his pocket. "Sure, got it right here."

"Give it to me," said Spaulding before turning to his assistant and handing her Eyebrow's phone. "Louise, could you please add our app to Mister St. Claire's phone?"

"Certainly Mister Spaulding. Give me a few minutes."

With Louise attending to the task of updating Eyebrow's phone, Spaulding explained what she was doing. "We're putting an encrypted app on your phone where you and I will communicate. We can pass messages and even call each other if need be. We do not use standard phone calls or text messages. Do you understand St. Claire? This protects both of us and keeps our communications one hundred percent secure and confidential."

"I understand," replied Eyebrow, before turning to an important matter of business. "How much do I need to pay you?"

Spaulding rubbed his chin while formulating his response, after which he smiled and reached toward Eyebrow, patting him on the arm. "Let's just see what I can find first OK?" Spaulding now stood and made his way to the door. "For now, it was lovely to see you again St. Claire."

Taking his cue to leave the office, Eyebrow followed before Spaulding stopped one final time to reiterate an important message. "Remember St. Claire, be very careful. Like I said, that slip of paper is your insurance policy so guard it wisely. I have the original here so in a worst-case scenario, disclose that information if it looks like it could save your hide. If you're in mortal danger, the fact that you can retrieve the key may be the leverage that you need." Spaulding now opened the door and ushered Eyebrow into the atrium where the conversation became less formal. "How long are you in town?"

"Just the one night," replied Eyebrow. "We're going home tomorrow."

"No time for sightseeing then?"

"No, but we kind of got a drive past of everything on the way in today."

"You drove in from Heathrow?"

"Yeah, we took a taxi."

"Oh St. Claire!" said Spaulding as he brought his hand down on Eyebrow's shoulder. "No, never a taxi from Heathrow. That must have cost you a fortune."

"Yeah, it wasn't cheap."

"Well, if you're back in town any time, you can catch the Elizabeth Line from the airport, directly here. You'll come out of the station about two minutes from the office."

"Jesus, that would have been handy to know earlier," bemoaned Eyebrow.

The two men had now sidled up to Louise's desk where she handed Eyebrow's phone back to Spaulding, who in turn flipped it around to show Eyebrow the screen. "Here's your app," he noted, pointing to a key icon on the home screen. "The first time you use it, it's going to ask you to set up fingerprint security. Once you've done that, you'll be the only person who can access it. I'll contact you ONLY by this means, do you understand?"

"Got it," replied Eyebrow firmly.

Spaulding handed Eyebrow the phone. "Where are you staying while you're in town?"

"A place called The Bloomsbury. Do you know it?"

"I do. A lovely hotel."

"It was hard finding something this weekend. There wasn't a lot of vacancy close to the city."

"No, you've chosen a particularly difficult time to try and book something at short notice," noted Spaulding. "It's the height of conference season and I know there's at least two big concerts on this weekend also. You were lucky to find a room at The Bloomsbury. Depending on what time you're leaving tomorrow, try to take a five-minute walk and visit the British Museum – it's just a stone's throw from the hotel. How are you planning on getting there?"

"I hadn't thought of that yet," replied Eyebrow. "I don't know my way around your subway, so I guess we'll probably just take a taxi again."

"It's called the Tube St. Claire. That's what our underground trains are called. It's not a subway, it's the Tube. Anyway, let me take care of that for you." Spaulding turned to his assistant. "Louise, could you please have a car brought around for Mister St. Claire and his associates? They'll be going to Bedford Square."

"That's very kind of you, thank you so much," replied Eyebrow as he extended his hand to Spaulding.

"Don't mention it. Again, it was lovely to see you St. Claire, and I'll be in touch as soon as I know anything. If you need me, reach out using the app." Spaulding now pulled Eyebrow in closer as he shook his hand. He lowered his voice. "And remember, be careful. What you seem to be involved in… it could get dangerous in a real hurry."

"I'll be alert, don't worry," muttered Eyebrow in return. "Thanks again for your help. We'll talk soon." And with a wave, Eyebrow made his way back to where Joe Purple and PQ had been patiently awaiting his return. Although buoyed by his conversation with Spaulding, he was also not without a distinct feeling of unease that the situation he now found himself embroiled in was a far cry from his old job of collecting monthly vig from an irate Greek shop owner. From this point forth, Eyebrow knew that he was now dipping his toe firmly into dangerous waters.

CHAPTER 22

No-Show at the Bloomsbury

Spaulding had been correct – *The Bloomsbury* was a beautiful hotel. Having seen off PQ at his hastily procured guest house that neither Jimmy Eyebrow nor Joe Purple bothered to note the name of, they both now stood inside the lobby of *The Bloomsbury*, marveling at its luxurious interior. "I must say Eyebrow, you've actually come through on this one," noted Purple, the appreciation in his tone genuine.

"It looks nice Joe, that's for sure. I didn't really know where we should stay so I kind of lucked into this to be honest."

"Well, I'm happy that we finally got a bit of luck going our way," added Purple as they both strode toward the reception desk to check in.

"Good afternoon, sir," said the man behind the desk. "Checking in?"

"Yes," replied Eyebrow. "I have a reservation for Von Steel. It was supposed to be for two nights, but we only need it for one now."

The man deftly fingered the keyboard in front of him, a look of concern slowly spreading across his face. "I'm sorry Mister Von Steel, but we were expecting you yesterday."

"Yes, I know. But we had a mix-up with dates, and we didn't arrive until today. So we don't need yesterday's booking, just tonight's."

"I'm afraid we won't be able to accommodate that Mister Von Steel. You were marked as a no-show yesterday when you didn't arrive, and we've subsequently accepted another booking for the room."

A heavy sigh emanated from the direction of Joe Purple, but Eyebrow dared not glance in his direction. "Well, is there another room we could have?"

The response was not encouraging. "Unfortunately not sir. We're fully booked for the entire weekend."

"What can I do then?" asked Eyebrow.

Despite there being no availability at *The Bloomsbury*, the man was nonetheless intent on helping where he could. "If you can give me a few moments sir, I'll make a phone call and see if I can organise something for you."

With the man busy making enquiries on their behalf, Purple shunted Eyebrow toward a corner nearby the reception desk. "Well fucking done Eyebrow," he hissed through gritted teeth. "Just when I thought you'd finally pulled one out of the bag, yet again we end up right back where we always seem to be, making shit up as we go along."

"I'm sorry Joe," whispered Eyebrow. "It's my fault for not knowing about the date thing."

"You'd better believe that it's your fault," grumbled Purple forlornly. "Here I was, getting excited that we could stay at a place like this, and now... no, let's just rip that rug right out from under my feet, as always."

With a slight wave of his hand, the man behind the reception desk now beckoned them back. "I'm sorry Mister Von Steel, I made a few calls to some other hotels where I have some colleagues, and I can't find any availability. I'm very sorry."

"So, what do we do?" asked Eyebrow meekly.

"Unfortunately, I've done all I can sir. The only remaining option is for you to try and secure alternative accommodation yourself."

Eyebrow sighed. "Ok then. Sorry to have wasted your time."

As the two men dejectedly exited the front door back into the mild London afternoon, Purple took the initiative. "Eyebrow, you're the world's worst fucking travel agent. I don't want you to touch another thing. This finding a hotel business... I'm taking charge now, got it?"

"All yours Joe," replied Eyebrow, happy to divest the responsibility.

But Joe Purple was soon to discover that the finding a hotel business wasn't exactly a simple enterprise. As the clock ticked into late afternoon, the two men had tried six different hotels in the vicinity of *The Bloomsbury*, none of which could accommodate them at short notice.

For the purposes of accuracy, one technically did have a single vacant room - their _Queen Victoria Suite_. But even though the threat of joining the ranks of London's homeless was looming, the price point was highly problematic. Thus, the two men continued their quest, eventually arriving at the steps of a boutique establishment named _The Jonmount_.

Striding toward the front desk, Purple assumed the lead role. "Do you have any rooms for one night?" he asked, pre-empting the greeting from the man behind the desk.

"I believe we might sir, just let me check," the man replied. Purple turned and shot Eyebrow a satisfied smile, along with a sharp thumbs-up. "Yes, we have one room available," said the man as he eyed Purple and Eyebrow. "It's two king-single beds, but they can be pushed together if desired."

"Yeah, there won't be any requirement for that," scoffed Purple in response. "How much is the room?"

"One hundred and eighty-five pounds for the night sir. Do you have a credit card?"

"We'd prefer to pay cash if we could," replied Purple.

"That's possible sir, but in that case we'll require a cash deposit to also be left."

Purple turned to Eyebrow. "Can you cover that?"

"Sure," replied Eyebrow.

Purple turned back to the counter. "OK then, we'll take it."

"Very well sir." The man retrieved a check-in form and slid it across the desk to Purple. "If you could fill this out for me please." The reception desk phone began to ring and the man motioned Purple to the far end of the desk to complete the administrative duties while he attended to the incoming call.

Purple beckoned Eyebrow over to him as he was completing the check-in form. "If we're paying with cash, then I'll be fucked if I'm checking in as Turd Ferguson," he whispered as he began to fill out the paperwork. Purple's pen now hovered over the "name" section momentarily.

"What's up Joe?" asked Eyebrow.

"Just coming up with a cool name. You're already Max Von Steel... I can be anyone I fucking want today." Eyebrow noticed a glint in Purple's eye, indicating that he'd settled on a new moniker and, sure enough, moments later the name _Donnie Mustang_ appeared on the form.

"Who the fuck is Donnie Mustang, Joe?" asked Eyebrow.

"Just made it up," replied Purple. "Sounds fucking awesome."

Eyebrow rubbed his chin in thought. "I've got a weird feeling that I've heard it somewhere else. Have you ever used that name before today?"

"I just fucking told you Eyebrow that I made it up on the spot. Right here. Right now. So no, I've never used it before."

"It's just familiar for some reason," mused Eyebrow. "Maybe I'm getting confused about someone back home. Like, *way* back home."

Purple had by that point finished completing the form. "Well, regardless, tonight I am no longer Turd Ferguson. Tonight, I'm Donnie Mustang. What do you think Donnie Mustang does for a living Eyebrow? I reckon he's a fucking race car driver."

"Sounds close to it I'd say Joe. Maybe a stuntman? But definitely something that's out there. Oh! Maybe he's one of those specialists that they bring in when things go to shit on an oil rig or something."

"Whatever it is, he's a man's man," replied Purple as he returned the form to the check-in desk. After a quick assessment that all was in order, the room key was passed across the desk and Eyebrow and Purple were on their way upstairs where, hopefully, a restful night of sleep awaited them. Entering their room, they found it to be quite agreeable – certainly not on par with Eyebrow's getaway at *The Bellagio*, but that bar was set so high that it would be almost impossible to compare any other room in good faith. But by normal hotel room standards at least, *The Jonmount* ticked all the boxes.

As Eyebrow fell face-first onto his bed, Purple, now free from the shadow of the ever-present PQ, probed for the details of the meeting with Spaulding. "So now that we've jettisoned that other prick, fill me in on what happened at your guy's office Eyebrow. Do you think he can help us?"

"It sounds like he might be able to Joe," came Eyebrow's muffled response, his face not rising from the mattress.

"Did he give any time frame?"

Eyebrow now rolled over onto his back. "No, but he did say that it might be a pretty big job. He didn't guarantee anything, but he sounded confident."

"So, what do we do now?"

"I guess we just go home and wait to hear from him. I don't think there's much else we can do."

"I'm happy with that idea Eyebrow," said Purple as he too now collapsed onto his bed.

Purple was satisfied that, despite the numerous hiccups, they'd still managed to meet their stated goal. Eyebrow had done all he could to locate Santiago's money, and no-one could ask any more. From that point, it was simply a case of returning home and awaiting any further contact from Spaulding. "We can spend a day sightseeing tomorrow and then just fly home," said Purple. "For once we seem to have done something that doesn't involve our fucking lives hanging by a thread. Let's go and find some dinner and then I'm planning on sleeping for as long as I can. My body clock's been put over a fucking barrel and reamed mightily during the last week, so I really need to rest and try to reset."

For both Purple and Eyebrow, rest would indeed be imperative, as it was soon to become a scarce commodity.

CHAPTER 23

The Remarkable Career of Donnie Mustang

Sleep thankfully did come to both Eyebrow and Purple – a deep restful sleep that had been in short supply of late. Despite the thriving city and its metro population of around fifteen million Londoners outside their window, *The Jonmount* was remarkably quiet, and both men had been able to drift through the night undisturbed. As the clock approached nine am, the two of them started stirring within minutes of each other, and both began their slow routine of rising in a scene reminiscent of a pair of Alaskan brown bears emerging from their winter hibernation.

"Ugh… what time is it Eyebrow?" groaned Purple, his eyes yet to fully open.

Eyebrow squinted at the bedside clock. "Almost nine," he muttered.

Purple rolled onto his back and rubbed his eyes. "We should find something to eat. Did you see whether they do breakfast here?"

"I didn't pay attention Joe, sorry."

"Well, can you find out?"

Eyebrow stretched his body along the full length of the bed. "Sure thing Joe, just give me a few moments." A couple of minutes later, Eyebrow threw his legs over the side of the bed, gave his eyes a vigorous rub, and shuffled to the bathroom to freshen up quickly before making his way downstairs to check whether the hotel did in fact have any breakfast amenities, or whether he and Purple would have to embark on a hunting and gathering mission.

"I'll be back in a minute Joe," he said as he opened the door and stepped into the hallway, with a click emanating from behind him as the door closed. Trudging downstairs, Eyebrow was surprised to find the lobby bustling with activity as several dozen men milled around, many clad in black leather from head to toe, while some of the more muscular men sported little more than shorts and tight mesh vests. Approaching the front desk cautiously, Eyebrow first enquired about the availability of breakfast, to which he was advised that while the hotel itself did not provide breakfast, a café only a few doors down traditionally performed that service for hotel guests.

Perusing the lobby again, Eyebrow's questioning then turned to the sudden influx of guests. "Is there a biker convention or something today? You seem like you've gotten really busy."

"I do have to apologise sir," said the man. "They're all here hoping to see your associate."

Eyebrow was understandably confused. "What do you mean?"

"Again sir, I do apologise, but it seems that our night manager saw that he'd checked in earlier in the day and... well, he may have alerted some friends of his, who in turn alerted others and... as you can see... it appears that word got around."

"Sorry, I'm still a bit confused," replied Eyebrow, again assessing the large mass of people mingling throughout the lobby.

"Well, it's not often we get a celebrity staying with us. We're not really one of those upmarket establishments where famous people generally lodge, so I have to say that it's quite the treat for us." The man paused for a moment, choosing his next words. "I mean, it's not really my scene, but I can understand the excitement."

Eyebrow also paused in thought, digesting the conversation in an effort to distil some intelligence about what was actually occurring. And suddenly, the penny dropped. Pulling the phone from his pocket as he bounded back up the stairs, Eyebrow keyed something in and awaited a response.

Inside their room, Joe Purple was soon roused by a persistent banging on the door, followed by Eyebrow's voice from the other side. "Joe, open up! I need to show you something!"

"Jesus Christ, hang on a moment," replied Purple gruffly as he eased himself out of his bed. As he opened the door, Eyebrow surged in brandishing his phone. "Fuck me Eyebrow. How incredible is this breakfast spread that you've got yourself this worked up?"

"It's not about breakfast Joe," replied Eyebrow, breathing heavily after his impromptu quick time ascent of the stairs. "I know where I've heard that name before."

"What fucking name?" snapped Purple.

"Donnie Mustang. Remember? You're Donnie Mustang."

"Fuck yeah, that's me," replied Purple triumphantly.

"You don't understand Joe, there's a heap of guys downstairs waiting to see you because they heard that Donnie Mustang's staying here. They're everywhere." Eyebrow handed his phone to Purple. "See? I knew that the name was familiar."

Purple looked at the phone and his face dropped instantly. "Jesus Christ! He's a fucking gay porn star?"

"Not just that Joe. Read more," added Eyebrow, directing Purple to scroll a little further.

Purple perused the accolades that had been bestowed upon Donnie Mustang and his eyes nearly sprung out of his head. "Five-time Golden Shaft winner???"

"That's like the top award in gay porn Joe. The guy isn't just an actor, he's like the biggest gay porn actor on the planet. He's a legend."

"Ahh, fuck me Eyebrow," moaned Purple. "And they think that's me?"

"Yeah. Some night manager called his gay buddies, and they've all come down here to see you. There's fucking hundreds of them." Eyebrow's estimate was of course significantly inflated, but it was nonetheless his best effort at conveying the gravity of the situation to Joe Purple.

"We have to get out of here," said Purple. "I guess we're skipping breakfast."

"You can't go down there Joe, they'll swamp you."

Purple looked at Eyebrow's phone again. Donnie Mustang did in fact have a shock of tightly permed dark hair, much like Purple's. But beyond that, the similarities were negligible. "I don't look a fucking thing like this guy," he noted.

Eyebrow seized the phone and looked at the photo. "It's the hair Joe, they'll see the hair."

"Well, have you got a fucking hat or something?" asked Purple.

"No, and trying to disguise yourself will only draw more attention to you," noted Eyebrow. A few moments of silence ensued before Eyebrow offered a solution. "Let's pack our bags real quick and then check out the hallway. I have an idea."

As Purple quickly dressed and began throwing whatever clothing he had left back into his bag, he made an observation. "Can I just point out Eyebrow how fucking nervous I get every time I hear you say that you've got an idea?"

"Hey, my idea about the video saved our arses when you were trying to land the plane," noted Eyebrow, accurately in this case.

"Fuck, I guess so," replied Purple begrudgingly. By that point both men had hastily repacked and as the two of them snuck into the hallway, Eyebrow performed a cursory safety check.

"Looks clear Joe," he noted, beckoning Purple to join him.

"OK, what's the big plan?" asked Purple as the door closed behind them.

"Follow me," said Eyebrow as he walked to the end of the hallway where it split into a short T-junction. Eyebrow looked to his right and then to his left where he identified what he'd been looking for. "This way Joe."

Purple followed as directed. "What the fuck do you have in mind Eyebrow?"

Eyebrow stopped at the window at the end of the short hallway and lifted it to reveal an external fire escape. "I'll go downstairs and check out, and you go out this way. I'll meet you outside."

Purple mulled Eyebrow's proposed solution and poked his head out the window to assess the fire escape. It appeared to be structurally sound and in good order. "This looks like it might actually work. OK, go ahead and check out, and I'll go out here and wait for you."

"Sure thing Joe," said Eyebrow as he departed, leaving Purple to effect his escape. Cautiously making his way down to the lobby, Eyebrow noted that the large throng of men was still there, although they seemed a little more interested in him this time. He sidled up alongside the reception desk, handed the room key back and after a few moments, the man behind the desk returned the cash deposit that had been left the previous afternoon. Eyebrow thanked the man, turned and made his way through the assembled crowd that silently parted before him, like Moses taking his first tentative steps into the Red Sea.

As Eyebrow reached the front door, he turned and noted that many of the men were still observing him – there was something different between this visit to the lobby and his earlier one only a handful of minutes before. It seemed as though he was now a known commodity, and he surmised that the reception clerk may have advised the Donnie Mustang fans that he was Mustang's associate.

Eyebrow stepped out the front door and looked to his left where Joe Purple's head cautiously emerged from the alley next to the hotel. As Eyebrow made his way toward him, he was unaware that one of the men from the lobby had followed him into the street.

"Hey! There he is!" the man shouted back to his colleagues in the lobby after he spotted the permed hair peering around the corner. "He's come out the side way!"

Instantly a teeming mass of leather and mesh poured onto the street and thundered towards Eyebrow and Purple. "Fuck Eyebrow! Run!" exclaimed Purple. Eyebrow didn't need any further encouragement and the two of them quickly decamped, the wheels of their small roll-along suitcases cranking out far more revolutions per minute than they were ever designed for. "Go, go, go!" yelled Purple again as they barreled across the road towards Hyde Park, the pursuing mob not giving them any quarter. These men had waited since the early hours of the morning in the hope of seeing their idol and they were not going to let the opportunity slip.

As they entered the park, Purple identified a pedal-powered rickshaw parked on the side of the promenade, its driver awaiting his next customer. "There!" said Purple as he pointed to the rickshaw. "Get in that!"

Eyebrow and Purple ran toward the rickshaw, their chests heaving. They threw their bags in and quickly followed. "Go pal!" barked Purple. "GO!"

The driver casually replied. "It's twenty pounds for ten minutes."

The mob was getting closer the longer the discussion went on. "I don't give a fuck!" snapped Purple. "Just go!"

The man slowly ambled away from his parking spot and began to give Purple and Eyebrow a running commentary about the park, all the while the Donnie Mustang fan club continued to close in at a rapid rate. "Skip the commentary pal," said Purple. "We know this is all a fucking scam and you'll try to keep us in here as long as possible, so let's just skip to the end. How much do you want from us?"

The driver looked sheepish. "I don't understand what you mean sir," he stammered.

"Stop the games buddy," replied Purple. "We know it's a scam and we know you just plan to keep us in here so that you can charge us a fucking fortune. So pal, please, just skip the scam element and tell us how long you were planning on keeping us on the hook." The driver knew that he had met his match and dropped his eyes sadly.

"I was planning on driving you around useless sights until you needed to pay about a hundred pounds," he replied.

"Right," said Purple frantically. "Eyebrow, pay the man his hundred pounds and pal, just fucking go, as fast as you can to the other side of the park. We literally don't give a fuck about sightseeing. Just get us out of here NOW!"

Eyebrow pulled a hundred pounds from his wallet and handed it to the driver. "Just go," he said as the following horde was now almost within reaching distance.

The driver began to pedal. "Do you want the disco lights on?" he asked.

"No, we don't want the fucking disco lights on!" yelled Purple. "Faster! GO!" The driver began to increase speed and, with what seemed like only seconds to spare, the rickshaw carrying Eyebrow and budget Donnie Mustang finally began to pull away from the chasing mob.

As the two men and their driver careened down the main promenade, Eyebrow peered over his shoulder to the group of men now standing motionless on the path, their enthusiasm for the chase now evaporated. "I think we're clear Joe."

Purple leant back with his eyes closed and rubbed his face. "Can we not do any sightseeing today, Eyebrow?" he said almost pleadingly. "I just want to go home. Can we just go back to the airport and sit there all day? They'll have restaurants and shit where we can wait. I'm fucking done with this." He opened his eyes and looked at Eyebrow. "Let's just go home."

At that moment, Eyebrow's phone buzzed with an incoming message. His heart sank as he saw who it was from. Going home was suddenly about to become problematic.

CHAPTER 24

Not the Hill to Die Upon

Joe Purple had wanted nothing more than to just relax at the airport in anticipation of the evening flight that would take he, Eyebrow and their skulking companion PQ back home after a whirlwind trip to London. But now, as Eyebrow and Purple sat in a coffee shop inside the terminal, several hours before their flight was scheduled to board, neither man could relax due to the text message that Eyebrow had received earlier that day.

The message was from Leo Bishop.

Where are you?

At the time, Eyebrow and Purple were careening through Hyde Park in their hundred-pound rickshaw and as Eyebrow turned the screen to Purple to show him the incoming message, Purple directed their driver to stop and let them out, satisfied that they were now clear from their earlier situation. They walked a short distance to a bench where they sat and pondered the development. "What do you think Joe?" asked Eyebrow.

"I don't know," replied Purple, rubbing his chin. "This might be a setup."

"I'll need to reply," said Eyebrow.

"Maybe just tell him you're at home. He said he was going to be away for the weekend, didn't he? He won't be able to check."

"OK," replied Eyebrow as he began to type.

At home. Why?

Bishop's reply came in quick time.

I'll come around to see you.

"Oh shit Joe!" exclaimed Eyebrow. "He says he's coming around."

"Fuck me! You have to stall him somehow."

"Shit, shit, shit…" muttered Eyebrow as he formulated his response.

You can't. I'm sick.

Bishop was insistent.

Just come to the window. I'm at your place now.

"Ahhh, we're fucked Joe!" lamented Eyebrow as he typed.

I can't, sorry.

Eyebrow could now see that Bishop was typing his next message and by all indications, this one was requiring more composition. When it arrived, Eyebrow knew that their fate was sealed.

Is that because you're too sick to get out of bed? Or is it because YOU'RE IN FUCKING LONDON????

Eyebrow dropped his head in defeat. "Jesus Joe, he knows. He knows where we are."

"Fuck me Eyebrow, this is bad."

"What should I say?"

Purple could offer little assistance. "I literally have no idea Eyebrow. Maybe if you don't reply at all, we can smooth it over when we see him on Monday."

As if reading Purple's mind, Bishop followed up with a further thunderous message.

DON'T FUCKING IGNORE ME!!!

Eyebrow tried to defuse the situation.

We'll explain on Monday.

Eyebrow hoped that this might buy them a little time, but his hope was soon to be demolished.

There won't be any explaining. You're going straight back to jail when you step off that fucking plane. And if that prick with you thinks that he's in the clear then think again because he aided and Albert you so he's going down too. I'm done with babysitting you two fuckups. You'll both be in jail where you belong.

…

*aided and abetted

Eyebrow passed the phone to Purple so that he could read the message himself. After perusing it, the response was exactly as Eyebrow had expected.

"Are you fucking kidding me Eyebrow? Now I'm dragged into this too?" Purple stood and paced, hands atop his head. "Jesus Christ, I knew it… I just fucking KNEW that somewhere along the line, I'd end up in the shit again because of crap that YOU did."

And thus, a couple of hours later at the airport, both men now faced a dilemma as they grappled with the repercussions of the development with Bishop. "Is there anything we can do Joe?" asked Eyebrow almost pleadingly, as if Purple could in some way affect the outcome.

"Short of emigrating Eyebrow, I think we're fucked," was Purple's succinct assessment of their dire predicament.

"I don't want to go to jail Joe," moaned Eyebrow.

"Well, neither do I Eyebrow. But thanks to you, it looks like I might be fucking joining you. As much as I hate to say it, I think our only option is to go home and face the music. Maybe we can hope that it doesn't turn out as bad as we're thinking."

"I don't like that option Joe," continued Eyebrow, which caused Purple to turn and glare at him angrily.

"Then what, pray tell, do you suggest as an alternative Eyebrow? Do we just stay here in England as fugitives and have Interpol chasing us the rest of our lives? How long do you think that bag of money of yours can last? What do you expect me to do for a living? Expand Turd's Pizza into a fucking international empire? This is not the hill we're dying on Eyebrow. We have to go back and face the consequences for our own fucking actions. I'm not going to become a fugitive again. Been there, done it, didn't like the lifestyle."

Eyebrow considered the points that Purple had just laid out. "I guess we don't really have an option do we," he said meekly.

The two men sat in silence for a short time before Purple slapped Eyebrow on the back. "Come on, let's walk around to our gate and settle in before PQ turns up here too. Hopefully we can get away with not sitting next to him again."

"I might go and get a magazine to help keep me occupied Joe," noted Eyebrow as they stood.

"They have colouring books and dot to dots I think," said Purple snidely.

"I was thinking more like a Hustler or something."

Purple shook his head in disbelief. "Jesus Christ, Eyebrow. They don't sell fucking skin mags at the airport."

"I'll find something else interesting then," replied Eyebrow.

"Well, whatever you settle on, you better not be whackin' off next to me on the plane. I'm not up for that kind of trauma."

Thankfully for everyone, Eyebrow settled on a puzzle book and a copy of *Inside Soap*, after which they consulted the departures board to locate the associated gate for their flight. "Joe…" started Eyebrow as he looked at the flight information.

"I see it Eyebrow, I see it. Fucking delayed. Just what we need. Why wouldn't this day end on this note?"

"Will we still be back in time Joe?" asked Eyebrow, mildly panicked.

"Yes, we have plenty of fat on that one Eyebrow, for what it's worth now anyway."

"What should we do now?"

"I guess we do the same as we were planning on doing, except we now have to do it longer. Looks like we're trapped here Eyebrow, so we may as well just go and settle in and accept it."

And settle in they did, eventually being joined by PQ and several dozen other passengers who were oblivious to the delay. "Engineering issue" was the official reason passed on by the customer service agents at the gate and so Eyebrow and Purple could do little more than sit, wait, and try to solve as many Sudokus as possible in the hours ahead.

Given that PQ had lodged separately, he was keen to get an update on their mission. "What did you two get up to? Did you find out anything more about the money?"

Purple was still recovering after fleeing at the head of a leather and mesh clad mob. "Fuck me, you don't want to know what we got up to," he groaned.

"Nothing about the money," added Eyebrow. "We're just going to have to wait until Spaulding contacts me."

"When will that be?" asked PQ.

"Whenever he's found something," replied Eyebrow. "There isn't a timeline, I just have to wait."

"How's he going to contact you?"

Eyebrow, remembering Spaulding's advice to be cautious, pointed to his phone. "Encrypted app on here. I'm the only one who can access it."

As the hours rolled on, the assembled passenger cohort was beginning to grow restless. It wasn't lost on many of them that the anticipated boarding time was rapidly approaching, yet there had not only been minimal movement at the boarding gate, but the flight and cabin crew were also yet to be sighted.

Some of the older, more experienced flyers were beginning to grow agitated at the lack of activity from the airline and, much to everyone's dismay, an announcement soon echoed across the waiting area.

Ladies and gentlemen, we thank you for your patience this evening. We regret to advise that issues with crew hours have required us to cancel tonight's flight. Our team is working to ensure that all of you are reticketed for tomorrow, however if you require assistance to make alternate plans, please don't hesitate to let us know and we will assist where possible. The airline apologises for the inconvenience that this may cause, and we thank you for choosing to fly with us.

Unsurprisingly, there was uproar from the floor and amidst all the pandemonium, Eyebrow and Purple tried to digest what it meant for them. Purple did some quick mental calculations and determined that even taking time differences into account, it was now highly unlikely that they could be back home in time for their Monday check-in with Bishop if they were forced to wait until the following day. Regardless, the requirement to meet Bishop seemed superfluous now as it was highly probable that both he and Eyebrow would be marched off to jail as soon as they arrived anyway.

Purple though still clung to the tiniest glimmer of hope that the combination of making their appointment on time as well as some slick talking might – just might – get them out of trouble. After all, he thought, maybe Bishop was just worked up when he sent the texts earlier that day and given time, perhaps he might be more amenable to compromise. But if they were no-shows, whatever glimmer of hope that may have existed would be permanently snuffed out. He had to investigate alternatives.

Even though there was a throng of irate passengers swarming the information desk, Purple barged his way through and barked at the customer service representative. "It's absolutely essential that we get out here tonight. Are there any other flights?"

"I'm sorry sir," replied the overworked representative. "There's nothing available."

"I don't care if we need to go at two in the morning," countered Purple. "Surely there's something."

"I'm very sorry sir, there's no possibility of us organising any other flights before tonight's curfew comes into effect. It's simply too late now. Again, I do sincerely apologise sir, but I promise you that we'll do our very best to get you out of here tomorrow morning."

Purple turned on his heels and left the information desk disgruntled. Departing the following morning wasn't a viable option. Yet again, the fates had conspired against he and Eyebrow, only this time they were thousands of miles from where they needed to be – a nineteen-seventies Cessna was not going to help them on this occasion. He walked back despondently to Eyebrow and PQ. "Looks like we're stuck here for the night."

PQ rose from his seat and began to walk off, brandishing his phone as he did so. "I'm going to make a call."

"There's nothing we can do Joe?" asked Eyebrow.

"Afraid not. They don't even have really late-night flights because the fucking airport closes. We're just going to have to find somewhere to sleep and then try again tomorrow. Fuck me, this is a disaster."

"Do you think we're going to jail when we get back Joe?" asked Eyebrow sadly.

"I'd say almost certainly. Bishop's gonna want to get this risk off his books now that he knows we can't be trusted. Ahh, fuck me, what possessed me to even suggest this? I should have killed it off when I had the chance."

As both men stood silently among the chaos engulfing the area, PQ returned with his phone to his ear. He beckoned Eyebrow and Purple to a neighbouring empty departure gate, away from the maddening commotion of distraught passengers demanding answers and venting their frustrations in equal measure. Once in the relative quiet, PQ handed the phone to Eyebrow. "It's Mister Santiago. He wants to talk to you."

Eyebrow took the phone and put it up to his ear. "Hello?"

"Señor Von Steel," came the voice from the other end. "I understand that you have a lead on my money."

Eyebrow glanced cautiously in Joe Purple's direction before answering. "Yes, that's right Mister Santiago. But we don't have much information for you just yet."

"I understand. But as I'm led to believe, you've found yourself waylaid, far from home. This has turned out to be good fortune for me, because I need you to do something."

"What's that Mister Santiago?"

"I'm attending to some business out of town at the moment and I need you and your colleague to join me. I've asked PQ to make all the necessary arrangements. You'll fly out tomorrow."

Eyebrow now began to feel somewhat uncomfortable about the path that the conversation was headed. He and Joe Purple were isolated and with no support network, so he needed to exercise caution, not just for himself, but for his friend also. Foremost in his thoughts also was the warning that Spaulding had left him with, and he instinctively slipped his hand into his pocket, seeking the reassurance of the decoy crypto key that he and Spaulding had created. It wasn't much of a shield – deception more than anything, but it was something at least.

"Where do you need us to meet you?" asked Eyebrow. As he awaited Santiago's response, no amount of mental planning could prepare him for the direction he was about to receive.

"I need you to be on the next plane to Colombia Señor Von Steel."

CHAPTER 25
No

To say that Joe Purple was far from impressed with Eyebrow's revelation that they were expected to fly to Colombia was an understatement of the highest order. Within moments of ending the telephone discussion with Santiago, Eyebrow had ushered Purple into a quiet alcove to discuss the direction that had been given to him. But Purple was far from supportive of the idea, with much of his argument focusing on the word "no," as well as many similar variants from the same general family.

"No, no, no," said Purple firmly as he shook his head. "You've had some idiotic ideas Eyebrow, but this one's setting the bar so high that it may never be topped. There's no way I'm getting on a fucking plane to Colombia. Do you know what they do to people they don't like there? Fuck me, we'll probably end up lying on the side of the road with our heads in a fucking hessian sack."

"Joe…" started Eyebrow before being cut off by Purple's unfinished rant.

"Do you know what a fucking Colombian necktie is Eyebrow? Think about it… they named it after the place that you actually want us to go to! No fucking way. Not a chance. Not happening. The answer is no."

"I can't go alone Joe, I need you," pleaded Eyebrow.

"It's time to fold up the tent on this one Eyebrow. This is getting way out of hand. We should never have gone to Cooper's house in the first place, but the Gods gave us a warning and let us walk away. But we ignored that and pushed our luck further, and now we've ended up stuck in this fucking airport, thousands of miles from home. We shouldn't even be here in England Eyebrow. We've pushed it to the limits. We need to wind it back. This can't go on."

"Well, what's the alternative Joe? We're going to jail if we go home. Bishop's already told us that."

"I DON'T FUCKING KNOW EYEBROW!" yelled Purple, drawing stares from some of the passengers one gate away. He lowered his voice. "I don't have a fucking alternative. I literally do not know what to do. If we go to Colombia, we'll probably last five minutes before we're bundled off to a fucking jungle camp in blindfolds. But if we go home, I'm going to jail. I don't care if it's just the holding area at that police station for a few days – I can handle that. But do you know what will happen if I end up in an actual jail and they find out that I'm a former federal agent? I'll be fucking dead inside a day."

Eyebrow mulled Purple's valid observations. This was indeed a situation where there appeared to be little chance of victory, regardless of which path was chosen. The house odds on this one would make even the most unregulated Indian casino weep in appreciation. Eyebrow beckoned PQ to join them, speaking quickly to Purple before PQ arrived. "If there was one option that I could offer you, would you consider it Joe?"

"Jesus, I'm skeptical Eyebrow," replied a very flustered Joe Purple.

By this point PQ had arrived, and Eyebrow turned to him. "Where are we meeting Mister Santiago?"

"In Colombia," replied PQ.

"Yes, I know that. But *where* in Colombia? In the city or do we have to go out into the countryside or something?"

"Why?"

"Because we're worried about what could happen to us. We'd rather be in the city somewhere."

"You won't even need to leave the airport," said PQ. "There's a hotel there where he's arranged to meet you. There's a lounge right in the lobby so you'll be in full view of everyone."

Purple now entered the conversation. "Why does it have to be in Colombia?"

"Mister Santiago's doing some business there and I think he needs you to give his business partner an in-person update on the situation. You know, just to show that he's handling it. It's nothing to worry about, I promise you."

Eyebrow looked at Purple and laid out his suggestion. "It looks like there's less chance that we'll be in trouble in Colombia than you originally thought Joe. If we don't even leave the airport area and we're meeting in a hotel, then we might be a lot safer than you thought."

Purple nodded along with Eyebrow's assessment. "Possibly." He now awaited the remainder of Eyebrow's proposal.

"We're probably going to jail when we get home, even if we go back tomorrow, right? It doesn't matter whether we go back tomorrow or go back after we've been to Colombia – we're going to jail. Do you think that's right Joe?"

"Yes," was Purple's resigned response.

Eyebrow probed further. "And you're worried about what could happen to you in jail?"

Purple was now growing agitated at the line of questioning. "Get to the fucking point Eyebrow."

"My point is Joe, that Esteban has influence, and maybe he could help *us* if we help *him*. Remember when I was in jail and Esteban's guy was looking out for me? Maybe if we help him out with this, he can make sure that you have protection in jail. You've already said it – we're going to be locked up no matter what we do now, so maybe it's best to get a favour in return from Esteban. What do you think?"

Purple said nothing at that point. He stared straight ahead, digesting the proposal. *God dammit*, he thought to himself. *He's fucking right.* But Purple didn't want to give Eyebrow the satisfaction of coming up with a perfectly rational solution to the problem. As history had shown repeatedly, that certainly wasn't Eyebrow's forte. Surely there must be some hole in the plan? For Christ sake, this was Jimmy Eyebrow after all. What glaring issue had Purple missed that would result in Eyebrow's idea falling into a screaming heap of mayhem like every single one before it? Try as he may to find fault with Eyebrow's proposition, Purple couldn't. The logic was sound.

"You're sure that we don't need to leave the airport in Colombia?" Purple asked PQ.

"Barely," replied PQ. "The hotel's, like, two minutes outside the arrivals hall. There's literally a walkway straight from the airport to the hotel."

"And when do we come home?"

"First thing the next morning. You can stay at the hotel, or you can go back over to the airport and sit near the police all night if it makes you feel safer."

Purple mulled the options before dismissing PQ. "I need to talk to my buddy for a moment, alone." He shunted Eyebrow a little further along the terminal, away from PQ, where he lowered his voice. "You sure that we can trust him Eyebrow?"

"I spoke to Mister Santiago myself Joe. It all sounds legit."

"Your guy in London told you to be fucking careful, remember?"

"I am Joe, I promise. If we don't have to leave the airport and we can come home the very next morning, then it should be pretty straightforward."

"We don't even know if what he says he wants you for is legitimate though Eyebrow. What if it's a fucking bait and switch?"

Eyebrow considered Purple's observation. "So long as we've got Esteban in our corner, I feel safe. I know that you don't really know Esteban yourself Joe, but he won't let us down."

Purple sighed deeply, knowing that like a gambler on a clearly unsustainable heater, he was yet again rolling the dice of fate – all while rubbing a rabbit's foot and praying that the dice would roll to a halt in his favour one more time. "Fuck it, I'm in," he announced reluctantly.

Joe Purple's original gut instinct had been "no," and Eyebrow had successfully coerced him into changing tack. But as most people will tell you, following your initial gut feeling before it's corrupted by external influences is often the prudent course of action if something doesn't feel right. Indeed, the thing about gut instincts is that they are, more often than not, right on the money.

* * *

Around a hundred kilometres, give or take, outside of Colombia's capital city Bogota, Alejandro Ortiz sat on his patio that overlooked the manicured grounds of his estate. Ortiz was not only the head of his family's prodigious drug empire, but also Santiago's business partner, although if one were to value accuracy, the power imbalance between the two meant that the term "partner" was relatively loose, with Santiago being about as much Ortiz's partner as Eyebrow had been Honest Dom's.

Ortiz was aggrieved because a significant sum of money that Santiago had been expected to funnel to him had disappeared into the void – the same money that Jimmy Eyebrow was now tracking. Having grown impatient with Santiago's lack of progress on the matter, Ortiz had now taken it upon himself to become significantly more active in resolving the situation.

As Ortiz sipped his coffee, one of his underlings approached, stood alongside the small table and delivered the news that Ortiz had been anticipating. "I've heard from our man. They're coming, both of them."

Ortiz didn't shift his gaze. "The one who talks secretly to the man in London? You're certain that he is coming?"

"I've been assured that is the case," replied Ortiz's man.

"And this is the man who holds the key?"

"That is what I'm led to believe Mister Ortiz, yes."

Ortiz took another sip of coffee before continuing. "Excellent. Arrange for them to be collected as soon as they arrive. You know where to take them. And Tito…"

"Yes, Mister Ortiz?"

"Make sure you have the hessian bags."

CHAPTER 26

Egregious Abuse of Rank

A sharp knocking on the door of his motel room roused Leo Bishop from the sleep that he'd only drifted into a short time earlier. He looked at the clock – 11:15PM. "Jesus Christ, what the hell is this?" he muttered to no-one in particular as he slid over to the side of the bed and attached his prosthetic leg. He grumbled further as he shuffled toward the door, still not fully awake after being jolted from his sleep that was less than an hour old. "This better not be some drunk trying to get into the wrong fucking room." Bishop tried to peer through the peephole in the door, but it was broken. "Who is it?" he yelled.

"Leo, open up, it's me," came the distinctive voice of Dennis Burnett from the other side of the door.

"Fuck me," muttered Bishop as he removed the safety chain and unlocked the door. He was understandably surprised by this unexpected development. "What the hell are you doing here Dennis?"

"We have a situation," said Burnet as he entered the room without waiting for an invitation to do so.

Bishop rubbed his eyes as Burnett was depositing his belongings on the small lounge in the room. "Is it an Eyebrow situation Dennis?"

"Yes, of course it's a fucking Eyebrow situation," snapped Burnett, who made his way to the bed and sat himself on the edge. "Which side are you sleeping on?"

Bishop was taken aback. "Whoa! What the hell Dennis. I don't have a *side*. I have the whole damn thing. You're not staying in here with me."

"Reception's closed and I can't get my own room."

"But…" started Bishop before he was cut off.

"Leo, I've been travelling all day, I'm tired, and I just want to go to sleep. It's nearly fucking midnight for Christ sake."

"Yes, I'm well aware of that Dennis," replied Bishop angrily. "But are you actually pulling rank on me to force me to sleep with you?"

"It's not 'sleeping with me' in the fucking code of conduct meaning of the term Leo. You won't even notice that I'm there. My wife says I fart through the night sometimes, but other than that, I'll be as quiet as a mouse. Leo, I'm fucking exhausted. Give me a break here."

"This is an egregious abuse of rank Dennis. I'd better not feel anything poking into me through the night."

"Cross my heart Leo. I just want to go to sleep, that's all."

"What about the Eyebrow matter?"

"Tomorrow, Leo. We'll deal with it tomorrow. Black and Dekker should be here sometime in the morning."

"Wait! They're coming too? What the fuck's happened? Something must have gone down for them to get off their fat arses and mingle with the peasants."

"You're right, it's escalated Leo. But we'll discuss tomorrow."

There it was, that phrase that had been uttered on so many occasions the last time they had an Eyebrow situation – *it's escalated*. Bishop felt a cold shiver run down his spine at the mention of those words. He was now stuck in a state of limbo by both wanting to know more, while at the same time not wanting to hear another word. To him, Eyebrow was a walking contradiction – supremely frustrating on one hand, though also delivering short bursts of exhilarating action on the other. If he was to be honest, the Vegas escapade had been one of the highlights of his career, especially given that he had been able to do it with his good friend, who at that moment was in a peaceful slumber a couple of doors down, completely unaware of Burnett's arrival.

Less than ten minutes later, with the lights out and Bishop lying awkwardly in order to avoid any unplanned touching of his sleeping boss, a fart from Burnett echoed across the room like a ceremonial cannon announcing the start of a yacht race. Burnett had not yet descended into a deep sleep and punctuated his impromptu French horn concerto by rolling towards Bishop and mumbling "all aboard," before once again drifting off.

Bishop had already had enough though and hopped out of bed, literally. Not even bothering to attach his leg this time, he retrieved a spare blanket and pillow from the closet, made himself a nest on the small lounge, and settled in to await what the following day would bring. Hopefully between then and tomorrow, sleep would find him.

Thankfully it did – a surprisingly good sleep under the circumstances. Rising and attending to his morning bathroom routine, he glanced toward Burnett who was still snoring steadily. Opening the door and stepping into the brisk morning air, Bishop made his way to McFadden's room and tapped on the door. It only took a few moments for McFadden to respond.

"Morning Leo," he said as he cracked open the door.

"Good morning, Mac, and what a fine morning it is," replied Bishop with a touch of the theatric.

"What are you up to?" asked McFadden warily.

Bishop motioned McFadden out of the room. "Maybe, instead of explaining, I could just show you." He began walking toward his room. "This way please."

Arriving back at his own room, Bishop eased the door open and pointed to his bed. McFadden squinted his eyes and looked back to Bishop in surprise. "Ahh, well… good for you Leo… I guess, even though it's a bit unexpected. But, if I'm being honest here, and this is genuinely me speaking to you as a friend… well… she's a bit… manly."

"No, you idiot. Look closer," snapped Bishop.

McFadden edged further into the room and leant down slightly, before turning back to Bishop with a look of shock on his face. "Is that Dennis?" he mouthed, to which Bishop nodded his head in confirmation. "What the fuck is he doing here Leo?"

Bishop quietly summoned McFadden outside. "I'd say the shit's hit the fan Mac. Something's happened with Eyebrow and whatever it is, it's big enough for Black and Dekker to be arriving today too."

"Shit, they're coming too? Did Dennis say what's happened?"

"No, nothing. He said he'd brief us today when the others arrive. What I want to know is what that prick was doing in London."

"Sounds like we'd better get some breakfast into us Leo. Might be a challenging day."

"Concur Mac. Let's see what culinary delights are on offer in the lobby today. I'd better get something for our guest as well."

McFadden quickly returned to his room to freshen up, after which both men ambled down to the motel lobby to indulge in their daily complimentary breakfast. The offerings generally consisted of donuts that Bishop suspected were leftovers from a donut shop a few doors down, industrial strength coffee, and a fruit bowl that was hit or miss, depending on the day.

Making their way back up to Bishop's room, they found Burnett awake and drying his hair following a shower, thankfully fully clothed by that point. Bishop tossed him a glazed donut. "What the hell is this, Leo?" he asked as he examined the suspect offering.

"Breakfast Dennis. That's what the department has been giving us for breakfast." He sat a Styrofoam cup on the bedside table. "And there's your coffee."

"Bullshit," replied Burnett. "This isn't breakfast. Come on, take me and show me where the buffet is."

Bishop and McFadden exchanged smiles before Bishop spoke. "Dennis, THIS is the breakfast you've had us on since we arrived. This is how we start our day, every day."

"Jesus, are you serious?" Burnett turned to McFadden. "Mac? Is he serious?"

"That's it Dennis," replied McFadden. "There's a diner up the road where we buy breakfast sometimes if we want."

"But then that's half our daily meal allowance gone before we've even got to lunch," added Bishop. "So, eat your day-old donut Dennis, or break out the corporate credit card and take Mac and I to breakfast."

CHAPTER 27

The Skeleton in the Closet

An hour later as the three men stepped out of *Rosie's Diner* and onto the sidewalk, Dennis Burnett made an observation. "I want you two to get breakfast there each day from now on. You'll have to pay for it, but it'll get reimbursed. Call it an authorization in the field. I'll deal with that pencil neck in the finance department when he inevitably makes a big deal about it."

"Thank you Dennis, that's very kind of you," replied Bishop.

"Can we get bumped up a star or two on our accommodation as well?" added McFadden.

"Let's not go too far there," replied Burnett as they rounded the corner into *Lucky's Motel* and began to walk past the lobby before a knocking on the window from inside caught their attention. The three of them stopped and saw Harry Black and Christian Dekker trying to attract their attention, the two federal agents having arrived during the breakfast adjournment. Burnett, Bishop and McFadden went inside where greetings were exchanged. "Gentlemen, welcome," said Burnett. "Lovely to see you again."

"Not sure if you're being genuine there Dennis," replied Black with a smile. "But it is nice to see all of you again."

Burnett made his way over to the front desk where he summoned the man whom he presumed was the owner of the motel. "Do you have a meeting facility that we could use?"

"No, we got nothin' like that," he replied.

Burnett produced his police identification to formalize his request. "Do you have any private space where we could all meet? We have confidential matters to discuss."

The man rubbed his chin in thought. "I guess you could use the old janitor's office. We ain't got no janitor anymore, so it's been empty for a while. Come with me, I'll open it up for you." The man opened a cupboard and grabbed an enormous set of keys before setting off outside with the other five close behind. "Down this way," he said, motioning with his hand.

It wasn't long before they arrived at an unnumbered door at the near end of the motel and, after the man tried four keys without success, he eventually jiggled the fifth one in the lock and the door sprung open, accompanied by a flurry of dust and stale air reminiscent of Howard Carter's unsealing of Tutankhamun's tomb. Bishop peeked into the gloomy interior of the room. "How long ago did you say the janitor left?"

"Can't remember when he left. All the years run into each other these days. Guy just stopped comin' to work one day and we never replaced him. I'm pretty handy myself so I do most of the maintenance around here now. Got my own tools and all."

Bishop nudged Burnett forward to inspect. "Jesus…" he muttered softly before turning to the man. "I guess this will do."

The man fumbled with the keys, eventually detaching the one for the door where they now stood and handing it to Burnett. "Just return this when you're done." He then moved forward and groped around inside the door, after which the fluorescent light flickered manically and ever so slowly began to fill the room with a soft glow. "Ain't been turned on for a while. Might take some time to get goin'."

As the motel owner turned and departed, Bishop and company stepped warily into the abandoned janitor's office. The place looked like a time capsule, and McFadden soon discovered a clue to the last time the janitor was in residence when he found an old-school *Firestone* nude calendar on the wall. "Jesus Leo, look at this." McFadden brushed the dust off the page that was displayed. "How old is this!"

Bishop leant in to look. "Holy shit," he muttered. "I tell you what, they don't make things like this anymore."

"A different world Leo," said Burnett who was opening the small refrigerator in the corner. "Christ, this thing's still on," he noted as he opened the door and peered inside before pausing in amazement. "Goddamn, you're not going to believe what's in here!" he exclaimed, before spinning around with an unopened can of *Tab* in his hand. "Look at this!" The significance of such a discovery was not lost on the other four men who all took turns in marveling at the pristine historical artefact being brandished by Burnett.

As much as everyone would have liked to continue exploring the cornucopia of retro pop culture that seemed to permeate every nook and cranny of the abandoned office, there was still the pressing Jimmy Eyebrow issue at hand, and Harry Black now cleared off the old desk and invited everyone to join him. "Gentlemen, if we could get down to business. Let me firstly bring you up to date with our investigation into Eyebrow's little sabbatical to the UK. We've run everything we can on their companion, this Charles Dunk character, and he's come up squeaky clean."

"That's the defence contractor guy, right?" asked Burnett.

"That's the guy," replied Black. "We've contacted his employer and he's been stood down from duties while we continue to investigate, but they say that he's been with them for twelve years and he's been a model employee. The only transgression he had was when someone complained to HR that Dunk was stealing their yoghurt from the lunchroom and then replacing it in bulk each payday. But beyond that, he's clean."

"The yoghurt matter could indicate financial distress," noted Bishop. "Could make him a prime target for extortion."

"Astute deduction," replied Black. "Hence why he's been stood down from duty while we probe a little further."

"Any idea what he was working on?" asked McFadden.

"Nothing sexy I'm afraid," said Black. "He does have high level clearance, but apparently he's not working on anything of significance at this time."

"So have we got any new information on what Eyebrow was doing in London?" asked Bishop.

"Nothing whatsoever," replied Black. "He's due back tonight, so I have people waiting to grab him as soon as he clears immigration. All we can hope is that no-one's tipped him off that we're waiting for him."

Bishop shifted uncomfortably and emitted a nervous cough, something that didn't go unnoticed by Burnett. "Do you have something to add Leo?"

"Well..." began Bishop before hesitating. "I may have lost my temper when I found out what he'd done, and I might have sent him a message telling him he's going to jail the moment he arrives back home."

"Jesus Christ Leo!" bellowed Burnett. "Why would you do that?"

"I was pissed off Dennis, I'm sorry," replied Bishop.

Burnett was now clearly frustrated. "Fuck me, he's probably already in the wind now Leo."

"He's not a fucking professional hitman Dennis," snapped Bishop. "He's a panty thief who pretends to be some big deal. He doesn't have the resources to turn to vapor and disappear."

Harry Black interjected as he pulled a large white envelope from his folder. "Well, on that subject, something else has now come across our desk, hence why we felt it necessary to meet with you face to face. It seems that Eyebrow may be involved in more than we currently understand."

Bishop dragged a chair from the corner, slapped the accumulated dust away and slumped into it. "Fuck me, here we go," he groaned as he began rubbing his eyes. "What the fuck has he done this time?"

"Several nights ago, there was a critical incident at Gatling International when an unidentified light plane landed without clearance. The occupants of the plane then crashed through the airport's perimeter before absconding into the night. We were able to get these stills from the airport's security cameras." Black spread a selection of photos across the table. The photos were from a reasonable distance and focused on two men decamping from a plane and fleeing into the surrounding undergrowth.

Bishop, McFadden and Burnett crowded around to assess the photos. "I'm not seeing anything Harry," said Bishop. "Is this supposed to be Eyebrow and Purple?"

"I agree that these photos are problematic," replied Black, who now slid two more photos across the table. "But *these* ones are a different story."

The three detectives leant in again to view two photos that this time very clearly identified Jimmy Eyebrow and Joe Purple in the back of a taxi. "Where did these come from?" asked Bishop.

"The investigation into the two mystery men was expanded into the local area in the hope that something might present itself. A local taxi driver said that he picked up two guys on the side of the road in the middle of the night – these two." Black tapped the photo of Eyebrow and Purple. "Care to take a guess where he drove them?"

Bishop took a moment as he mentally retraced the timeline for the incident. "Holy shit! They turned up in a fucking taxi for their daily check-in that day! They came straight here!"

"If I could address the elephant in the room here gentlemen," added Burnett. "I don't recall either of them owning a plane or being trained pilots."

"You are correct Dennis," replied Black. "The plane, or what's left of it at least, has been identified as belonging to one Lester Hartley. It took off from an airport quite a distance away from here on the evening of the incident and arrived with Eyebrow and Purple, but minus Mister Hartley. The airport of origin is located in Cedar Falls, and remember that, because we'll be revisiting it shortly."

"They stole a fucking plane?" asked Bishop.

"Not exactly," said Black, who now produced a newspaper and pointed to the story *Man Falls From Sky*. "It would appear that on that same evening, the now late Mister Hartley has had a fall from a significant height. I would estimate, without knowing the details, oh… about… ten thousand feet."

Bishop was snapped to attention. "What? Are you telling me that Eyebrow threw the guy out of the plane?"

Dekker now entered the conversation. "We're trying to determine if Hartley had any sort of background that would make him of interest to Eyebrow, but at this stage, we're coming up empty. He's just the general hand at the local airfield, as well as an avid amateur pilot."

Burnett held his hand up to pause any further conversation. "Gentlemen, a moment to regroup please. I'm certain that you all recall vividly… God knows I do… the last time we went down this same path with Eyebrow. We had him pinned for a bucket load of shit that ended up being nothing but a massive goddamn coincidence. He didn't do any of the stuff that he was suspected of."

"Except the guy who had the dildo rammed down his throat," noted Bishop.

"I stand corrected Leo," said Burnett. "He did *one* thing that we accused him of. But surely we need to be a little more cautious this time about jumping to conclusions, wouldn't you agree?"

"I would normally agree with you there Dennis," said Black. "However, working backwards, we still haven't finished. As it turns out, earlier that day, Eyebrow and Purple took a commercial flight to… Cedar Falls. Told you we'd circle back there. Care to guess which one of them flew business class?"

Bishop placed his face into his palms. "Fuck me," he muttered. "What were they doing in Cedar Falls?"

"Interesting you should ask that," said Black as he pulled another document from his folder. "Cedar Falls is the home to Mister Julian Cooper, an accountant who one day recently just vanished into thin air."

"What makes you think he's associated with Eyebrow?" asked Burnett.

"The local police received a call from a concerned neighbor about intruders at Cooper's house. Upon arrival, an unknown number absconded, but they left behind a hire car in the driveway."

"Let me guess," said Bishop. "Rented to Eyebrow?"

"No," replied Black. "A man named Yuri Sikorsky."

"So, nothing to do with Eyebrow?" asked Bishop.

Black screwed up his face in response. "Not quite that simple Leo. You see, we ran Sikorsky's name and lo and behold, he's also on the same flight to Cedar Falls as our two guys. And, when we ran a background on Sikorsky, he's an associate of a man named Rafael Santiago, a Latin American drug lord who is in turn associated with…"

"Wild assumption here – Esteban Gutierrez," said Bishop as he fell back into his chair.

Black clicked his fingers and pointed directly to Bishop. "Bingo."

Bishop was by now rubbing his face vigorously. "So, we can't just let him roam around out in the wild now, right? If his unauthorized visit to England wasn't enough to lock him up, then this surely is, don't we agree? I mean the guy's tried to set up a murder for hire business for Christ sake." Bishop turned to Burnett. "I can't take responsibility for this anymore Dennis. It's escalated too far."

"I agree," said Burnett. "Hold that thought Leo, I need a piss. We'll discuss it further when I get back."

"There's a toilet just down there," said McFadden, directing Burnett down a short hallway.

In Burnett's absence, Black resumed the discussion. "I'd have to agree with you Leo. I think he needs to be in a place where we all know exactly where he is. Does the detective who arrested him here know that Eyebrow's taken off to London?"

"Shit no!" exclaimed Bishop. "As far as he's concerned, everything's hunky dory over here at Lucky's Motel. Question for you though – why the fuck did they get issued with… you know… valid passports? How come they didn't get flagged up at the airport?"

"Any reinvention like what Eyebrow and Bloom went through is all legitimate," replied Black. "Everything they have is registered and official. We can get an alert pushed to us if they move through a port of entry or exit, but unless they have a detainer, we can't stop them."

The conversation was interrupted by Burnett from near the toilet, in an area that the men had not yet explored. "Guys! Could you come here please."

"You're not stuck in your zipper are you Dennis?" asked Bishop with a smile as the four of them began to make their way down the small hallway.

"No Leo, it's a bit more serious than that," replied Burnett.

"*Nothing* is more fucking serious than that Dennis," said Bishop.

Burnett was standing beside an open door that led to what appeared to be a storeroom of some sort. "Remember the owner of the place said that the janitor just stopped turning up for work one day?"

"Yes," replied Bishop. "I remember him saying that."

"Well… I think it's more the case that the guy never left. Check this out." Burnett pushed the door of the storeroom open to reveal a toppled set of shelves with various items strewn across the floor, and a wheeled swivel chair up-ended in the corner. Protruding from under the set of shelves was a fully skeletonized set of legs with the material of the pants almost completely deteriorated over time. "I think the owner might be up for a bit of overtime here," added Burnett.

"Jesus Christ Dennis, what's happened here do you think?" asked Bishop.

Burnett pointed to the swivel chair. "I'd say he's been using the chair with wheels as a step to get something from the top shelf and it's moved on him. He's panicked, grabbed the shelf, and brought the whole fucking thing down on himself."

Bishop turned to McFadden. "Can you believe this shit Mac? We've got a rogue hitman on the loose and now, as if that's not enough, we've been holding our meeting in an office with a fucking dead body on the other side of the door. Is this shit beginning to feel all too familiar?"

"I think so Leo," replied McFadden. "It feels like we've booked ourselves another ticket on the Eyebrow train."

CHAPTER 28

Le Bilan de Monsieur Longchamp

One kilometre down, eight thousand four hundred and ninety-nine to go. As the plane bound for Colombia eased into the air carrying the optimistic Jimmy Eyebrow as well as a reluctant Joe Purple, Eyebrow turned to Purple and made a light-hearted observation. "It's a shame we didn't sign up as frequent flyers Joe. We'd have a few miles this week."

"You've got that right," grumbled Purple. "We'd probably be fucking platinum members by now." Purple turned and stared out the window. "I have to say Eyebrow, even in my wildest alcohol-induced fever dreams, I would not have envisaged the shit that we've done this week."

Unfortunately, they had not been able to separate themselves from PQ on this flight and unlike their flight to London, the three of them now sat abreast of each other, with Purple ensuring that he claimed the window seat while using Eyebrow in the middle seat as a buffer between he and the ample-framed PQ. Despite the fact that Joe Purple had willingly agreed to accompany Eyebrow, he nonetheless remained a very reluctant participant in this escapade. As such, he was determined to ensure that as a reward, he would take advantage of any benefits that may arise and securing the window seat on yet another long-haul flight was a prime opportunity right out of the gate.

For Jimmy Eyebrow though, as the hours ticked by and darkness set in, the situation was far from ideal. PQ seemed to be able to sleep with ease and sandwiched as he was between PQ's snoring and Joe Purple's seismically active arse, middle seat life was challenging. With an appreciation now for what their hapless large-headed companion had endured on the previous flight, Eyebrow awkwardly climbed over PQ and stumbled along the aisle toward the rest rooms at the rear of the cabin where he intended firstly to relieve himself and then use the extra space in the area to stretch his legs for a short period. Unfortunately, all the rearward facilities were in use, leading to Eyebrow having to make the trek back up the aisle to the restrooms in the middle of the plane, this time thankfully finding one available.

With his ablutions attended to, Eyebrow exited the small restroom and glanced to his right, back to where his seat was. The whole cabin was a biomass of open mouths, limp body parts and more than a few sets of bare feet protruding into the aisle, all punctuated by the sporadic glow emanating from the few in-flight entertainment screens that were still in use by the handful of insomniacs.

Turning his attention to the left, Eyebrow sensed a greater aura of calm and he resolved to investigate, quickly finding himself entering the realm of the plane's first class cabin. Given that the majority of the passengers were in a state of rest at that late hour, the cabin crew were likewise taking the opportunity to operate on reduced responsibilities, and with minimal oversight within, Eyebrow was able to slide into the first class cabin undetected. Remembering fondly his recent, albeit short-haul, experience in business class, Eyebrow resolved that he would try to avoid returning to his middle seat in economy for as long as possible.

The first class cabin was not full and in fact appeared to be operating at something close to only half capacity. As such, Eyebrow had little trouble identifying a vacant seat close to where he had entered the cabin. Quietly easing himself into the seat, Eyebrow scanned the cabin for any indication that the flight attendants had identified his intrusion into their restricted space, but there was nothing. It appeared that he had remained, thus far, undetected. Eyebrow suspected that the first class crew would be familiar with their passenger manifest so he accepted that he would likely be moved on within a short time, but for now he intended to make the most of the lie-flat seat and try to catch up with some of the rest that had eluded him further down the plane.

Surprisingly, Eyebrow's rest extended far longer than expected – his sleep state coupled with a lack of in-flight service requests keeping his clandestinely procured upgrade undetected. And then, without warning, Eyebrow was roused from his slumber by the cabin lights quicky coming up, accompanied by a sudden flurry of activity as the words "Oh no! Won't someone help my husband!" came from further toward the front of the plane.

Eyebrow leapt to attention and identified the origin of the commotion as he saw a well-dressed man lying on the floor and another man who appeared to be a doctor gently rolling him onto his back. Given that Eyebrow was an uninvited squatter in the first class cabin, a hasty retreat to his original seat seemed to be the appropriate course of action now.

He quickly made his way back down the aisle, doing his best to step aside as two members of the cabin crew frantically rushed toward the incident unfolding in the forward cabin. As he arrived back at his original row, Joe Purple had been awoken from his sporadic sleep by the sudden increase in activity around him. "Where the fuck have you been Eyebrow?" he snapped.

"Just went to the toilet Joe," replied Eyebrow only partially honestly.

"Where? Up the front? What the fuck's going on up there?"

"I'm not sure, but there's a guy lying on the ground. Something's going down, but I only saw it for a second." Eyebrow climbed over PQ and resumed his seat. "How long until we arrive?"

Purple looked at his watch and tried to make some quick mental calculations. "I'm not sure, but it's still a few hours I think." Several minutes of uncertainty about the current situation elapsed before an announcement came across the speaker.

Ladies and gentlemen, your first officer speaking. Unfortunately I have to advise that due to one of our passengers experiencing a serious medical episode, the captain has made the decision to divert to the nearest suitable airport to ensure that the passenger receives the best care possible. On behalf of myself and the captain, as well as the cabin crew, please allow me to take this opportunity to apologise for this unexpected change to your travel plans. We'll be making a slight left turn towards Caracas in the next few minutes, after which we'll begin our emergency descent, and we should have you on the ground within the next thirty minutes or so. I'd ask that when we land, all passengers please remain in your seats until advised otherwise in order to allow emergency medical personnel full access. Your understanding at this time is greatly appreciated and we'll be sure to provide you with updated information as soon as possible once we've landed.

"Fuck me Eyebrow," groaned Purple. "Just what we fucking need."

"Where's Caracas Joe? Where are we landing? Is that like, Mexico?"

"No, it's in South America somewhere," replied Purple. "Fucking Bolivia, or somewhere like that."

"Venezuela," noted PQ, entering the conversation.

"Where's that compared to where we need to be?" asked Eyebrow.

"Next country over," replied PQ who by that point had his mobile phone out trying to connect to the in-flight Wi-Fi. "You got a credit card?" he asked Eyebrow.

"No," replied Eyebrow.

"What about you?" he asked Purple.

"No, and even if I did, I wouldn't be fucking giving it to you," replied Purple gruffly.

"I have cash," said Eyebrow, reaching into his pocket.

"What good is cash for trying to pay for something on my phone?" said PQ. "What am I supposed to do with cash? Push it through the fucking screen?"

"Just wait until we're on the ground," said Purple. "The airport will have free Wi-Fi I'm guessing." He turned and peered out the window. "Can't see a fucking thing out there yet."

"I wonder what'll happen when we arrive Joe," said Eyebrow. "Do you think we'll take off again pretty soon?"

"No idea Eyebrow. Let's just wait and see how it plays out."

In his earlier address to the passengers, the first officer had estimated around thirty minutes or less to their destination and, true to his word, the plane was soon descending towards Simon Bolivar International Airport. Eyebrow leant across Joe Purple to glance out the window as they approached the city, its lights stretching out into the distance. "This is actually bigger than I thought Joe."

Purple gently guided Eyebrow back to his seat as he resumed his own observation duties. "Same here Eyebrow. I thought it was some fucking country town or something." The plane soon eased itself onto the runway and Purple could see the illuminated airport terminal coming into view. "Jesus, this is like a legitimate airport," he muttered, partly to himself and partly to Eyebrow.

"Can I tell you something a little bit embarrassing Joe?" asked Eyebrow.

Purple turned and looked at Eyebrow warily. "Jesus Christ, you're not going to tell me you've shit your pants or something are you?"

"No. It's just that I thought we might be landing on dirt or something, not a real airport like this."

"Jesus Christ," noted PQ, entering the conversation. "Have you two ever been away from home at any point in your entire lives?"

"We've been plenty of places dickhead," snapped Purple. "Like most of the fucking population though, we just haven't been to South America."

"Well, stick close by when we get off," replied PQ, still toying with his phone.

After landing, the pilot made haste to the gate where Purple could see emergency personnel waiting to board the plane. Though he could not identify what was happening in the forward section, it was only a short time until the unfortunate first class passenger was hurried off, presumably to a nearby hospital. All that remained now was for the announcement to be made as to what the next course of action would be for the plane and its passengers. The minutes went by, eventually turning into half an hour. Passengers were becoming visibly restless about the lack of information being passed to them, and Purple was no exception.

"Fuck me, how much longer do we have to wait?" he grumbled to no-one in particular, prompting the woman in front of him to turn around.

"I know right?" she said in a thick British accent. "It's bloody ridiculous."

Half an hour became forty-five minutes when, eventually, an announcement came across the speaker, this time from the Purser.

Ladies and gentlemen, thank you for your patience. We know that it's been a long day for you and we appreciate your understanding. At this time, the captain has advised that due to operational restrictions, we'll be unable to continue our journey this evening.

Unsurprisingly, this announcement triggered an immediate uproar that the Purser did his best to set aside as he continued.

We will begin deplaning everyone shortly however due to immigration controls, we ask that everyone remains within the terminal. Please do not attempt to pass through immigration into Venezuela. This is particularly important for those of you holding United States passports as any attempt to enter without a valid visa may result in you being detained. We will have staff waiting for you in the terminal for further assistance. We are expecting our flight to Bogota to resume tomorrow morning and we'll keep you updated as we know more details.

"What about our luggage?" yelled one irate passenger.

All checked luggage will remain on the plane, however we ask that everyone take their carry-on baggage and personal items with you when you leave the plane. If you don't have any toiletries, some will be provided to you in the terminal, along with water and food. We sincerely apologise for this inconvenience and be assured, we are doing everything we can to get you back on your way first thing tomorrow morning.

Purple buried his head in his hands. "For fuck sake," he sighed.

"Well at least we didn't check our bags this time Joe," said Eyebrow.

"We've still got all our stuff."

Most of the passengers were now beginning to stand and arrange their personal affairs before making their way off the plane. "Come on, get up," said Purple, directing his comment to PQ in the aisle seat. "I want to get out of here. Let me get my bag."

It appeared that PQ hadn't risen from his seat for the duration of the flight, and his movements were unsurprisingly sluggish, leading to a long sigh emanating from Purple's direction. "I'll get your bag for you Joe, don't worry," said Eyebrow, leaning forward and probing the overhead locker above PQ's head, eventually locating both his and Purple's small suitcases. After what felt an eternity standing in the aisle, a slight movement from the front of the plane signaled that disembarkation had begun and in little over a minute, the three men were shuffling their way toward the exit and whatever Caracas airport held in store for them.

Stepping into the terminal, Eyebrow was shocked to see that the airline crew were joined by at least six heavily armed guards, presumably to ensure that no-one left the terminal or attempted a clandestine entry into the country. For all intents and purposes, he, Purple, PQ and around two hundred other passengers were essentially prisoners for the night. Having been immobile since the moment he sat down, PQ now found that he needed to visit the restroom as a matter of priority and promptly joined the throng of other men with the same intention, all being accompanied by a handful of armed officers likely awaiting one of their unexpected guests to nervously shit out a condom full of narcotics.

With PQ gone, Eyebrow pulled out his phone and checked it. "Doesn't look like I can make phone calls from here Joe."

Purple checked his phone as well. "Same. No network."

"I think I should try and call Esteban and let him know what's going on," said Eyebrow, glancing around for an option. "Do you think the airline would let me use their phone?"

"No idea," replied Purple. "Can't hurt to ask. Let's go." The two of them walked to the desk where one of the customer service agents was standing. "Excuse me," said Purple. "My friend here needs to make an important phone call. Can he use your phone?"

The customer service agent glanced around. "I don't think we can do that sir, sorry."

Purple was undeterred. "He's on his way to Colombia for an important medical procedure, but he's going to miss that now. He needs to call them and let them know. It's a groundbreaking new operation that can make people less retarded and he's one of the first test patients."

"In that case sir, we may be able to make an exception," said the agent as she picked up the phone and place it atop the counter. "Just press that button to get an outside line," she said, pointing to a green button at the top of the keypad.

"Thank you," said Eyebrow as he scrolled on his phone to identify Gutierrez's contact card. He slowly dialled the number on the airport phone, ensuring that he added the correct prefix codes to connect internationally. After ringing for a long time, a voice eventually came from the other end.

"Hola."

"Esteban, it's Jimmy."

"Jimmy, what is going on? Why are you calling me from this number?"

"I wanted to tell you that we've been delayed."

"Delayed where Jimmy?"

"On our way to Colombia. There was an emergency on the plane, and we've had to stop in Venezuela for the night. But we're going to be leaving again tomorrow."

There was a long pause before Gutierrez spoke again. "Jimmy, why are you going to Colombia?"

"Mister Santiago sent us."

There was another pause. "Mister Santiago is staying with me in my guest house Jimmy. Please hold on while I get him."

Eyebrow stayed on the line awaiting Santiago's arrival. A full four minutes elapsed before he heard rustling from the other end, followed by Santiago's voice.

"Hola Max?"

"Hello Mister Santiago. I'm just keeping you up to date. Our flight to Colombia had to make an emergency stopover but we'll be on our way first thing tomorrow. If you could let your business partner know that we're going to be late, that'd be great. I'm really sorry about this."

"Max, I'm a little confused. Why are you going to Colombia and why do you think I need to know?"

"Because you sent us here. I spoke to you on the phone, remember? Wait a minute… how come you're there with Esteban and not on your way to Colombia like you said you were?"

An unsettling pause set in on Santiago's end of the line. "Max, if you spoke with someone, it wasn't me."

Eyebrow's heart immediately sank. "I didn't speak with you?"

"No Max, it was not me."

"But PQ said that it was you."

"Is PQ with you?" asked a somewhat surprised Santiago.

"Yes, he's here with us in Venezuela. And he came to London with us as well. He told me that you said he had to come with us."

Eyebrow awaited a response as he listened to Santiago breathing on the other end of the line. This situation seemed to have suddenly escalated, possibly dangerously, and Eyebrow's hand was now visibly shaking.

Eventually Santiago spoke. "Max, you need to listen very carefully. I don't know what's going on, or who you've been talking to, but I have not seen, nor heard from PQ since the day I despatched all of you to visit Cooper's office. Whoever you spoke to, it was not me. I haven't spoken to PQ, or you, in over a week."

CHAPTER 29

The Many Husbands of Aunt Sofia

Joe Purple had been watching Eyebrow on the phone and the instant that he saw the colour suddenly draining from his face, he knew that something was amiss. Whatever was happening on the other end of the line, it appeared to be dire, and he couldn't help but be concerned about the seriousness of the situation they appeared to have now found themselves embroiled in. Whatever it was, the expression on Eyebrow's face indicated that trouble had found them. Eyebrow turned to Purple and motioned him over. "Joe, you've gotta keep PQ occupied when he comes back," he whispered.

"What the fuck's going on Eyebrow?" asked Purple.

"I'll explain later," replied Eyebrow who had spotted PQ returning from the men's room. "Keep him busy," he added frantically.

Purple could tell that whatever was happening was serious, so he quickly followed Eyebrow's direction. "Who's he talking to?" asked PQ as Purple intercepted him.

Gleaning what he could from Eyebrow's demeanour and his desire to exclude PQ from proceedings, Purple surmised that the topic at hand must involve PQ in some manner. As such, he was determined to run as much interference as possible until such time as Eyebrow could brief him on the matter. "His guy in London," replied Purple, not wanting to alert PQ to the actual nature of Eyebrow's conversation.

"What's he talking to him about?" asked a now visibly nervous PQ.

"Just a status update, that's all. I think he got a message to call him or something, I don't really know."

"How long will he be?"

"Fuck me, how am I supposed to know?" snapped Purple, who then ushered PQ to a row of seats. "Let's just sit here and let the man fucking finish."

The two of them waited, both keeping their eyes trained on Eyebrow – PQ anxiously, and Joe Purple with interest about what was happening. Purple was not one who enjoyed being kept in the dark, especially as it pertained to his own safety, so it was his hope that a little clarity would soon be forthcoming. Eyebrow continued talking for ten more minutes before hanging up and sauntering toward them. He did not say a word as he sat. PQ made to speak but Eyebrow simply held up his hand to halt him. Purple likewise tried to initiate a conversation and again, Eyebrow repeated the simple gesture.

Amid the chaos of the terminal with irate passengers demanding attention and airline staff rushing hither and yon, silence descended across the three men. Purple and PQ shifted uncomfortably in their seats, both occasionally rising to stretch. And all the while, Eyebrow sat stone-faced, staring straight ahead. Purple had never seen him like this before, which filled him with equal parts curiosity and anxiety about what Eyebrow knew. What was he waiting for there in his monk-like state?

The answer came after nearly an hour as three heavily armed officers entered the terminal and spoke to the man who appeared to be the supervisor. After exchanging words, the officers looked in the direction of Eyebrow and his associates and strode toward them with purpose. Stopping directly in front of them, one of the officers spoke. "Señor Von Steel? Señor Ferguson?"

"Yes, that's us," said Eyebrow as he stood.

"Come with us please," said the officer without further elaboration.

Joe Purple was now clearly worried about this unexpected turn of events. "What the fuck's going on Eyebrow?"

Eyebrow answered confidently and reassuringly. "Don't worry Joe. It's OK, trust me. Grab your bag and make sure you have everything."

"What about me?" asked PQ.

Eyebrow stooped a little to look PQ directly in the eye. "You're staying right here you double-crossing piece of shit."

This brought Purple instantly to life. "Oh fuck yes! I *knew* there was something about you. You fucked with the wrong guys this time!" As Purple and Eyebrow made their way to the terminal exit in the company of the armed officers, Purple spun and gave one final middle finger to PQ who was now sitting alone in stunned silence, trying to comprehend what was happening.

But it wasn't just PQ trying to piece together what the hell had just happened, but Purple also. "You're gonna have to tell me what's going on here Eyebrow," he said.

"Real soon Joe, just hang in there," replied Eyebrow.

As they now approached the immigration hall, the man who appeared to be the senior officer gestured to an immigration official with a click of his fingers before turning to Eyebrow and Purple. "Open your passports to a blank page," he instructed curtly. Both men did as instructed, and the officer directed the immigration official to their passports with a single point of his index finger, after which a stamp was quickly placed in each, with no further formalities required.

After exiting the immigration hall, Eyebrow and Purple were directed towards a man in a suit, and the three officers then swiftly departed without a word exchanged. The suited man extended his hand and flashed a broad smile. "Señor Von Steel?" he enquired.

"Yes, that's me," replied Eyebrow. "And this is my friend…"

"Ferguson," added Purple quickly.

"Good to see that you have made it safely," said the man. "I am Ernesto by the way. Please, follow me to the car. Mister Ventura is looking forward to meeting you. It will be a drive of about twenty minutes."

Purple looked at Eyebrow. "I'm still waiting to find out what's going on here Eyebrow."

"I'll tell you in the car," replied Eyebrow.

Soon enough, they were on the road, winding their way to the home of Rudy Ventura, a senior minister in the Venezuelan government. Relaxing in the back seat, Eyebrow now got down to the business of laying out the sequence of events for Purple. "Mister Ventura's a good friend of Esteban's," he began. "When I called Esteban, he put me onto Mister Santiago who was there with him. He told me that he hadn't heard from PQ since our trip to Cooper's house."

"But PQ told us that Santiago had sent him to be with us," noted Purple.

"Yeah, that's what PQ told us. But it was bullshit. He'd never spoken to Santiago."

"So he made that shit up?"

"Sounds like it," replied Eyebrow.

"Fuck me," mumbled Purple. "And what about this trip?"

"Santiago didn't know a thing about it."

Purple was confused. "But you spoke with him on the phone."

"That's the thing Joe, I didn't. It wasn't him. Fuck, I should have known because the guy called me Señor Von Steel, but Santiago calls me Max. This is all on me Joe. Whoever it was, it was someone that PQ was working with. I guess they thought they could sneak another guy's voice past me."

"Well… they were right."

"I'd only met the guy once before. How could I tell if it was him on the phone? I bet you wouldn't be able to tell either."

"Yeah, you're probably right," replied Purple. "Who was it then?"

"No idea," said Eyebrow. "But whoever it was, they were working with PQ to try and get us to Colombia, and I bet it's got something to do with that key."

"I fucking told you didn't I! I was right. We were going to end up in a fucking bag at the bottom of a river. Jesus Christ Eyebrow, I should have stuck with my gut on this one."

"Well, we're safe now Joe. This guy we're going to see, he's going to let us stay for a few days. He's got security and shit because he's a pretty big deal. That's what Esteban says anyway. Esteban's sending help for us and then we can just go back home."

Purple offered up an observation that, from his perspective, had a solid foundation of historical evidence to support it. "I tell you what Eyebrow, you have a remarkable way of finding new and exotic ways to get us out of the equally exotic and shitful situations you continually put us in. You're like… I don't know… the fucking arsonist who turns up to put out the fire."

Before Eyebrow could respond, Ernesto turned slightly and spoke, pointing up the road as he did so. "Mister Ventura's house is right up here." Within moments they were slowing down outside a large gate as Ernesto waited for it to steadily open in response to the electronic signature of their car. Eyebrow glanced around and even though the neighbourhood was still urban, he could tell that this was far more upmarket than some of the areas they had traversed on their journey from the airport. This appeared to be an exclusive gated community, likely inhabited only by those with power and resources. As a senior government minister, it was likely that Rudy Ventura had both in abundance.

As the car rolled to a halt at the front of Ventura's house, a man casually dressed in shorts and button shirt, most likely Ventura himself, descended the front steps to meet them. This was confirmed moments later as he greeted Eyebrow warmly, like an old friend that he wasn't. "Señor Von Steel, so lovely to see you. I am Rudy."

Ventura was around fifty years old, tall, though slightly built, and balding. He also sported a pair of oversized and very thick glasses. "Mister Ventura, thank you for having us," replied Eyebrow. "This is my friend…"

"No need for introductions," interrupted Ventura as he pressed his hand firmly into Purple's. "This is your assistant, Señor Ferguson I am guessing?"

"That's me," grimaced Purple before lowering his voice. "Good old Ferguson the assistant." The final utterance was accompanied by a now familiar glare in Eyebrow's direction.

"Please, come inside," said Ventura as he beckoned them up the steps. "You must be hungry. I have some food prepared for you. I understand that it is late, so we can chat briefly tonight and then the two of you can get some well-earned rest." Ventura ushered them into a casual dining room that abutted the kitchen. Despite the late hour, there was an older lady preparing herself a drink in the kitchen as they approached. She appeared to be in her eighties, with deeply tanned leathery skin, and wearing a small silk dressing gown.

"Aunt Sofia, what are you doing up?" asked Ventura. "It's late."

Sofia walked over towards Ventura and patted him on the shoulder while flourishing some form of cocktail in the air. "Just making myself a drink Rudy my dear."

Ventura looked at his watch in dismay. "Really Aunt Sofia?"

Sofia walked over to Eyebrow and Purple and sized them up. "I see we have guests." She moved closer to Eyebrow and rubbed her hand up and down his arm. "My… you look a lot like my fifth husband," she noted.

Eyebrow was unsure how to respond. "Your fifth husband? How many have you had?"

"Four," she replied, touching her finger lightly on his chin. She turned to Rudy. "I'll go back to bed and get out of your way." As she walked past Eyebrow she glanced slyly at him. "I don't lock the door of my room, so please be careful that you don't mistake my room for yours," she added with a wink.

"That's my Aunt Sofia," noted Ventura after she had departed. "She's got no-one, so she stays with me."

"Has she really had four husbands?" asked Eyebrow.

"She has indeed," replied Ventura. "She has been close to having a fifth two times before, but each time, it ended… shall we say… unfortunately."

"What do you mean?" asked Eyebrow.

"First there was Nestor. He was a manager at the sewerage treatment plant who drowned when he fell into a tank of effluent. And then about a year later there was Luis. His death wasn't very pleasant so I don't know if I should talk about that."

"Jesus Christ!" said Purple. "How much fucking worse can it be than drowning in a vat of other people's shit?"

Ventura lowered his voice and began relating the tragic story of Luis. "Luis was a university professor… very smart man. An anthropologist, I think is the term. One day he embarked on an expedition to study Guyanan red howler monkeys and never returned. Several days after failing to check in, a search party was sent for him and he was found, dead."

"What happened to him?" asked Eyebrow.

"It appeared that the howler monkeys entrapped the good professor, beat him and then…" Ventura took a deep breath and averted his eyes. "They violated him. Guyanan red howler monkeys are known to be quite sexually aggressive and by the time the search party found Luis, he had probably been dead for around three days. His clothes were shredded, and it appeared that the monkeys had been using him for their own satisfaction the whole time."

Eyebrow brought his hand to his mouth. "Oh shit."

"Fuck me," added Purple. "So, he was humped to death by monkeys? Jesus, that's fucked up."

Ventura gently nodded his head, allowing the silence to hang in the air for a short time before slapping his leg in glee, a broad smile breaking out over his face. "I'm only messing with you," he screamed through fits of laughter.

Eyebrow was taken aback. "What, so there never was anyone named Luis?"

"Oh yes, Luis was real," replied Ventura. "But he was a used car salesman."

"Did he actually die?" asked Purple.

Ventura nodded. "Unfortunately, yes. He choked on his food at Macho Burger. Not quite worthy of a story like the other sadly. Have you ever been to Macho Burger?" Both Eyebrow and Purple shook their heads. "I will take you there tomorrow night. Do you remember the legendary wrestler, Macho Man Savage? If you order their famous Double Macho with cheese using Macho Man's voice, you get the burger for half price." Ventura now looked toward Eyebrow and shifted gears. "Fair warning Señor Von Steel. The fifth husband of Aunt Sofia is indeed a cursed space. Beware if you plan to go there."

"I… do not plan going there," replied Eyebrow. "Once we're done here, I'm on my way home. Without a wife… who's eighty years old."

"Wise move," said Ventura, patting Eyebrow on the shoulder.

Purple now entered the conversation. "Exactly how long are we planning on staying here?"

"Esteban has asked if you can be my guests for at least two days," replied Ventura. "He is dispatching some help for you as a matter of priority, after which you will be able to return home. I will ensure that you have safe passage when the time comes."

"And we're safe here?" asked Eyebrow.

"Yes, Señor Von Steel, you are safe. The neighbourhood is the home of many government ministers, and we have excellent security providers who monitor the entire precinct. Aunt Sofia is not my only associate here in this house, but as the hour is late, everyone else, except Ernesto who has returned home… they have all retired for the evening. I will introduce you to the others tomorrow, but for now, you should eat and rest."

"And what about PQ?" asked Eyebrow.

"I am presuming PQ is the unsavoury character who was accompanying you?"

"Yeah, the guy we left at the airport."

"Then he will be stuck there until he's loaded back on the plane to Colombia tomorrow morning. Given that it's an emergency stopover, no foreign passport holders will be permitted entry into the country." Ventura smiled and gave a subtle nod in Eyebrow and Purple's direction. "Present company excluded of course – one of the benefits of, shall we say… influence."

All seemed in order for Eyebrow and Purple, and for now, they could relax, safe in the knowledge that they had dodged a bullet of significant magnitude. Both men yearned for a good night's sleep in a comfortable bed and if they were to be lodging with Ventura for two days, such a prospect was now firmly on the cards. But as with everything associated with Jimmy Eyebrow, flies were circling the ointment, waiting for the right moment to dive in.

CHAPTER 30
The First Fly

Rudy Ventura had been correct about one thing – without high-level intervention such as that which he had rendered to Jimmy Eyebrow and Joe Purple, no foreign nationals on their diverted flight would have been permitted entry into Venezuela. And by using that logic, it would be reasonable to presume that the conniving PQ was still confined to the transit terminal at Caracas International Airport. But there was one major variable that had not been factored in – a variable that became starkly apparent when PQ rummaged through his luggage and retrieved his passport. He sat there momentarily, caressing the document, sliding his thumb across the cover that read: *Mercosur República Bolivariana de Venezuela.*

Soon after Eyebrow and Purple disappeared in the company of their armed escort, PQ himself was making his way to the immigration hall. But without the benefit of expedited entry as Eyebrow and Purple had received, by the time he had completed his formalities, his former companions were nowhere to be seen. He presumed that they were somewhere in Caracas, but beyond that, he had no clue.

PQ's silent partner in the deception that led Eyebrow and Purple to be on a plane to Colombia was the head of the Ortiz crime family, Alejandro Ortiz. And now, the first order of business was to get a message to Ortiz to apprise him of the unexpected development that saw both Eyebrow and Purple whisked away under what appeared to be diplomatic protection.

In addition, PQ's cover was now also certainly blown so it was only natural that Ortiz must be advised of the situation. Given that Ortiz was in Colombia, it was not possible for him to arrange a meeting at short notice. However his reach was wide, and he did have mid-level minions residing in Caracas, one of whom he despatched to meet with PQ, who now sat on the edge of the fountain in the city's central plaza, awaiting his arrival. The hour was late, and there were hardly any other people frequenting the plaza at that time. After what seemed an inordinate amount of time, another man eventually strolled across the plaza in his direction before stopping about ten feet in front of him.

"Are you PQ?" he enquired.

"Yeah, that's me. You Ortiz's guy?"

The man moved closer. "Yes. My name is Roberto. You have a situation, yes?"

"You could say that again," replied PQ. "A big fucking situation."

"Come," said Roberto, beckoning PQ to follow him. "We cannot conduct business here, but we will go to my house, and we'll call Mister Ortiz from there."

Thankfully for PQ, who was on the tail end of a very long and stressful day, Roberto's car was not far away and within half an hour, the two men were sitting at the dining table in Roberto's modest, but tasteful house. Off to his left, PQ was eyeing a luxurious plush sofa, but as Roberto had chosen the table for their meeting, PQ felt it best to play his role as guest dutifully. Roberto placed his phone in the middle of the table and dialled. The phone only rang once before a voice came from the other end.

"Si," was all that Ortiz uttered, not even in question form. It was spoken in a manner indicating that he wanted to get straight to the point, without feigned formalities.

"I have your man here with me," noted Roberto.

Ortiz spoke. "PQ, your earlier message mentioned that you have a situation. Please fill me in."

"It's serious, Mister Ortiz. Both of them are gone."

"Both?" asked Ortiz. "Longchamp as well?"

"Longchamp's dead," replied PQ. "I contacted him like you told me to, I got him to London, and I organised for us to all be on the same plane. He wasn't happy about being rushed like that though. But then he collapsed while we were in the air, and the plane ended up being diverted here to Caracas."

"And the one who knows about the money?"

"That's Von Steel, and he's gone, along with his buddy. Somehow, they got taken through immigration and someone picked them up."

There was a momentary silence from the other end before Ortiz offered his observation. "Gutierrez..." he whispered, before pausing in thought again. "I needed both of those men. I needed this Von Steel character to tell us everything he knew about the location of the money. One way or another, I cared not how we got it. And I needed Longchamp to weave his magic and fix whatever was going on. Von Steel was expendable, but not Longchamp – he was indispensable. He's been with us for generations. This is not good PQ. This is turning out nothing like how I had planned it."

PQ leant a little closer to the phone. "I have to tell you something Mister Ortiz. I'm starting to think that this Von Steel guy has a bit more going on than I originally thought."

"Please explain," replied Ortiz.

"It's just that, well... he seems to have some big-ticket contacts, like the guy we went to see in London. I don't know what game the guy's in because Von Steel wouldn't tell me, but he seems like a connected player."

"Did you get a name at least?"

"Spaulding. He runs a place called Iron Key Consulting. I checked it out and it just says that it's a security place. Other than that, I have no clue what it specializes in though. All I know is that Von Steel flew all the way to London to see him about something, and it's got to be about the money. Von Steel has to know something, but he wouldn't tell me jack shit."

"Interesting..." replied Ortiz before PQ continued.

"But that's not all. I know this is a big call Mister Ortiz... but I can't shake the feeling that Von Steel had something to do with Longchamp's death. The guy disappeared for fucking hours on the plane and then when he gets back, Longchamp's on the floor. It's gotta be him that did it Mister Ortiz. He must have known what was going on. All this time, he knew, and he was playing us. Maybe..." PQ paused to summon up the courage to mention his next thought. "Maybe he *wanted* to be on that plane. Maybe... he's coming for *you*."

"What do you mean he disappeared on the plane?" asked Ortiz, surprised.

"I mean, he got up and went to the can at the back of the plane, and then the next time I see him is when he's wandering back all casual from the front of the plane where all hell's breaking loose and Longchamp's gone down."

"You truly believe that this assassin manipulated us to get on the same plane as Longchamp?" asked Ortiz, by now clearly annoyed at the state of affairs. "You feel we may have been played? And you think he might be coming for *me*?"

"It's just a guess Mister Ortiz. Being diverted to Caracas might have thrown his plan out and that's why he had to call in a favour to get out of there."

"So, where is he now?"

"No idea to be honest. He could still be here, or he could already be on his way to you."

There was silence from the other end of the call – this time a silence of the long variety. Eventually Ortiz spoke menacingly, as if his persona had completely switched in the period he had been silent. "If what you say is true, then he has made a terrible mistake that will cost him dearly." Ortiz now addressed his associate. "Roberto?"

"I'm here Mister Ortiz," replied Roberto.

Ortiz was succinct in his order. "I want all our available resources in Caracas looking for this Von Steel. I want him captured and brought to me." There was another brief pause from Ortiz before he continued with an ominous warning. "And if this hitman is already coming to me of his own free will, then be assured that I will be waiting."

CHAPTER 31

Beware the Dog That Isn't Barking

From a very early age, Charles de Klerk was fascinated by the visual elements of the world around him. The colours, the relationships between objects, the effects of light and shade – his young mind analysed and processed every aspect of the fascinating realm that is life. As a child he was a prolific artist and before the age of ten, he had developed a skill for image composition that most people do not achieve in a lifetime.

Though not destitute, his parents were also not bathing in cash so it was quite the treat when on his twelfth birthday, young Charles received his first camera – a gift that would herald the beginning of what would become a decorated career in photojournalism. Charles sought out and absorbed every book and article he could about photography, and he scoured the newspapers and magazines to study how the masters of photographic composition made their works jump off the page and into the viewers' consciousness.

In particular, de Klerk spent countless hours analysing the great works of photojournalism such as Rosenthal's immortal image of the flag raising on Iwo Jima and Robert Jackson's incredibly timed capture of the moment when Lee Harvey Oswald was shot. And if one were to identify a seminal influence on de Klerk's studies, it would be the haunting "Saigon Execution" photograph snapped by Edward Adams in 1969 – a point in time captured so hauntingly that it sent shockwaves around the globe and demonstrated to de Klerk the colossal influence that a single photograph can wield. One moment in time – one split second among an infinite number of seconds in the lifetime of the universe – the power that de Klerk possessed with a single perfectly-timed squeeze of the shutter release button was intoxicating.

Over time, de Klerk honed his talents and took them to locations still so mysterious that they often lived solely locked within the pages of a *National Geographic*. This was long before the advent of the Internet and the ability for people to travel to the farthest reaches of the planet from the confines of an office cubicle. One of de Klerk's first major photojournalism expeditions was in what was then Rhodesia where he was embedded with an army unit dedicated to tracking poachers who were decimating the black rhino population.

The poignant nature of what he saw through his viewfinder during that three-week expedition not only exposed him to the dark underbelly of human nature, but it also illustrated starkly to him that no matter how much he may wish to the contrary, he held no control over events – he was nothing more than an observer to the worst that humanity could offer. It was de Klerk's early work in Rhodesia, and later Cambodia, that not only honed his skills in working within danger zones but also reinforced that his role was to document history, nothing more and nothing less. Wars would be started and finished, political earthquakes would shake the globe, leaders would rise and fall – and through it all, the world would always keep turning, and he was just along for the ride.

As successful as he was at his chosen craft, one of de Klerk's biggest professional regrets was his failure to identify the developing situation that was primed to explode in East Berlin in November of 1989, leading to him not being in attendance on one of the most consequential nights in modern European history when the Berlin Wall fell. To be fair to de Klerk, there were few people who could have anticipated the alarmingly swift escalation of the situation that had slowly been simmering to a boil in the weeks prior to the night in question. He, along with dozens of other photographers and journalists from across the world, had certainly identified that *something* was in the air and were already en route, but unfortunately for them, the unprecedented speed with which the situation escalated through the night would mean that they would only capture the aftermath and not the main event.

As disappointing as the Berlin experience was for de Klerk, it served as a pivotal moment in his career, and it fuelled his resolve to never again miss the warning signs that something big was brewing. He observed, he listened, and he analysed. He would call in favours and most of all, he had used the relationships that he had developed over what was now decades in the game to tap into intelligence channels that would give him an advantage over the many thousands of other photojournalists crisscrossing the globe at any given time.

The career of Charles de Klerk had been remarkable indeed and he was now considered to be one of the eminent photographers of his time. As he had studied the works of Rosenthal, Jackson and Adams decades earlier, so too did budding photojournalists now turn their studious eyes to his body of work that was, by that point in his life, prodigious. But unlike the idols of his own youth, de Klerk was still to capture that one iconic image that would ultimately define him. He had spent a lifetime in pursuit of the supreme photo, yet it always seemed to elude him.

And now, as de Klerk 's taxi wound through the streets of Caracas on the way to his hotel, he gazed across the placid nature of the scene outside his window. The whole place exuded a calmness that de Klerk suspected may not be built to last. There is a saying among the intelligence community – "beware the dog that isn't barking". Up until recently, de Klerk's contacts had kept him abreast of significant back-chatter emanating from Venezuela – an indication that something was brewing. What it was, no-one could determine but a little over twenty-four hours earlier the chatter had slowed, and then ultimately ceased.

A lifetime of research and observation had taught de Klerk that when the dog that has been barking incessantly suddenly falls silent, the odds increase markedly that something is afoot, hence his hasty arrival in the Venezuelan capital. Whatever was going down, Charles de Klerk was determined that this would not be another Berlin. If his destiny was waiting for him, then this time he would be ready.

CHAPTER 32

The Second (Much Larger) Fly

Entirely unaware that the full Caracas-based resources of the Ortiz family had been mobilised in an effort to locate him, Jimmy Eyebrow now found himself in a state of blissful relaxation on the pool deck of Rudy Ventura's luxury villa. It hadn't taken long for Aunt Sofia to again seek Eyebrow out that day, with Eyebrow already succumbing to her desires for him to apply tanning lotion to her… liberally… twice already, even though it was not yet noon.

Now as Eyebrow stretched out on the deck, basking in the warm glow from the cloudless sky, Ventura and Purple sat close by at a small table, each with an ice-cold drink that had been provided to them by Juan-Carlos, Ventura's young in-house concierge. Both men sat and gazed across the scene lying before them on the pool deck, Ventura not sure how to start the conversation.

"I…" he began before stumbling.

"It's OK," replied Purple. "You can say it."

Ventura tried, but again was stumped. "I'm just…"

"I know," said Purple, nodding his head gently.

Ventura rubbed his chin in heavy contemplation, finally finding some diplomatic words to convey his thoughts. "That is… one hell of a bathing outfit."

Purple took a sip of his drink. "Not even close to the words I'd use. We almost got arrested at the airport in London because he had that fucking thing in his bag. I think on the scale of seriousness, customs have stuff like heroin and weapons at the top of the list, and immediately below that, they have his jocks. Just above freeze-dried scorpions and other shit that Asians are always trying to smuggle in."

"I think Aunt Sofia has a soft spot for him," noted Ventura.

"Wouldn't be surprised if he's got a semi-hard spot for her," replied Purple with a chuckle. Taking another sip of his drink, he relaxed and assessed Ventura's estate. Within the grounds he had identified three members of Ventura's security detail, two of whom were on constant patrol with a third sitting in what appeared to be a small guard house. Eyebrow and Purple had also been introduced at breakfast to two other residents of Ventura's estate – Mariano and Humberto.

Mariano was a rugged man in his forties who appeared to be a Mr. Everything for Ventura. Currently he was attending to some gardening, but Purple surmised that Mariano was also the resident handyman and general hand. In addition, Purple had also noted that Mariano carried himself like a soldier, however he did not press the matter with Ventura, who in turn did not offer any background when he introduced Mariano to his two guests.

The second man, Humberto, was elderly and infirm – likely in his late seventies, maybe even in his eighties. Humberto was confined to a wheelchair and operated on a single-digit percentage of his lung function, necessitating the constant presence of an oxygen bottle and mask. As a result, he was barely able to raise his voice beyond a whisper and in order to attract the attention of anyone further than two feet away from him, Humberto's wheelchair had been fitted with a squeeze horn from an old bicycle.

Ventura had explained to Eyebrow and Purple earlier that Humberto was the original gardener for the estate and had resided there long before the ravages of old age caught up with him. Having never lived anywhere else for the majority of his life, Ventura felt obliged to allow Humberto to remain in residence into his retirement years, even after he made the first two replacement gardeners so uncomfortable that they each left within a week of being appointed.

Ventura then brought in the no-nonsense Mariano who did not tolerate Humberto's cantankerous nature. Over time, Humberto slowly began to accept Mariano's presence in his old role, though he still offered advice from time to time – advice that Mariano eventually came to appreciate did in fact come from a position of authority on the subject.

As Purple and Ventura sat, Humberto's horn honked. "What's up Humberto?" asked Ventura.

Humberto wildly gesticulated toward Eyebrow and then pointed to his own crotch, followed by the universal hand signal for *what the hell?*

"What can we do Humberto?" said Ventura. "He is our guest for a couple of days. If he wants to wear that, so be it. Go inside and watch some TV or something." As Humberto wheeled himself away to the guest house, Ventura turned to Purple. "How does your friend know Esteban?"

"I have no idea whatsoever. I've only spoken to the guy once myself." Purple brought his fingers to his mouth and whistled in Eyebrow's direction, grabbing his attention instantly. "Come here, Rudy wants to ask you something," he said firmly.

Eyebrow rose and sauntered over toward them, his skin luminescent from the vast amount of tanning oil that Aunt Sofia had lathered over him during a mutual oiling session earlier. In fact, the quantity of oil she had sensually coated him with was so prodigious that if he were to enter the water in his current state, it would likely trigger an Environmental Protection Agency response similar in scale to the *Exxon Valdez* incident. "What's up?" asked Eyebrow as he neared Purple and Ventura.

"Rudy wanted to ask how you know Gutierrez."

Eyebrow went to take a seat, but given his current state of lubrication, it proved to be problematic, and he was unable to securely position himself without continually slipping forward. "I think I might have to stand," he noted after several unsuccessful attempts to sit. Eyebrow looked toward Ventura and spoke. "How do I know Esteban? We met on a cruise, and we kept in touch after that. He saved my skin a couple of times, so I owe him big time."

"He speaks very fondly of you," replied Ventura as he leant forward in Eyebrow's direction. "Myself, I have known Esteban for around thirty years. He is a good man, if you're on the right side of him." Ventura flourished his hand around the house and gardens. "He has helped me immensely in getting where I am today. And of course, I reciprocate that friendship wherever possible. Tell me Señor Von Steel, have you been friends for long?"

"No, not really," said Eyebrow.

"I see. Well, if I were to offer you any advice, it would be to always ensure that you water and tend to that friendship. Because over time, it could grow to be something more powerful than you could imagine."

Eyebrow nodded his understanding before Ventura continued. "But just remember, you have only ever seen the generous and benevolent side of our mutual friend. Esteban is not a violent or cruel person by his nature, but if it comes to survival, be assured, he will do anything to ensure that he is the man left standing at the end. Esteban's influence is due to respect, not violence, but sometimes… sometimes violence becomes a necessary evil in his world. Thankfully you have not yet seen that, and pray that you never will Señor Von Steel."

Eyebrow and Purple did not possess a hive mind, but it was clear that on this occasion, both were thinking the same thing and were beginning to develop an appreciation for the world in which they now walked. The days of collecting loan money from Greek shopkeepers and performing unpaid janitorial duties for a disagreeable pizza shop proprietor were now becoming a distant memory. Sitting, or standing in Eyebrow's case, around a pool deck in Caracas, they knew that their lives had become far more exotic, but Joe Purple for one was unsure as to whether it was for better or worse. They were roused from their thoughts by the sound of Humberto's bicycle horn honking from the guest house. Ventura looked at Eyebrow, who was already standing. "Would you mind?"

"Sure thing," replied Eyebrow, who made his way to the small sunroom in the guest house where Humberto was watching TV. "What's up Humberto?" he asked, to which Humberto just pointed to the blank screen in annoyance. "I don't understand," said Eyebrow.

Humberto beckoned Eyebrow to within speaking distance and removed his oxygen mask. "The TV… the station just went black," he whispered. Eyebrow took the remote control from Humberto and cycled through several neighbouring channels – nothing. Humberto whispered again. "All of them, they just stopped."

Eyebrow checked the television itself, unsure of what he was actually looking for, but nonetheless attempting to look competent. Everything appeared to be in order. "I don't know what's happened I'll go and let Rudy know." Eyebrow returned to the pool deck and relayed the situation to Ventura. "The TV's stopped working."

"It is completely dead?" queried Ventura.

"No, I should have rephrased that," replied Eyebrow. "The TV itself is working, like, it's turned on and everything, but there's no channels coming through."

"Not to worry. I'm sure it will work itself out." Ventura summoned Juan-Carlos. "Could I please have a coffee Juan-Carlos. Thank you. And please check to see if Humberto would like one also." Ventura turned to Eyebrow and Purple. "Coffee?"

"No thanks," replied Eyebrow before Purple also politely declined.

"Just for me, and maybe Humberto too then," said Ventura as he dismissed Juan-Carlos.

"What's the deal with Mariano?" asked Purple after Juan-Carlos had departed. "He looks like a soldier. Is he ex-army?"

"Very perceptive Señor Ferguson," replied Ventura. "He is indeed. Bolivian army in fact. He was an engineer – building bridges, blowing up unexploded bombs… that sort of thing. He is the nephew of an old friend of mine, sadly passed away now. My friend asked me if I could try to find some work for Mariano when he left the army so, he ended up here. And he has been here ever since. He's very handy around the place, plus he's like an extra security resource on top of what I already have."

"He doesn't talk much," noted Eyebrow.

"You are strangers to him. He's a quiet man, yes, but he would open up more if he knew you, I'm sure of it. But as you're only staying for a couple of days, I am guessing that he is choosing to just keep to himself."

At that moment, Aunt Sofia beckoned to Ventura. "Rudy darling!"

"Yes, Aunt Sofia?"

Aunt Sofia eased herself out of her deckchair and strutted towards the three men. "My phone isn't getting any signal darling. Can you check to see if yours is working?"

Ventura pulled his phone from his pocket and checked its signal. "No, I don't have anything either." After looking at the phone for a few moments, something seemed to register in his mind and Ventura stood bolt upright, his face suddenly ashen.

"What's happening Rudy?" asked Eyebrow, but Ventura waved him off without a word. Eyebrow turned to Purple and whispered. "Something's going on Joe."

"I sense that too Eyebrow," said Purple. "Stay alert."

Ventura stood statuesque and vigilant, a sense of dread beginning to wash over him, like a Vietnamese villager in his rice paddy who suddenly hears *Fortunate Son* begin playing in the distance. He clicked his fingers toward the security detail and directed them to lift their alert level.

In the background, a rumble that had been barely perceptible moments earlier was now becoming more prominent. Ventura ushered Aunt Sofia away from the pool and toward the guest house. "Get inside Aunt Sofia. Go with Humberto." Ventura now beckoned Mariano toward him. "Something's not right Mariano," he noted ominously. "Something's definitely not right."

CHAPTER 33

The Devil's Brew

Rudy Ventura stood silently, flanked by Jimmy Eyebrow and Joe Purple – all three men now assessing the uneasy feeling that had descended across Ventura's estate. Mariano, who had been standing alongside Ventura moments earlier had slowly edged his way toward the garden shed, while all three members of Ventura's security detail were now ready at arms. The rumble that had been slowly growing in the background had now transitioned to a constant drone, and whatever it was emanating from was now very clearly just outside the perimeter of Ventura's estate.

Mariano was the first to identify the imminent nature of what was at play and urgently beckoned Eyebrow and Purple to join him at the garden shed. Whatever was going on, this was far beyond their scope of normal operations so they both obeyed Mariano's direction without hesitation, placing their fate in the hands of someone who clearly knew his way around what was happening. Mariano stopped – he had heard something that the others could not register. "GET DOWN!!! NOW!!!" he bellowed.

Ventura hit the grass and lay as flat as he could behind a small wall near the pool, his hands covering his head and his feet facing the direction of where the rumble was coming from. Eyebrow and Purple, meanwhile, dived into the garden shed a millisecond before an ear-splitting explosion caused Ventura's perimeter wall to shatter as if it were made of little more than honeycomb, raining rubble throughout the garden and the street.

"HOLY FUCK!" yelled Purple before glancing toward Eyebrow who was now cowering in fear.

"WHAT THE FUCK IS THAT, JOE?" screamed Eyebrow frantically.

Purple did not have time to respond as Mariano quickly retrieved two M16 automatic rifles from the wall and thrust them into Eyebrow and Purple's hands. "GO!" he ordered. Eyebrow quickly composed himself and looked around the interior of the garden shed for the first time, noting that it bore much more resemblance to a mini-armory than a repository for gardening equipment. Eyebrow peeked outside and identified the source of the earlier rumbling as a tank was now forcing its way across the rubble and into Ventura's garden. Eyebrow glanced across to Ventura and saw that he was still secreted behind the small wall that, for now at least, remained intact.

Purple now joined Eyebrow as the tank continued its slow march into the interior of Ventura's estate. By now, at least half a dozen foot soldiers were flanking the tank and were pouring through the gap in the wall, now engaging in a firefight with the two security guards who remained after their other associate fell in the initial explosion. "Quick Joe, over here!" yelled Eyebrow, directing Purple to the small wall where Ventura was hiding. "We need to protect Rudy."

"Screw Rudy. We need to fucking protect ourselves," said Purple as he bounded toward the wall with Eyebrow, emptying his magazine into the oncoming attackers.

The two men slid to the turf next to Ventura. "Are you OK?" enquired Eyebrow over the roar of the gunfire.

"Yes! Don't worry about me," replied Ventura.

Eyebrow and Purple now took up their position behind the cover of the wall, providing supporting fire from an additional angle to Mariano and the security guards. Or to be more precise, the lone remaining security guard – his second comrade having been cut down by the soldiers who held a superiority in numbers. But the superiority was dwindling as between Eyebrow, Purple and the other two of Ventura's men, they began slicing through the attackers until only two remained.

It was then that another thunderous roar rolled through the air, followed by a high-pitched whirring sound that felt within touching distance above Eyebrow's head. Behind him, a mighty explosion rocked Ventura's house as the second ferocious round from the tank wrought havoc throughout the structure.

Eyebrow and Purple's bullets were impotent against the impervious exterior of the tank but thankfully, Mariano was up to the task as he now strolled out of the garden shed with what looked like a bazooka perched atop his shoulder. The tank slowly turned its turret toward him, but it was all in vain as Mariano unleashed the high-explosive projectile toward its target. "HOLY SHIT!" exclaimed Eyebrow as the round slammed directly into the turret, causing an immediate chain reaction within the tank's interior.

"Get down!" yelled Mariano as the tank began the grotesque process of what combat soldiers term "brewing up," with flames now screeching from any opening in the tank like a blast furnace. Whatever was going on inside there, neither Eyebrow nor Purple wanted to consider it. They had both reluctantly been pushed into resorting to violence themselves in the past, but this was now taking it to another level. This was life or death combat – legitimate warfare – that neither of them had even had the slightest opportunity to prepare for.

The shooting had now stopped as the proximity of the two remaining soldiers to the brewing tank carcass resulted in them now being lost to the carnage also. Other than the hellish sound erupting from the tank, the battlefield had fallen silent. Joe Purple rolled over to look at Ventura, who was now beginning to rise from his prone position. "What else does he keep in that fucking tool shed?" Purple asked incredulously.

"As I said before, an extra layer of security," said Ventura as he dusted himself off. He turned to look at the house, flames now beginning to take hold. "Juan-Carlos!" he yelled as he jumped to his feet. "I sent him inside for coffee!" Ventura took off at a frightening pace toward the house as Mariano now approached Eyebrow and Purple.

"What the fuck is going on Mariano?" asked Eyebrow, his voice beginning to waver now that the initial surge of adrenaline was wearing off.

Mariano squatted before Eyebrow and Purple. "That, my new friends, is what the start of a military coup looks like. This city is about to descend into chaos, and I assure you, we do not want to be here when that occurs because Mister Ventura, and any of us alongside him, will be high value targets. The fog of war will be heavy for a short time yet so if we're going to move, we need to do it now, before these rebels begin reorganizing themselves."

Mariano exuded authority and experience, and both Eyebrow and Purple knew that their survival in what had suddenly become a life-or-death situation, rested on placing their faith in his leadership. Mariano motioned towards the gaping hole in the wall. "You two go and check to see if we're clear outside. I'm going to check on Humberto and Sofia."

Mariano quickly scurried off to the guest house leaving Eyebrow and Purple with their assigned task. While Purple was already clothed, Eyebrow was still clad only in his tiny American flag bathing suit and was also without footwear. He quickly grabbed a pair of sandals from the pool deck – whose they were, he had no clue, and he also shuffled over to a deck chair and took the sash from a red dressing gown and wrapped it around his head.

"What the fuck are you doing with that, Eyebrow?" asked Purple.

"My wig, it keeps slipping off," replied Eyebrow as he tightened the sash behind his head. "This'll keep it in place."

The two men now followed Mariano's earlier direction and, rifles at the ready, cautiously made their way toward the remains of what was once Ventura's stone wall. They had caught the eye of the lone remaining security guard and, using hand signals between the three of them, had organized to inspect the carnage from both sides of the burning tank – Eyebrow and Purple to the left and the security guard to the right. Approaching the wall slowly, Eyebrow peeked around the corner – nothing. He turned to Purple. "Have a look, Joe. Can you see anything?" Purple warily poked his head out into the street and quickly jerked it back. "What is it Joe? Is there something out there?"

Purple whispered back to Eyebrow. "No, just making sure there's no fucking snipers or anything." Purple again peered into the street, this time for longer. "I'm not seeing anything Eyebrow. There's people running everywhere, but I'd say they're just regular citizens. I don't see any soldiers or anything."

"I'm going for a better look," said Eyebrow as he made his way into the street. "Just be ready to give me some cover if something happens."

Purple trained his weapon on the street in readiness. "For fuck sake Eyebrow, be careful."

Eyebrow slowly emerged from the gaping hole in the wall to assess the scene. Like Purple, he too saw a lot of commotion further up the road, but it appeared to be, as Purple had surmised, civilians who were in the process of making themselves very scarce, lest a second rebel force roll around the bend. Eyebrow glanced over his shoulder towards the house. The flames from the earlier explosion had now firmly taken hold and there would be no saving Ventura's beautiful residence. He also saw Ventura supporting an obviously shaken, but thankfully very alive Juan-Carlos as they slowly shuffled across the lawn towards the intact guest house.

Eyebrow now returned his attention to the streetscape. The area was strewn with remnants of the short, but ferocious battle. Smoke from both the burning tank and Ventura's house was beginning to hang heavily in the sky. Ahead of Eyebrow was a large pile of smoldering rubble among which a wrecked car was embedded. Eyebrow scrambled across the rubble and checked the car – empty, much to his relief. Eyebrow now climbed to the apex of the rubble to further assess the landscape, his M16 in hand and clad only in a pair of sandals, a makeshift headband to secure his hairpiece, and his American flag jocks. He gazed across the street, his oiled skin shimmering in the rays of sunlight that broke through the backdrop of smoke rising from the carnage behind him.

Nearby, an unseen player in the situation was ready and waiting, showing both the steely resolve and calm demeanor of a man who had heavy experience on the front lines. A set of crosshairs settled on Jimmy Eyebrow standing atop the rubble and the mystery actor slowed his breathing and composed himself. Standing heroically and glistening as the sun bounced off his oiled body, the image of Jimmy Eyebrow was carefully centered into view as the incognito man paused… exhaled… and squeezed his finger.

Click.

Charles de Klerk had his legacy photograph. After a lifetime of waiting, this was going to be his Iwo Jima.

CHAPTER 34

Party of Seven

Per Mariano's earlier observation, the fog of war was indeed heavy as Jimmy Eyebrow and Joe Purple tried their best to process the events that had just unfolded before their eyes. Somehow, the two of them had found themselves as active participants in a Latin American coup – the M16 rifles that nestled in their hands, along with the near empty magazines were testament to that. In the space of half an hour, they had gone from relaxing on the pool deck to climbing over smoking rubble and sidestepping at least half a dozen bodies, and that was without even pausing to consider the horrors that were inside the still flaming tank.

Joe Purple wiped the rapidly accumulating grime from his face. "Eyebrow, I don't need to say this, but we are in a fucking shitful predicament here."

"I know it Joe. We're not going home now, are we?"

Purple maintained his vigilant gaze on the street outside Ventura's property as he spoke. "I would say the probability of that is about zero percent right about now Eyebrow." The two of them crouched in silence for a few moments as they both assessed their next course of action. This was clearly the most danger they had been in together. True, they had previously been stranded ten thousand feet in the air without a pilot, but at least in that situation they were still able to exercise control over how everything ultimately played out. In this instance, they were most definitely not calling the shots, and this game was only just getting started.

It now fell to them to wrestle back some semblance of control and begin playing the game on their terms. Purple placed a hand on Eyebrow's shoulder and slowly guided him backward. "I'm feeling pretty exposed out here Eyebrow, and I'm not even the one wearing nothing but his fucking jocks. Let's go, we need to get back inside."

As they made their way across the rubble-strewn lawn, Mariano, who was beginning the process of marshalling the troops, beckoned for them to join him as the assembled group of residents, guests and employees convened on the pool deck. His first order of business was to check on his boss. "Are you OK Mister Ventura?"

"Yes, thank you Mariano," replied Ventura. "Are any of you injured?" he added as he looked around the group, before settling his gaze on the lone remaining security guard. "Cisco, your colleagues?" he asked forlornly. Cisco the security guard solemnly shook his head to indicate the worst. "I am very sorry," added Ventura.

"Thank you, Mister Ventura," replied Cisco.

Ventura looked around the group. "Is everyone else OK?" he asked, to which they all answered in the affirmative, though with differing degrees of enthusiasm. Juan-Carlos was OK in the broad sense of the term, as in, he was not about to die, but he was nonetheless sore and very shaken up after having come within inches of taking a round of high explosive to the face.

Ventura now spoke directly to his assembled associates. "Gentlemen... and lady," he began with a nod toward Aunt Sofia. "I don't need to tell you that we are currently involved in a very dangerous situation. The comrades of these men that we've stopped today will be back, and likely in much larger numbers. Everyone here is in some danger of being rounded up at some future point, but until we know the extent of this coup that's underway, I have no way of knowing when, or even if, that will happen."

Ventura paced for a few moments, catching his breath before continuing. "But one thing is certain – the only person in immediate danger is me. I am the one that they are after, and they *will* be returning for me... soon. The rest of you all have time to make your exit and get as far away from here as you can if you wish. There is no shame in wanting to be with your family at this stage." Ventura gazed around the group and noticed that Juan-Carlos was shifting uncomfortably. "Juan-Carlos, it's OK. Go and make sure that your family is OK."

"Are you sure sir?" asked Juan-Carlos.

"Absolutely," replied Ventura as he stroked his young employee's arm reassuringly. "Go, please, and stay safe." As Juan-Carlos departed, Ventura addressed the rest of the crew. "If you are going, then now is the time."

Mariano stepped forward, a little closer to Ventura. "Where you go, I go," he said firmly.

"Same here," added Cisco.

Ventura shifted his gaze toward Aunt Sofia and Humberto. "I'm going with you Rudy my dear," said Sofia. "I can't imagine the indignity of what would happen if those savages got their hands on me." Humberto gave his horn a solid toot and pointed firmly toward Ventura, confirming his desire to also stay by his side.

The eyes of the group then collectively refocussed on Eyebrow and Purple. "How about you Max? What are your plans?" asked Ventura.

"Can I see you for a moment?" whispered Purple as he grabbed Eyebrow's arm and guided him off to the side. "I'm fucking uncomfortable here, Eyebrow. This is no joke. We need to find a fucking embassy or something and get help."

"I understand Joe. But by the looks of it, we won't be able to get much help here."

"What, you're all of a sudden a fucking expert on foreign affairs now are you? How do you know that?"

"Let me ask Rudy then," said Eyebrow as he turned back to the group. "Are there any embassies that could help us?"

"Unlikely," replied Ventura. "Embassies will be on lockdown and the entire area around the embassy district will be the epicenter of what's currently going on. You must understand how a coup works Max. The critical infrastructure and power base will be seized swiftly in those first few hours. What you saw happen here would have happened at the residences of all government ministers at the same time and this city is now a powder keg. We cannot be seen roaming the streets. We need to get far away until the situation settles."

"What about Maracaibo?" offered Mariano. "They might be able to find safe passage from there."

"Certainly a possibility," replied Ventura after contemplating Mariano's suggestion. "Maracaibo may not be under siege as we are here, and it's close to Coronado, which is where my intention was to take us."

"I guessed that would be the case," said Mariano. "Does he know we're going there?"

"Not yet. I'll let him know once we're on our way."

Clearly Ventura and Mariano were reading from the same playbook, but Eyebrow was completely unfamiliar with any of the locations mentioned and had no clue about who, or what, was so important about the town of Coronado. All he knew was that he and Purple needed to stay safe and under the current perilous circumstances, in a completely foreign environment, safety would be found in numbers. "I think we'll stick with you Rudy," said Eyebrow, accompanied by a glance toward Joe Purple.

"Wise choice I think," whispered Purple, albeit begrudgingly.

"It's settled then," said Ventura firmly. "From this point, Mariano is in charge." Ventura now ceded the floor. "Mariano, over to you."

Mariano looked at his watch. "We move in ten minutes." Mariano pointed to Eyebrow and Purple. "You two will come with me to the shed. There are supplies in there that we need to take with us." He then turned to Cisco. "In the garage, I need you to bring the Land Rover around for us. Keys are in it. Fill the water cans, all of them." Finally, Mariano swivelled to Ventura. "Mister Ventura, you make sure that you have everything you need and please prepare Humberto and Aunt Sofia. I don't have any clothes packed for her, so you'll need to see if there's anything suitable in the guest house."

Behind them, Ventura's house was now burning vigorously thanks to the earlier explosion and given the crisis currently gripping the city, it could be safely concluded that help to extinguish it was not coming. As Joe Purple gazed across the inferno, a thought suddenly dawned on him as he turned to Eyebrow. "Ahh, fuck. All our shit's in there. Our spare clothes are fucking toast." Purple paused again and his face fell even further. "Jesus Christ, I just realised something. Our fucking passports are in there too." Purple cupped his face and yelled into his hands. "Goddamn it!"

Eyebrow glanced toward the small table by the pool deck. "I've still got my wallet and phone Joe. I've got money. The phone won't work here though." Eyebrow scooped up his meagre belongings and walked over to Mariano. "What do you need us to do?"

"Come with me," said Mariano as he began walking toward the garden shed. "I have go-bags in here that should have everything we need." He turned to Purple. "I have clothes for you, don't worry."

"Well thank fuck for that," replied Purple as he glanced toward the scantily clad Jimmy Eyebrow. "I wasn't looking forward to spending however fucking long we'll be on the road looking at THAT!"

Mariano retrieved several bags from a storage unit inside the shed and tossed them on the floor. "The go-bags have clothing, food for several days, basic tools and such. There's even a small amount of emergency cash in each one." Eyebrow and Purple each opened a bag and retrieved two pairs of black fatigues and jungle boots. "Get into those quickly," said Mariano looking at his watch. "I want to be out of here in seven minutes."

Purple tried to ease himself into the fatigues from his bag but quickly ran into trouble with the sizing. "Fuck me!" he exclaimed as he tried in vain to stretch the buttons across his chest. "Who were you expecting to be traveling with you? Fucking Gary Coleman?"

While Eyebrow wasn't having the same issue with his clothing, he instead found himself slipping on a pair of boots that were at least three sizes too big. "How are your boots, Joe? Mine are a bit loose."

Purple tried his boots on. "Mine aren't actually that bad. You'll have to make do with your clown shoes there, because I ain't swapping."

"Let's go you two," snapped Mariano as he handed them both additional weapons and ammunition. "Grab those bags and weapons and come with me." If the pre-emptive stocking of the shed with all the essentials required for a quick exit was indeed Mariano's doing, then it was a remarkable, and commendable, display of preparedness. Eyebrow and Purple knew that they were dealing with a professional in this field, which was something that they hoped would serve them well in their immediate future.

The three men departed the shed and strode across the yard – Ventura's house burning freely on one side and the destroyed tank finally beginning to settle into a steady smoulder on the other. Haphazardly re-clothed, carrying six go-bags and a surprisingly sizeable cache of weapons and ammunition, they were ready to hit the road. Mariano checked his watch again. "Three minutes."

Ventura, Humberto and Aunt Sofia were waiting at the Land Rover that Cisco had brought around for them. The heat from the house fire was now radiating over them, prompting Ventura to note that if they were going to leave, now was the time. Mariano threw open the tail of the vehicle. "Supplies, in there, quickly," he shouted to Eyebrow and Purple who complied with military-like obedience. "Now into the vehicle, all of you. I'll drive with Mister Ventura up front. Cisco, in the back with these two and Aunt Sofia." Humberto gave a vigorous honk to attract Mariano's attention. "Yes, yes… I'm thinking Humberto, I'm thinking." Mariano turned to Ventura and whispered. "I can't fit him in."

"You have to Mariano," replied Ventura firmly.

Mariano surveyed the situation, alternating his glance between the Land Rover and Humberto in his wheelchair. He beckoned to Eyebrow and Purple. "You two, come here. I need your help. We need to get Humberto up top." This prospect drew an immediate procession of angry honks from Humberto, who had to be calmed by Ventura.

"We don't have an option Humberto," he said softly. "We've already got more people in the vehicle than it has seats. We need to put you and your chair up top, even if it's just for a short time. We'll make sure that you're strapped down securely." Ventura turned to Mariano. "We'll ensure that he's firmly secured, won't we Mariano."

"Absolutely. You won't be going anywhere Humberto, I promise." Mariano now climbed atop the front of the Land Rover and directed Eyebrow and Purple to commence their lift.

Humberto summoned Ventura closer and removed his oxygen mask to speak. "Not fucking happy," he whispered, pointing his finger at Ventura in anger.

"We'll try to fix it, I promise," said Ventura as he motioned for Eyebrow and Purple to continue. Between Eyebrow, Purple and Mariano, they soon had Humberto, along with his wheelchair and his oxygen tank, atop the Land Rover and being tightly secured by cargo straps threaded through the wheels of his chair. They also concocted a makeshift seat belt to further assist in keeping Humberto and his wheelchair in place and, after testing the integrity of the bindings, the unorthodox group of seven were ready to begin putting distance between themselves and the chaos erupting in Caracas.

Mariano pulled a map from the glove compartment and discussed the logistics of the escape with Ventura. "We can't take the highways. We're going to have to go through the countryside using back roads. I estimate that it will take us a day or two to get to Coronado under the circumstances." Mariano glanced at his watch, noting that the day was already half over. "Do you have any thoughts about where to go from here?" he asked Ventura.

Ventura pointed to a spot on the map that was probably around two hours from where they currently were. "We'll be safe there for the night, and we can regroup with clear minds, ready for tomorrow."

"Very well," replied Mariano as he turned the engine over and quickly checked on everyone sitting in the back. The situation in the back seat was outside of the standard operating guidelines for the Land Rover, with four people crammed in where three would normally sit. But the current state of play was itself far outside a standard operating environment. Whatever needed to be done had to be done, which had led to Aunt Sofia now being perched on Eyebrow's lap and Humberto strapped to the roof. "We good to go back there?" asked Mariano.

Everyone nodded, and Purple punctuated everyone else's non-verbal response with an observation of his own. "I was ready to get the fuck out of here five minutes ago. Let's go."

As Mariano exited the estate for likely the last time and made his way onto the road, Ventura turned to him. "Do we have the satellite phone?"

"Glove compartment," replied Mariano, pointing to the dash in front of Ventura. Retrieving the phone, Ventura dialled and waited for an answer – nothing. He tried again, this time receiving a response. "Hola, mi amigo," he said. "It's happening, just as we suspected it might one day. It took a lot longer than we thought, but it started, less than an hour ago. We are making our way to Coronado. Party of seven."

Ventura paused as the person on the other end spoke, after which he glanced into the back seat and responded to whoever was on the other end of the line. "Yes, he's with me. Both of them are."

CHAPTER 35

No Hay Gasolina

Amid the mayhem engulfing the streets of Caracas, the odds of Jimmy Eyebrow and his cohorts remaining inconspicuous as they edged their way out of town would, under normal circumstances, likely be tilted ever so slightly in their favour. But there would be few things that could draw unwanted attention more than a wheelchair-bound octogenarian strapped to the roof of one's vehicle, which is what now led to Mariano discreetly easing the Land Rover from alley to alley in an effort to remain off the city's main thoroughfares.

The party of seven was still within the city limits of Caracas at this stage. What would usually be little more than a fifteen-minute drive to their current location had now consumed nearly an hour and a half, such was Mariano's cautiousness with regards to extracting them from the immediate danger currently enveloping the streets. While the tedious pace was infuriating at times, both Eyebrow and Purple knew that Mariano was doing exactly what he was required to do – keep Rudy Ventura, and by extension the rest of them, safe. Just as one would not rush the surgeon performing surgery on your brain, so too Eyebrow and Purple knew not to press Mariano to expedite the process. On this matter, he was the surgeon, and he was proving to be a highly proficient one.

It took nearly three hours of meticulous navigation through the back streets and tight alleyways before they emerged from the city's confines and with the afternoon rapidly progressing, they began to pick up the pace as they finally hit the country roads. Hurtling along – "hurtling" being a relative term for the vintage Land Rover – they had been accompanied by the constant honking of Humberto's horn emanating from atop the vehicle for at least the past ten minutes.

Either Mariano did not hear Humberto, or he was ambivalent to the sound and chose to ignore it. But Joe Purple eventually reached a point where he could no longer cope with the constant drone in his ear. "For fuck sake, can we stop for a moment and see what he wants upstairs! The honking's driving me fucking insane."

Ventura motioned to Mariano. "Find somewhere suitable to pull over when you can. We'll check on what Humberto wants."

"I wouldn't advise it sir," replied Mariano. "We need to stay mobile."

Ventura dismissed Mariano's concern. "It's OK Mariano. It'll just be for a moment." Ventura turned toward the back seat. He looked first at Eyebrow who had Aunt Sofia perched on his lap, and then to Purple, to whom he spoke. "When we stop, check on Humberto, but please be quick."

A little over five hundred metres further down the road, Mariano identified a siding where he could safely pull off the road. Easing to a stop, he turned to Purple and spoke firmly. "Thirty seconds, and then we're back on the road."

Purple quickly exited the vehicle and clambered onto the roof. "What the fuck's going on up here?" he barked, completely devoid of empathy for the elderly man completely exposed to the elements. Humberto in turn flashed his middle finger to Purple and then pointed to his face that was covered in dead bugs, or at least the remains of dead bugs.

Humberto removed his oxygen mask and beckoned Purple closer. "This is fucking disgusting," he whispered.

Purple took a moment to assess the situation. "Wait here," he said as he jumped to the ground.

"Where the hell am I going to go?" wheezed Humberto in response to Purple's somewhat redundant directive.

Purple motioned for Ventura to wind his window down. "Humberto's covered in fucking bug guts up there. Do we have any goggles or anything he could use?"

Ventura opened the glove compartment to investigate. "I can't see anything in here," he said before turning to Mariano. "Do you have anything?"

"No goggles, sorry," replied Mariano. "Come on, we have to get going again."

Aunt Sofia now entered the conversation from the back seat. "Wait a moment my dear, I might have something." Sofia rummaged through her handbag briefly before producing a pair of enormous tortoiseshell ladies' sunglasses. "Are these suitable?"

"They'll have to be," Purple said as he snatched the glasses from Sofia's hand, glancing at an agitated Mariano as he did so. "This guy looks like he's giving me about three more seconds before he abandons me." Purple swiftly climbed aloft and passed the sunglasses to Humberto. "This is all we have," he said as he began his equally swift descent, lest Mariano speed off unannounced with Purple flailing from the side of the vehicle.

"Is this a joke?" wheezed Humberto as he slid the glasses over his ears.

"Wish it was pal, but that's it," replied Purple as he disappeared back inside the vehicle. He was about to direct Mariano that they were good to resume their journey, but Mariano had no intention of waiting, and they were peeling out of the gravel siding before Purple's arse had even touched vinyl.

As they continued their journey, thankfully unthreatened by roaming rebels who were unlikely to have strayed far from the major urban centres at that stage, Ventura unfolded the map in the front seat. He beckoned to Mariano to view it with him, though understandably, Mariano could only glance briefly each time before returning his eyes to the road. Ventura placed his finger on the map. "We're about here." Mariano quickly flicked his head around to assess Ventura's positioning. Ventura now moved his finger an inch or so, to rest on a crossroad. "And up here… this is where we need to turn off."

Mariano again took a quick peek at the map. "Looks like it's only about fifteen minutes away. Which way am I going?"

"Right," replied Ventura.

"Where to?" asked Mariano.

"Don't worry. You just drive, and I'll let you know when we're there."

Mariano did as he was instructed and even though his estimate was short by about eight minutes, Ventura was soon directing him toward a lone petrol station on the side of the road around fifty metres ahead. As the Land Rover slowed and departed the tarmac, an old man dressed in overalls emerged from the auto-shop waving his arms and mouthing something that they could not hear.

Both Mariano and Ventura rolled their windows down. "No hay gasolina… no hay gasolina," the man yelled, continuing to wave his arms.

"What's he saying?" Eyebrow asked Aunt Sofia.

"He has no gasoline," she replied softly.

They pulled to a halt where the man moved to Ventura's window to repeat his advice that the facility was *sans* petroleum. But as he leant through the window, his face broke into a broad smile, and he clutched firmly at Rudy's arm. "Rudy!" he said excitedly. "What are you doing here?"

"We're on our way to Coronado," replied Ventura. "There is trouble in Caracas."

"So I hear. Are you needing a place to stay?"

"That is exactly why we're here. Just for the one night if that's possible. We'll leave for Coronado first thing tomorrow. I don't want to put you in danger though."

"Don't worry about it. You're most welcome to stay my friend." The man opened the door and Ventura stepped out of the vehicle, stretching as he did so. After so many hours crammed into such a tight space, the rest of the travelling party followed suit, prompting Ventura to make an introduction.

"Everyone, this is an old friend of mine, Armando."

"Quite the band of companions you have here Rudy," he replied before shifting his gaze to the top of the Land Rover where the bug-splattered, but flamboyantly bespectacled Humberto sat. "Humberto – lovely to see you again. I'm loving the new look." Humberto simply responded with a disagreeable glare, accompanied by a sharp honk of his bicycle horn. "Come, let's get you inside and off the street," said Armando as he began to wind open the door to the auto-shop. "You can put your vehicle in here."

"Thank you," replied Ventura as he placed a friendly hand on Armando's upper arm. "It is very much appreciated." Ventura turned to Mariano. "Could you please take care of this? I'm going to take a walk with Armando."

"Of course, Mister Ventura."

Aunt Sofia tugged at Mariano's shirt. "I need to find the ladies' darling."

Mariano turned to Eyebrow, Purple and Cisco. "You three get Humberto down from up there. I'm going to try and find the restroom for Aunt Sofia."

Eyebrow glanced toward Humberto before turning back to Mariano. "Can you try and find some wet wipes or something so that we can give Humberto a bit of a clean-up? It's pretty nasty up there."

"I'll see what I can find," replied Mariano. "Just get him down and inside for now."

Eyebrow and Purple deftly climbed atop the Land Rover and with Cisco's assistance, soon had Humberto offloaded and safely sequestered in the office. With Mariano and Aunt Sofia having now returned from the restroom, Mariano set about organising logistics. First up was removing the vehicle from view. "Go and look around in the auto-shop," said Mariano to no-one in particular. "Make sure I have room to get in there."

The air in the lubritorium was heavy with the smell of grease and motor oil as Eyebrow and Purple assessed the area, which was full of an abundance of automotive-related material – spare parts, tyres, cans of all shapes and sizes, as well as an extensive collection of promotional material that had been left by travelling vendors over the years. There was evidence that cars had certainly been worked on in there recently, but the general clutter around the place indicated that those vehicles must have been small – much smaller than the Land Rover. The two men began shifting some of the material in order to create adequate space for the Land Rover to fit in without hinderance, eventually beckoning Mariano and the vehicle inside and deftly guiding him such that it sat astride the mechanic's pit.

Satisfied that the Land Rover was secure, Mariano retrieved a duffel bag from the back and beckoned for Eyebrow and Purple to reconvene with Humberto, Aunt Sofia and Cisco in the office. Opening the bag, he distributed several packets. "We have plenty of food here. This is freeze dried, all it needs is some hot water." Mariano looked around the area. "Does Armando have a kettle here?"

Eyebrow and Purple perused the area nearby, while Cisco checked through the small door to the rear of the office. "In here," he announced. "Looks like a break room or something."

The six of them slowly filed through the door to assess the area, with Cisco's initial observation correct – this was the break room with a small kitchenette, including a kettle, as well as a table, some chairs, and a small lounge set against the wall. Mariano clicked his fingers towards Eyebrow. "Get some water going here," he said before moving towards the lounge. "Aunt Sofia, you can sleep in here tonight. This looks to be the most comfortable spot."

"Thank you Mariano darling," replied Aunt Sofia. "That's very kind of you."

"Are you and Humberto OK to prepare some food for yourselves?" Mariano asked.

"I'll be fine, thank you dear." Aunt Sofia's words were accompanied by a honk from Humberto indicating that he too would be OK preparing his own meal from the freeze-dried options.

Mariano now summoned Eyebrow, Purple and Cisco back to the auto-shop where he opened the back of the Land Rover and distributed automatic weapons to each man. "We should be safe here for tonight. But just in case, we need to be ready to mount a defence. The four of us will rotate through the watch overnight – two-hour shifts. Any questions? If not, let's get something to eat." There were no questions. They'd been on the road all day and breakfast felt like an eternity ago. Food was the primary driver at that point, with any operational questions able to be shunted off until later in the evening.

A short time later, with their meals rehydrating, Eyebrow and Purple made their way into the auto-shop and sat down on an old bench seat that had been removed from a car at some point in the past and for some reason was never returned. Neither man spoke immediately, with Eyebrow eventually breaking the silence, motioning towards Purple's packet. "What have you got there Joe?"

"Ravioli apparently. What about you?"

Eyebrow checked his packet. "Lamb casserole."

There was further silence before Purple spoke. "How the fuck did we end up in this mess Eyebrow?"

"We were conned Joe. That's how we ended up here. If that prick hadn't convinced us to get on the plane with him, we'd be home right now."

Purple nodded. "Bishop would've had our heads on a fucking platter, but yeah, we'd be home at least."

Eyebrow lifted the first forkful of his meal into his mouth. "Holy shit, this isn't too bad Joe. Try yours."

Purple spiked some ravioli and put it into his mouth, eliciting an immediate reaction. "Fuck, fuck fuck… hot!" he said, fanning his mouth vigorously, eventually reaching the point where he could chew and swallow. He nodded in agreement. "Not that bad actually. Might have to keep a few of these on hand when we get home."

"How do you think we're gonna get out of this Joe?" asked Eyebrow through a mouthful of lamb casserole.

"No fucking idea Eyebrow. I just hope that they can get us to that place where there's an embassy. Might be a couple of days, might be a week… I have no idea. We're just going to have to put our trust in Mariano I guess."

"What do you think is at this town we're going to tomorrow Joe? Rudy wasn't giving much away about it."

"Coronado? No fucking idea." Purple stood and walked over to the Land Rover.

"What are you doing Joe?" asked Eyebrow.

"Getting the map. Let's see where that fucking place is." Purple rummaged in the glove compartment, retrieved the map and returned to the car seat. Spreading it out, he first identified Caracas and then traced a line with his finger in the general direction of where he suspected they had driven. "I'm pretty sure that we're in here somewhere," he said, circling his finger. "We're not even in a fucking town though, so I can't be sure." Purple moved his finger westward, settling on Maracaibo. "Here's where I think they said we're going, so this Coronado place must be somewhere on the way there."

Both of them examined the map, searching for the town of Coronado. "I'm not seeing it Joe," said Eyebrow.

Purple was also scanning the map methodically with his finger. "Same. Can't seem to find it." Purple now moved his finger east from Caracas. "I'm pretty sure we didn't go this direction," he said as he continued his search for the mystery town. "No, it's not that way. We didn't go that direction." He correctly motioned his hand across the swathe of countryside that they were indeed in at that time. "We're definitely up around here somewhere."

The two of them continued their search, but it was ultimately in vain. "It's not on here Joe," said Eyebrow eventually.

"Gotta agree with you there Eyebrow. I can't see it either."

"Should we try to find out from Rudy or Mariano?"

Purple paused in thought before answering. "No, let's keep this to ourselves for now. But I think we need to stay alert. I'm not sure what's going on here."

Purple re-folded the map and made his way back to the Land Rover to return it from whence it came, after which he and Eyebrow settled back into their evening meal. Recent events had conditioned them to be wary, and the inability to locate the phantom town where they were supposedly headed the following day was just one more noise among the symphony of alarm bells currently ringing out.

Still, they had little control over their present situation, so their accepted strategy was one that had been their standard operating procedure for some time to that point – ride it out and deal with any situation if and when it arose. For now though, they needed sustenance, and they were soon scraping the bottom of their meal packets, pleasantly surprised by the quality while at the same time disappointed that there wasn't more on offer. In addition, they were hopeful of a decent night of rest because tomorrow, they would be back on the road to Coronado. Wherever the hell *that* was.

CHAPTER 36

Guarding Aunt Sofia

Joe Purple stood on the road verge outside Armando's lonely service station, the first warmth from the new day's sun beginning to settle on his face. The air was crisp and still and the smoke from Purple's cigarette would briefly hang like a morning mist before slowly dissipating.

Despite Armando's proclamation the previous afternoon of "no hay gasolina," Purple still felt it was prudent to err on the side of caution and avoid lighting up within the vicinity of the pumps. And now, as he stood alone on the edge of the road in the middle of El Nowhere, he closed his eyes and thought of home, the only thing missing in the moment being a pair of ruby slippers.

The night had been uneventful thankfully, and even though his sleep was fitful at times, Purple was as rested as one could be under the trying circumstances. He had commandeered the back seat of the Land Rover as his bed for the evening, and it was an inspired choice as he was able to stay both warm and relatively comfortable. Purple did have to share his accommodation with Cisco in the front seat, but thankfully Cisco was equally as exhausted and had no desire to indulge in any sleepover rituals with his bunkmate.

The rest of the group had dispersed to various parts of Armando's establishment for the evening, with Humberto claiming the old bench seat where Eyebrow and Purple had taken dinner, and Aunt Sofia sequestered in her own private quarters in the office. Mariano for some reason had secured a patch of ground outside for his bed, while Eyebrow had constructed a nest from old rags and towels that, other than the associated smell of grease and grime, ended up being surprisingly comfortable. Not that he spent long nestled within though, as during a toilet visit a little before midnight, he was summoned by Aunt Sofia's voice from the office.

To be completely accurate, she wasn't specifically summoning Eyebrow when the words, "Mariano, is that you?" came from beyond the door. But nonetheless, Eyebrow gently cracked open the door and responded.

"No Aunt Sofia, it's me," he whispered.

"Is that Max?" she asked.

"Yes," replied Eyebrow. "Is everything OK?"

Aunt Sofia's voice quivered, indicating that this was not one of her usual devious attempts to lure Eyebrow into her embrace. This was genuine. "I'm frightened Max. Will you sit with me for a short time?"

"Just give me a moment Aunt Sofia. I'll be back after I've gone to the toilet, and then I'll stay with you."

"Thank you Max darling."

Eyebrow attended to his business and returned to his sleeping place to retrieve his M16. As he fumbled around in the dim light, he noted that Mariano was in the process of prodding Joe Purple awake for his shift on watch. Eyebrow carefully made his way over to where Purple was slowly beginning, very reluctantly, to ease out of his slumber for his two-hour swing on guard duty. Eyebrow leant in through the open door and spoke. "Go back to sleep Joe, I've got this."

Purple rubbed his eyes. "What do you mean Eyebrow?"

"I'm up anyway Joe. I'll do your shift. Don't worry about it. Get some rest."

There was certainly no push-back from Purple. "Thanks Eyebrow, I owe you one," he mumbled as he gratefully laid back down.

M16 in hand, Eyebrow stepped quietly back toward the office where Aunt Sofia was awaiting his return. "Aunt Sofia, are you still awake?" he whispered through the door.

"Yes Max, I'm here," came the reply.

Eyebrow edged his way into the office. "What can I help with?"

"I just need to know that someone's here, my darling," replied Aunt Sofia from the darkness.

Eyebrow shuffled across the room and retrieved a chair from beside the small table. "I'm going to sit outside the door and guard it. I won't go anywhere. No-one will come in here. You've got nothing to worry about, OK?"

"Oh thank you Max. You really are a dear," replied Aunt Sofia, the happiness resonating through her voice in stark contrast to the anxiousness of only a few minutes prior.

"Don't mention it," said Eyebrow as he dragged the chair outside the door and settled in. And it was there, guarding Aunt Sofia, where he would remain for the rest of the night.

Eyebrow stayed awake all night, so technically he wasn't the first one to wake up in the morning as he'd not gone to sleep in the first place, save for a couple of hours before his nocturnal bathroom visit. The early riser honour still rested with Joe Purple who was now finalising his cigarette on the roadside. His eyes still closed, dreaming of anywhere but there, Purple heard the crunch of gravel behind him, signaling that he was about to have company. Sure enough, a moment later, Mariano sidled up to him and tapped out a cigarette of his own. "How did you sleep Señor Ferguson?"

Purple drew the last of his cigarette down to within a millimetre of the butt and dropped it on the gravel, extinguishing the remnants underfoot. "It's Purple, not Ferguson."

"I'm sorry?" asked Mariano, mildly confused.

Purple tapped out another cigarette from his packet and brought it to his lips. "My name's Joe Purple, not Ferguson. It's a fucking made-up name." Purple lit the cigarette and inhaled mightily. "It's official and all, but it's still fucking bogus. You and I are in this shitshow together, so there's not much point in continuing the charade. If I'm going to end up dead from this, I'm sure as hell not going out as fucking Turd Ferguson."

Mariano was taken aback at Purple's revelation. "You are a government agent?"

"No, not a government agent."

"Then what?"

"It's… complex," replied Purple, avoiding eye contact.

"And they gave you the name Turd Ferguson?" asked Mariano incredulously.

"Yeah, can you believe that fucking shit?"

Mariano shook his head mournfully. "That's savage my friend." Like Purple, Mariano also drew on his cigarette. "Does Rudy know?"

"No, you're the first one I've told."

"And your associate?" enquired Mariano.

Purple flicked away the ash from his cigarette and scuffed the gravel with his foot. "Same deal. He's not fucking Max Von Steel. He's Jimmy Eyebrow."

"And what is he? Is he a government man? Military maybe?"

"Eyebrow? Fuck no. I'll tell you what he is – he's a fucking walking paradox, that's what *he* is."

Mariano's confusion was evident. "I'm sorry, my English is quite good I think, but I do not know this word. What is this word ... *paradox*?"

Purple took another drag of his cigarette and paced a little before answering, choosing his words. "It means something that shouldn't exist, yet it does. Like... two completely opposite things existing in the same space. *That's* Eyebrow. I have never in my life met anyone better than Eyebrow at screwing up everything that he touches. He doesn't even really need to touch it... he just needs to be in the area, and it'll all go to shit. He's a complete and utter, weapons-grade fuckup. But then, and here's the fucking infuriating part, he also has this incredible way of having shit just work out for him, so that no matter how fucked up the situation is, he always seems to get out of it. Somehow, it just... it just fucking works for him."

"So, this Jimmy Eyebrow, he is the one that Rudy must help?" asked Mariano. "He is Esteban Gutierrez's associate?"

"Yeah," replied Purple. "Fuck knows how the two of them became buddies, but Eyebrow would do anything for him apparently." Purple took a few steps forward before turning and looking directly at Mariano. "And that's the fucking thing that gets Eyebrow in trouble all the time. He always wants to do the right thing by people. Anyone who asks him to do something, Eyebrow always just wants to please them, no matter how fucking ridiculous the task might be."

"That is not the worst quality in a man."

"Yeah, I know. But it's how we always keep getting into these shit situations with our arses always on the line. It's fucking exhausting."

Mariano tilted his head slightly, a perceptive expression lingering on his face. "You are not obliged to join him, yet you are here. You care for him, yes? He is your friend?"

"Friend?" chuckled Purple. "Yeah, if you mean 'friend', like that fucking orangutan from the Clint Eastwood movie." Purple pulled a mint from his pocket and flipped it into his mouth. "Good fucking movie that one. Did you ever see it?"

"Cannot say I have," replied Mariano.

Before Joe Purple could launch into a synopsis of the Clint Eastwood classic *Every Which Way But Loose*, both he and Mariano were beckoned by Ventura who had spent the night with Armando's family next door to the service station and was now walking in their direction. "Buenos días gentlemen!" he called out as he sauntered toward them, brandishing a basket that had been supplied by Armando and his wife. "I have fresh bread and fruit for us."

"Did you sleep well Mister Ventura?" asked Mariano as Ventura joined the pair on the side of the road.

"I did, thank you for asking Mariano. I trust you are rested also. We should have something to eat and move out. We do not want to put Armando in more danger than he already is with us here."

"I'll go and make sure the others are up," said Mariano as he dropped his cigarette and ground it into the gravel with his foot. Mariano then looked at Joe Purple before returning his attention to Ventura. "I think you two should stay here and talk for a few moments Mister Ventura. I believe Mister Ferguson has something that he'd like to share with you."

CHAPTER 37

The Road to Coronado

The steam from Rudy Ventura's cup of budget instant coffee drifted across the wildly diverse selection of freshly baked bread, fruit and ration packs that comprised the breakfast buffet at Armando's garage that morning. With the full contingent of travelling companions present, Ventura was still processing the information he had received from Joe Purple minutes earlier. And now, with the entire party briefed on the Max Von Steel/Turd Ferguson charade, Ventura looked at Purple as he broke a piece of bread from the loaf.

"I would not have picked Joe Purple as your name. You do not strike me as a Joe."

"Well, what *do* I look like?" asked Purple.

Ventura's gaze lingered on Purple as he considered his options. "Don. You look like a Don."

Ventura now turned to Eyebrow. "But... as for you Jimmy Eyebrow... yes, I can understand that. You do look like a Jimmy Eyebrow." Ventura took a bite from his chunk of bread while waving his free hand over Eyebrow's forehead. "I do see though that your eyebrows today are less... what is the word?"

"Traumatizing?" suggested Purple from the side.

"No, that is not the word I was looking for," replied Ventura, still puzzling over the correct English terminology as Purple offered a further option.

"Objectionable?"

"No. Let me think. In English it means, 'very clearly seen'… *prominent*, that is the word I'm looking for. They are less *prominent* today."

Eyebrow brushed some grime from his face. "It's been a crazy couple of days Rudy. I haven't had a chance to touch them up, especially since we lost all our shit back at your house."

"You need to fix those," added Mariano. "They're not good my friend."

"It's on my to-do list," replied Eyebrow as he took a sip of coffee.

Aunt Sofia offered her own supportive, though clearly fictional, observation. "Well, I think they look just wonderful Jimmy. I had no idea they weren't real until now."

"Thank you, Aunt Sofia," replied Eyebrow blushingly.

As the group continued with their breakfast, talk began to turn to their plans for the day's journey to Coronado. However with discussions barely underway, a small sedan suddenly, and equally unexpectedly, pulled to an abrupt stop at the front of the garage in a cloud of dust. A young man quickly exited from the driver's side and charged towards Armando who indicated immediately that he knew who the mystery man was.

"Paolo, is everything OK?" asked Armando.

Whoever Paolo was, his voice was filled with urgency, and he spoke firmly and deliberately. "Rebels! They are coming this way!"

Mariano and Ventura quickly leapt to their feet. "How far away?" barked Mariano.

"Ten minutes maybe," replied Paolo.

"Quickly, you must go," said Armando. "Leave all of this with me, I'll clean it up. You pack up and make your way to Coronado."

"I doubt they know we're here, it's probably just a routine patrol," said Ventura as he began to gather his belongings. "It's day two, so it's to be expected that they'll be expanding their operations wider. We must be careful as they could be everywhere now." Ventura turned to Armando. "Thank you for your hospitality my friend. I really do appreciate it."

"You're always welcome," replied Armando as he hugged Ventura. "We must get together again when this is over. For now, you have to leave quickly. I will run interference for you if they come here."

Fortunately, Mariano had put the crew on a standing two-minutes' notice to move footing since the previous evening and he was backing the already loaded Land Rover out of the auto shop when he beckoned Purple from the window.

"You, Eyebrow and Cisco get Humberto back up on top. And be quick. We're leaving in ninety seconds."

Purple quickly marshalled Eyebrow and Cisco. "We need to get Humberto up top now! GO GO GO!!!" Cisco swiftly climbed atop the Land Rover, while Eyebrow and Purple retrieved Humberto and began the lift. Temporarily setting him down on the hood, both men quickly stepped up and proceeded to lift Humberto the remainder of the way where Cisco secured him in quick time.

While Mariano was ushering Ventura and Aunt Sofia into the vehicle as quickly as he could, Armando was rummaging through some old tools in the auto shop where he retrieved a welder's mask that he brought to Humberto. "Here you go Humberto," he said as he handed it up to him. "This should give you more protection than the sunglasses," to which Humberto honked what seemed to be an appreciative reply as he slipped the mask over his head.

As Eyebrow was preparing to climb into the vehicle, Mariano pulled him aside. "Not this time," he said firmly. "We need firepower on both sides of us, so you're driving this time. Cisco, Purple and I will provide the cover out the windows if needed. Let's go!"

There was no time for discussion – the situation was dire, and the clock was ticking. They needed to decamp, and they needed to do it now. With Mariano in the passenger seat, and Cisco and Purple in the rear with a combined firepower that could have single-handedly won the Battle of Waterloo, Eyebrow jumped into the driver's seat of the already running Land Rover, shifted it into gear and peeled away from the garage with Armando bidding them farewell as they sped off. "God speed my friends!"

Eyebrow had no clue whatsoever where they were headed, and he was soon approaching a crossroad. "Turn right up here," said Ventura pre-emptively. "And then keep following that road until I tell you to turn off."

Turning right as directed, Eyebrow soon identified a vehicle approaching from the opposite direction and after quickly alerting his armed companions, Mariano signalled to Purple and Cisco to be ready to engage if necessary. Safeties off and fingers hovering near the triggers, everyone breathed a sigh of relief when the vehicle passed by benignly, its lone occupant likely oblivious to the situation developing in the surrounding countryside. "We have to stay on alert," noted Mariano. "If something's going to happen, it'll happen quickly."

And happen quickly it did. Less than ten minutes later as they were rolling swiftly along the open road in a small valley, Joe Purple spotted another suspect vehicle travelling in the same direction on a parallel road, a little further up the embankment. "Heads up, nine o' clock. Might be trouble."

Mariano leant across to Purple's window to assess the situation. He could see that the vehicle was an older model two-door Land Rover with a drab green tarpaulin covering at the rear. "Definitely looks like trouble," he cautioned before speaking to Eyebrow without removing his gaze from the other vehicle. "Just keep driving as you are. Don't draw attention to ourselves. Let's see what they do." It didn't take long to see what they would do as at the first opportunity available to them, the mystery vehicle lurched sharply to the right and down a narrow dirt track in an effort to intercept the Land Rover. "GO!" barked Mariano. "GO NOW! DRIVE!"

Eyebrow floored it but without the torque of more modern vehicles, the Land Rover's acceleration was laborious, mitigated only by the fact that the pursuing vehicle was also far from a well-oiled machine and was experiencing its own performance issues. Second by painfully frustrating second, the Land Rover picked up pace and they were able to put a small gap between themselves and their pursuers. With the screaming of the engine and rattling of the old interior dominating the soundscape, it soon became evident that they could now hear the sound of gunshots emanating from the rebels' vehicle.

"Fuck, they're shooting at us!" yelled Purple with fear in his voice.

"Don't worry about it," replied Mariano calmly. "They're a long way behind us and their accuracy will be very poor under these circumstances. The shooting is really just for show. We're pulling away so we'll be OK soon." Mariano turned to Eyebrow and offered some encouragement. "Well done Jimmy, you've done a good job there."

They may well have been pulling away from their original pursuers, but trouble now loomed ahead as Eyebrow quickly identified a second rebel vehicle almost identical to the first emerging from a side road and turning directly towards them. They'd successfully achieved a moment of respite after putting distance between themselves and the gunshots originating from the rear, but the distance from the new danger that had appeared in front was now closing rapidly. Mariano vigorously slapped Eyebrow's shoulder and pointed to the right toward a small side road that disappeared into the forest. "Down there, quick!"

Eyebrow jerked sharply right and barrelled down the small road, barely wider than the Land Rover. Thankfully their vehicle was made for this sort of corrugated terrain, for if they were travelling in any form of standard family car, their fate would be well and truly sealed. Eyebrow's quick evasive action had brought them an advantage of a few moments, but they could not yet stop as the pursuit was still very much active, with potentially deadly consequences attached.

"For fuck sake, keep going Eyebrow!" yelled Joe Purple as he, Mariano and Cisco all readied their weapons in the event that they might encounter additional rebels and become dangerously trapped in a pincer operation.

Eyebrow checked his mirrors. "We may have lost them."

Mariano wasn't so sure. "We haven't lost them. If they're on this road, they're still behind us. Don't let up, keep going!"

The road became narrower as it wound further into the valley, but Eyebrow kept up the pace. Among the many things that he wasn't trained for, jungle combat was now the pressing deficiency, and he was justifiably fearful of becoming trapped in such an unforgiving environment. Up ahead the road appeared to disappear until Eyebrow noticed that instead, it actually continued through a small tunnel cut into the hillside. "Do I drive through here?" he asked Mariano.

"Yes, keep going!"

"Fucking floor it, Eyebrow!" added Purple.

"It's gonna be tight," said Eyebrow, wincing as he hurtled toward the opening that appeared only slightly larger than the Land Rover. Suddenly, a faint, though mildly familiar, sound could be heard over the rush of noise from outside. All too late – almost simultaneous to the sickening thud that accompanied their entrance into the tunnel – Eyebrow came to the shocking realisation that the sound he had heard was in fact the frantic honking of a bicycle horn.

"Ahhh, fuck me!!! I forgot about Humberto!" he yelled as he hit the brakes and stuttered to a stop.

Aunt Sofia quickly brought her hands to her mouth, speechless, while Ventura simply shook his head as he spoke softly. "Oh dear, this is indeed an unfortunate turn of events." Ventura gazed at the floor. "Mariano, can you please go and check on Humberto?"

"I'll come too," said Eyebrow. "This is my fault."

Mariano handed his weapon to Purple. "Hold this for me while I see what's happened."

Purple shook his head and glared at Eyebrow. "Well fucking done, you idiot. Just fucking brilliant."

"It was an accident Joe," replied Eyebrow forlornly as he exited the vehicle. "I just forgot he was up there."

As Eyebrow walked around to the back of the vehicle, Mariano was already assessing the grisly scene at the entrance to the tunnel. Eyebrow called out to him. "Is he OK?"

Mariano turned and shook his head. "There is no place further away from OK than where Humberto is right now."

"Should we take him with us?" asked Eyebrow.

Mariano gazed upon the situation on the road before him. "Unless you have a shovel, I don't think that would be possible."

Before Eyebrow could respond, the sound of the rebels' vehicle suddenly increased in volume, so quickly in fact that neither man had time to react before it roared around the corner barely fifty metres from where they stood. Mariano patted his hip, struck by the sudden realisation that he'd left his sidearm in the Land Rover. He turned to Eyebrow. "GO! Get back to the vehicle!"

"What are you going to do?"

"Don't worry about me," barked Mariano. "Get back to the vehicle and get ready to go!"

As Eyebrow hurried back through the tunnel to the idling Land Rover, Mariano scanned the area and identified Humberto's oxygen tank that had landed several metres away from where Humberto and the wreckage of his wheelchair had fallen. With the rebels rapidly approaching and gunshots beginning to ring out, Mariano scurried to the side of the road and grabbed a heavy rock around the same size as a softball. With bullets now whizzing past him, Mariano spun the oxygen tank and carefully positioned it to face the oncoming vehicle.

With the rock firmly in his hand, he struck a mighty blow to the oxygen tank's regulator. As it snapped off and instantly released the intensely compressed contents from within, the oxygen tank roared directly towards the vehicle like a torpedo from an Akula class attack submarine. As it turned out, Mariano's calibrations had been remarkably precise, with the makeshift projectile slamming into the defenceless vehicle's engine block and exploding shrapnel throughout the passenger cab. The mortally wounded light truck and the equally incapacitated rebels rolled to a slow halt across the road, not only resolving the immediate issue, but also providing some well-needed interference from anything following.

Mariano wasted no time in getting back to the Land Rover and had directed Eyebrow to make haste out of there, even before he'd had a chance to secure the door. With a vehicle on one side of the tunnel spewing steam from its crushed radiator, and another speeding away in a cloud of dust on the far side, Rudy Ventura's travelling crew pressed onward to Coronado. Inside the Land Rover there was a mix of emotions among the six remaining members – sadness at the loss of Humberto, hope that Coronado would be their safe haven, and fear that they might not be the first ones there.

CHAPTER 38

Madre

Jimmy Eyebrow could do nothing more than stare at the bug crawling across his arm as he laid prostrate in the Venezuelan jungle – it was enormous, like nothing he had ever seen before. But Mariano had assured him that it was harmless and there was nothing to be concerned about, so he simply let it go on its way, wherever that may be. Eyebrow and the rest of the travelling party, minus Aunt Sofia who refused to venture into "that filthy environment," had taken up a position atop a small hill, observing a collection of buildings a short distance further down the slope.

As it turned out, the reason that Jimmy Eyebrow and Joe Purple could not locate the town of Coronado on a map was because it wasn't a town at all, but rather a large estate. Spread out below them was a sprawling assortment of buildings and landscaped gardens, all built with one purpose in mind – to serve as the Gutierrez family compound.

Mariano and Ventura alternated with the one set of binoculars observing the compound for any sign that it may have been compromised by rebels before their arrival. But after quarter of an hour of constant observation, there was nothing apparent to give either man cause for concern. As Mariano scanned the area, Ventura leant towards Eyebrow and whispered. "This place was built, or at least financed, many years ago by Esteban who wanted somewhere safe and comfortable for any of his family members to live should they wish to."

"Was Esteban married?" asked Eyebrow.

"No, he never married. He was always too consumed with his business activities to settle down."

"Kids?" enquired Eyebrow further.

"No, none. In his golden years, I feel that he may have grown to regret that in some way." Ventura placed a hand on Eyebrow's shoulder. "The way he speaks of you and how he wanted to make sure that I kept you safe Jimmy… I believe he cares for you. You may be the beneficiary of that regret."

Eyebrow motioned towards the estate below. "So, who lives there now?"

"Extended family and friends. Anyone associated with Esteban who wishes to live there is free to do so. It is very safe, which is why we've come here."

Mariano now shuffled over and handed the binoculars to Ventura. "It all looks clear to me Mister Ventura."

Ventura didn't need to look again, he had seen enough. "I agree Mariano. I believe that we are safe to proceed."

Mariano waved to Eyebrow, Purple and Cisco. "OK, let's go. I'll drive this time, with Mister Ventura up front. You three in the back with Aunt Sofia."

Moments later, and with Aunt Sofia resuming her favoured seating position on Eyebrow's lap, they were descending the road to Coronado. Slowing down as they approached, a pair of large muscular men who appeared unarmed, but likely weren't, emerged from a small guardhouse to greet them. One of the men approached the window of the Land Rover and quickly identified Ventura. "Mister Ventura, we heard you were on the way. Seven of you we were told."

"Ah, yes. Only six now unfortunately," replied Ventura. "Is everything OK here? No trouble yet?"

"Nothing so far," replied the man. "We're prepared though."

"Excellent, that is good to hear," said Ventura, grabbing the man's arm firmly. "Where would you like us?"

The man waved them down the road. "Two down on the left would be the best place to set up. If you need anything, just let us know."

"Thank you," replied Ventura as he signalled Mariano to continue to where the man had directed them.

Eyebrow leant over to Purple as they entered the estate. "Looks nice Joe."

"Yeah, it's a real fucking resort Eyebrow," replied Purple dismissively. "In case you'd forgotten though, let me just remind you that we're not here on holiday. This is still a literal fucking war zone AND, might I add, even though we've managed to scrape through by the skin of our nutsacks so far, I'm still not fucking happy that we're even here in the first place. I can tell you now, we'll be having a serious fucking talk when we get home."

Aunt Sofia snapped her fingers sharply in Purple's face. "Mister Ferguson, or Purple, or whatever your name is… language, please."

"I apologise," replied Purple sheepishly. "I'm just a little tense."

Aunt Sofia was unmoved. "That's not an excuse to be uncouth, please remember that."

The Land Rover had by now rolled to a halt outside a neat two-storey chalet and the six occupants stepped out, stretching as they did so and happy in the knowledge that they were back among friends, for now at least. Several people came to assist with the unpacking of the vehicle, while Eyebrow and Purple took a short walk to a small fountain in a manicured garden where Purple tapped out a cigarette, offering one to Eyebrow as well. Purple's tone was serious as he spoke. "We've gotta get to that fucking embassy Eyebrow. This is serious shit that we're involved with here."

Eyebrow looked over his shoulder to where the Land Rover was being unpacked and bags moved inside the chalet. "I'd say we're staying here for tonight at least Joe. Maybe they'll take us to the embassy tomorrow."

"When we get there, do me a favour will you Eyebrow. Just let me do the fucking talking. We've got no passports, and no ID, so it's gonna be a fucking diplomatic nightmare. The last thing I want is my fate on foreign soil being tied to a fucking lobotomite like you. Just… let me manage everything, OK?"

"Sure thing Joe. I don't know anything about how all of that works anyway."

As the two men stood next to the fountain, dragging on their cigarettes, they were approached by an attractive dark-haired young woman who sidled up beside them. She looked at them with a warm and disarming smile. "Hello gentlemen. Welcome to Coronado."

Purple gulped slightly before responding – she was pretty indeed. "Hi," he stuttered. "You live here?"

"Yes," she replied, extending her hand in greeting. "I'm Rosita."

"Joe," replied Purple as he took her hand.

Rosita released her grip from Purple and turned to Eyebrow. Purple could see Eyebrow preparing to respond and pre-empted him. "Don't fucking do it Eyebrow," he said before turning to Rosita. "He's got a mental condition where he thinks he's this international man of mystery named Max Von Steel. It's like, a psychosis, or some sort of shit like that. No matter what he says, don't believe him. His name's Eyebrow."

"I can't just call you Eyebrow," replied Rosita as she shook his hand. "Do you have a first name?"

"Jimmy... call me Jimmy."

"Pleased to meet you Jimmy," said Rosita with a smile as she slowly waved her hand over the expansive grounds. "Do you like our estate?"

"It's impressive," replied Eyebrow. "How many people live here?"

"About forty. Family, friends and support people – cooks, gardeners, security... that sort of thing."

"Any relatives of Esteban's?"

"He is my uncle," replied Rosita.

A broad smile spread across Eyebrow's face. "Really? I'm happy to meet you. He's a good man."

Rosita had a slight look of surprise. "You know Uncle Esteban?"

"I know him well. He's helped me out of a few jams, including this one. We found ourselves stuck here in Venezuela, so he arranged for Rudy to help us. He's really your uncle?"

"Well, not exactly. If you want to be technical, he's like a cousin, twice removed, or something like that. I don't know how it all works. But I've always just called him Uncle Esteban." Rosita took Eyebrow's hand. "If you really are a friend of Uncle Esteban, I'd like to show you something." She then turned to Purple. "You can come too Joe, if you'd like."

"All good here," replied Purple. "I think I need a few minutes with my thoughts." Purple waved his hand across the compound. "This whole thing... today... I just need to process it all."

"Very well," said Rosita as she guided Eyebrow through the garden towards another chalet a little further down the hill, this one a more modest single-storey building. As they approached closer, Rosita directed Eyebrow's attention to an elderly woman sitting on a lounge overlooking the valley below, with another person who appeared to be some sort of home help standing nearby.

"Who's that?" asked Eyebrow.

"That's my great-great aunt Ana," replied Rosita.

"OK," said Eyebrow, a little confused. "We have Aunt Sofia back up the hill. Does your Aunt Ana need a friend?"

"I don't think you understand Jimmy." Rosita placed her hand on Eyebrow's arm and pointed again to the elderly woman. "This is my great-great Aunt Ana... Ana Gutierrez."

"A relative of Esteban's?"

"Jimmy, that's Esteban's mother."

Eyebrow's jaw almost hit the ground. "Holy shit! That's Mrs. Gutierrez?"

"Miss. She never married. After Uncle Esteban became successful, he made sure that she was taken care of. He has never visited Coronado, but his money is what built this place, and everything around it. He wanted to make sure that Aunt Ana never wanted for anything, and most importantly, that she was always safe."

"She must be old. What is she... a hundred or something?"

"She was only young when Esteban was born. She is ninety-one." The two stood in silence for a few moments before Rosita beckoned for Eyebrow to accompany her. "Come, would you like to meet her?"

"I'm not sure about that," replied Eyebrow, nervous about the prospect of meeting someone obviously so important to Esteban – the equivalent of royalty within his circle.

"It'll be fine Jimmy. Come, we'll say hello. She does not speak English so I'll help, OK?" Eyebrow hesitantly ceded to Rosita's direction and accompanied her to the verandah. Just before they stepped up to where Ana was sitting, Eyebrow pulled Rosita aside.

"Is 'hola' the Spanish word for hello? I think it is, but I want to make sure. I don't want to mess up."

"Yes, that is the correct word Jimmy," she replied reassuringly as they stepped onto the verandah. Rosita leant down to Ana and spoke to her in Spanish – Eyebrow able to discern only the words 'Jimmy', as well as 'amigo' and 'Esteban'.

Ana rose from her lounge and stepped towards Eyebrow, her arms outstretched. "Hola Miss Gutierrez," he said with an equal mix of confidence and fear that he'd messed up the pronunciation.

Ana grasped Eyebrow's arms, as firmly as a ninety-one year old could at least, and spoke to him with a light in her eye. He again understood the words 'amigo' and 'Esteban' but was unable to glean anything further from her speech. He looked to Rosita for help, which thankfully came immediately.

"She is thrilled to meet a friend of Esteban's," said Rosita with a smile.

Ana continued on, with Rosita translating accordingly. "She wishes to know when you last saw Esteban, and whether he is well."

Eyebrow nodded to Ana and spoke. "Tell her that I spoke with him not that long ago and he sounded well. Tell her too that he's been a good friend to me."

Rosita relayed Eyebrow's message and Eyebrow thought that he could see small tears of happiness spread across Ana's eyes at his reply. She patted Eyebrow on the arms, looked directly at him and spoke again. "She says that any friend of Esteban's is welcome at Coronado for as long as they wish. And she thanks you for being a friend to Esteban."

"Gracias Miss Gutierrez," replied Eyebrow before turning to Rosita. "Did I say that right?"

"You're a natural Jimmy," replied Rosita with a smile as the two of them bade Ana farewell and began the walk back up the hill to where Eyebrow had left Joe Purple a short time earlier. Purple was sitting on the edge of the fountain with a smouldering cigarette hanging out of his mouth – whether it was the one he lit with Eyebrow, or a second one, Eyebrow could not tell. "I'll leave you here Jimmy," said Rosita. "You're both welcome to join my family for dinner tonight if you would like to," she added as she began to walk off.

"Thank you Rosita, that'd be great," replied Eyebrow with a smile. Purple though was too caught up in his thoughts to offer anything more than a cursory wave to the departing Rosita, and as she walked away, he looked at Eyebrow and spoke.

"This is great and all Eyebrow, but for fuck sake, we need to keep our primary mission in focus. We need to get to that fucking embassy, that's all we should be working on." Purple scanned the compound before continuing. "I don't like this Eyebrow. I don't like any of it. We're acting like we're out of danger and I can tell you right now that we're fucking not."

Purple had every right to be wary because outside the Coronado Estate, trouble was brewing. He and Eyebrow had ridden a remarkable streak of luck to that point, but luck has its limits, and the limit was rapidly approaching. Unknown to Eyebrow and Purple at the time, the event that would ultimately come to be known as The Battle of Coronado was now imminent, and on this occasion only one of them would be walking away unscathed.

CHAPTER 39

Maximum Escalation

There was something about Jimmy Eyebrow that brought out the worst in people who would otherwise abide by stringent professional standards. Having never done so before in their respective careers, federal agents Harry Black and Christian Dekker had now ignored their second dead body in an effort to not interrupt the momentum of a Jimmy Eyebrow investigation. After once leaving the body of international hitman Wolfgang Dietrich broiling away in a vacant Las Vegas lot for twenty-four hours in order to avoid alerting Eyebrow to their presence, today they were operating in the new Eyebrow HQ at *Lucky's Motel* with a long-deceased janitor's skeleton sequestered behind a closed door nearby.

The reasoning was twofold. Firstly, they wanted to avoid disruption to their investigation and, furthermore, the janitor's demise clearly occurred a considerable time ago. As such, another day or so would not make much difference to the inevitable investigation once they called it in, which of course they knew they were morally and legally obliged to do – eventually. It just wasn't going to be *that* day.

The new version of the Eyebrow taskforce was still in its embryonic stages and over the past days, they had not been able to develop much more of an insight into Eyebrow's movements, beyond the fact that he had failed to return from London as had been expected. The focus had quickly shifted, unsuccessfully to that point, onto identifying his present location. However any further investigation was brought to a screeching halt by a call to Harry Black from his boss, Jerry McNeil.

Bishop, McFadden and Burnett, along with Black's colleague Dekker watched on as Black listened to what was obviously a development of some significance. "You're shitting me!" said Black abruptly. He looked in the direction of his colleagues. "Yes, they're all here. Yes, Christian is as well. No, no-one else. OK, wait a moment…"

Black placed the phone on the table and touched the speaker button. "OK Jerry, you're on speaker." McNeil's voice came from the phone.

Gentlemen, I won't waste time with formalities because frankly, we don't have that luxury. All five of you are required here as a matter of urgency. We have a ticking clock that needs to be addressed immediately.

Burnett was the first to speak. "Jerry – Dennis Burnett here. I have Leo and Ike with me as well. Surely you don't mean us, do you?"

Especially you three Dennis.

Bishop, McFadden and Burnett exchanged concerned glances. "Where exactly are we going?" asked Burnett.

Washington.

"What the fuck!" exclaimed Burnett. "As in, Washington DC?"

No, I need you in Spokane… YES, of course DC!

"Can I enquire as to what's happened Jerry?" asked Dekker.

It's complex apparently. I don't even know the details myself, other than the fact that all of us – me, and you lot, have been called for. Gentlemen, this has come from the highest level. Something's escalated here, clearly.

"OK Jerry, we'll make arrangements," said Black.

No need to. It's already organized. You leave in less than two hours, so throw on some deodorant, grab an overnight bag and get to the airport. No checked baggage, you don't have time. I'm already here and someone will meet you at Reagan as soon as you arrive.

"Thank you Jerry. We'll leave immediately," replied Black. "See you in a few hours."

The five men stood in silence for a few moments before Bishop spoke. "Just so you know, I'm fucking uncomfortable about where this is going."

"You and me both," added Burnett. "We're fucking street cops for Christ sake. We don't belong in Washington, wading into all the high-level secret shit that they get up to."

"Clearly an Eyebrow situation," noted McFadden. "There's no conceivable reason for us to be involved otherwise."

"Fuck me, what could he have possibly done?" muttered Bishop as Black began to tidy up the small amount of material that they had scattered throughout the makeshift office.

"No idea Leo," replied Burnett. "But it looks like the road trip continues. And God help me, it seems as though I have to fucking tag along this time."

"You'll be in your own room though Dennis," said Bishop with a smirk as the team made their way out the door and on to their respective vehicles for the drive to the airport.

A handful of hours later, after being collected with utmost efficiency from *Reagan National Airport*, the five men were being whisked across the river toward the heart of Washington in a van being driven by a suit-wearing, though otherwise unremarkable driver. Leo Bishop gazed out the window, noting the Washington Monument in the distance. "You ever been here before Mac?" he asked.

"No, first time," replied McFadden. "To be honest, there's a couple of things that I was kind of expecting, but it's not actually the case."

"What's that?"

"Well, maybe I've watched too many movies… but we're all in one van. Usually there's three vehicles that all travel in a tight formation." Bishop nodded his understanding as McFadden continued. "And the van's blue. Like… it's no different to a basic family van really. I've never seen a movie involving shit like we're doing where the vans aren't black."

"Fuck, you're right," noted Bishop as he pondered his own cinematic understanding of official Washington DC transport.

Black and Dekker were also both consumed by thought. "They're right, you know," said Dekker. "The vehicles we use are pretty much always black aren't they Harry?" – a question that drew a nod in return.

Bishop leant forward to speak to the driver as they exited the bridge. "Are we going to drive past the White House?"

"No, we're almost here," replied the driver dryly as he made a turn and eased into a slip lane that led to a large building swarming with security.

"Oh shit," whispered Black.

"What's that for?" asked Burnett. "Why did you say 'oh shit'?"

Black beckoned for the five of them to huddle as best they could in the back as he lowered his voice. "This is the fucking State Department."

"What the fuck are we doing at the State Department Harry?" asked Burnett with thinly veiled anger. "What's going on?"

"I don't know Dennis, I swear."

"You've kept shit from us before. What do you know?"

Black replied defensively, but at the same time sincerely. "Swear on my life Leo, I'm as much in the dark as you."

After clearing several layers of security, the van now edged its way into a courtyard where the five of them could see Jerry McNeil awaiting their arrival. As they exited the vehicle, McNeil greeted each of them in turn, ending with Burnett. "Dennis, great to see you again."

"Likewise," replied Burnett as he grasped McNeil's hand firmly. "But we'd sure as hell like to know what's going on here Jerry."

"Me too Dennis, I assure you." McNeil proceeded to usher the five men inside. "All I know is that something big must have gone down."

"How do you know?" asked Black.

"Trust me, when you see who's waiting for us inside, you'll understand," replied McNeil forebodingly.

As they walked along the hallway in silence, Bishop had to suppress the urge to hurl, the worry about what was brewing threatening to overwhelm him. Soon enough, they arrived outside a large door where McNeil stopped to address them one last time before they entered. "A reminder, gentlemen, to be respectful in here. Speak clearly and concisely. Think before you speak and if you're not sure about something, don't mention it. Do you understand?"

All five men nodded, after which McNeil swung the door open and the six of them strode into a large conference room – the centrepiece of which was a long hardwood table, around which a handful of other people sat awaiting their arrival. McNeil did a quick introduction of the key people in attendance, though the dimensions of the room did not permit any associated handshakes.

"I'd like everyone to meet Harry Black and Christian Dekker, who work for me," said McNeil as he directed his open palm toward his agents. "And next to them we have Dennis Burnett and detectives Leo Bishop and Ike McFadden, our subject matter experts."

Bishop looked to McFadden, who was equally bemused about their new title. *Subject matter experts?* mouthed Bishop to McFadden, who subtly shrugged his shoulders in return.

McNeil now introduced the people seated around the table, beginning by extending his hand toward where a grey-haired man in his sixties sat. "Gentlemen, this is my Director, Gene Woodley."

"I believe I may have met your men once before Jerry on a visit into the field," replied Woodley, before turning his eyes toward Burnett, Bishop and McFadden. "And nice to meet you gentlemen for the first time. I've heard a lot about your work."

McNeil continued around the room, settling on a tall square-jawed man who appeared to be in his early fifties. "Robert Van Pelt, Deputy Director of Intelligence Operations." Van Pelt replied with a slight nod but remained otherwise mute. He was flanked by two associates whom Bishop assumed were lower-level associates. Neither were introduced by either McNeil or Van Pelt – likely because McNeil had no idea who they were, and Van Pelt considered them inconsequential.

Dekker leant over and whispered to Bishop. "I don't know what's going on Leo, but that guy's a big deal."

McNeil then moved onto another man, also flanked by several associates. This man appeared younger, possibly early forties. "And this is Nicholas Bradshaw from the State Department."

Bradshaw waved McNeil off. "Please, it's Nick. Nice to meet you." Bradshaw now turned to one of his unnamed colleagues. "Can you let the Secretary know that we're ready to begin." The underling was summarily dismissed to a neighbouring room, after which Bradshaw motioned towards several large chairs nearby. "Have a seat, please. Secretary Garrison will be with us momentarily."

As they sat, Dennis Burnett leant in on McNeil and spoke with barely a whisper. "Secretary Garrison? As in, Myles Garrison? That's who I think it is, right?"

"I believe so Dennis," replied McNeil, as bewildered as Burnett was. "Whatever this is that we're involved in, it's escalated all the way to the Secretary of State."

CHAPTER 40

Hang it in The Smithsonian

The mood throughout the large meeting room deep within the State Department was tense, with several sub-groups of people around the table actively whispering among themselves, but with no cross-group discussion occurring at that stage, not even the simplest of pleasantries. Leo Bishop glanced around the other two groups – Intelligence and State, trying to determine if they were any the wiser as to why this meeting was taking place.

He had never been involved with anything this high-level before – the closest he had come was one occasion a year earlier when he was called upon to give a PowerPoint presentation to the Assistant Commissioner. As such, he was unsure about the behaviour he was expected to conform to. His only hope was that he could take guidance from others before he was called upon to speak, if indeed that was going to happen at all.

After several minutes, the door to the adjoining office opened and a man who Bishop recognized instantly as Secretary of State Myles Garrison strode in, flanked by two associates. Burnett leant over to Bishop and McFadden, whispering as he stood. "Stand up you two." As Bishop looked around the room, he noted that all other attendees were doing likewise – his first introduction to high-level protocol.

"Please, be seated," said Garrison as he took his own seat at the head of the table before getting straight down to business. It appeared that he had been suitably briefed about the attendees, hence no requirement for introductions.

Garrison looked at his watch before he spoke. "Gentlemen – yesterday, a military coup was initiated in Venezuela, clearly with the intention of toppling the current government. To the best of our knowledge, government forces are continuing to resist the coup, however reports are that the rebels are beginning to gain the ascendancy, and it will only be a matter of time until the government, and any forces loyal to it, succumb."

Garrison turned to his associate Bradshaw before continuing. "Mister Bradshaw, if you could please pass out the papers." Bradshaw rose and began distributing folders to the assembled groups while Garrison resumed his briefing, again glancing at his watch before speaking. "Approximately eight and a half hours ago, the State Department received a request for information from the Associated Press about our involvement in the coup, of which I assured them that we have none. I was then advised that a photograph of some significance had been captured within the opening minutes of the coup that would indicate otherwise. We were further advised that as a courtesy to the Department, AP would hold off publishing the photograph for twelve hours to allow us time to develop a response, again as to the nature of our involvement in the affair."

Once again, Garrison looked at his watch. "By my reckoning, that gives us three and a half hours to deliver a suitable response, otherwise AP will be reporting, just in time for the evening news, that the United States has not only initiated this coup, but we are actively involved on the ground. If you would like to open your folders, you'll see the cause of our current issue."

Folders had been provided to all attendees, however Bishop balked at opening his. Given that he and his team had been summoned to the meeting and subsequently introduced as subject matter experts, he suspected that he knew the general content of the material inside, and every second that he could stubbornly avoid the reality was one more second of Eyebrow-free serenity. He turned to McFadden. "I can't look Mac. I just can't do it. You'll have to tell me if it's something that I need to see."

McFadden eased open his folder. "Holy shit…" he muttered. "Uhhh, Leo, I think you're going to have to see it."

Bishop could hear Burnett off to the side as he too opened his folder, but he was far less subtle in his response. "Jesus Christ! LEO!!! What the fuck is this?" Resigned to the fact that he was committed, Bishop took a deep breath and flipped the folder open.

Thankfully he had taken that deep breath, because an ordinary breath may well have seen Bishop's entire oxygen supply sucked out in an instant. Staring directly back at him was Charles de Klerk's photo of Jimmy Eyebrow, standing heroically and proud atop the rubble outside Rudy Ventura's estate with his M16 rifle provocatively poised and ready for action. Eyebrow's near-naked oiled body glimmered in the eerie light that was streaming through the smoke and haze in the background. And front and centre, proudly displayed for the world to see, were Eyebrow's star-spangled jocks.

"Dear God," muttered Deputy Director of Intelligence Van Pelt. "It's magnificent!"

Garrison was less enthusiastic than Van Pelt. "Yes, yes, Robert, I'm sure that in time it'll be hung in the Smithsonian. But for now, I need to know what the hell is going on here. First and foremost, I need to know, and I need to know NOW, about your knowledge of our involvement in this coup."

Van Pelt stood. "This was not an Agency operation sir."

"Are you telling me everything?" snapped Garrison.

"There's nothing more I can tell you sir," replied Van Pelt. "This was not our doing."

"Last chance to come clean on what you know Deputy Director. I am number four in line to the presidency. But if you're not telling me something because you believe, erroneously might I add, that I don't have the authority to ask, I can get number one here with a single phone call." Garrison now aggressively slammed his finger onto his copy of Eyebrow's photo. "Do – you – know – about – this?"

"No sir. Whoever that is, he's not ours."

"I was trying to determine your knowledge of any role the United States may have played in this matter Deputy Director, not the subject's identity." Garrison now pivoted toward Jerry McNeil's boss. "We know who he is, don't we Director Woodley."

Like Van Pelt before him, Woodley stood. "We do Mister Secretary." But Woodley had no interest in addressing the matter himself, instead passing it deftly off to McNeil. Woodley hadn't risen to the position he was in without knowing when to distance himself from something career-threatening, and in this case, he had metaphorically pulled the pin from a grenade and tossed both items to McNeil with the directive to try and put the pin back in. If the grenade blew up, then it wasn't Woodley's fault – he had after all given McNeil everything necessary to avoid catastrophe.

McNeil though had also played this game before and as quickly as the grenade landed on his lap, he had passed it off to his subordinates in equally swift time. He pointed towards his own two agents and the three local detectives seated to his right. "These are the gentlemen who are the real experts in this field."

Garrison assessed the men seated before him before leaning back in his chair and speaking. "What do *you* know about this situation in Venezuela?" The five men exchanged glances. As Burnett made to stand, Garrison responded gruffly. "Please, there's no need to stand every time you speak. We're time limited here so let's just skip formalities and talk."

"Very well sir," replied Burnett. "I understand that we're tight for time, but I'm going to need thirty seconds to confer with my colleagues."

Garrison again looked at his watch. "It's ticking."

Burnett quickly motioned for his colleagues to huddle, including McNeil. "Do any of you know anything about this? This is fucking serious shit and if anyone knew what Eyebrow was up to, then now is the time to say it." Burnett glared at his federal counterparts. "Does this have your shit-stained fingerprints on it?"

McNeil quickly countered. "Nothing whatsoever to do with us. We'd never interfere in a foreign country, and certainly not using Eyebrow."

Burnett stared at Black and Dekker for several seconds before Black took the cue. "We know nothing about it Dennis, I swear."

Burnett pivoted towards Bishop and McFadden. "You two?"

"For fuck sake Dennis," snapped Bishop. "Are you seriously asking whether Mac and I planned a fucking Latin American coup from our motel?"

"OK," replied Burnett as he swung around to face Garrison again. "We have no knowledge whatsoever about what's happened sir."

"But your agency is responsible for this man's welfare is it not?" asked Garrison.

"Well, to a degree sir," replied Black.

"But we don't monitor his every move," added Bishop.

"Well, clearly that's the case," noted Garrison, who stood and opened the folder in front of him. "Let me apprise you of what we've been able to ascertain thus far. Are you aware that he travelled to London recently?"

"We are sir, yes," replied Bishop.

"Do you know what business he had in London?"

"No, we don't."

"Well up to this point, we're in lockstep, because neither do we. Now, do you know where he went from there?"

Bishop looked around his colleagues. "I'm presuming Venezuela, sir."

"Yes, that would be the logical conclusion, but incorrect. He instead boarded a plane bound for Colombia." Garrison retrieved a photo from his folder and flipped it around for the group to see. "On board that plane was this man, Gabriel Longchamp. His photo is also in your briefing file. As it turns out, Longchamp is, or *was* at least, the long-time money man for a Colombian drug lord named Alejandro Ortiz. It would seem however that en route to Colombia, on the same flight as your man, Mister Longchamp has suffered an as yet undetermined medical episode that resulted in his death. The plane was subsequently diverted to Caracas where the passengers were deplaned for several hours before the flight resumed. However, and here's where things take an interesting turn, when the passengers were returned to the plane, three were missing – your man, his associate Turd Ferguson, and a third man named Pasquale Ramirez."

Bishop leant forward to address the room. "Let's set the table here so that everyone's on the same page sir. Our man, as you refer to him, is Jimmy Eyebrow. Following recent events, he was reinvented by our federal colleagues as Max Von Steel, which is likely the name he travelled under in this instance."

"That is correct," noted Garrison.

"And his associate is Joe Purple. His journey is a little more complex…"

Garrison interrupted Bishop. "He was a former federal agent named Marcus Bloom, I've been briefed on that."

"Just trying to set the scene for everyone else sir," countered Bishop. "Originally Marcus Bloom, later Joe Purple, and now officially Turd Ferguson, though I believe he uses that name only through necessity now. The one I don't recognize is Ramirez. Who's he?"

"Unsure. What we do know is that not long after your man Eyebrow absconded in Venezuela…"

Bishop quickly broke protocol to interrupt the Secretary. "He's not *our* man sir." Bishop looked around the assembled group to reinforce his point. "We just need to be clear on that. Whatever he's done, it's completely independent to us."

"Be that as it may," said Garrison as he resumed his briefing. "Soon after Eyebrow absconded, the coup began. And the photograph that you have before you was captured within the government residential precinct, specifically at the home of senior minister Rudolfo Ventura. At this stage, we have no indication as to Ventura's wellbeing, but we're working on the assumption that Eyebrow has taken him prisoner."

Bishop closed his eyes and shook his head gently. "Why would he do that? Are you suggesting that he's become a mercenary?"

"No idea. That's why you've been included in this taskforce as subject matter experts." Garrison turned to Van Pelt. "Deputy Director, I believe that the 'I' in your agency's title refers to 'intelligence' does it not?"

"Yes, it does Mister Secretary," replied Van Pelt.

Garrison, who was already standing, now buttoned his jacket to indicate that his part in the meeting was nearing its conclusion. "Then by God, let's get some of that intelligence." Garrison again glanced at his watch. "I want to be briefed in two hours about what we know with regards to this mess."

Garrison gathered his files and began to make his way to the door. Stopping briefly, he pointed to Bishop and his crew, and then to Van Pelt and his associates. "This room is yours. Work together, share everything. I need to know what *you* know. We'll reconvene in two hours." With the deadline set, Garrison and his State Department associates departed, leaving Bishop, McFadden and Burnett, who not long ago were simple city detectives, in the company of the Deputy Intelligence Director, working on the orders of the United States Secretary of State.

Bishop turned to Burnett and McFadden. "What the fuck is going on? How the hell did we end up here?"

Burnett rubbed his eyes vigorously. "I don't know what that man of yours is up to Leo, but I can guarantee that leading a fucking military coup in South America was not on my bingo card."

"I'm with you Dennis," added McFadden. "I did not see this coming."

Bishop spoke to Burnett. "You know how Mac and I received the Meritorious Achievement Medal after the last Eyebrow case?"

"Yes, of course I remember that Leo. I recommended both of you for it."

"Well, do we get, like, an oak leaf cluster or something for it this time around, considering we've been recognized by the US Government as the world's foremost experts on Eyebrow? Maybe the department could strike a commemorative Eyebrow medal to recognize the fucking shitshow that working on any of his cases involves."

"I'm balls-deep in this one myself now, aren't I," noted Burnett forlornly. "So you can be assured that we'll be fucking recognized in some way. But for now, pack up your shit and move over to the other side of the table." Burnett glanced toward Van Pelt. "That guy's not moving over here to be with us peasants, so it looks like we need to go to him. Buckle up gentlemen, because this fucking fiasco has taken the express elevator to the top floor."

CHAPTER 41

Hiding in Plain Sight

Despite his menacing initial impression, Bishop's team quickly discovered that Deputy Director of Intelligence Robert Van Pelt was actually a pleasant guy. Professional to a fault for sure, but also quite affable. The first indication of this was immediately after introductions when he dispatched one of his associates to retrieve some food and drinks for the assembled team – a task that soon resulted in ample amounts of coffee and a plate of croissants being deposited on the table in front of them.

Van Pelt took a bite from his crescent of yeasted dough as he discussed the matter at hand with the four original members of the Eyebrow taskforce – Bishop, McFadden, Black and Dekker, along with their respective superiors, Burnett and McNeil. "Best place to start here I think is for me to lay out what we know about your guy, and then you can fill in the blanks, of which I assume there are plenty." Van Pelt looked toward McNeil, the ranking man among the six.

McNeil was quick to set a scene where he was little more than a background character. "I'm involved in more of an oversight capacity. Harry and Leo are probably your information suppositories on this, so I'll cede to them in the first instance."

"I think you mean repositories Jerry," noted Black.

"What did I say?" asked McNeil.

"Suppositories."

McNeil looked confused. "Bullshit, no I didn't."

"Yeah, you did Jerry," added Burnett, to which Bishop, McFadden and Dekker all nodded in agreement.

"Well, you know what I meant," grumbled McNeil before turning to Van Pelt. "They're the information *repositories*." McNeil flipped his attention back to his colleagues. "There, you happy?"

Bishop smiled. "Come to think of it, with what we've had to go through, the original description probably isn't far off the mark."

This comment led to Burnett intervening. "On point please Leo. Unless you missed the memo, we're on a pretty fucking tight timeline here, so let's switch on please."

"Absolutely Dennis," replied Bishop, who quickly shifted his gaze to Van Pelt. "What have you got on Eyebrow?"

Van Pelt opened a large folder in front of him. "I'll work backwards. Secretary Garrison laid out the current situation for you. Do you have any questions on that?"

"About a fucking million," replied Bishop sharply. "I'm curious about the French guy that died on the plane. Was there a known cause of death?"

Van Pelt flipped through several pages until he landed on the one he needed. "That would be Longchamp – Gabriel Longchamp, the money man for Alejandro Ortiz. Whatever it was that killed him, it seems to be exotic. According to reports, he just began seizing on the plane and even though they tried their best, he was dead not long after arriving in Caracas."

Bishop closed his eyes and rubbed his forehead before turning to McFadden. "Exotic poison Mac," he said softly.

"Andronikov," whispered McFadden in reply.

"Who's Andronikov?" asked Van Pelt as one of his associates who had been working off to the side placed more papers on the table next to him.

"Muscle for an organized crime outfit who was allegedly taken out by Eyebrow in a similar manner to Longchamp. In the end, it wasn't Eyebrow, but the similarities are there."

"If it wasn't Eyebrow, who was it?" asked Van Pelt.

"We don't know," replied Bishop. "His manner of death remained partially unresolved. The victim's heart stopped, but the coroner never was able to determine exactly why."

Van Pelt pressed the matter. "So, you cleared Eyebrow?"

"In essence," replied Bishop.

"How so?" asked Van Pelt.

Bishop glanced toward Black who took the cue to speak. "Eyebrow confirmed to us that it wasn't him who did it."

Van Pelt leant back in his chair as another associate entered the room and deposited more papers on the growing pile. "He confirmed it? As in – he *told* you that he didn't do it? But you investigated his claim, right?"

Black shifted uncomfortably and peered toward Dekker, who did not return eye contact. "The situation at the time was complex. We didn't have cause to doubt his sincerity in the moment."

Van Pelt shifted his eyes back to Bishop who motioned his head in the direction of Black and Dekker. "We just went with what they told us."

Van Pelt glanced at his watch and rubbed his eyes. "Very well then, let's continue." His associate directed him to one of the papers that had been brought into the room during the earlier conversation. Van Pelt perused it before speaking. "It looks like we have more information on the third man who absconded from Caracas – Ramirez. It seems that he's tied up with a mid-level Latin American drug boss… let me check his name here… Santiago. Rafael Santiago."

"Holy shit!" snapped Bishop. "Santiago's the same one who that other guy was associated with. The one at Cedar Falls. Hire car guy… what was his name?"

Burnett clicked his fingers repeatedly in frustration trying to recall their earlier briefing back in the janitor's office at *Lucky's Motel*. "Fuck me…" he muttered in frustration before suddenly settling on the name. "Sikorsky! Like the fucking helicopter."

"That's right," replied Bishop. "And Santiago's associated with Gutierrez, so there's the connection right there."

"Wait a moment," replied Van Pelt. "Gutierrez? Do you by chance mean, Esteban Gutierrez?"

"That's the guy," replied Bishop.

"How is Eyebrow associated with Esteban Gutierrez?" asked Van Pelt, somewhat startled at this development.

"They have some sort of close connection," replied Bishop. "Gutierrez is Eyebrow's benefactor, or something like that."

Black added his thoughts. "Whatever the dynamic, Eyebrow's loyalty to Gutierrez is strong."

"Well, it adds another layer to the matter if that's the case," said Van Pelt, turning to one of his associates. "I believe Esteban Gutierrez is Venezuelan by birth, isn't he?"

Van Pelt's associate deftly touched his keyboard and replied succinctly a few seconds later. "Yes, he is."

"OK, so we're forming a broad association here." Van Pelt turned back to Bishop. "What else can you tell me?"

"Well…" began Bishop with a sigh. "Several days ago…"

Van Pelt cut him off. "Is this before, or after the London excursion?"

"Before. Eyebrow, Purple and that Sikorsky guy…"

Again Van Pelt interrupted. "That's the other guy associated with Santiago?"

"That's the one… Eyebrow, Purple and Sikorsky were in a place called Cedar Falls."

"What for?"

Black took his turn to add commentary. "Unsure. But Cedar Falls is the home to a man named Julian Cooper, an accountant. Cooper recently vanished into thin air, and Sikorsky's hire car was found at Cooper's residence by local police."

"The hire car was found on the same day that Eyebrow, Purple and Sikorsky flew to Cedar Falls," added Dekker.

"Was that Ramirez character with them?" asked Van Pelt.

"Again, unsure," replied Black. "We didn't examine the passenger manifest in depth once we found Eyebrow and Purple on it." Black quickly turned to Dekker. "Let's get on that."

"Sound strategy," noted Van Pelt, who scribbled something on a piece of paper and handed it to an associate. "Julian Cooper – see what you can find on him."

"There's a curveball in this episode though," noted Bishop forebodingly. "Neither Eyebrow nor Purple were on their return flight from Cedar Falls. It appears that they instead hijacked a light aircraft, threw the pilot out of the plane along the way, and made an unauthorized landing at the Henry J. Gatling International Airport, before absconding."

"What sort of plane?" asked Van Pelt. "Not that Cessna that I saw recently?"

"That's the one."

"Holy shit!" said Van Pelt. "We had to look into that! That was your guy? Seriously?"

"That was indeed our guy," replied Bishop with a nod, accompanied by a theatric flourish. "Mystery solved!"

"Jesus Christ," muttered Van Pelt. "So, in between these two episodes, we have the London matter. The timeline we have is that your two guys, plus Ramirez, travelled to London on an overnight flight and were due to return soon thereafter, however their original return flight was rescheduled, and they failed to board. Instead, they boarded the plane to Colombia, and, well… we know the rest."

"What the fuck was Eyebrow doing in London?" asked Bishop softly, primarily to himself given that he didn't look at anyone else while raising the question.

While Bishop was pondering, Van Pelt's associate made a contribution. "I've checked on Cooper sir, and there's nothing in our system. Not on our radar at all."

"Very well," replied Van Pelt, who then turned back to Bishop who maintained his earlier contemplative state. Noticing this, Van Pelt pivoted instead to Burnett. "What other deaths has your guy been linked to in the past?"

"Jesus, where to start," said Burnett. "There was Ray DeVecchio, but in the end, Eyebrow had nothing to do with it. Ended up being some other scumbag who needed DeVecchio taken out."

"Waheed as well," added Black.

"Whoa, whoa, whoa there!" said an obviously startled Van Pelt. "We're not talking about Muhammad Waheed here, are we?"

"No, his son Omar," replied Black.

"Jesus Christ, your guy was involved in Waheed Junior's death?"

"No, not in the end," said Black.

"Cleared?"

Black twitched nervously in his seat. "Uhhh… again he confirmed with us that he wasn't involved."

Van Pelt now adopted a sterner tone. "Wait a moment. Are you telling me that you cleared him of this incident as well because he simply told you that he didn't do it? Tell me that you investigated his claim before cutting him loose… please."

"Again, the situation was complex," stammered Black.

"So just to confirm, you did NOT corroborate his claim?"

Black again glanced toward his partner Dekker before answering. "Technically speaking, that's probably correct. But you must understand…"

Van Pelt quickly cut Black off. "Just so there's no ambiguity or misunderstanding on my part here – this is TWO deaths where you suspected his involvement, but your sole reasoning behind clearing him was because... he *told* you he didn't do it?"

"As we mentioned..." began Black.

"Not interested in discussing any nuances," interrupted Van Pelt sternly. "Yes, or no – did you investigate Eyebrow's claim that he was not responsible?"

"No, we did not."

"And the earlier guy? The one who was poisoned?"

"Same," replied Black softly.

Van Pelt inhaled deeply. "Right. Are there any more unresolved deaths where he was cleared solely based on him telling you that he didn't do it?"

Silence filled the room for a few seconds before Bishop, who was resting with his head face down on the desk offered a muffled observation. "St. Claire."

Van Pelt closed his eyes and rubbed the bridge of his nose between his thumb and forefinger – Eyebrow's event horizon had now claimed another unsuspecting victim who wandered too close. "Please tell me, who is St. Claire?"

Bishop lifted his head, rubbed his eyes and sighed deeply before answering. "Eyebrow played a poker tournament in Las Vegas masquerading as a man named Conrad St. Claire. The real St. Claire was found strung up on the back of his hotel door, while Eyebrow played the tournament in his name. It was written off as auto-erotic asphyxiation gone wrong." Bishop swiveled toward McFadden. "But we had our concerns at the time, didn't we Mac?"

"We did Leo. It had a distinct whiff about it."

"And let me guess," opined Van Pelt. "No further investigation because he told you that he didn't do it?" There was no verbal confirmation from Black this time, just a simple thumbs-up. Van Pelt continued. "So, this St. Claire. What was his background?"

"Nothing of relevance," said Bishop. "We looked into him, and he was just a regular guy. School teacher I think, from memory. Nothing, that we could find at least, tying him to anything that might necessitate a hitman."

Van Pelt now stood and paced a little. "Surely he wouldn't murder someone just to get entry into a poker tournament that he could just pay to enter himself? A thrill kill maybe?"

One of Van Pelt's associates now offered a perceptive thought. "If there's nothing at all tying Eyebrow to St. Claire, then maybe it had nothing to do with St. Claire himself."

"Go on," said Van Pelt.

The man looked around the table, ensuring that he had the attention of his audience. "Poker tournaments don't have open seating – it's always assigned. If it wasn't about St. Claire personally, maybe it was all about St. Claire's seat. Maybe he needed that particular seat for some reason."

Van Pelt paused in thought for a moment before responding. "That is a very sound observation." He turned to Bishop. "Is there any way that we could find out more information about this poker tournament?"

Bishop nodded his head gently. "We probably could, yes. When do we need it?"

Van Pelt glanced at his watch. "Before we meet with the Secretary again."

"Fuck," muttered Bishop as he stood. "OK, let me make a call." Bishop turned to McFadden and brandished his phone. "He's not going to be fucking happy Mac." Before Bishop could leave the room, Van Pelt offered an observation.

"I've been in the intelligence game for thirty years. I've studied the best and I know how they operate. There's more to this Eyebrow than meets the eye and I fear gentlemen that he's clever enough to have been secreted right where you least expect him to be – right in front of you. He's been hiding in plain sight leading up to this moment. I can tell you now, he's not one of ours, and that's what I'll be telling the Secretary. But as to what his ultimate game is here… we're going to have to do a whole lot more digging."

CHAPTER 42
The Third Fly

When it came to upmarket North African cuisine, *The Barbary Kitchen* was the undisputed king of the greater Washington DC area, and among its many high-profile patrons, Secretary of State Myles Garrison was a regular customer. Garrison had developed a taste for North African food two decades earlier when he was posted to the US Embassy in Tunisia, hence his choice of venue for that day's meeting. He had arrived ten minutes earlier and was by now becoming more aggrieved by the tardiness of his guest, Gustavo Torres, as each subsequent minute came and went.

Torres was the former Venezuelan ambassador who had been on a bungee cord of diplomatic postings as the government of Venezuela constantly closed embassies across the globe, before backflipping on those decisions, after which yet another alternate foreign policy posture would inevitably be adopted. At this point in time, Torres was between positions and his role with the present government, both currently and into the future, had no more certainty than a random roll of the dice. And given the situation currently unfolding back in his home country, it was probably understandable that he might have had a number of things on his mind that all contributed to his delay in responding to Garrison's unexpected, and very short notice, demand to meet.

When Torres finally arrived, sixteen minutes past the agreed upon time, Garrison quickly directed his minders to take their leave, as did Torres – whatever the two men were going to discuss, it was for their ears only.

Garrison remained seated and looked at his watch. "You need a little more urgency Gustavo. Time is of the utmost essence at the moment."

"I do not operate at your pleasure Mister Secretary," replied Torres curtly as he sat. "And could we not have met somewhere a little more… discreet?"

"What were you expecting Gustavo? The two of us wearing trench coats and sunglasses in an underground parking garage?" Garrison looked around the restaurant theatrically. "Right here is fine. If we're out in the open in a public place, what sort of business could we possibly be up to?"

"Very well," replied Torres. "What did you need to see me about?"

Despite Garrison's earlier assurance that the restaurant was a suitable venue to discuss whatever business they had pending, he nonetheless lowered his voice and leant slightly forwards. "We have a situation evolving that may be… problematic."

Torres sat back in his chair and rubbed his chin, a subtle look of annoyance spreading across his face. "You assured me Mister Secretary that all contingencies had been considered."

"I'm dealing with it," replied Garrison in a hushed tone. "It looks like AP might be about to publish a photo that… may… possibly create an illusion to the casual observer… that the United States is involved in the coup."

A look of fury now exploded across Torres's face as he spoke through gritted teeth. "How did that happen? You guaranteed me that no-one would know. If anyone even suspects that there has been United States assistance, we'll lose all popular support with the people of Venezuela. I did not sign on to be Vice President in waiting for a puppet regime of the United States."

Garrison looked at Torres and raised his eyebrows in response. "I'm pretty sure that's *exactly* what you signed on for Gustavo."

"But the people must never suspect that," countered Torres. "Has this been contained in your own circles?"

"I just had an initial briefing and no-one knows a thing. Even the Agency hasn't picked up a single thread linking the situation to either of us. The whole operation has been done off the books. I could count on one hand the number of people who are in the loop on this. I pressed everyone in the briefing earlier, and they've assured me that they know nothing, so there's been no leakage of intelligence from inside our circle. For now, the operation is proceeding as we planned, except for this one fly in the ointment."

"And what is the nature of this fly?" asked Torres.

"A mercenary of sorts. The photo that AP is threatening to release is of this mercenary at the residence of minister Rudolfo Ventura."

"And why would anyone believe that this mercenary is linked to the United States based solely on a photograph?"

Garrison shifted uncomfortably before answering. "I'd rather not divulge that information right now, suffice to say… the link could be made."

"And what are you doing to counter this?" asked Torres angrily.

"Everything I can. I've put pressure on AP to not run the photograph, but they're insisting that they will. They have however given us the courtesy of time to develop a response before they do so."

"Is that it?" snapped Torres. "A response?"

"We'll be vigorously denying any involvement, I can assure you of that. We'll disavow any knowledge of who this alleged mercenary is."

"And *do* you have any knowledge of who he is?" asked Torres.

Garrison again squirmed in his seat. "Yes, we do. It would appear, from first indications, that he's an international hitman who is a part of our federal witness relocation program."

Torres now leant as far across the table as he was able, directly toward Garrison. "Are you fucking serious? He's a goddamn US government asset? And you think that this won't have blowback? Do you understand what you've done?"

Garrison tried to placate the situation. "Gustavo, please. He's not an *asset* as you refer to him. He's simply…"

Torres unceremoniously cut him off. "He is your responsibility, so tell me, how did he get to Venezuela without you knowing?"

"It seems that he secretly boarded a flight to the United Kingdom, where he booked another ticket to Colombia. While in the air, that flight was subsequently diverted to Caracas, where he then decamped."

Torres looked skeptical. "A coincidence yes that his flight was diverted to Caracas?"

"Indications are that he murdered someone on the plane to ensure that it was rerouted to Venezuela."

Torres buried his face in his hands. "Dear God…" he muttered. Garrison made to speak but Torres held up a hand to halt him. He needed a few moments of silence to compose himself. "How are you planning to contain the situation?" he asked without raising his head.

"There's nothing I can do to prevent the story from getting out, but the United States government will be providing a very firm denial of any involvement. I'll do whatever I can to ensure that you and your associates…"

Torres, his head still bowed, interrupted Garrison. "*OUR* associates Mister Secretary. You cannot unlink yourself from this carriage now."

"Of course. I'll do whatever I can to ensure that *our* associates are distanced from it all Gustavo, you have my word on that."

Torres now lifted his head and offered his own perspective. "What you need to do first and foremost Mister Secretary is locate this mercenary. Can I presume that you have some inkling as to where he is currently?"

"We're working on it."

"Then I would suggest that you work on it a little harder. You need to find this man, dispose of him, and then openly discredit him after he has no means of rebuttal. This coup MUST succeed Mister Secretary. Might I remind you that as alluring as our oil reserves are to you, the risk to reward ratio associated with your backing, no matter how clandestine, is extreme. You and I are in this together, but it is not me who has the most to lose if this blows up publicly, remember that."

"I can assure you Gustavo, I'm fully aware that it's my neck on the block here." Garrison glanced at his watch. "I have a follow-up briefing with my taskforce in less than an hour. If it's clear that none of them have turned up anything that could be damaging, I'll shut them down and then move on to the next phase."

"Which is?" asked Torres.

"Finding this guy and closing the book on him. It will be sorted Gustavo, I assure you. Whoever this guy is, I guarantee you that he hasn't come up against what I'm going to throw at him."

Garrison's plan sounded solid, but it was grounded in one key prerequisite – that the taskforce he'd left behind in the State Department meeting room did not turn up any further information of interest. But if they did, they'd be like a pack of hyenas, and if that scenario came to pass, Garrison would have a much more difficult time pulling them from the carcass.

CHAPTER 43

Seat Number 7

Rufus Hardcastle, the Operations Manager at *Caesar's Palace*, sat peacefully in his office – the serene sounds of Mozart's Violin Concerto Number Five wafting through the room. On his desk was a tabletop Japanese Zen garden that was a coping mechanism suggested by his therapist as a part of his return-to-work program following the debacle some months earlier that had become known as *The Disgraceful Eight Affair*. The desk was immaculately devoid of clutter, with every pen and notebook aligned perfectly and nothing out of place.

As Hardcastle delicately dragged the small rake through the Zen garden, his desk phone buzzed. Using his free hand, he pressed the button and answered. "Yes Barbara?"

Barbara's voice came from the speaker. *Mister Hardcastle, I have a Captain Parker from the Las Vegas Police Department here to see you if you're free.* The sudden twitch of Hardcastle's hand at this request sent grains of white sand sliding across his desk, while at the same time his respiration rate increased markedly. Barbara spoke again. *Mister Hardcastle? Are you there sir? Is everything OK?*

"Yes, yes, I'm here Barbara. You can send Captain Parker in but wait about thirty seconds please." Hardcastle opened the top drawer of his desk and retrieved a bottle of pills. Popping the lid, he tapped out two and without the benefit of water, flicked them into his mouth and swallowed with a grimace. Several moments later, Duane Parker knocked and entered, having been successfully preoccupied by Barbara for the thirty seconds that Hardcastle had requested.

"Mister Hardcastle, how lovely to see you again," said Parker as he strode forward to greet Hardcastle.

"I wish I could say the same," deadpanned Hardcastle as he took Parker's hand limply and offered a cursory shake in return. "Are you here to befoul our reputation once more Captain Parker?"

"No, I am not sir. I'm here seeking your assistance actually."

"And what is it exactly that I can do for you?" asked Hardcastle as he sat. "Do I need legal counsel here?"

"No, not at all Mister Hardcastle. Just to prepare you though, I'm here in relation to… you know…"

"The infamous poker tournament?" replied Hardcastle, his eye twitching at the very mention of the event that had sent him' on a months-long sabbatical to repair his frayed nerves.

"Yes sir, that's correct. I received a phone call a short time ago from one of the detectives who was here with us on the day, and he asked if it would be possible to get something from you."

"And what exactly would that be?"

"He was wondering if you still have the surveillance footage of the tournament."

"And why is that?"

"The request has come from the highest office Mister Hardcastle. There's some sort of national security matter that's going down and he needs to see his guy on the floor. Needs to see who he was interacting with on the day."

"That's it!" snapped Hardcastle as he picked up his phone. "I'm getting Legal up here right away."

Parker quickly headed him off. "Sir, apparently this is a time critical affair. If we could access the footage without the need for your legal team to stifle the process, we'd be deeply indebted to you."

Hardcastle gently sat the phone back down. "What's the nature of the issue?"

"Hand to heart Mister Hardcastle, I don't know. But he called me from Washington, so something's going down. We could really use your help sir." Hardcastle sat in contemplation for quite some time before he again reached for the phone.

"Very well, Captain Parker, allow me to make a call. But if I help you with this, I expect to never see your shadow fall across my doorway again." He dialled and waited. After several seconds, Parker could tell that someone had answered and Hardcastle began speaking.

"Hello Angus, it's Rufus Hardcastle. Yes… I'm well, thank you. I'd ask you too, however it appears that we have a somewhat time critical matter that I'm hoping you could assist me with. Yes… oh dear… oh that's no good… please pass on my best wishes. Angus, if I may… hospital you say? Well, that's no good… so, Angus, to my request… yes, yes, the state of the health system is a concern, I understand your frustration, but if we could… no, I'm not really up to date with health insurance rules Angus… yes, I think it would very much depend on who your provider was… Angus, I'm sorry but I really am going to have to stop you there because I do need your help, and it's very important."

Parker shuffled impatiently while Hardcastle navigated his way through his colleague's complete lack of situational awareness on the other end of the line. "Angus, I need access to some archived surveillance footage… no, it's from a few months ago… yes, The Incident, that's the one." There was a pause while Angus relayed something back to Hardcastle, after which Hardcastle thanked him and hung up the phone.

"That was an ordeal," noted Parker.

"Indeed," replied Hardcastle, who now stood and made his way to the door, beckoning for Parker to follow him. They were on their way to the casino's security bunker where hopefully the footage was not only available, but able to be shared with Bishop and the team back in Washington.

As it turned out, the footage was indeed there, archived simply as "The Incident" – apparently never to be destroyed, such was the infamy now attached to that particular poker tournament. The second aspect however had proven to be a little more problematic and at the State Department, Deputy Director of Intelligence Van Pelt had to call in the resident IT experts to enable a sharing session to exist between the two parties. It was of course understandable that there would be barriers in place to prevent remote sessions being initiated from random computers within the State Department, however after some brief adjustments that made sense only to the IT guy, the two parties were now connected.

Bishop could see Parker and Hardcastle on the other end of the video and he gave them a wave. "Duane, great to see you again. Thank you for organising this hookup."

"No problem Leo, happy to be of assistance. What's that guy of yours been up to now?"

"It's complex Duane. We just need to look at the video first." Bishop turned his attention to Hardcastle. "Mister Hardcastle, how are you doing sir?"

Hardcastle remained stone-faced. "I would rather be doing anything else than revisiting this abomination," he replied. "Please, let's just get down to business and get this over and done with. And for the love of God, no surprises, I beg of you."

"We'll do our best sir," said Bishop. "Could you please show us the start of the tournament when our man first arrives."

"Certainly," replied Hardcastle before speaking to someone off-screen. "Angus could you please wind forward the video of the tournament check-in area. Mister St. Claire arrived late." The men at the State Department could see the video skip forward quite some time before the unseen Angus and Hardcastle then began jumping the video forward in smaller increments. They could hear Hardcastle speaking softly to himself. "It should be around here somewhere."

Eventually the video landed on Eyebrow standing in front of the seat allocation screens. "There he is," noted Bishop. "Can we wind it back a little to see if he arrives with anyone?" The video was taken back a minute or so as requested to the point where Eyebrow was yet to arrive. "Just let it roll from here," said Bishop. After a few moments, Eyebrow entered the room at pace.

"There he is Leo," said McFadden from the side. "He looks like he's in a hurry."

"He certainly does Mac. Look at him checking the door. Something's got him spooked." The video rolled a little further before Eyebrow was approached by a tournament official. "Here we go," noted Bishop. "He's on his way to St. Claire's seat. Mister Hardcastle, can we switch to the specific table now please?"

"Certainly," replied Hardcastle before turning to his associate off camera. "Table twenty-six please Angus." The view on the screen now settled upon Eyebrow taking his seat at table twenty-six, easing himself gingerly onto the only vacant chair, seat number seven – the seat belonging to the recently deceased and, at that point, still undiscovered Conrad St. Claire who was fated to become a far more influential figure post-mortem than he ever was during his living years.

"Here he goes," said Bishop in anticipation of something remarkable happening right out of the gate. But nothing did, with the exception of Eyebrow winning his opening hand and his eliminated opponent subsequently storming off in a huff.

"He's certainly riling them up Leo," noted McFadden.

"That he is Mac. He has a way of doing that."

"What are we looking for here?" asked McFadden.

"Not sure," replied Bishop. "There's nothing jumping out at me, not at this stage anyway."

As vision of Eyebrow shaking hands with the man next to him played, Hardcastle enquired as to whether they wanted him to roll the video further along, noting that there were many hours of vision, and limited time. Bishop was poised to give Hardcastle the go-ahead to do so when Van Pelt muttered ominously. "Holy shit…"

"What?" asked a suddenly concerned Bishop. "What is it?"

Van Pelt stood and tapped the screen, but did not respond directly to Bishop. Instead, he scrawled something onto a piece of paper and passed it to one of his associates. "I need you to call this person at the British Embassy." The seriousness of his direction was now clear in his voice. "Tell him that I need him here immediately. If he's doing something else, tell him to stop and get here as a matter of priority." Van Pelt pointed to a firmly underlined word written on the slip of paper. "Use THAT word in your communication."

Bishop was taken aback by whatever was developing. "What the fuck's going on here?"

Again, Van Pelt did not respond, instead continuing the order to his subordinate who was now standing, phone at the ready. "Whatever traffic laws he needs to break to get here, tell him to do it. I need him here five minutes ago." Finally, Van Pelt turned to Bishop and spoke. "I suspect that your man is something far more significant than you might think."

CHAPTER 44

The Full Package

The British Embassy sits less than three miles from the State Department – a journey by car of somewhere between nine and twelve minutes, depending on traffic. But whatever code word Van Pelt had conveyed to Simon Barber, his British contact, certainly appeared to have had the desired effect as Barber arrived at the gate, at speed, approximately eight minutes after receiving the communique.

With the security formalities complete, Barber joined the team in the State Department meeting room where he was greeted warmly by Van Pelt, who in turn performed the perfunctory introductions around the table, as well as to Parker and Hardcastle who were still on the video link. Barber was introduced simply as a "security attaché" for the British diplomatic corps, which Bishop took to mean that he was likely a spy, or at minimum something in that broad family. "What's arisen here Robert?" asked Barber as he took a seat next to Van Pelt, seemingly keen to get down to business.

Van Pelt slid the now infamous de Klerk photo over to Barber. "We have a situation that's come about with this guy," he said as he tapped the image.

Barber looked at the photo incredulously. "Good Lord!" he exclaimed. "What on Earth is going on here?"

"This photo was taken at the outset of the coup in Venezuela yesterday, and Associated Press is preparing to go public with it. Secretary Garrison is rightly concerned about the optics on this one."

Bishop offered his own observation from the side. "He's got every right to be concerned about the optics of that fucking defilement of our senses. I feel like I need to put a few drops of pure bleach into my eyes every time I look at it."

"Leo, please," said Burnett. "Let the professionals handle this." Burnett turned to Barber. "Sorry about that. Carry on. We're here for questions if you have any, which I'm willing to bet a buck you will."

Barber examined the photo of Eyebrow. "Given your communication earlier Robert, I presume this is relevant to me somehow."

Van Pelt took up the briefing again. "This man is an associate of Esteban Gutierrez and he is under federal supervision by these guys." Van Pelt pointed in Bishop's direction, causing Bishop to quickly shake his head and redirect Barber's gaze toward Black and Dekker. "Several days ago, he slipped out of the country and paid a flying visit to London. We were initially unsure as to why, however we've now had some new information come to light that I need to share with you."

Van Pelt turned his attention to where they had now transferred Parker and Hardcastle's video call from Las Vegas to a large screen on the wall. "Mister Hardcastle, could you please play the video from the start." As the video of Eyebrow's arrival in the ballroom played, Van Pelt gave Barber the background of the issue at hand. "This man, Jimmy Eyebrow, recently played in a poker tournament at Mister Hardcastle's casino…"

"We wouldn't have known about this man," came Hardcastle's voice defensively from off-screen.

"It's OK Mister Hardcastle, we wouldn't expect you to have," replied Van Pelt reassuringly before resuming his briefing. "Eyebrow also goes by the name Max Von Steel, however for this tournament he assumed the identity of one Conrad St. Claire, who was later found deceased in his hotel room."

"Murdered by this Eyebrow character?" asked Barber.

"Open for interpretation," replied Van Pelt. "He was cleared by our friends across the table, however the new information we have may, shall we say, reinvigorate the possibility that St. Claire was a pawn in Eyebrow's long game."

Van Pelt's colleague now added his own observation – the same one that had triggered the renewed interest in Eyebrow's gambling activities. "Seating for a poker tournament isn't random. The initial seating at least is assigned at the outset, and we had a working theory that St. Claire's seat might have had a particular significance, hence its interest to Eyebrow."

Van Pelt pointed to the screen where Eyebrow was now being led to the table. "If you watch here Simon, I'd like you to pay particular attention to who he gets seated next to." Barber leant forward and watched intently as Eyebrow was seated. Van Pelt watched Barber's expression and noted a subtle change as the situation began to reveal itself. Van Pelt spoke to Hardcastle. "Please roll it forward to the end of the first hand."

As Eyebrow raked in the chips from his opening hand win, he turned and shook hands with the man next to him, engaging in conversation as he did so. Barber now leant to the farthest edge of his seat. "Holy shit," he muttered.

"So, I'm not the only one who sees it?" asked Van Pelt.

Barber was incredulous in his response. "That's Stuart Spaulding!"

Van Pelt slapped the table. "I think we've worked out out why Eyebrow was in London."

This was Bishop's cue to re-enter the conversation, annoyed by the cryptic nature of Barber and Van Pelt's exchange. "What the hell is going on here?"

"Shall I?" Barber asked Van Pelt.

"Go ahead, you're the authority," replied Van Pelt.

"The person that your guy met with here is named Stuart Spaulding. He is former MI6, now in private enterprise. One of the foremost security experts on the planet… a brilliant analytical mind. He works with some of the biggest clandestine operators in the world, and not always the wholesome ones either. He's a gun for hire, at a price – a *very* expensive one."

"What does that even mean?" asked Bishop. "The guy's a hacker?"

"Hardly," replied Barber. "We're talking about the ability to compromise the entire security apparatus of even the most sophisticated actors. It's not just about digital penetration, but the whole ecosystem – physical resources, social engineering. The harder the target, the more exhilarating the challenge is for him."

"Even your systems?" asked Bishop.

"Please… Spaulding engineered our systems. No doubt he put backdoors in there that we'd take a century to find. We just accept that."

A loud thud suddenly emanated from the speakers of the wall mounted TV. "Jesus Christ!" came Duane Parker's alarmed response. "Hardcastle's hit the deck here guys."

"Shit, is he OK?" asked Burnett.

Parker was now off-screen, attending to Hardcastle. "He's breathing, and his eyes are open," they could hear him say. "He's had some sort of turn by the look of it."

Burnett looked to Van Pelt. "Are they needed anymore?"

"I think we've got what we needed for now."

Burnett turned back to the screen. "You can terminate the call Duane. Just get Mister Hardcastle the assistance that he needs. Thanks for your help on this."

With the screen fading to black, Bishop returned to the matter at hand. "Ummm… a question that clearly must have an answer then. If Spaulding's that much of a security risk, why isn't he behind bars?"

"He operates under the protection of the Home Office," replied Barber. "No-one could move on him without the approval of the Home Secretary themself."

"Why?" asked Bishop.

Barber sighed, as if he'd had to explain this to more than a few other people previously. "Because he's a weapon… a missile that we can launch and then hide in our bunker when it goes off. He has high-end clients across the world, and he serves only the highest bidder. Some of his clients are friends to the UK, and some… some are not so much. Sometimes, with the right client, he finds himself disrupting the activities of players, or governments, that might not necessarily be aligned with the values and long-term vision of the United Kingdom. In those circumstances, by default Spaulding ends up acting as a de facto arm of the UK Foreign Office… BUT, being a private citizen, we're completely at arms-length."

"So, he ends up doing the shitty jobs where you don't want to get your hands dirty?" asked Bishop, nodding his understanding.

"He's not ours, but we end up with the desired result," replied Barber.

McFadden now added his own question. "And what about if he's working for the other side?"

"The cost of doing business," said Barber calmly. "So long as the long-term scales remain tilted in our favour, it's a price we're willing pay. What I'm now intensely interested in is what relationship your man has with Spaulding. If they know each other, then your man must be a significant player."

"No, he's not," replied Bishop defiantly, trying his best to deny the evolving situation. "He's a fucking underwear thief who somehow got tapped to be a hitman, and a shit one at that."

Barber raised his eyebrows in response. "You sure about that? Spaulding's top tier."

Van Pelt added an observation. "Their guy knows Mohammad Waheed as well."

Barber's eyes instantly became the size of a pair of dinner plates. "Seriously?"

"No," replied Bishop. "It's a misunderstanding. He doesn't know Waheed."

"But you said that you suspected him of Waheed Junior's murder," noted Van Pelt.

Bishop fumbled in response. "Yes… but… it's complex."

"It always is with these types," replied Barber. "Do we know how he travelled from London to Venezuela?"

"Via a commercial flight to Colombia," replied Van Pelt.

"I wasn't aware that anyone offered commercial flights to Colombia with a stopover in Venezuela. Certainly not from the UK," noted Barber.

Bishop placed his hands over his face, knowing what Van Pelt's next contribution was going to be. "The plane was diverted to Caracas, possibly because Eyebrow murdered someone on board."

"Hey, we don't know that!" snapped Burnett defensively.

"It was Gabriel Longchamp," added Van Pelt, sidestepping Burnett's point of order.

"Longchamp, the cartel money man?" asked Barber.

"Yes," replied Van Pelt.

Burnett now took the floor. "Gentlemen, can you give me a couple of moments to have a few words with my colleagues here?"

"Absolutely," said Van Pelt with a wave.

Burnett ushered his three federal associates, along with Bishop and McFadden away from the table where he lowered his voice. "They're making some pretty valid fucking points here. Are you sure that you haven't underestimated this guy?"

"He's a fuckup Dennis," replied Bishop sharply. "He doesn't have the fucking mental capacity to keep up with the people they're talking about over there. I have no idea how he knows Spaulding, and Waheed's the biggest fucking arms dealer on the planet. They're not associated, end of story."

Harry Black coughed. "Leo, a wrinkle in this if I may. The flight to London… there was that other guy flying with them."

"Which one?" asked Bishop. "What are you talking about?"

Black walked the short distance back to the table and retrieved his leather travel satchel. Rummaging through the papers within, he located the file that they had shared back at *Lucky's Motel*. "The defence guy Leo," said Black as he thumbed through the file. "Let me find his name here – Dunk... Charles Dunk. From Triochron Industries."

"He's got a point there Leo," said Burnett. "There's some pretty fucking compelling evidence that things might not be what they seem."

Bishop rubbed his eyes. "I don't know about this Dennis."

"We've gotta tell them about Dunk too," said Burnett.

"I concur," added Black. "We can't sweep this under the rug now. It's escalated too far. They need to know everything."

Bishop was lingering in the purgatory between anger and despair and just waved a silent response, which Burnett took to mean "go ahead".

Burnett walked back to Van Pelt and Barber. "Ahh, gentlemen, there is one more thing that we need to add to the mix here, and Robert, I apologise that we neglected to mention this earlier. When Eyebrow flew to London, he and his associate appear to have travelled with a man named..." Burnett turned to Black for assistance.

"Charles Dunk," said Black. "He's an engineer for the defence contractor, Triochron Industries."

Both Barber and Van Pelt sat back in their seats and exhaled deeply, side by side, as if performing a synchronised routine. Van Pelt gathered his thoughts before speaking. "So, let's summarise what we've learnt here today. Eyebrow has secretly travelled to London to visit a former MI6 operative, in the company of an engineer from one of the United States' biggest private defence contractors. After that, he's boarded an international flight, during which he's murdered a Colombian drug lord's money man in order to get the plane diverted to Venezuela, where he's then decamped, obviously with assistance on the ground, and subsequently kidnapped a government minister during a military coup."

There was silence from the other side of the table before Burnett added his assessment. "Yeah... when you hear somebody else say it, I guess it does sound pretty bad."

Van Pelt looked at his watch. "We have about twenty minutes before we need to brief Secretary Garrison again. Does anyone have anything further to add?"

"God I fucking hope not," said Burnett. "Leo?"

"Nothing," replied Bishop, his eyes still closed as he sought sanctuary in the Eyebrow-free darkness.

Burnett looked at Black. "Harry? Anything?"

"Nothing here."

"Very well," said Van Pelt. "Toilets are in the hall if you need to go, and coffee's in the next room if you want something before we reconvene."

As they all stood, Barber made an observation. "I don't know who, or what, this guy of yours is, but he's sure as hell not a garden-variety underwear bandit, that's for sure. Spaulding, Gutierrez, Waheed, Longchamp – this guy's running with the top tier. He's certainly no two-bit crook like he's got you believing... absolutely not. This Eyebrow character – he's the full package."

CHAPTER 45

Bring the Trench Coat

At a facility named Orfield Laboratories, there is a special room dubbed "the quietest place on Earth". Unfathomably silent, the room, or anechoic chamber if one were committed to accurate naming conventions, has been used for all manner of acoustic testing and is so devoid of background noise that the only sound a person would experience if standing inside is the internal sound of their own body operating. Coming in a close second for the quietest place on Earth, on this day at least, was the State Department briefing room as Secretary Garrison sat unmoving, trying to digest the information that had been relayed to him by Intelligence Director Van Pelt.

Garrison had hoped that the unexpected, and very inconvenient, appearance of Jimmy Eyebrow front and centre at the Venezuelan coup was going to be easily explained away, however the updated brief delivered by Van Pelt had now thrown a spanner of extraordinary proportions into the works. Garrison's thought process was twofold. Firstly, given the newly discovered complex web of Eyebrow's professional relationships – some genuine, and some entirely misinterpreted but taken as fact – Garrison was now going to have to find a creative method of explaining the situation away to the Associated Press.

But more pressing for Garrison was Eyebrow's choice of attire for the photograph that was soon to be blasted across the world. The coup in Venezuela had been brewing for at least two years, however the agitators had neither the organisational skills nor, more importantly, the funds to raise a successful rebellion. To resolve that situation, Garrison had unilaterally used a tightly sequestered network of back channels to funnel clandestine United States support to the rebels, in exchange for increased access to Venezuelan oil reserves following the successful transfer of power. It was a bold, and even potentially treasonous, plan given that it was backed by no-one else in government, and Garrison had strayed so far off the reservation by that point that he was in uncharted territory – this was Iran-Contra on steroids. But if it was pulled off, he would be able to deliver an economic bonanza to the President on a golden platter.

The plan however had a major, and non-negotiable, caveat – the United States could not in any way be seen to have any involvement in the rebels' actions. This would be problematic not only for the United States, but it would also erode popular support in Venezuela for the rebels. And it was precisely Eyebrow's choice of star-spangled jocks for his impromptu photo shoot with Charles de Klerk that now threatened to derail the entire, meticulously planned operation. Any other outfit choice from Eyebrow and the de Klerk photograph, while still impressive, would nonetheless be a political non-event.

The silence in the de facto second most quiet place in the world was finally broken as Garrison leant forward in his chair and rubbed his face vigorously. "I'm really not sure how I spin this to AP."

The extended period of silence hadn't been wasted though. The cogs in Bishop's head had been turning and formulating a potential solution. It was a ridiculous option, and he used every second of peace and quiet trying to develop an alternative course of action. But every time he tried, his mind kept wandering into the same cul-de-sac where his original idea resided. It's difficult to say whether Bishop's reluctance to fully pursue the idea was due to his belief that it wouldn't work, or his wounded pride that it actually *had* worked before. But there weren't many other options available so, with a deep breath to kick off proceedings, he offered his thoughts. "Sir, I might have a solution for you."

"What the fuck are you doing Leo?" whispered Burnett.

"Something so fucking ridiculous that it might work," replied Bishop.

Garrison turned to Bishop. "And what might that solution be detective Bishop?"

"May I have a quick conference with my colleagues?"

Garrison shuffled in his seat while glancing at his watch. "I need to deliver my response to AP in less than an hour, so make it quick."

Bishop, McFadden and Burnett swung around in their seats and huddled. "What's on your mind Leo?" asked McFadden.

Bishop rubbed the bridge of his nose. "God help me Mac, but I think I might know how Garrison can deflect this."

* * *

The cursor hovered over the "join meeting" button on the large screen in the State Department briefing room while Secretary Garrison composed himself and went over in his head one more time the response that he was about to deliver. He glanced toward Bishop and gave him a thumbs-up, with Bishop returning the gesture. "You've got this sir," said Bishop in support.

"OK, let's join Nick," said Garrison as he assumed the air of dignity customary for the United States' chief diplomat. Garrison's associate joined the meeting where, thankfully, only one other person was present – Kenneth Marks, the Executive Editor for *Associated Press*.

"Good evening Mister Secretary," said Marks. "Thank you for taking the time to meet with me."

"Good evening Ken, lovely to see you," replied Garrison. "I have to say though that I'd prefer it if we weren't meeting under these circumst…"

"You're on mute I think, Mister Secretary."

Garrison turned to Nick who was managing the technology logistics. "Am I on mute?"

"Yes, sorry about that sir, it joined the meeting that way." Nick quickly made the necessary adjustment. "You're unmuted now sir."

Garrison turned back to the screen and began his opening formalities anew. "I was saying Ken, that it's lovely to see you, although it would be nicer if we were meeting under different circumstances. You've really put me through the wringer here."

"I'm just doing my job sir, I hope you understand that."

"I do Ken," said Garrison before launching into the key issue that had brought both men together. "Ken, I'm writing up a statement that I'll have for you shortly, but I wanted to brief you on the position of the United States with regards to the individual you've photographed in Venezuela. The man in your photograph is not working in any capacity for the United States now, nor has he ever done so in the past." It was Garrison's hope that this simple rebuttal would satisfy Marks, thus avoiding the need to transition into Bishop's plan. That hope was soon dashed, as the logical follow-up question came in quick time.

"Do you know who he is?"

This was where Garrison now had to get creative, because leaving such an enormous loose end for a journalist of all people would result in problematic threads being pulled. And given the day's revelations about Jimmy Eyebrow, Garrison most certainly did not want those threads picked at. "We do Ken. Our intelligence team has identified this man as a mercenary operating out of Mexico who goes by the name 'La Tormenta'. He has been implicated in a significant number of incidents and our people have been tracking him for some time. I'd like to take this opportunity to thank AP for bringing his presence in Venezuela to our attention."

Garrison could see that Marks was preparing to speak but pre-empted him. "I expect that one of your supplementary questions will be about his attire, and I assure you, that got me angry as well. You see Ken, the man hates the United States and has openly taunted us in the past. This would simply be another of his perverse attempts to thumb his nose at us from afar."

"So just to confirm – this man is NOT aligned with the United States government, or military, in any manner?"

"That is correct Ken. And the formal statement to follow will reiterate that."

"And the United States has not engaged this mercenary's services for the purposes of proxy participation in the coup currently underway?"

"Correct again Ken."

"And is the United States supporting this coup in any way? Be it covert activities, diplomatic actions… *financial support?*"

Fuck, he put emphasis on the money bit. Does this prick know? thought Garrison to himself before quickly responding, lest his pause be interpreted with interest. "None whatsoever Ken. And the statement that we'll provide you within the hour will attest to that."

Marks remained silent for several seconds as he digested the substance of the conversation. "Very well Mister Secretary, thank you for the clarifications. We'll be sure to include your quotes as a supplement to the story."

That response was nowhere near decisive enough to satisfy Garrison. "I need to confirm Ken, that you'll be stating very clearly that the United States is not associated with this coup."

"What we'll be reporting Mister Secretary is that the United States has *told us* that they are not involved in the coup attempt. But we don't create facts. What we *will* do is report accurately on what you've quoted. You have said that you're not involved, so we will report faithfully what you've said."

Garrison understood the nuance associated with the slight variation that Marks had placed on Garrison's simplistic request. Marks was correct – it was not the role of AP to create facts, and the fact of the matter was that a man wearing American flag briefs was photographed at a Venezuelan government minister's house, actively participating in the coup. How the public interpreted that was up to them, but AP would at least be reporting that the United States government was firmly distancing itself from any involvement, either direct or covert. All Garrison could hope was that the denial was prominent enough within whatever article AP planned to run alongside the photograph.

With the meeting winding up, Bishop was expecting a short debrief with the Secretary, however within moments of the video call terminating, Garrison rose and gruffly left the room without a word. Given his assistance in extracting Garrison from the mess that Eyebrow had put him in, Bishop felt that at minimum, a cursory show of appreciation would be offered, but it was not to be.

Secretary Garrison instead walked into a side room, closed the door behind him, and pulled out his phone. Every new revelation about Jimmy Eyebrow had escalated his current situation further – a phenomenon that was new to Garrison, but all too familiar for everyone in the other room. He may have deflected AP in the short term, but he also knew that it wouldn't take long before their journalistic fervor took over and the quest for more information about the mythical "La Tormenta" would be underway. Garrison opened the text function of his phone and typed a short message to Gustavo Torres, his co-conspirator in the matter at hand.

We have a situation. Meet in 30 minutes. Car park at the Plaza. Bring your trench coat.

CHAPTER 46

Possibly the Hill to Die Upon

Half a world away from the events unfolding in Washington, the smoke from Joe Purple's cigarette barely wavered from the perpendicular from where it was smouldering in the ashtray – testament to the perfectly still morning that had dawned over Coronado that day. There wasn't even a whisper of wind, the sky was cloudless, and the morning air held a crispness that was customary among the lush, low hills where the Coronado Estate sat. Under any other circumstances, it would have been an idyllic setting for enjoying the breakfast platter that sat unattended next to the ashtray. But not that day.

The coffee mug that rested nearby still had steam rising from it when it catastrophically exploded, sending shards of ceramic flying everywhere, courtesy of the stray bullet that had just slammed into it. The scene inside Coronado at that moment was chaotic, a ferocious battle having erupted only moments earlier with little forewarning.

Not long before, Joe Purple and Jimmy Eyebrow had been taking coffee together after a restful night in the Venezuelan countryside. Both had attended dinner with Rosita's family the previous evening – Eyebrow enthusiastically, Purple somewhat less so, before retiring to their own comfortable rooms. Joe Purple in particular found the concept of private quarters to be refreshing given that he and Eyebrow had essentially been in each other's pockets for more days than he could remember recently. He gratefully took advantage of the peace and quiet to rest and rejuvenate as best he could.

And now, that morning as he sat chatting in the garden with Eyebrow, alternating sips of coffee and drags of his cigarette, Purple was soon to learn how important being rested was going to be. Without warning, a thunderous alarm sounded, much like a collision warning on a cargo ship. "What the fuck is that?" yelled Purple as people inside the estate began running everywhere.

"Something's happening Joe," replied Eyebrow.

"Jesus, you think so, captain fucking obvious?" snapped Purple. "What the fuck's going on?" The answer soon came via the sound of automatic gunfire filling the air.

"Fuck, we're under attack!" screamed Eyebrow.

Purple ducked and dragged Eyebrow down with him. Looking around, he pointed to the Land Rover around twenty metres away. "We need to get over there! That's where the weapons are."

The two of them leapt from their concealment and ran like they'd never run before. At the entrance to the estate, the guards were securing the area and Eyebrow could see a swarm of vehicles thundering down the hill toward the rapidly closing gates. The sound of gunfire echoed across the hillside as one of the guards fell, followed soon by another. The gate had been successfully closed, but it was more ornamental than siege-resistant, and it would only be a matter of time until it was breached. That is if the attackers, whom Eyebrow had by now identified as rebels, even bothered with the gate when there were numerous other open avenues to enter the estate at various points around the perimeter.

Sliding in a cloud of dust behind the Land Rover, Eyebrow and Purple were soon joined by Mariano who had the same idea. "The rebels have located us. Cisco is inside with Mister Ventura and Aunt Sofia. We need to load up, NOW!" He swung the door of the vehicle open and distributed the M16 rifles, tossing them a bag at the same time. "Extra ammo. You're going to need it."

An explosion suddenly rang out from the front gate, followed in short order by another. "Are they coming through?" yelled Eyebrow over the noise.

"No," replied Mariano. "They were claymores. This place is well defended."

Purple poked his head out from the side of the Land Rover. The gate was still intact, but there was carnage on the other side of it. He couldn't tell how many rebels had fallen victim to the twin blasts, but coming to a halt as they had, they'd unknowingly strayed directly into the kill zone and had paid the price.

But still more vehicles appeared on the hill above and it soon became clear that even with the reasonable contingent of armed personnel who had poured out of the neighbouring buildings now returning fire, they were significantly outnumbered. The siege of Coronado had begun.

Mariano directed Eyebrow and Purple to a low wall back near where they had originally been. "Get behind there and spray anything that comes through that gate. GO!"

Both men took off once more, this time with weaponry in hand. Eyebrow again glanced up the hill and saw additional vehicles arriving from the other direction. But they weren't rebels this time – they were different. His hope that they may be friendly was soon dashed when instead of making toward the front of the estate, they diverted down the hill in a flanking manoeuvre. "Fuck Joe, there's more of 'em," he said, tugging at Purple's sleeve as they ran.

The two of them quickly dove for cover behind the wall, the air now heavy with the sounds of battle. "Fuck me, this is bad Eyebrow. Who are this other lot?"

"Different vehicles Joe. I don't think they're with the rebels." Eyebrow looked around the scene and saw that most of the defenders were focused on the frontal assault and rightly so, because the rebels were not going to fall into the same trap again, and this time began to plough through the hedges on each side of the gate. While the vehicle to the right found itself strung up on obstacles, on the left side, one vehicle had managed to break through and even though under intense fire, secured a breach for attackers on foot to slip through the perimeter and quickly spread.

The defenders, Purple and Eyebrow reluctantly among them, were valiantly holding ground, even as many had now started to succumb to the relentless fire from the rebels. The situation was deteriorating and from the corner of his eye, Eyebrow saw Mariano beckoning for he and Purple to retreat to a more defensible position closer to where he was. As the two of them hurried toward Mariano, Eyebrow spotted Rosita charging down the hill, firing her own automatic weapon furiously toward the lower part of the estate where the second unidentified attackers had now breached the lesser defended perimeter.

Eyebrow froze. In an instant, he knew where Rosita was going. "Holy shit! Miss Gutierrez!" he bellowed.

Purple had noticed that Eyebrow was rooted to the spot, out in the open. "For fuck sake Eyebrow, get over here!" he yelled at the top of his lungs.

But instead, Eyebrow sprinted toward Rosita, turning quickly to call to Purple. "I've gotta help Miss Gutierrez!" he screamed over the top of the carnage before careening down the hill.

With the battle continuing to rage behind him, Eyebrow caught up to Rosita and between the two of them, began fighting a rearguard action against what looked like approximately ten attackers, give or take. Glancing toward the veranda of Ana Gutierrez's cottage, Eyebrow and Rosita identified a terrified Ana taking cover on the floor. Turning to face the attackers, Eyebrow's heart sank when he saw who was among them. As an open top four-wheel drive rolled into the estate, Eyebrow was shocked to see the forgotten PQ posing majestically atop the vehicle's open tray, chest pushed forward like Erwin Rommel assessing the Libyan Desert.

It now became clear that these were not rebels like those involved in the frontal assault – these attackers were members of the personal army loyal to whoever PQ was originally ferrying Eyebrow and Purple to. Eyebrow and PQ locked eyes, with a maniacal grin radiating impending revenge spreading across PQ's face. Suddenly, an already diabolical situation had somehow gotten worse, with the battle now being fought on two fronts against two different enemies. There was clearly no scenario now where Eyebrow and Purple survived if they could not repel the attackers, who were now far greater in number than those defending the estate.

Further up the hill, the situation was grim. The Coronado menfolk had fought bravely, but the flow of rebels was becoming insurmountable, and ammunition supplies were beginning to wane. Mariano had mustered all the remaining defenders, and they had retreated to a reinforced strong house where, on the proviso that heavy weapons were not deployed, they could hold out for a significant period of time.

Down the hill however, it was an army of two – Eyebrow and Rosita. Their priority at that point, beyond staying alive, was ensuring the safety of Ana Gutierrez who had found herself terribly exposed, though thankfully undetected at that stage. Eyebrow was the first to arrive by her side and he gently guided the elderly Ana to her feet in order to move her inside, all the while with Rosita providing covering fire. When suddenly, out of nowhere, one of PQ's men leapt from behind a wall and levelled his rifle directly at Ana. Rosita took aim and quickly dropped the attacker, but it was a split second too late.

As the crack of the rifle rippled through the air, Eyebrow instinctively cradled Ana and spun her away from danger, shielding her with his own body. The bullet from PQ's man smashed into Eyebrow's shoulder, sending a searing pain coursing through his body. Eyebrow had been in many a painful situation in the past and had been beaten to within an inch of his life more than once, but nothing compared to the pain that suddenly overwhelmed him at that moment. Still, he maintained his grip on Ana and stumbled through the door with her in his arms, followed soon by Rosita who was strafing the attackers outside and had already halved the force that the two of them were facing.

"Are you OK Miss Gutierrez?" asked Eyebrow through gritted teeth as he set her down on the floor.

"Si, si, mi héroe," she whispered, patting his face softly.

Eyebrow turned to Rosita. "I'm fucked Rosita. This hurts so much. I can hardly move my arm."

Rosita knelt at the window and unloaded another fusillade to keep the attackers at bay momentarily before she shuffled over to Eyebrow. Ripping open his shirt, she identified a hole in the back of his shoulder, but no corresponding exit wound. "It's still in there, Jimmy…" she said as she continued her examination. "I need to stop this bleeding. Stay here." Rosita unloaded the remainder of her magazine out the window and then scurried across the floor to the kitchenette where she rummaged through the drawers.

The sound of gunfire from outside had not abated and the exterior of the building was being peppered with bullets. Rosita returned to where Eyebrow was huddled and sought to reassure him. "The walls of every building in the compound are reinforced so we're safe behind them Jimmy. We just can't let them get inside." Rosita quickly popped her spent magazine and inserted a new one before directing a few more diversionary shots out the window.

Rosita flipped Eyebrow around to face the wall and prodded at his entry wound, eliciting a muted cry of pain in response. "I can only do a quick patch job here. We'll need to get you help when we get a chance." She slapped a folded tea towel against the wound and began winding cello tape across his shoulder and under his arm – once, twice, at least half a dozen times until Eyebrow's shoulder was covered. It wasn't going to be pleasant to peel off when the time came, but it was the best that Rosita could muster under the circumstances.

The sound of breaking glass was heard from the back of the building, indicating that the aggressors were now flanking around the outside, having determined that a frontal attack was not the only means of taking the objective. Given that PQ knew Eyebrow was inside the building, the attackers were unlikely to relent of their own accord. Rosita was low on ammunition and Jimmy Eyebrow was operating with one arm. Together they needed to somehow defend their stronghold, not only to protect Ana Gutierrez, but also to stay alive themselves.

Back when Eyebrow and Purple had been stranded in London, Purple cautioned Eyebrow that his determination to accompany PQ to Colombia was, metaphorically of course, not the hill to die upon. But *this* hill – the hillside where Coronado sat – this was shaping up to be a different story entirely. This hill gave every indication that it could indeed be the one.

CHAPTER 47

The Siege of Coronado

The situation inside Coronado was as dire as any since the day Colonel Custer rallied his men to what would become known as "Last Stand Hill" with the guarantee that "the savages will have no chance against our highly disciplined fire up here". The Battle of Coronado was now being fought, and lost, on two fronts – in the upper portion of the compound, Purple, Mariano and what remained of Coronado's small security detail had retreated to a safe house, while in the lower estate, Rosita and the wounded Jimmy Eyebrow were hunkered down and battling against the odds in Ana Gutierrez's villa.

And now the two attacking groups – the rebels at the top of the hill, and PQ's men at the bottom, were readying themselves to deliver the final blow. It was not through coordination that the two groups had found themselves arriving at Coronado within minutes of each other, but more pure coincidence. Each had their own objective – the rebels to capture or kill Rudy Ventura, while PQ's men had been sent to locate Jimmy Eyebrow and the rumored crypto key that he held in his possession.

Inside Ana Gutierrez's villa, Eyebrow quickly took stock of his rapidly diminishing ammunition supply. He had a handful of bullets left in his current cycle, and two full magazines remaining in reserve, while Rosita was already halfway through her final magazine. They had defended valiantly, but the odds were now against them. Eyebrow slid one of his full magazines across the floor to Rosita and inhaled deeply, resolving to go down fighting.

If this was to be his end, as it looked more likely to be with each passing minute, then he was going to go out on his feet. As Eyebrow contemplated his fate, he thought back to the last telephone conversation he had with Esteban Gutierrez when he and Joe Purple had been stranded at Caracas airport. Not only had Eyebrow been apprised of PQ's treachery during the call, but Gutierrez had also arranged for Eyebrow and Purple to be safely billeted with Ventura. And while that hadn't gone precisely to plan, Gutierrez had also promised something else – that he would send help. Sitting there on the floor of the villa with the gunfire unrelenting outside, Eyebrow thought to himself that some of that promised help certainly wouldn't go astray at that moment.

It may or may not have been by design, but Esteban Gutierrez's track record of providing Eyebrow with assistance right when he needed it the most was strong indeed – Eyebrow's guardian angel certainly seemed to have a flair for the dramatic. More gunfire now erupted from outside the villa, but Eyebrow detected a subtle change in its cadence and tone. It appeared that now, the fire was directed *away* from the building. He knelt to peek cautiously out the window and found that his initial observation was correct – PQ's men were now rushing to a point away from the villa. "Rosita! Something's going on! Can you see?"

Rosita slid to a halt next to Eyebrow and performed her own assessment. "Something's definitely going on out there, Jimmy," she noted as she began creeping toward the door. "I'm going to have a look."

"Be careful," said Eyebrow as Rosita eased the door open and slipped onto the veranda.

Within moments, Eyebrow could hear Rosita's jubilant cry. "YES! Jimmy! Come out here!"

Eyebrow ducked below the window and made his way cautiously out the door where he could immediately see the source of Rosita's joy. Eyebrow had no inkling who it could be, but PQ's men were now engaged in a pitched battle with a new armed group that had attacked them from behind. They were larger in number and had the element of surprise, such was the preoccupation of PQ with taking the villa that he had clearly felt that the need for a rearguard was moot. And now, PQ and his men were paying a heavy price for their tactical arrogance. One by one, they were brought down in quick succession thanks to the barrage coming from the new entrants to the battle. In addition, enfilade fire was now pouring in from Rosita and a one-armed Eyebrow who had also opened up and were depositing the last of their inventory of ammunition into the hapless enemy.

With a newfound air of confidence, Eyebrow alighted from the veranda and strode out to join forces with his new comrades who were still streaming through the lower reaches of the estate, even as the vanguard of the force was already making its way up the hill to relieve Joe Purple and his besieged comrades. The rebels in the upper compound had seen what was occurring not far away and had begun their own tactical retreat under fire, although similarly to PQ's squad, they too were now under counterattack on multiple fronts as Purple and Mariano's crew spilled out of the safe house to complement the fire coming from below.

As the pitifully small number of remaining rebels now fled, Eyebrow turned to see who his saviour was. Just as PQ had ridden arrogantly into Coronado atop his vehicle, now it was the victor who rolled into the compound in the same triumphant manner – the Montgomery to PQ's Rommel. Gutierrez had told Eyebrow that he was sending help, but he didn't say it would be someone familiar.

"Yuri! What the hell!" cried Eyebrow as Yuri stepped from his vehicle. "Who the hell are these guys?"

"Locals," replied Yuri. "It's not just the people in Coronado who get looked after by Mister Gutierrez. Everyone from the nearby towns and this whole community benefits from his generosity. They all live very comfortably because of him, so if he needs assistance, they all stand ready to help."

Eyebrow shook Yuri's hand vigorously. "Jesus Christ, you couldn't have timed it better."

"Well, we could have arrived an hour earlier. There's that."

"Yeah, come to think of it Yuri, that probably would've been handy."

Yuri now examined Eyebrow's left arm. "You're injured there Max. Have you been hit?"

Eyebrow waved Yuri off. "It's not Max, Yuri. My name's Jimmy. Max was just a cover. And yes, I took a bullet to the shoulder. It fucking hurts like hell, but Rosita here patched me up." Eyebrow beckoned Rosita to join them, introducing her to Yuri as she arrived. Looking around the carnage, Eyebrow ushered Yuri toward a vehicle that had been disabled during the earlier firefight. "Did you see who the fuck was with these guys?"

"No?" replied Yuri, more in question form than statement.

Eyebrow rounded the vehicle and found who he was looking for. He pointed to the ground where a wounded, but still very much alive, PQ stared back at them. "This prick. Can you believe it?"

Yuri was stunned. "What is this asshole doing here?"

"He fucking tricked us into coming here," replied Eyebrow.

"Yes, Mister Santiago mentioned that. But I didn't expect to see him actually *here*, in Coronado." Yuri squatted before PQ and spoke directly to him. "What the hell is going on here you fucking snake?"

"Screw you," replied PQ. "I should have just killed you when I had the chance."

"What does he mean Yuri?" asked Eyebrow.

Yuri turned to Eyebrow. "The reason I didn't hook up with you after the incident at Cooper's house is because this prick here plunged a kitchen knife into my leg and left me there to take the rap, while he took off like the weasel he is."

"Why the fuck aren't you in jail?" wheezed PQ.

Yuri turned back to PQ and towered over him. "Well, your little plan ran into a bit of an issue. Cops turned up, I'm on the floor with a knife sticking out of me… didn't take much to convince them that I was just checking on my friend Cooper and I disturbed an intruder. Hardly going to stab myself am I. Like you said, you should have finished me off instead of trying to get cute."

"I'll fucking keep that in mind next time," hissed PQ.

"There's not going to be a next time you prick," replied Yuri menacingly before turning to one of his associates and pointing at PQ. "Whatever happens, don't let this prick find a way to get out of here." Yuri now called for Eyebrow to accompany him up the hill. "Let's check on your friends."

As they trudged up the hill, Eyebrow's arm hanging limply by his side, Joe Purple emerged from the chaos ahead and upon sighting Eyebrow, made a beeline directly for him. "Holy fuck Eyebrow, you're alive!" he yelled in obvious delight.

"We made it Joe," replied Eyebrow with a broad smile.

"Jesus, what happened to you?" asked Purple as he suddenly noticed Eyebrow's arm and its associated makeshift repair.

"I got hit. They were about to shoot Miss Gutierrez, but they got me instead."

"Fuck me Eyebrow, you took a bullet for her?"

"Just did it on instinct, I guess." Eyebrow now pointed toward Yuri. "See who it was who organised our rescue, Joe?"

"Christ, this day's full of fucking surprises," said Purple as he extended his hand to Yuri. "Thanks for showing up."

By that point, Mariano and Ventura had also made their way over for a reunion. "Are you OK Jimmy?" asked Ventura, seemingly oblivious to the damage that Eyebrow was carrying.

"Not really Rudy," replied Eyebrow as he motioned his head toward his arm. "I might be in a bit of trouble here."

"Let me look," said Mariano as he peeled back some of the tape and lifted the hastily applied tea towel from the back of Eyebrow's shoulder. "Didn't go through?"

Eyebrow winced in unison with every poke and prod by Mariano. "No, still in there."

"This will need to be seen to. Come with me. We have medical supplies so I can clean and re-dress it properly, for now at least. But we need to take you to a doctor. This entire thing needs to be properly cleaned out and the bullet removed if possible. You'll need medication. You can't let a wound like this fester for too long in a tropical environment."

As Eyebrow and Mariano made their way to the Coronado aid post, Joe Purple pondered Mariano's comment about needing to maintain the wound adequately if spending time in the tropical environment. For Purple, he had no intention of spending any more time in the tropical environment – he was ready to move on to wherever the nearest embassy was.

Whatever forward plan Eyebrow and Mariano might cook up in the aid station, Purple now suspected that he was going to have to be firm and reassert control of their significantly off-the-rails escapade. He knew that there would be trouble the moment they touched down back home, but given the carnage now littered around him, he was willing to accept his fate. This world where he and Eyebrow had found themselves was brimming, one could even argue overflowing, with far too much risk of the life-threatening variety for his liking.

But as much as he wanted to plant his feet firmly on home soil, the landscape there was also rapidly changing. Secretary of State Garrison's treasonous plot to clandestinely fund the Venezuelan coup was threatening to blow up in his face and as he scrambled to salvage the situation, eliminating Jimmy Eyebrow and anyone associated with him had become the operational plan. Notwithstanding their great victory at the Battle of Coronado, Purple and Eyebrow were soon to find that the threat lurking in the shadows was not going to be confined to Venezuela for much longer.

CHAPTER 48

Parting of the Ways

From the moment Jimmy Eyebrow, Joe Purple and the rest of the party of seven had fled Rudy Ventura's rapidly crumbling villa in Caracas, strong bonds of camaraderie, some might even say friendship, had formed among the travelling party. But unless Eyebrow and Purple were considering emigrating to Venezuela, a parting of the ways had always been inevitable, and two events had now hastened that occurrence.

The original plan had been to rest and recuperate in the friendly confines of Coronado for a few days before continuing to Venezuela's second largest city, Maracaibo. But the rapid expansion of the rebel theatre of operation had now placed Coronado firmly on the map, and even though the rebel force had been repulsed, there was no guarantee that they wouldn't be back, and possibly better resourced. As such, the timeline for not only Eyebrow and Purple, but also Ventura, to seek a more stable safe haven had been accelerated, and they would need to depart while the rebels were still in disarray. That window of opportunity was currently pried open, albeit precariously, and no-one knew how long it would remain so.

More pressing though was Eyebrow's status as a battle casualty. The adrenaline flushing his veins was now subsiding to the point where the pain from his wound was beginning to wash over him in increasingly large waves. The risk of carrying an untreated open wound for too long in the jungle was very real and while Eyebrow had been patched and sterilised in the field to the best of Coronado's capability, he still required elevated medical assistance. And if the city of Maracaibo had embassies, it would also have doctors and hospitals. The hope now was that Maracaibo had not fallen to the rebels.

There was a lot to do around the compound to fortify it against any future incursions and through the combined efforts of the residents, as well as the locals who had been rallied by Yuri, rapid progress was already being made in remediating the carnage of that morning. Eyebrow, however, had been placed on bed rest while preparations were underway for the imminent departure of himself, Purple, and Ventura.

Accompanying them on the next leg would be Cisco, who had argued successfully that he had signed on to protect Ventura, and he would fulfil his duty, resting only when Ventura had reached safety. Mariano had chosen to stay at Coronado to assist in overseeing the refurbishment of the defences, while Aunt Sofia had no intention of venturing out onto the road again, preferring to recuperate in her private quarters.

The arrival of Joe Purple in Eyebrow's room signalled that the time to move was approaching. "Fifteen minutes Eyebrow," said Purple as he entered, before slumping into a chair in the corner. "You doin' OK?"

"Hurts Joe, but I'll be OK." Eyebrow began to rise, his arm secured by a sling that was remarkably well constructed given the current medical care limitations.

"You better not go and die on me you prick. We've come too far for you to pull that shit on me."

Eyebrow sat on the side of the bed. "Don't worry Joe, I don't intend to do that. Are we still going to that other city?"

"That's the plan as far as I know. You, me, Ventura and Cisco."

Eyebrow slipped his shoes on and rummaged through his pocket, pulling out his phone. "I hope we can charge this somewhere and get a signal. Spaulding's probably been trying to get in touch with me."

Purple stood and adopted a firmer tone. "Do I need to go over this again Eyebrow? This fucking escapade is finished. For fuck sake tell me that you have some sort of appreciation for the situation we're in. The money's gone. We didn't get the job done. We need to cut our losses and just try to fucking survive. For the love of all things holy, show me that that you have a degree of appreciation for what our priorities are at the moment. I'll give you a hint to get you started Eyebrow – it's not the fucking banking."

"I understand that, Joe. I was just thinking that if somehow…"

Eyebrow was abruptly cut off by Purple. "There's no 'somehow' Eyebrow. It's finished." Purple beckoned for Eyebrow to make his way outside in preparation for departure. "Come on, it's time to fly this fucking coop and get home."

Walking outside, Eyebrow could see that it was a hive of activity in and around Coronado. Ventura spotted him exiting the villa and made his way over. "Jimmy my friend, how are you feeling?"

"Not great Rudy. But I can push through."

"We'll get you to a doctor Jimmy, don't you worry about that."

Eyebrow glanced to his left where he saw Rosita approaching. "Rosita! Are you OK?"

Rosita flashed a broad smile "Hola Jimmy. Yes, I am fine thank you." She leant in and hugged her new friend – a gesture that elicited a surprised wide-eyed stare from Joe Purple. Rosita stepped back, firmly grasping Eyebrow's free hand in her own. "Thank you for everything. Your bravery here today will never be forgotten." Rosita paused and stared directly into Eyebrow's eyes as she delivered her next words. "I would be honoured to fight alongside you any day Jimmy Eyebrow."

"Same here Rosita," replied Eyebrow with a smile. His gaze shifted across Rosita's shoulder to further down the hill where Ana Gutierrez stood, supported by her care nurse. Miss Gutierrez raised a hand to her lips, kissed it and waved to Eyebrow – a simple, but very powerful gesture. Eyebrow waved back, a knot forming in his stomach. He knew that it was likely to be the last time he would see Ana Gutierrez and although their time had been fleeting, for Eyebrow it had still been powerful. He felt privileged to have met such an important person in his benefactor's life.

As tender as the moment standing hand in hand with Rosita was, Eyebrow was abruptly pulled away from the side by none other than Aunt Sofia who had also emerged to bid her hero farewell. "Goodbye Jimmy," she said as she firmly clamped his face between her two leathery hands and planted a kiss squarely on his lips – a kiss that the observing Joe Purple felt may have lingered somewhat longer than necessary.

When Eyebrow was finally released from Aunt Sofia's embrace, his face had turned as red as a beet. "Jesus Christ, are you done here Hugh Hefner?" said Purple as he grabbed Eyebrow's arm and ushered him towards the Land Rover that was now packed and ready for departure.

Eyebrow looked around the compound and saw Mariano and Yuri working side by side near the front gate. "Give me a minute Joe." Eyebrow brushed Purple aside and made his way toward the two men. "Mariano," he said as he approached them. "Thank you for everything. You really saved our skin back at Rudy's place."

Mariano turned. "And you saved ours here Jimmy." He took Eyebrow's hand and gripped it firmly – a handshake of genuine appreciation, and friendship. "I wish you the best of luck on your onward journey. May you find whatever you need at your next destination. Please say goodbye to Joe on my behalf."

Eyebrow turned to Yuri and shook his hand as well. "You're not coming with us Yuri?"

"No, I should help trying to clean up here before I leave to go home."

"What's going to happen to PQ?"

Yuri glanced toward one of the buildings where several armed men milled around outside, presumably where PQ and any other prisoners were being held. "Leave that to me. He'll be taken care of." His words were accompanied by a menacing grin. "We may meet again Jimmy, hopefully under less stressful circumstances next time."

"Drinks will be on me," said Eyebrow as he smiled and bade both men farewell. Walking back to the Land Rover where Purple, Ventura and Cisco were already waiting inside the idling vehicle, Eyebrow hoisted himself up awkwardly and shut the door behind him. With one last wave through the window, the four men slowly made their way through the gate and out onto the road. Yet while the Coronado estate soon disappeared from sight behind Jimmy Eyebrow and Joe Purple, the memory of their short time there would be forever etched in their collective memories – a permanently dog-eared page in their book of life.

They were only minutes into their journey when a first heavy drop of rain fell on the windshield, followed by a second and then a third and fourth in quick succession, after which the next hundred fell in unison as a rainstorm typical of Venezuela suddenly enveloped them. In the space of around twenty seconds, the weather had somehow gone from mildly overcast to torrential downpour. Purple, who was sitting in the back seat, had to raise his voice to account for the pounding of the rain. "How long until we get to this next place?"

"I was going to say probably around two hours or so, but with this weather, maybe three now," replied Ventura. "We have no idea of rebel activity around here, so we'll need to be mindful of our path."

Yet even though Ventura had championed caution, the battle of earlier in the day was indicative of increased activity in that region of Venezuela, and it wasn't long before the inevitability of the next round of contact became reality. Barely thirty minutes into their trek toward Maracaibo, a small convoy of military vehicles rounded the bend ahead of the four travellers and, after several seconds, came to a halt at the same time as Cisco. Neither party moved, both now deadlocked in a stare down on the straight stretch of quiet country road, the rain cascading down between them.

"Who the fuck are they?" asked Purple nervously.

"I don't know," replied Ventura. "I count three vehicles so I'm not sure we have the firepower to fight our way out of this one."

Cisco looked over his shoulder to the road behind. "The rain's made the edges wet Mister Ventura. I don't think I can turn us in time to get out of here. My only escape route would be to drive full speed in reverse."

"I don't think that would be wise Cisco," said Ventura. Silence descended while each group continued to assess the other. Ultimately, the doors to one of the vehicles on the road ahead opened and five men disembarked and began walking toward the stationary Land Rover. "You three stay here," said Ventura as he unbuckled his seat belt. "If they're rebels, then they'll only be after me. Let me deal with this."

"Are you sure sir?" asked Cisco as he reached for his weapon.

"Please, put that away," said Ventura. He turned to Eyebrow and Purple to reinforce his earlier observation. "This is not a fight that we can win with bullets. Stay here, all of you, and let me try to resolve this."

Ventura grabbed his hat, for whatever nominal value that could offer in the downpour outside, opened the door and stepped out. As he slowly made his way toward the advancing strangers, Purple offered a thought that the other two undoubtedly also had on their minds. "I hope he fucking knows what he's doing."

CHAPTER 49

Parlay in the Rain

As it turned out, it appeared that Ventura did in fact have a good read on the developing situation because as the three men peered through the rain from the Land Rover, it was soon evident that the only thing being exchanged was not gunfire, but handshakes. "Looks like they know each other Joe," noted Eyebrow.

"We might actually be in the clear here Eyebrow," replied Purple, breathing yet one more deep sigh of relief to add to the already extraordinarily long line of such sighs in recent times.

The parlay in the rain between Ventura and his counterpart did not last long before Ventura quickly returned to the vehicle and hurriedly sought shelter inside. "What's going on Rudy?" asked Eyebrow.

"I'll explain shortly," replied Ventura before directing Cisco to follow the vehicles ahead of them. "There's a farm around ten minutes away. Follow them and they'll take us to it. We'll talk more once we're there."

They soon pulled off the road to where a small barn sat alongside an equally small farmhouse. The three vehicles that blocked their passage earlier were already parked outside the barn and the uniformed occupants were in various stages of seeking shelter within. Eyebrow and his associates alighted from the Land Rover and joined the gathering inside where one of the men was already well into the process of starting a small fire, while another was beginning to distribute bags of snacks.

Ventura and his entourage approached what appeared to be the senior man among the group. This was the man with whom Ventura had engaged briefly in the middle of the road earlier, and the two of them once again shook hands. Ventura turned to his associates and introduced him. "Cisco, Jimmy and Joe, this is Colonel Bautista from the Venezuelan army."

"Pleased to meet you sir," said Cisco.

Eyebrow turned to Purple and whispered. "Am I supposed to salute him Joe?"

"Absolutely Eyebrow. He'll appreciate it."

Eyebrow promptly snapped his hand to his forehead. "Nice to meet you Colonel."

Bautista gave a sideways look to Purple who was biting his lip, before responding to Eyebrow. "You don't salute me unless you're in the Venezuelan military my friend." Instead of returning Eyebrow's gesture, Bautista extended his hand. "And your name is…"

"Jimmy. And this is my friend Joe," he added, pointing to Purple.

"Joe, welcome," said Bautista as he shook Purple's hand firmly. "It sounds like you two are not from around here. Your tour bus left you behind maybe?"

Purple had lived on the edge for too long on this expedition and had cheated death on far too many occasions for Bautista's remark to go unchecked, even if it was in jest. "We're not fucking tourists pal," he snarled, prompting Ventura to intervene.

"It's OK Joe, I'm sure the Colonel meant nothing by it." Ventura turned to Bautista. "It's been a stressful day for all of us. Let's sit by the fire and discuss the current situation, shall we?"

With the rain relentless outside, the group of men made their way to the fire that was by now well underway – a pot of water destined to be coffee poised near the edge. "The Colonel and his men have come from Maracaibo," said Ventura. "Regrettably, they have some unfortunate news for us."

"What's wrong?" asked Eyebrow.

"I'm afraid that Maracaibo has fallen to the rebels," replied Bautista. "The bridge has been taken and there's no way in from this direction."

"Can we get in any other way?" asked Purple.

"You could divert around the Lake, but under the conditions, that would take days. But even if you did that, whatever you were seeking in Maracaibo will most likely not be there."

"Fuck me," muttered Purple. "Are any of the embassies still open?"

"No," replied Bautista.

"Can you fight your way in?" asked Eyebrow. "You're the army, aren't you?"

Bautista waved his hand around the barn. "This is all that I could salvage from my men. A third of them joined the rebels when the coup began, while many of those who stayed were lost in the fighting. I remain loyal to the government and to Minister Ventura, but I simply do not have the manpower at my disposal to mount a counterattack."

Eyebrow and Purple exchanged worried looks before Purple spoke. "Ahh, can I see you privately for a moment Eyebrow?"

The two men hurried off to a quiet corner of the barn. "What's up Joe?" asked Eyebrow nonchalantly.

"What's up? What's UP??? Jesus Christ Eyebrow, what the fuck is wrong with your brain? There's got to be some sort of fucking traumatic head injury somewhere in your past, it's the only explanation for the way you are. What's up? Did you hear what the man said? We have no fucking way home now. THAT'S what's up."

Eyebrow appeared to still not grasp the magnitude of the situation. "Could we get to another embassy maybe?"

Purple rubbed his eyes in frustration. "No, we can't Eyebrow. We can't go back, and we can't go forward."

"Can we go over the border?" asked Eyebrow, trying his best to offer a logical resolution.

"What, to fucking Colombia? We wouldn't last a fucking day on the backroads there. We're fucked Eyebrow, it's as simple as that. There is no solution… nothing… zero solution Eyebrow. ZERO!"

Ventura, who had wandered over from the fire, now interrupted their conversation. "Gentlemen, we may have found a solution."

Eyebrow smiled at Purple and reassuringly placed his one functioning hand on his shoulder. "See, you worry too much Joe." Purple could do little but grimace in response, annoyed beyond words with what appeared to be Eyebrow's complete lack of awareness about the never-ending cavalcade of life-threatening situations they had managed to escape thanks to one quirk of fate at just the right time. Surely, Purple reasoned, the fact that Eyebrow currently had a bullet embedded in his shoulder should have been a wakeup call about the severity of the situation. But no… here was Eyebrow, yet again, with his trademark "she'll be right" attitude on full display.

The two men accompanied Ventura back to the fire – Eyebrow brimming with enthusiasm, and Purple annoyed. "Colonel Bautista may have a solution for all of us," said Ventura as he ceded the floor to the Colonel.

"When we happened across each other, I was on my way to an airfield, probably about thirty minutes from here. Over the duration of my military career, I have made some… shall we say… strategic investments. And, given the current situation, I feel that now might be the time to depart Venezuela, temporarily of course, to… how can I put it… to check on my portfolio."

"And where might this financial portfolio be located?" asked Purple.

"The Cayman Islands," replied Bautista. "I have offered Minister Ventura a seat on the plane, but he has indicated that he will not join me if you two and his associate are not also afforded safe passage with us. I personally have no concerns about leaving you behind, but I am committed to ensuring the safety of Minister Ventura so given that you seem to be… what is the English term… a package deal, I am also offering the two of you an opportunity to accompany us."

Eyebrow was about to turn to Purple to discuss the proposal, but Purple was already far ahead of the curve. "Yes!" said Purple joyously. "We would most definitely like that opportunity."

"Then it's settled. Take some time to grab a coffee and dry any wet clothes you might have, and we'll be on our way shortly."

Joe Purple was now struck by a sudden thought that he had not considered in his haste to sign on to Bautista's escape plan. "What sort of plane is it? Is it a passenger jet or military plane?"

"No, it's a small private plane," replied Bautista.

Purple closed his eyes and rubbed his temples. "For fuck sake, tell me that you have two pilots."

CHAPTER 50

The Hungry Iguana

Given the particularly unpleasant outcome the last time Jimmy Eyebrow and Joe Purple took to the air in a private plane, it was entirely understandable that they were filled with a distinct reluctance to part with the surface of Venezuela as Colonel Bautista's plane picked up speed down the small dirt runway. But as the ground rapidly receded beneath them, their anxiety was tempered somewhat by a combination of factors, not the least of which was the fact that they were finally making positive progress toward returning home.

Adding to that joyous development were two additional elements. Firstly, unlike Lester's dilapidated Cessna, this plane was slightly more spacious, more modern, and was powered by twin engines. And secondly, much to Purple's satisfaction, the flight crew consisted of two pilots, so at least this time they could afford to have one of them fall out of an open door without the need to call upon the passengers to finish the journey successfully.

Along with Eyebrow and Purple, the plane's passenger manifest included Ventura and Cisco, as well as Colonel Bautista and two of his aides. "How long will the trip take?" asked Eyebrow.

"A bit over three hours," replied Bautista. "In-flight service will start shortly."

Eyebrow nudged Purple. "I could use a coffee, Joe."

"Jesus Christ," replied Purple with a sigh. "He's fucking with you Eyebrow. Just... I don't know... close your eyes and try to rest." Purple leant over Eyebrow and peered out the window, the coastline of Venezuela now receding behind them. "Finally on our way home," he whispered.

Eyebrow did as Purple directed over the course of the next hour, but rest did not come to him easily. "My shoulder Joe, it's fucking hurting," he said dolefully.

"Well, you *do* have a bullet lodged in there Eyebrow. Once we get to where we're going, we'll get you some proper medical help. Just try to push through." Purple turned and leant across the aisle toward where Ventura was sitting. "Do you have any pain killers for Eyebrow? He says that his shoulder's hurting like hell."

Ventura peered over the seat in front of him to where Bautista and his entourage sat. "Do you have painkillers?"

One of Bautista's associates reached for his duffel bag and replied. "I have morphine."

"Fuck me," said Purple. "We don't need to go that big. Do you have, like, an Aspirin or something?"

"On the battlefield, we don't administer Aspirin and a lie down with a hot water bottle," replied the soldier. "We only carry heavy duty pain relief for heavy duty injuries."

"Your friend *has* sustained a battlefield injury," noted Bautista. "If he's in pain, a shot of morphine might be helpful."

Purple paused in thought before turning to Eyebrow. "Is it actually hurting Eyebrow? Like, is it genuinely painful, or just a fucking hurty shoulder?"

"Yeah, it's really hurting Joe. I'm actually in a lot of pain here."

Eyebrow's misery seemed genuine. Purple stood and made his way into the aisle, beckoning the soldier to come to Eyebrow's aid. "He's actually hurt. Go ahead and give him a shot."

The soldier retrieved a morphine syrette from his kit, shuffled over to Eyebrow and with neither a warning nor a request for permission, jabbed his thigh and sent ten milligrams of the drug coursing into his system – a relatively insignificant amount in the greater scheme of things, but enough to temper Eyebrow's pain at least. "That should start taking effect in a few minutes," said the soldier as he slipped the empty syrette into a small bag and returned to his seat.

"You happy now Eyebrow?" said Purple.

"I probably will be soon Joe." Eyebrow closed his eyes in anticipation of the euphoric wave of relief that he hoped would soon wash over him. But the wave that began looming ominously on the horizon was certainly not euphoria, and no more than five minutes after receiving his dose, Eyebrow turned to Purple and whispered, "I don't feel too good Joe."

Barely had the words "what's the problem Eyebrow?" escaped from Purple's mouth, when Eyebrow leant forward and deposited what appeared to be at least a litre of vomit all over Purple's legs. "Holy shit!" screamed Purple as he tried to escape the seat before the next inevitable wave hit him, only partially succeeding in doing so as Eyebrow's encore performance landed firmly in Purple's vacated seat. "Fuck me Eyebrow, do that somewhere else!" bellowed Purple before he sought assistance from Bautista's man. "What the fuck's going on here? Is he allergic or something? It looks like his fucking head's about to spin around."

"Common side effect with morphine," replied the soldier calmly. "He'll be OK. It won't stop the pain relief from working."

"I don't give a fuck about his pain relief," snapped Purple as he pointed to his vomit-soaked pants. "Is this going to keep going? Christ, don't tell me he's going to shit himself too?"

"Unlikely," came the reply that accompanied a third, thankfully less prolific, hurl from Eyebrow. "It's the initial hit that triggers this reaction."

Purple pointed mournfully toward his soaked pants. "Jesus Christ, you could have fucking warned me. Look at this shit. I've got Eyebrow's fucking street chowder all over me. What am I going to do about this?"

"You'll just have to wait until we get to our destination," replied Ventura. "We'll find a change of clothes for you then."

Purple continued his journey of self-pity, gesturing wildly to his former seat that now had a pool of vomit slowly soaking into the fabric. "Fuck me, where am I going to sit? I can't sit there." There was no response from any of the other passengers. "What, I just have to fucking stand for the next two hours?"

"You may have to I'm afraid," replied Ventura. "The time will pass quickly, I'm sure."

"I'm sorry Joe," whispered Eyebrow sombrely. Purple took a deep breath to compose himself, slowly coming to terms with the fact that despite the repugnant inconvenience of the situation, it was hardly Eyebrow's fault.

"It's OK Eyebrow," he eventually said supportively. "Try and get some rest."

Rest did find him this time, and he spent the next two hours in a pain-free, morphine-induced slumber. Purple on the other hand, soaked in vomit, stood in the aisle and despite Ventura's earlier assurances, the remaining journey did *not* pass quickly – far from it in fact. Thankfully the plane eventually began descending and in quick time, they had rolled to a stop at the Cayman Islands airport.

Or at least that's where Joe Purple *thought* they had landed. Instead, as he departed the plane with a still limp Jimmy Eyebrow supported at his side like a drunk exiting a nightclub, Purple looked around what appeared to be a rural landing strip. "Where the fuck are we? I thought the Cayman Islands was some big tourist hub."

"Grand Cayman is, Joe," replied Ventura. "But we've landed at Little Cayman. This is far more discreet and the immigration process is a lot more, shall we say… relaxed." Ventura pointed over Purple's shoulder to where a small police vehicle was now approaching. "Even you, without your passport, must admit that there are some complexities to our situation. Please, let me handle the formalities." Ventura began walking toward the grass verge to greet the imminent arrival.

The police car came to a halt and a short, rotund officer stepped out, his uniform straining under the stress across his midsection. "Ventura?" he asked.

"Yes, that's me. I'm looking for safe passage for myself and my travelling companions."

The officer gazed across the assembled party milling around on the tarmac beside the plane. "I presume your customs affairs have been taken care of?"

Ventura reached into a leather satchel and retrieved a thick envelope that he proceeded to pass to the officer. "Yes, we've all been cleared. I'm sure you'll find all the paperwork you require in there."

The officer weighed the envelope in his hand. "It feels like everything is in order. If there's anything I can be of assistance with, please let me know."

A cough from the vomit-caked Joe Purple summoned Ventura's attention. Ventura looked briefly to Purple before returning to the officer. "You wouldn't have any spare clothes by chance? Or a large hose?"

"I'm not a charity," replied the officer, prompting Ventura to again reach into his satchel and retrieve a handful of cash, after which the officer's demeanour underwent a noticeable change.

"But I may have a couple of spare uniforms in my trunk," he said as he sauntered to the rear of his car. The officer retrieved two plastic sealed Royal Cayman Island Police Service uniforms and tossed them to Purple. "Welcome to the force."

Purple propped Eyebrow up and pressed the fresh clothing into his chest. "I'm not fucking undressing you Eyebrow." He waved his hand across the space between the two of them. "There's a fucking line, and it's right here. There's no way in hell that my hands will be over that line touching you. Sort yourself out."

Purple quickly peeled off his spew-stained shirt and tossed it to the side, even before tearing open the plastic bag that contained the sharp white shirt and stylish dark pants within. Eyebrow did the same, albeit slower – the effects of the earlier morphine hit still having a residual, though now much lesser, effect. As Eyebrow eased out of his pants, to reveal the infamous star-spangled jocks, Purple groaned. "Fuck me, I'd forgotten about them. You've been wearing those since Ventura's place?"

"I haven't had a chance to change Joe," replied Eyebrow.

Eyebrow's jocks had now caught the attention of Colonel Bautista. "What in the name of God are those?"

"They're for swimming," replied Eyebrow. "We were at Rudy's pool when all that shit went down a few days ago." Eyebrow now turned to Purple. "Anyway, you've probably been wearing the same jocks since then too."

"Not me," replied Purple as he stepped out of his pants. "I've been free-ballin' since Armando's gas station. Only way to go in the heat... no crotch rot."

"Jesus Christ!" bellowed Ventura, averting his eyes.

"Ugh, for God's sake," added Bautista as he too looked away from the spectacle before him – Purple buck-naked and Eyebrow sporting his form fitting, and by that point visibly stained, stars and stripes bathing suit.

"I could arrest them if you'd like," said the police officer.

Ventura waved off his offer of assistance, though not before fleetingly considering it as a valid possibility. "It's OK," he said before turning gingerly to Eyebrow. "Just let us know when you're both decent again."

"Is there anywhere we can get something to eat and drink around here?" asked Eyebrow as he slipped into his fresh clothes.

"Just down that path," said the officer, pointing past a shed that appeared to be the airport's terminal building, at least when it was being used for a more legitimate arrival than today's. "There's a café called the Hungry Iguana."

Ventura gestured for Bautista to begin walking with him, before turning over his shoulder to the still re-dressing Eyebrow and Purple. "We'll meet you down there. Try to be respectable when you arrive, please."

"You must be feeling better if you want something to eat," said Purple as the others departed for the cafe.

"I'm not feeling sick Joe. My shoulder's still hurting through."

"We'll be able to find a doctor here I guess," said Purple as he buttoned his shirt. "Let's get some food and take it from there."

Eyebrow had finished re-dressing, and he now rummaged through the pockets of his discarded fatigues. He retrieved his mobile phone and checked it – dead, as expected after so many days. "I wonder if they have a way for me to charge the phone at the café Joe."

"You could ask. Don't know why though. What are you going to do? Order a fucking cab or something?"

"I just want to see if Spaulding's sent me anything."

Purple sighed. "It doesn't matter if he has Eyebrow. We're slowly clawing our way back home and this fucking money chase is finished. It's over Eyebrow, get it through your frustratingly thick head."

The two men began the short walk to *The Hungry Iguana* where they found the bulk of their travelling companions already seated. Ventura directed them to the counter area. "No table service here. Order up there."

After ordering coffee and a serving of coconut shrimp, Eyebrow enquired as to whether there was any capacity to tend to his phone. "Sure, there's an outlet over there," said the man behind the counter.

"I don't suppose you have a cord that I could use?" asked Eyebrow. "I lost mine a few days ago."

The man fumbled under the counter for a moment before producing a charging cable. "Here you go. Just remember to return it when you're done."

"Thanks pal," said Eyebrow as he collected the phone and charger and made his way to the power outlet. "Do you have Wi-Fi here?"

The man flipped a small a-frame sign around to face Eyebrow and tapped it to identify the café's Wi-Fi network, along with the words "no password". As the phone began charging, Eyebrow waited a few moments as the screen eventually came to life before he connected to the Wi-Fi and then left the phone to replenish its battery while he retired outside to join his associates.

Keen to edge ever closer to home, Joe Purple was already discussing logistics with Ventura. "So, when are we moving out?"

"Colonel Bautista and I will be staying here for the foreseeable future," replied Ventura. "We'll work out something for the two of you, I promise."

Bautista retrieved a map from his pocket and unfolded it on the table, his finger coming to rest on the Cayman Islands. "We are here," he said, before tracing his finger east. "If we can arrange for you to go to Cuba, there's a United States Naval base where you could be taken to."

Purple paused in thought for a moment before the realization dawned on him. "Uhhh… are you talking about fucking Guantanamo Bay? Because if you are, then forget about it. Jesus Christ, are you suggesting we just roll into Guantanamo Bay unannounced, without passports or anything? Fuck me, what could possibly go wrong there? Surely there must be another option."

Bautista, now traced his finger in the opposite direction. "If we go west, you end up in Mexico." He perused the map for a few moments before settling his finger at a specific location. "Cancun… maybe Cancun is an option."

Purple threw his hands in the air excitedly. "Cancun! That's the place. There would have to be a way home from there. Plus, there must be an embassy or something nearby. And the bonus is that we can hit the beach with a fucking Pina Colada before we go home!" Purple turned to Eyebrow. "What do you say Eyebrow? Cancun sound good to you?"

"Happy to go with whatever you think Joe," replied Eyebrow.

Purple turned back to Bautista and Ventura. "Cancun it is. How do we make it happen?"

"I'll see what I can arrange," said Ventura, looking at his watch. "It won't be today, but we'll get you out of here one way or another."

"I can spend the night here," said Purple, waving his hand across the turquoise water lapping at the sand in front of *The Hungry Iguana*. "No coup, no fucking rebels trying to kill us… I can most certainly handle this."

But back inside the café, Eyebrow's unattended phone had begun to rise from its slumber. First one notification, followed soon by another, after which a Beethovian symphony of message and missed call notifications rang out, prompting the café manager to open the door and summon Eyebrow.

"Sir, I think you need to come and check your phone. It sounds like someone's really been trying to reach you about something."

CHAPTER 51

Coming Up Empty

Twenty-six messages and ten missed calls – all from Spaulding. That's what confronted Jimmy Eyebrow as he examined his resurrected mobile phone. "Something's going on Joe," he noted – a point that hardly needed emphasizing given the prodigious amount of incoming traffic.

"What is it Eyebrow?" asked Purple.

Eyebrow began scrolling through the messages. "It's about the money, but I'm not sure what he means."

"Leave it alone Eyebrow," snapped Purple. He held his thumb and forefinger aloft, separated by less than an inch. "We are THIS fucking close to getting home. I am not going off on another fucking wild goose chase for this mythical pot of gold."

"I'll call him Joe and find out what he wants."

"Please don't," replied Purple mournfully. "I just want to go home Eyebrow."

"I just need to find out what he wants, that's all," said Eyebrow as he put the phone up to his ear.

The call didn't even reach its third ring before it was picked up by Spaulding. "St. Claire! Where have you been? I've been worried sick."

"We got a bit sidetracked," replied Eyebrow. "Ended up in Venezuela and got caught up in a bit of trouble there."

"I see," muttered Spaulding before continuing. "Where are you now?"

"Cayman Islands."

"Are you just?" replied Spaulding, his voice suddenly exuding a little more pep. "Well, that is indeed a highly fortuitous situation St. Claire."

"Why's that?"

"Well, as it turns out, my people were able to get into the crypto account that you were looking into."

A broad smile of anticipation broke across Eyebrow's face. "And? Is the money there?"

"I'm afraid the account is currently empty. However, in examining the transactions – very large transactions might I add – there appears to be a strong connection to one particular bank account. What would be of significant interest is if I was able to identify the owner of that account. Now, and here's the exciting part, do you care to guess where that bank account might be domiciled, St. Claire?"

Eyebrow covered the speaker with his hand and whispered to Joe Purple. "What does *domiciled* mean Joe?"

"Where something lives," replied Purple.

Eyebrow returned to Spaulding's question. "No idea."

"Go on, take a guess," pressed Spaulding. "Just think for a moment."

"I don't know… Africa?"

Spaulding's frustration was evident, even from thousands of miles away. "What? Why the hell would you think of Africa? The Cayman Islands, St. Claire… the Cayman Islands."

"Where I am right now?"

"Oh, for God's sake. Yes! Where you are right now. You're not very sharp today, St. Claire. Is everything OK?"

Eyebrow winced as he tried to wriggle his shoulder. "I've had a bit of an incident, but I'll be OK."

"Well, if you can push through, I have a task for you. I'm going to send you the bank account details and what I'd really like you to try and do is identify who the account holder is for that account. Do you think you can manage that?"

"Sure, I'll do my best," replied Eyebrow, notwithstanding the fact that he had no clue whatsoever as to how he might accomplish that assignment.

"I'll send you the details now. And please St. Claire, keep me updated. You had me worried for a while there."

"I promise I will. I might not have any signal sometimes, but I'll make sure that I keep checking in with you."

"Let me know how you go with that account," said Spaulding as he signed off. "I'll speak with you again soon I hope."

Eyebrow ended the call and turned to Purple. "Before you say anything Joe, it's not anything dangerous."

"Fuck me, I've heard that before," replied Purple snidely. "What's going on this time Eyebrow? Do we have to steal nuclear launch codes from a fucking submarine? Storm the gold depository maybe?"

A notification rang out from Eyebrow's phone. "Nope." He turned the message around for Purple to see. "We just need to find out who owns this bank account. It's right here in the Cayman Islands."

"What about the crypto account? What's happening there?"

"Spaulding got into it, but it's empty. He thinks that this bank account is tied to the money somehow and he wants us to try and find out who it belongs to."

"And how do you suggest we do that? You don't just walk into a bank, drop the account number on the counter and ask who it belongs to. There's a thing called privacy Eyebrow, especially in the Cayman Islands. It's like fucking Switzerland here."

"Can you think of anything Joe?"

"What, you're outsourcing your jobs to me now? That's not how it works pal... *I* outsource to *you*." Notwithstanding the fact he was not Eyebrow's contractor, Purple nonetheless drifted into thought, tempted by the challenge. At least a minute of silence ensued before he reached for Eyebrow's phone. "Give me that thing." He initially got Eyebrow to open Spaulding's message and then opened a web browser, searching for the *First National Bank of the Caymans*. Locating the bank's phone number, he dialled and put the phone to his ear.

"What are you doing Joe?" asked Eyebrow, to which Purple simply raised his finger to request that Eyebrow give him space and silence.

"Yes, hello," said Purple as the call was picked up on the other end. "I have an account with you. May I give you the account number?"

"Of course sir," came the customer service clerk's voice from the other end.

Purple proceeded to reel off the account number. "857... 000... 529...774... 01."

"Was that triple zero sir?"

"Yes, triple zero. 857, triple zero."

"OK, thank you sir. Just one moment. And who may I be speaking with?"

Purple grimaced and mouthed a silent *fuck* – he was hoping not to have gone down this path. "What's the name you have there?" he asked, in hope now more than anything.

"I'm sorry sir, I do need to identify you before we go any further," replied the clerk.

Sensing the dead-end looming in front of him, Purple pivoted in the hope that he could salvage at least one morsel of intelligence from his deception. "You know what, I've just had a client come into the office, so if you could arrange for someone to give me a call back, that would be terrific."

"Certainly sir. What's the best number to get you on?"

Purple gritted his teeth. "Uhhh… what's the number you have on file for me? Just so… you know… I can confirm that it's correct."

"Again, I'm very sorry sir, but I can't give out that information. If you could just leave me your best contact num…"

Purple terminated the call and turned to Eyebrow, defeated. "They were fucking onto me Eyebrow. I don't know how you'll get any information out of them."

"Maybe I could go in there and try. I might have more luck in person than on the phone."

"Jesus Christ Eyebrow," muttered Purple, rubbing his eyes. "If I couldn't get anything out of them on the phone, how the fuck do you think they'll give you any information when you just rock up without a shred of ID and no corroborating information about the account whatsoever."

"It couldn't hurt to try Joe. I couldn't do worse than you."

"I beg to differ," countered Purple. "What if they call security on you? At least all I had to do was hang up the phone."

"I'll take that risk Joe."

Purple stared back, wide-eyed. "Oh, you will, will you? Well, here's a little newsflash – I'm not fucking coming with you. I'm not getting involved. If you do that, then it will be all on you."

"I need to ask Rudy how to get to the main island," said Eyebrow as he began to make his way to where Ventura was sitting outside.

As they approached, Ventura turned and beckoned them closer. "I've arranged transport to Cancun for you. You'll leave by boat tomorrow afternoon, so you have until that time to enjoy this beautiful place."

"About that Rudy. How do I get to Grand Cayman? I need to do something there."

"Grand Cayman?" replied Ventura with a quizzical look. "What business do you have there?"

"Personal. Can you get me there?"

Ventura looked at his watch. "Certainly, but it's unlikely to be today."

"That's OK," said Eyebrow. "Could I get there tomorrow morning?"

"We could organize that, I'm sure. For the two of you?"

Joe Purple threw his hands up defensively. "Nope, not me. I'm happy right here, thank you very much. This is all him."

"Very well then," said Ventura. "Remember that your boat to Cancun will be leaving here in the afternoon, so you'll need to make it a quick visit."

"I'll be quick, don't worry," replied Eyebrow. "In and out."

Joe Purple's earlier observation about bank confidentiality was accurate, and under normal circumstances, Eyebrow's plan to deceitfully acquire the information he and Spaulding sought would have little chance of even leaving the starting gate. But Eyebrow's universe rarely conformed to what most people would class as normal and tomorrow, even though he had no inkling at that point, a man named Hendrik Visser was going to have a very bad day. And if the stars aligned, Visser's misfortune might just be the back door into the system that Eyebrow needed.

CHAPTER 52
The Misfortune of Hendrik Visser

Twenty years. That is the length of service where an employee of *The First National Bank of the Caymans* would ultimately unlock some quite generous long-service benefits. Nineteen years and eight months. That was the present length of Hendrik Visser's tenure.

Two decades earlier Visser had uprooted his life in his native Holland and relocated to the Cayman Islands in order to pursue a career with the *First National Bank*, and for the entirety of his employment, he was a loyal and dedicated worker. Many workplaces have a cavalcade of unsavoury individuals including, but not limited to, the closet racist, the person who insists on microwaving fish in the lunchroom, and the most despicable of all – the dreaded phantom shitter. *The First National Bank*, like so many other organisations, was not immune to this, however Hendrik Visser was none of these characters and was in fact described in all of his annual performance reviews as a model employee.

Never transgressing the rules of his employment and rarely taking leave, the summoning of Visser to the Human Resources office on that day did not set off any alarm bells. Indeed, Visser presumed that the meeting would be related to preparations for his looming long-service milestone. But it was not to be. With his accumulated leave entitlements taken into account, Visser was officially being let go with a final length of tenure clocking in at nineteen years, ten months and twenty-eight days – a whisker short of the benefits that would have flowed his way on the twentieth anniversary of his appointment.

Visser was, understandably, devastated at the news, especially given that the bank was not at that time undertaking any downsizing or "repositioning" activities, nor had Visser fallen foul of any of his employment conditions – a point confirmed by the Human Resources Manager at the time. The only reason given was that the bank felt it was "time for a change" and they even grubbily attempted to spin the news as a positive for their distressed employee by arguing that their motivation was to propel Visser along to the next exciting adventure in his banking career.

But Visser knew what their motivation was, and it had not a single altruistic thread running through it. This was purely about voiding the benefits and associated financial impacts that were on the radar – nothing more, nothing less. Walking out of the office and back to the banking chamber with his crumpled two weeks' notice letter clutched in his trembling hand, Visser felt as if his soul and body had separated. *The First National Bank* had been his life and now it had been cruelly taken from him by a pompous, gold tie-wearing ponce who was at least ten years his junior, along with his power-suited female associate whose hair was pulled back so tight that her face looked like a tri-slot moneybox.

It was at precisely this moment, as he stumbled forlornly back to his post, that he crossed paths with a customer who had approached him for assistance – Jimmy Eyebrow. A minute less, or a minute longer in the meeting, a diversion to the restroom or even a left turn instead of a right, and the crossing of paths would not happen – the two men would pass by like the proverbial ships in the night. But cross they did, and for Eyebrow it was a most fortuitous meeting.

"Excuse me," said Eyebrow as he approached Visser. "Could you help me with an enquiry about an account?"

Visser assessed Eyebrow, inhaled and reset himself. "Certainly sir, please come this way." Ushering Eyebrow toward a small office, Visser probed as to the nature of Eyebrow's enquiry. "What exactly is it that I can help you with?"

Eyebrow retrieved a slip of paper from his pocket and passed it to Visser. With no subtlety whatsoever, he cut straight to the point. "Could you tell me who owns this account?"

If Eyebrow had asked that same question on any one of the previous nearly five thousand days when Visser had been working at *The First National Bank*, the answer would unquestioningly have been in the negative, with the maintenance of customer confidentiality utmost in the fiercely diligent Visser's mind.

But today was different – what loyalty did he owe them after what they'd just done to him? He'd been tossed to the kerb with the same indifference that a smoker flicks a cigarette butt out the car window. While in some parts of the world, the events of that morning would have resulted in the terminated employee attending work the next day dressed in a black overcoat and carrying a large duffel bag, Visser's response to his betrayal would be more nuanced. He teetered on the moral edge for a moment before reaching for the paper in Eyebrow's hand. "Let me have a look for you sir."

And so it was that a short time later, Jimmy Eyebrow set foot back on Little Cayman and sauntered triumphantly toward Joe Purple, proudly brandishing a piece of notebook paper above his head like Neville Chamberlain stepping off the plane from Munich. "I got it Joe," he said with a broad smile.

Purple rubbed his eyes vigorously in disbelief, the confusion clearly evident in his voice. "How the fuck did you manage that Eyebrow?"

"I just walked in and asked."

"No you didn't," snapped Purple. "It doesn't work that way. You must have done some sort of fucking perverted favour for the guy, or was it an eighty-year-old woman? Because beyond that, you don't just walk into a Cayman Islands bank, slap an account number down on the table and expect them to just give you a complete info dump of everything you want to know."

"Well… that's exactly what happened Joe. Except for the perverted shit. I didn't have to do that. The guy just gave me the name of the customer."

"Fuck me. How you manage to pull off shit like that is one of life's biggest mysteries," said Purple as he held out his hand asking for the paper. He perused the details that Eyebrow provided. "The JP Mears Foundation. Based in Cocoa Beach, Florida. Ever heard of 'em?"

"No idea Joe," replied Eyebrow. "Does the name mean anything to you?"

"Not a fucking clue. So what now Eyebrow? Do you give this to Spaulding?"

"I guess so. He'll just do whatever it is that he does." Eyebrow quickly typed the details into his phone and dutifully forwarded them to Spaulding – his assigned task successfully completed.

"Can I confirm Eyebrow, that we're now no longer chasing this mysterious pot of money? Have you done what you set out to do?"

"Not much more we can do Joe. The crypto account was empty and whatever Spaulding's looking into, it probably doesn't involve us. I'll have to let Mister Santiago know."

Purple continued pressing for a commitment from Eyebrow. "And then after that, we're just focussed on getting home, right? No more side missions, no more wild goose chases?"

"Absolutely Joe. I want to go home. I just need to sit down for a bit before I do anything else… I don't feel that good."

"What's wrong?" asked Purple.

"I just feel sick. Not like I'm going to throw up. But just sick all over. Like something's not right."

Purple moved next to Eyebrow and placed a hand on his injured shoulder. "What's going on here? Is this sore?"

"Yeah. It's just constant now."

"Let me have a look," said Purple as he eased Eyebrow's shirt away and pried open the bandage. "Ugh, fuck me!" he exclaimed as he peeled back the dressing. "This looks fucking disgusting. I'm surprised there isn't a bunch of maggots in there." Purple called out and beckoned for Bautista's associate to assess Eyebrow's wound.

Perusing it with a critical eye, the diagnosis was succinct. "This is infected. I can do a surface cleanse and put a fresh dressing on, but your friend needs a doctor."

"Is there one here?" asked Purple.

"Not that I know of," said Ventura, who had also wandered over to assess Eyebrow's situation. Ventura looked at his watch. "Your boat to Cancun leaves in an hour. We can get you back to Grand Cayman, but you'll miss your ride. Or you can push on and see the doctor at your next destination." Ventura turned to Bautista's man who was cleansing Eyebrow's wound. "Does he have another twenty-four hours in him?"

"Easily."

Joe Purple now re-entered the conversation. "Twenty-four hours? How fucking long is this boat ride?"

"Nearly a full day," replied Ventura. "Mexico isn't just a quick hop across the lake."

"Fuck me," muttered Purple. "What do you think Eyebrow? We're almost there. Are you good to go?"

"I should be OK Joe," replied Eyebrow before he stood and turned his eyes to Ventura. "Let's go. Let's get to this boat and get out of here."

Thankfully Little Cayman Dock, where their boat was departing from, was less than a ten minute drive from their current location and after a brief farewell with Bautista, Eyebrow and Purple, accompanied by Ventura and Cisco, were soon edging into the small dirt parking lot at the dock. It had only been a handful of days since the opening shots of the Venezuelan coup rang out, but these four men who had been unexpectedly thrown together in their quest for survival had developed a bond that is forged only under the direst of circumstances.

Yet as the group exchanged their farewells, Ventura chose a sporting metaphor to underscore their new friendship. "There is an old saying among football players, that you will always wave to someone who you played on a team with, but you will cross the road to talk to someone you shared a championship with. Jimmy Eyebrow and Joe Purple – I consider myself privileged to have met both of you, and I hope that one day in the future, we may cross the road to talk once more."

"It's been a pleasure Rudy," replied Eyebrow, extending his hand. "We wouldn't have lasted long without your help."

"I agree," added Purple as he shook first Ventura's, and then Cisco's hand firmly. "Without you, we'd probably be fertilizing some fucking coca plantation in Colombia by now."

"I'm glad that I could be of assistance," said Ventura as he began ushering Eyebrow and Purple down the path toward the dock where a sleek, jet-black cigarette boat was awaiting. Emblazoned on the side was the boat's name – *The Penetrator.*

"Holy shit!" exclaimed a startled Joe Purple. "Is this our ride?"

"Certainly is," replied Ventura. "You'll be eating dinner in Cancun tomorrow night."

Purple assessed the boat's name, a smirk breaking out on his face. "Jesus Christ, a long black boat named The Penetrator? Some serious over-compensation going on there Rudy."

"I'm not sure I see your point Señor Purple," replied Ventura.

"The *Penetrator,*" reiterated Purple as he looked around his associates. "You're not seeing it?"

"It's very good at discreetly slipping into places where maybe it shouldn't," replied Ventura. "I think the name is very appropriate. I don't understand what's amusing you."

Purple rubbed his eyes. "Forget it," he said dismissively before turning to Eyebrow. "I'd be willing to bet a buck that you own a movie with the same title."

Eyebrow ignored Purple's comment and instead turned to Ventura. "Looks fast Rudy."

"You will certainly be travelling fast," said Ventura. "But it will still take the better part of a day for your full journey." Ventura beckoned for the boat's driver to join them. He was tall, with rugged looks, a shock of black hair and a large moustache. "Gentlemen, this is Rene – he'll be taking you to Cancun." Rene nodded in the direction of Eyebrow and Purple but was otherwise indifferent. "You have some water and food for our guests?" asked Ventura.

"Yes sir," replied Rene.

"Very well," said Ventura, extending his hand one more time. "It is here where we part ways. I wish you all the best on your journey home and trust that you will get there safely."

"Thank you Rudy," replied Eyebrow. "We'll certainly try our best." And with a final wave, Eyebrow and Purple climbed aboard *The Penetrator* with Rene and began edging away from the dock. It had been less than a week since they arrived in Venezuela, yet it felt like half a lifetime, such was the unrelenting chaos that had engulfed them of late. But now, finally, they were starting to make their way home and, most importantly, the danger was receding behind them.

CHAPTER 53

Cocaine Slumber

As *The Penetrator* left Little Cayman Island in its wake, Eyebrow and Purple were standing aloft, gazing over the vast vista of the Gulf of Mexico opening up before them, the cool ocean wind lapping at their faces. Rene turned to Eyebrow and pointed to his hairpiece. "You might want to hold onto that my friend. I'm about to open it up."

Seconds later, Rene pushed the throttle to its full capacity, the boat feeling like it was about to leap out of the water. The acceleration was instantaneous – *The Penetrator's* ocean racing capability now on full display. As instructed, Eyebrow clamped his hand firmly atop his head but even that was proving to be a potentially fruitless endeavour. "Fuck me Joe, this thing's fast!" he yelled above the roar of the boat skimming along the surface, bouncing as it encountered even the slightest swell.

"Holy shit!" replied Purple, who by the look on his face appeared to be having the time of his life. "This is fucking incredible!"

"I've gotta go below deck Joe!" yelled Eyebrow as he clutched at his hairpiece.

"What?" replied Purple as Eyebrow's words were lost to the wind.

Eyebrow pointed to himself and then the door leading to the interior of the boat, to which Purple gave a thumbs-up in acknowledgement. Eyebrow stepped down from the perch, opened the small door and stepped inside, the relief from the wind immediate as he closed the door behind him.

Looking around inside, Eyebrow stopped in his tracks before returning topside and sidling up to Purple where he leant close to his ear. "Joe, you need to come downstairs with me."

"Is it too scary for you to be alone?" replied Purple.

"I'm serious Joe, you need to come with me right now."

"Fuck me Eyebrow, what is it?" Purple was clearly frustrated. All he wanted was a few moments of peace to enjoy the freedom that came with skimming across the open ocean with the fresh nautical air cleansing his airways. But instead, Eyebrow couldn't even go a full minute without demanding his attention. But as Eyebrow opened the door and ushered Purple into the space below deck, he could see why he'd been summoned. "Holy fucking shit!" he exclaimed as he turned to Eyebrow wide-eyed. "Is that what I think it is?"

"I think it probably is Joe. I didn't check."

Purple shuffled over to where a pile of plastic-wrapped blocks sat and did a quick count across and up. Using the math skills that his high-school teacher always assured him he'd need as an adult, he calculated the volume of the pile. "Jesus Christ Eyebrow, if each of those is a key, then there's over a quarter of a fucking ton of cocaine here!" Purple paused in thought before the realization dawned on him. "Ahh, for Christ sake Eyebrow, we're on a fucking drug run!"

"Should we do something Joe?" asked Eyebrow.

"What the fuck would you suggest? We're in the middle of the goddamn ocean. There's nothing we can do except go along for the ride. Fuck me… what have we gotten ourselves into?"

"He's still taking us to Cancun though, right?" asked Eyebrow.

"How the fuck would I know Eyebrow? I've got no fucking idea what his plan is." Purple paced, at least as much as he was able in the confined space. "Fuck it, I'll just go ask him."

Purple flung the door open and stepped up to where Rene was sitting. "Rene, I need to ask a question." Rene looked at Purple and offered the slightest nod in return, which Purple took as an encouragement to continue. "I've gotta ask… what's the deal with the manifest?" Purple now braced himself. Would Rene's response be reasonable, or would Purple find himself bobbing in the Gulf of Mexico with the boat rapidly disappearing from view sometime in the following five seconds?

Thankfully, Rene seemed ambivalent, as if hauling a pile of cocaine worth around ten million dollars was all in a day's work, which in retrospect, it probably was. "We have one stop to make," said Rene calmly. "Maybe fifteen or twenty minutes and then we'll be on our way again."

"Can you drop us off first?" asked Purple.

"Sorry sir, no can do. Don't worry, you won't have to do anything. I'll be in and out before you know it."

Purple muttered something unintelligible to himself and stayed by Rene's side in silence for a few more minutes. He had done some quick mental calculations earlier and couldn't work out why at their speed, Ventura had said it would still take the better part of a day to get to their destination. With the previously unmentioned stop now factored into the itinerary, at a location that remained unknown to Purple, it now made more sense. Purple eventually retreated back below deck where he found that Eyebrow had done some interior redesign. "What the fuck is this Eyebrow?" he yelled. "What have you done?"

"I need to lie down Joe. I don't feel that good. I'm not great on the water."

Purple sighed heavily at the sight before him. "Jesus Christ Eyebrow. That's all well and good, but you've rearranged everything and built a fucking bed? Seriously? What if he can't fucking count his stash accurately now? He might think we've stolen some. He probably had that laid out like he did for a fucking reason."

"It's all here Joe. It's just moved around a bit."

Purple sat at the end of Eyebrow's makeshift bed and rubbed his face. "Wherever he's going Eyebrow, we're going along with him by the look of it. So we may as well settle in." Purple assessed the inside of the cabin, noting that there wasn't much free space. He slid over toward one of the seats and lifted the cushion – it was attached by nothing more than Velcro. He began removing cushions and tossing them to Eyebrow. "Here, grab these Eyebrow. Those blocks of cocaine are packed so fucking tight that they're like goddamn bricks. Lay these out to make it all a bit softer."

Eyebrow did as he was directed and in no time had laid down what looked like a marginally comfortable and serviceable, even if haphazardly constructed, mattress. Eyebrow patted the cushions. "Feels good Joe."

"Good, move over then," said Purple as he slid in alongside Eyebrow. "I had to stand up on that fucking plane, and I'm not doing the same here. If you're lyin' down, then so am I."

The journey was far from comfortable though as the roar from nearly two thousand horsepower of thrust as well as the abrupt bouncing of the hull conspired to create a less than serene cruising experience. Purple and Eyebrow rested as best they could atop their cocaine bed for nearly five hours before the sound of the throttle being eased back signaled that they may have been nearing a point of interest. Sure enough, within a minute, the throttle was wound back completely, and the boat came to a halt, the roar of the engine now little more than a dull idle and the crunch of high-speed travel replaced instead by a gentle, almost comforting, rocking.

Purple rose from the bed and made his away above deck to assess the current situation. It was still light, but his watch indicated that it was by now early evening. He could see that they were becalmed and while distances across water are notoriously difficult to estimate, he reckoned that they were maybe a kilometre, possibly two, offshore. His first observation was that this was definitely not Cancun, but as to where they were, he had no clue. "Is that Mexico?" he asked, in the hope that at least they had gone in the direction they wanted to go.

"Yes, that's Mexico," replied Rene.

Thank fuck for that, thought Purple to himself. "What now?"

"Now, we wait," replied Rene dryly.

"How long?"

"Until four am. That's when the exchange will happen. If you want to sleep, now is the time. We'll be here until then."

Purple slipped back below deck to relay the information to Eyebrow. "This is where he's going to offload this shit Eyebrow." Purple looked at his watch. "We've got until about four in the morning to wait, so try to rest. We'll start stacking this fucking bed back up around three."

Purple's original intention was that he too would try to rest, but try as he did, the circumstances of the situation did not allow it. Eyebrow, however, had been snoring prodigiously for several hours when Purple finally forewent any further efforts on his own part and instead, stepped atop once more where Rene had been engaged in a supreme feat of endurance by remaining at his post from the moment they left the dock at Little Cayman.

Purple looked at his watch – a tick past one am. "What's the deal?" he asked Rene. "Will they be coming out here?"

"No," replied Rene. "I'll get a signal from the shore to come into the dock. The cargo will be unloaded, and we'll be on our way."

Purple rubbed his arms. The cold night air was in stark contrast to the daytime weather and his cotton short-sleeved shirt provided little to no respite from the chill. Perceptive to his associate's plight, Rene tossed him a jacket that he'd retrieved from behind his seat. "Here, put this on."

Purple accepted the offer gratefully and settled in with Rene to await the next phase of the operation. He remained hopeful that it would be seamless and they could soon be back on their journey. As the two men sat there in silence for the next couple of hours, Rene identified a signal emanating from the shore a little before three am – an indication that the exchange might be occurring ahead of schedule, much to Purple's delight.

"Is that it?" he asked Rene.

Rene slowly throttled up the boat and began edging closer to the shore. "Looks like it."

"I'll go down and wake Eyebrow," said Purple.

Rene didn't take his eyes off his destination as they crept closer at low speed. "You two stay down there when we get to the dock," he said firmly.

"Absolutely," replied Purple as he disappeared through the door. On this, he had no intention of getting involved. Walking over to Eyebrow, he slapped him on the cheek. "Time to get up, let's go." Eyebrow didn't respond initially, prompting Purple to repeat the process. "Come on Eyebrow, it's time." Eyebrow showed signs of rising from his slumber, but it wasn't fast enough for Purple who now pressed his thumb into Eyebrow's wounded shoulder. "I said, get the fuck up Eyebrow!"

This elicited a much more vocal response from Eyebrow. "OW! Fuck me Joe, why did you do that? That fucking hurt."

"I'd already tried waking you twice Eyebrow, We don't have time to fuck around. This shit's going down soon. Get up."

"Is it four already?" asked Eyebrow.

"Three. We're an hour ahead of schedule, which I'm fucking pumped about. Means we'll get to Cancun earlier." Purple started pulling the cushions off Eyebrow's bed. "We need to fix this pronto."

As the two men attended to the refurbishment of Rene's shipment, the boat slowly edged its way toward the dock where, after a few minutes, Eyebrow and Purple could feel that they were coming to a halt and sidling up next to the jetty. The door swung open slightly and Rene poked his head in. "Stay here," was his succinct instruction, to which both Eyebrow and Purple were more than happy to comply.

They felt the boat bump up against the dock and the throttle wind all the way back to the idle position. Even though they couldn't see it, they sensed Rene alighting to the jetty and the sound of muffled voices suggested that he was in discussions with someone. Without warning, two shots rang out, followed by an uptick in activity not far from the boat. "What the fuck was that, Joe?" asked Eyebrow nervously.

"Fuck me, I have a reasonable idea," replied Purple forebodingly. "I'll have a look, wait here." He quietly eased the door open and crept aloft in an effort to observe what was happening outside, steeling himself for what he suspected was at play. Sure enough, as he gingerly peered toward the dock, he saw what he feared he was going to – Rene lying prostrate in a pool of blood.

Scurrying back below deck, he summoned Eyebrow. "It's a fucking setup Eyebrow. They've shot Rene."

Eyebrow became frantic. "Fuck! What do we do Joe?"

"They probably don't know that we're down here. They would have expected that Rene came alone."

"We're fucked if they find us Joe. What's the plan?"

Purple flicked his fingers. "I'm thinking Eyebrow… I'm thinking. Just shut up and fucking let me work it out. This is fucking bad." Purple paced as his thoughts ticked over, knowing that time had never been more of the essence. If he was going to come up with a plan, it had better be quick. "Fuck this," he said as he moved toward the door. "Hold on Eyebrow."

Purple again crept through the door onto the deck where Rene recently stood. He assessed the dock again, noting three men standing there, and several more now alighting from a vehicle a little further away. They would soon be boarding the boat to steal Rene's shipment and the moment they discovered two unexpected associates secreted inside, Eyebrow and Purple would be able to measure their life expectancy in seconds. If Purple didn't do something now, the opportunity would be lost.

The boat's engine was still running, albeit in the idle state and Purple slid along the floor to the main controls. Reaching up, he pushed the throttle forward and felt the boat surge ahead momentarily before snapping to a halt only moments later. "Jesus fucking Christ," he muttered to himself as he realized that the boat was still tethered to the dock. He'd lost the element of surprise as the thugs on the dock raced toward him, now aware that the boat, still laden with the cocaine they'd planned on stealing, was undertaking an unexpected emergency departure.

Purple reached over the side of the boat and fumbled with the rope, thankfully freeing it in quick time as bullets began whizzing past him. With the rope free, he pushed the throttle as far forward as he could and *The Penetrator* leapt from the water and roared away from the dock, the sound of gunfire heavy in the air behind him. He kept his head down and barely peered across the bow, unable to see where he was going and operating on blind faith that he was heading toward open water instead of a cliff face.

Given *The Penetrator's* match-grade speed, it was less than a minute before they had cleared the initial danger and as Purple eased the throttle back, he summoned Eyebrow upstairs. "Are we safe Joe?" asked Eyebrow.

"For now," replied Purple as he began to examine the boat's controls. It came as a huge relief to find that the boat was equipped with a state-of-the-art GPS that identified precisely where they were – a life-saving development for them as they bobbed on the ocean in the pitch dark. Purple played with the controls before turning to Eyebrow excitedly. "Look at this shit! This is the same as a car GPS, except it's made for boats. Look, I just pump in my destination, and it'll draw it on the map for me." Purple typed in "Cancun" and the map quickly returned a red coloured path for him to follow. "Fucking bingo!" he exclaimed.

"So you can get us there Joe?" asked Eyebrow.

"Looks like it Eyebrow. We're carrying quarter of a ton of A-grade blow, and it looks like we might technically be South American drug smugglers, but fuck it… we're goin' to Cancun baby!"

CHAPTER 54
Ping

The Jimmy Eyebrow taskforce in Washington had been convened earlier that morning – early enough in fact to warrant a catered breakfast spread across the conference table, courtesy of the State Department. As Leo Bishop bit into his second egg and bacon roll of the morning, he passed an observation to Dennis Burnett. "You see, *this* is how breakfast should be done when we're on the job Dennis."

"Very easy to do when you have an unlimited line of credit Leo," replied Burnett who was busy assembling a fruit bowl. "I need to scratch around for every dollar like a fucking chicken loitering under the kitchen window."

One member of the taskforce who was not there at that moment was Intelligence Director Van Pelt and as Bishop transitioned from breakfast roll to coffee, Van Pelt strode in to convene the morning's activities. Unexpectedly, Van Pelt was accompanied by Secretary of State Garrison, resulting in everyone quickly leaping to their feet as he entered the room.

Garrison waved them off. "Please gentlemen, as you were. It's early, enjoy your breakfast while we talk." Garrison joined them, pouring himself a cup of coffee before taking his seat and tossing a copy of *The Washington Post* onto the table. On the front page was Charles de Klerk's perfectly composed photograph of Jimmy Eyebrow – his oiled body and American flag jocks on show for the entire world to see. Accompanying the photo was the headline *LA TORMENTA: Venezuela Crumbles as the World Watches On.*

"It would appear that we've had limited success in getting this story buried," said Garrison. "I expect that at least half of the newspapers in the goddamn world will be carrying this today. So, with the genie most certainly out of the bottle, let's hear why Director Van Pelt has gathered us here this morning."

"We've had a couple of significant developments sir," replied Van Pelt. "The most pressing was brought to my attention by Agent Black a short time ago." Van Pelt motioned for Black to take the floor.

Dennis Burnett leant in toward Bishop. "Do you know anything about this?" Bishop simply shook his head in response – whatever Black was preparing to present was news to him.

Black shuffled some papers, stood and jumped straight to the point. "When Eyebrow was placed in the witness relocation program, he was issued with a mobile device. As you would all likely understand, mobile devices can be geo-located if need be. Following Eyebrow's disappearance, we'd been trying to pick up his location using his device, with the last record being in London. This was presumably during his visit to Spaulding. From that point, he went completely dark. That was, until yesterday when his device pinged a tower in the Cayman Islands."

"The Cayman Islands?" said Bishop. "What the fuck would he be doing there?"

"Attending to some banking I'd say," replied Black as he opened a folder and passed several copies of a photograph around the table. "The first ping came from Little Cayman, while a second one was tracked to Grand Cayman. Given the larger proliferation of mobile infrastructure in Grand Cayman, the second one could be isolated with more accuracy, specifically, within an area of the town where the First National Bank is located." Black now summoned Van Pelt to continue.

"Given that this was now an international matter, Agent Black engaged with us to investigate further, and we were able to secure surveillance footage from inside the bank." Van Pelt motioned toward the photos being distributed. "If you examine the photos in front of you, you'll see that your man not only appears to have attended to some business there, but he's also disguised as a Royal Cayman Islands Police officer."

"Fuck me…" muttered Bishop.

"What's he up to Leo?" whispered McFadden.

"Who knows Mac… who fucking knows," replied Bishop, his forehead resting on the table as he spoke.

"Is there any sign of Purple?" asked Burnett.

"Would appear not at this stage," replied Van Pelt.

"Do we know what he was doing there?" asked Garrison, perspiration beginning to bead on his forehead.

"We do not sir," answered Van Pelt.

Garrison pressed further. "Are you certain? Have you been able to speak with anyone at the bank about what he was there for?"

"Not as yet sir. The hour was late when we pieced this together, but we'll be making further enquiries later today."

"So, where is he now?" asked Burnett.

Black took carriage of the presentation once more. "As of now, he's gone dark again."

"But you mentioned that you could track him using his mobile phone," said Burnett. "Can't you tell where he went?"

"It doesn't work like in the movies," said Black. "We can't watch him in real time rounding a corner into your street like the delivery driver arriving with your Kung Pao Chicken. This is a very reactive technology. We can tell where he *was* recently, but we can't identify his real time location right *now*."

"So, you can only tell where he's been after the fact?" asked Bishop.

"Correct," replied Black. "There's no tracking him on some futuristic wall-sized monitor like a Mission Impossible movie. We can't reposition a military satellite and zoom in on him."

Garrison re-entered the conversation. "Right, so what was your last location for him?"

"One more check-in on Little Cayman later that day and then nothing. Radio silence," said Black.

"Could he still be there?"

"Possibly sir, but more likely he's moved on. We'll just have to wait for the next time his phone checks in with a tower."

"Any idea whatsoever where he'll likely bob up next?"

"No, sir. It would only be a guess. The direction he's moving… it certainly looks like he's making his way back here. But again, there's no scientific evidence backing me up there. It's just pure speculation on my part at this point until we get another ping."

"Very well, let's move on please," said Garrison. "You said there are other developments as well Director Van Pelt?"

"Yes sir," replied Van Pelt. "I'll defer to Agent Black again if I may."

Black, who was still standing, shuffled some papers before beginning. "We've been looking into the Julian Cooper affair…"

Black was interrupted by Garrison who had quickly leant forward in his chair. "What's the Julian Cooper affair?"

"Sorry sir," replied Black. "I forgot that we hadn't briefed you on that aspect. Prior to recent events, Eyebrow and his associates visited the town of Cedar Falls on business unknown. What we do know however is that while there, they attended the residence of Mister Julian Cooper before decamping when the local police arrived to investigate suspicious behaviour at Cooper's residence." At this point, Black turned to Burnett, Bishop and McFadden. "We did find out one unfortunate fact during our enquiries and that relates to the guy who accompanied Eyebrow and Purple – Sikorsky."

"The hire car guy," noted Bishop.

"That's correct," replied Black. "The regrettable thing – we discovered that Sikorsky was actually questioned by police at the scene and subsequently released without charge."

"How the hell did that happen?" asked Burnett.

"According to the report, Sikorsky was found at the site suffering from a stab wound and maintained that he was a friend of Cooper's who was simply checking on his welfare when he was attacked by an unknown assailant who then fled the scene."

Burnett was less than pleased at this revelation. "And the locals bought that story?"

"It would appear so. Sikorsky was transported for medical treatment and released not long after." Black took a sip of water before continuing, turning his attention back to Garrison. "Returning to the Cooper issue sir, he's an accountant, and after some investigation it appears that he may have been involved in some less than reputable activities with regards to moving money around off the books. Hearsay only from our very preliminary enquiries at this stage, but something worth pursuing further I'd suggest. This could have relevance to Eyebrow."

"I doubt it's pertinent to our current situation," replied Garrison gruffly. "Is there anything else we need to be briefed on?"

"I have some operational matters sir," said Black. "But probably nothing that you need to concern yourself with."

"Very well then," said Garrison as he rose and eased himself back into his overcoat. "Please keep me updated. There's probably less urgency now that we've failed mightily in keeping this story out of the media."

"We'll be sure to do that sir," said Van Pelt.

Garrison quickly made his way out the door, after which he dispensed with his minions and ascended the stairs to the rooftop sundeck. There would be no lounging in the sun that day though, and not just because it was overcast and drizzling. Garrison's reason for seeking out solitude was to attend to business matters – business from which his co-conspirator Gustavo Torres had maintained arms-length separation. Whoever Garrison was calling, it was not Torres.

He pulled two phones from his inside pocket, quickly examined them, and slipped one back inside his coat. Dialling the second phone, Garrison was forced to wait several seconds before it was answered. Wasting no time with formalities, he jumped straight to the crux of the discussion. "They're starting to sniff around about Cooper."

"How do they know about Cooper?" asked Garrison's man on the other end.

"Some goddamn wildcard put it on the radar. I need to know that they're not going to find anything."

"They won't."

"The Cooper job was clean?"

"It was clean."

"Are you sure?"

The previous answer was repeated firmly. "It was clean."

Garrison paused and rubbed his forehead momentarily before speaking again. "What about the others?"

CHAPTER 55
Red Notice

The Penetrator sat bobbing in the water offshore from Cancun with Jimmy Eyebrow and Joe Purple topside taking in the morning sun and assessing the shoreline off in the distance. Purple looked at his watch. It was well after eight in the morning, and the beach was already beginning to fill with the early-risers keen on their morning beach session. Given Purple's unfamiliarity with Rene's boat, along with his lack of knowledge about marine navigation, the two of them had ploughed through the darkness at a much lesser speed than that which Rene had made the first portion of the journey. The boat's GPS though had proven to be a godsend and had thankfully delivered both men to their destination with pinpoint accuracy.

Now, as they gazed at the beach from afar, the issue turned to how they planned to make their way ashore. Joe Purple offered his thoughts. "I suggest that we get a bit closer and then we swim for it. I can just imagine you sauntering out of the water up onto the beach wearing those fucking swimmers Eyebrow."

Eyebrow of course immediately identified the flaw in Purple's plan. "Uh, Joe. I can't swim with one arm. This fucking thing's killing me at the moment. There's no way I could swim to shore. Or anywhere for that matter. I can't even lift it." Eyebrow winced in pain as he attempted to illustrate the point to Purple.

"Fuck me, I'd forgotten about that," replied Purple. He stood in silence for several moments as he mulled his options, scanning the vast swathe of beach in the distance. "I don't see a dock or anything Eyebrow. There's nowhere for us to tie up."

"There'd have to be Joe, wouldn't there? They have cruise ships come to Cancun don't they?"

"Probably a cruise terminal somewhere around here, but I can't see it." Purple continued his assessment of the topography. "I've got no fucking idea of the layout of this place. I've never been here before." He paused in thought again before issuing directions to Eyebrow. "Make sure you've got all your shit together and your running shoes on Eyebrow. This might get a little wild."

"What the fuck do you have planned Joe?"

Purple was not forthcoming as he gunned the throttle. "Just hold on Eyebrow."

Eyebrow did as he was told, not through obedience, but survival instinct. As the boat hurtled ever closer to the beach, it became obvious to Eyebrow that Purple was not slowing down. "What the fuck are you doing Joe?" he screamed above the roar of the engine.

Ahead of them, swimmers in the water began to scatter as they saw the boat approaching, followed soon thereafter by sunbathers on the beach quickly leaping to their feet and fleeing. Thankfully at that time of the morning, the beach was nowhere near as packed as it would be later in the day, but nonetheless, the sight of *The Penetrator* charging beachward sparked panic among the small crowd. "Hold on Eyebrow!" yelled Purple as the boat entered the low surf just off the beach.

Moments later, *The Penetrator* hit the sand at full throttle and barrelled up the beach, finally coming to a shuddering halt at least a hundred feet from the shoreline. Eyebrow and Purple were thrown to the floor of the cockpit, but were otherwise physically unscathed, if not a little mentally frayed. "Fuck, I hope we didn't flatten anyone," said Eyebrow as he quickly gazed over the side of the boat. "We didn't hit a kid or anything did we Joe?"

Purple was already making his way over the edge of the boat with haste. "Levelled a few sandcastles I reckon, but no people. Come on Eyebrow, we need to get as far away from this shitshow as possible."

Eyebrow quickly joined his friend in decamping. "Where are we going Joe?"

"Anywhere but here," replied Purple, who was already setting off. "Just fucking run Eyebrow and we'll make up the rest as we go along."

"I can't run far Joe," said Eyebrow. "I feel like shit. I don't think I've got much in me."

Purple returned and placed a hand on Eyebrow's arm. "Let's just get off the beach Eyebrow, and then we can work out the rest after that."

The two men made their way off the beach as briskly as Eyebrow's deteriorating condition would allow and soon found themselves on what appeared to be the main promenade behind the ocean front. They continued straight but didn't get far before encountering more water. Looking around, Joe Purple assessed the situation. "Fuck me, this is really narrow."

Eyebrow gazed into the distance to where a larger urban area sat. "That looks like the main city over there Joe."

Purple gazed left and right. "Yeah, but how the fuck do we get off this bit?"

"Should we try to find the embassy?" asked Eyebrow.

Purple assessed the area for any indication as to where they may be. "Good idea for once Eyebrow. Let's do that." Following a little assistance from some tourists, they were soon able to get directions to the United States Consular Office, which thankfully was not too far away from where they were currently marooned.

Standing outside the building, Eyebrow passed an observation. "It's smaller than I thought it would be."

"I don't think it's a full-blown embassy Eyebrow. That'd be in Mexico City. This looks like some sort of satellite thing. Probably for all the American tourists who finds themselves fucked up here." As they approached the door, Purple halted Eyebrow and discussed the plan of attack once inside. "Just let me do all the talking OK Eyebrow. We've got no ID and, importantly, no fucking passports. They'll probably have to do a shitload of work to verify us so… just let me handle it OK?"

"I'm fine with that Joe," replied Eyebrow as they entered the building and approached the enquiries counter.

"Good morning, we have a problem that we need assistance with," said Purple to the consular officer. Concocting a story about being robbed and beaten, while pointing to Eyebrow's injury as proof, Purple explained how their passports and all forms of ID had been stolen. The consular officer was empathetic, though naturally officious, and after typing in the names "Max Von Steel" and "Turd Ferguson," she directed them to a small waiting area.

"This might take a while Eyebrow," said Purple. "Better make yourself comfortable."

Eyebrow took out his phone and found, much to his delight, that he still had a minimal amount of charge and more so, that the consular office offered free Wi-Fi. Successfully connecting, it didn't take long for the notifications to begin sounding. Not as many as before, but certainly Spaulding had been trying to reach him about something.

Eyebrow perused the messages and then turned to Purple. "Hey Joe, what's a Red Notice?"

"A Red Notice? Why the fuck do you want to know that?"

Eyebrow flipped the screen of his phone around to Purple. "Because Spaulding says we have one on us."

Purple immediately leapt to his feet. Directing his attention behind the counter, he saw the consular officer with whom they had been speaking moments earlier discussing something with two security guards. Thankfully at that stage, they had not seen Purple watching them and he swiftly turned to Eyebrow. "Get up Eyebrow. We need to get the fuck out of here."

Purple grabbed Eyebrow, who was confused about the development, and dragged him toward the door. "What's going on Joe?"

"I'll explain in a moment," replied Purple. "Trust me, we need to fucking move NOW!" Purple bundled Eyebrow outside and down the road, scanning the area for any means of concealment. "Quick, in here," he said, pushing Eyebrow into a café. Purple gazed through the window to ensure that they were not being followed before turning to Eyebrow. "They're onto us Eyebrow."

"What do you mean Joe?" asked Eyebrow.

Purple now returned to Eyebrow's thus far unanswered question from earlier. "A Red Notice is something that Interpol puts out to make sure you get detained if you bob up anywhere. It's so that whoever's after you can come and get you. Jesus Christ, I fucking saw this coming didn't I! I fucking said back at the airport in London that we'd end up as fugitives on the run from Interpol. It's played out exactly as I fucking called it." Purple now paced, hands atop his head as he looked out the window in a panicked state. "We need to get out of this part of town Eyebrow, as a matter of priority."

"I can't walk very far Joe," said Eyebrow. "I'm feeling sick."

Given that where they currently were was a tourist hub, there appeared to be an abundance of taxis cruising the street outside. "Come on Eyebrow, let's go," said Purple as he ushered Eyebrow outside where, within moments, they were in a cab. Once safely on the move, it didn't take long before the tourist strip was receding behind them, bound for the urban sprawl and associated anonymity of the downtown district. With an Interpol Red Notice now in effect, staying below the radar had suddenly become more of a priority than ever.

CHAPTER 56

Crazy Jose's Big TransAction

Eyebrow and Purple's taxi crept around the downtown district of Cancun, waiting for Purple to select an appropriate location to disembark. Not knowing the city at all, he had asked the driver to take them to an area where there was an abundance of hospitality venues, figuring that such a location would also be home to elevated foot traffic. As they rounded a corner to what appeared to be the very thing he was seeking, Purple signaled to the driver to pull over. "Pay the man Eyebrow, I'll be waiting outside," he said as he opened the door and stepped onto the sidewalk.

The morning had progressed and by now, the sun was beating down relentlessly as the clock neared midday. The heat was not bothering Purple so much as it was Eyebrow, who tugged on Purple's arm. "I need a drink, Joe. I feel like I'm about to collapse."

Purple looked at Eyebrow and was taken aback by his visible deterioration since hitting the beach. "Jesus Eyebrow, you look like shit. Let's get some hydration into you, and then we need to find a doctor to check you out."

Eyebrow gazed around the street. "Not sure about this neighbourhood Joe. It doesn't look as nice as down near the beach."

"It certainly has a different feel to it Eyebrow, I grant you that," replied Purple as the two men began walking toward a small café nearby. As they approached however, two local police officers stepped out, much to the surprise of an already nervous Joe Purple.

"Fuck," he muttered as he spun Eyebrow around and quickly directed him in the opposite direction and eventually down a side street. "If we get pulled up by the cops for anything, that fucking Red Notice will come back to bite us on the arse. We need to keep our heads down."

Eyebrow perused the small street they were on, settling on a neon sign one door down. "That place looks like its open Joe." Eyebrow wandered to the front of the business that gave every indication that it was a club of some sort. He looked at the sign – *Crazy Jose's Big Transaction*. "Weird name. I wonder what that means Joe."

"No fucking idea Eyebrow." Purple poked his head through the door in an effort to glean some information about what *Crazy Jose's* was. "Looks like a bar of some sort. We should be able to get a drink in here, I guess. And truth be told, I could use one too. I hadn't noticed it until now, but I'm fucking thirsty. Let's grab something to drink and then find you a doctor."

Eyebrow and Purple stepped into *Crazy Jose's*, noting that there was no cover charge at that time of day – admission only kicking in after seven pm according to the sign. The club was quite large inside, but given the hour, it only had a small pool of patrons milling around. Clearly this was more of an evening hotspot than a lunchtime retreat. Eyebrow sat at a small table while Purple attended to the drinks, soon returning with two Cokes, each adorned with a wedge of lime and a small umbrella.

"Here you go, get this into you," said Purple as he placed the drink in front of Eyebrow. Purple sat and glanced around the bar area, his eyes ultimately settling for a little too long on three extravagantly dressed women, leading to them rising and beginning to make their way over to the two men. "Ahh, fuck me," whispered Purple. "Don't look Eyebrow… don't make eye contact."

Eyebrow immediately proceeded to do everything that Purple told him not to, making a meeting of the two groups now imminent. As the three women approached nearer, Purple was able to get a closer look at them. The evening gowns were flamboyant, one bejeweled with sequins and another adorned with a large floral embellishment on the shoulder – outfits certainly not in keeping with the time of day. The other thing that Purple immediately noticed was the over-reliance on makeup that nonetheless did little to disguise the stubble, along with the distinct evidence of three Adams' Apples. Looking closer he even detected a faint indication of a moustache on one of them.

"Well hello there," said the taller of the three as they sidled up to the table.

"Ladies…" replied Purple with a subtle head nod in their direction.

Eyebrow stood and grabbed Purple's arm, dragging him away from the table. "Joe, I don't think these are ladies," he whispered.

"Oh, really?" replied Purple sarcastically. "Whatever could have given it away? Is it because one of them looks like fucking Ernest Borgnine?" Purple glanced around the club, his eyes coming to rest on the sign that he now took a little more time to assess. "Ahh, fuck me Eyebrow. We didn't read the sign properly."

Eyebrow checked the sign himself. "Crazy Jose's Big Transaction. What's wrong with it Joe?"

"Transaction isn't one word Eyebrow, look at it again. There's a fucking space in there. It's two words. Fucking cursive… no wonder we couldn't work out what it meant."

Eyebrow squinted. "Oooh, you're right. That makes a shit ton more sense now. What should we do?"

"Just be polite Eyebrow." Purple turned around to greet their guests again. "Ladies, how are you today?"

The taller of the three replied. "We are doing well thank you Señor. My name is Alexandra, and these are my good friends, Brandy and Victoria."

"I'm Joe," replied Purple as he gently shook each hand in turn – Alexandra's and Brandy's handshakes quite delicate, with Victoria, the mustachioed of the three, somewhat firmer. Clearly these "ladies" had not been ladies forever, and it was Purple's guess that Victoria was the newest among the three. Purple turned to Eyebrow. "This is my associate, Jimmy."

Alexandra extended a hand to Eyebrow while Brandy and Victoria exchanged a whisper between themselves. "I do like your uniforms," said Alexandra. "Are you police officers?" Eyebrow looked down across his shirt, having completely forgotten that he was still wearing the clothes given to him on Little Cayman. "These? No, these were given to us as spares. I threw up all over myself on a plane and then Joe sat in it."

Purple closed his eyes and grimaced as he listened to Eyebrow's vivid exposition. "I think you need to watch a few old James Bond movies Eyebrow, so that you can get some lessons on how to open conversations."

"You don't look well there Jimmy," noted Brandy. "Are you still feeling poorly?"

"I threw up because of the morphine I was given," replied Eyebrow. "What's killing me is my shoulder."

"What happened," asked Brandy.

"I got shot," said Eyebrow, eliciting gasps from around the table.

"Oh my. Victoria, can you have a look?" said Alexandra before turning to Eyebrow. "Victoria used to be in the army during another life."

Eyebrow felt his shirt being lifted and a pair of rough, calloused hands probing his wound. "This is not good," noted Victoria. "He's going to need medical assistance."

"We can't go to a hospital," noted Purple swiftly, cognizant of the Red Notice lurking in the shadows behind them.

"OK," said Alexandra skeptically, sensing correctly that there was more to these two characters than met the eye. "What brings you here to Cancun?"

Purple was in no mood for deflection or lies – it had got him nowhere to that point, so he simply laid out the situation for his three guests in abridged fashion. "Where can I start? We're on the run with no passports and no identification. We've been balls-deep in a fucking coup in Venezuela, Eyebrow's been shot, a few hours ago we crashed a boat carrying a quarter of a ton of cocaine on your main tourist beach, we found out that Interpol is looking for us, and all we want to do is get to the United States border. We just want to go home."

Purple's revelation brought a soft squeal of excitement from Brandy who turned to Victoria. "I told you it was him!"

Victoria stepped back and looked directly ay Eyebrow before responding. "Oh my God! You're right!"

Joe Purple was confused. "What the fuck is going on here?"

Brandy's gaze had not moved from Eyebrow. "You're La Tormenta!"

"Wait, what the fuck?" snapped Purple. "La... *what?*"

Eyebrow was equally confused. "Yeah, I think you're getting me mixed up with someone else."

Alexandra stood and walked to the bar, returning moments later with a newspaper. Holding the front page up, Purple and Eyebrow could see the headline story, complete with the now iconic de Klerk photograph of Eyebrow standing heroically atop the rubble in his red, white and blue.

Purple's jaw almost hit the ground. "What... the fuck... is THAT???" he shrieked as he reached for the newspaper. Turning to Eyebrow, he repeated his redundant question. "What the fuck is this Eyebrow?"

"I have no idea Joe. Looks like the photo was taken at Rudy's. I never saw the guy taking it. Did you?"

Purple was reading the accompanying story when he paused, grabbed Eyebrow's arm and shunted him off to a nearby corner. "Do you have any fucking idea what they're calling you in this story?"

"I haven't read it Joe. I've got no clue."

Purple paced before handing the newspaper to Eyebrow and pointing to the article. "Apparently Eyebrow, you're a fucking international mercenary known as La Tormenta. No wonder these three think you're a fucking celebrity. Where the fuck did the news people get that from?"

"That might explain why everybody suddenly seems to be after us," noted Eyebrow as he now perused the article.

Purple snatched the paper from Eyebrow's hand. "The way it's written, it makes it look like we're fucking involved in the whole thing – like you're a fucking ringleader." Purple glanced toward their new friends and lowered his voice. "We need to be careful Eyebrow. This lot might be fucking bounty hunters or something."

Silence fell as Eyebrow and Purple returned to their seats – Brandy and Victoria excitedly awaiting words of wisdom from the famed La Tormenta, Eyebrow with no clue about how to proceed, and Purple wishing it was all just a bad dream. Eventually it fell to Alexandra to speak. "Well, you've certainly found yourselves in a bind. Under the circumstances, it sounds like you might have to engage a specialist to get you across the border."

"You got a copy of the Yellow Pages?" replied Purple. "I've got no idea how to organize that sort of shit."

Brandy reached across and clasped the still wary Purple's hand. "We might be able to help you."

Before Purple and Brandy could explore that avenue further, Victoria directed everyone's attention to Eyebrow who was now beginning to sway on his seat. "Something's wrong, look at him."

Purple slapped Eyebrow around a little, but there was no response. Eyebrow's eyes rolled back, and he began to slump in his chair. The infection that had been progressively building in his system since Coronado had now reached a critical mass. Of all the risks he had faced, this invisible enemy now posed a bigger threat than any other that he'd encountered. The bacteria attacking him was now rampaging through his body and was bent on complete destruction. If unchecked, there would be only one inevitable outcome. Eyebrow needed professional medical help, and he needed it immediately. Even now, it may have been too late, and as Purple cradled his friend in his arms, he knew that the clock was ticking.

CHAPTER 57

A Different Category of Serious

Leo Bishop and Ike McFadden stood at the base of the Lincoln Memorial's lower steps overlooking the iconic reflecting pool, partially for sightseeing purposes, together with an equal measure of business. Both men had initially used a break in proceedings that afternoon to take in some of Washington's landmarks, however no sooner were they gazing across the imposing sculpture of President Lincoln in his cavernous abode than Bishop's phone buzzed – a request from Harry Black and Christian Dekker to meet with them outside the confines of the State Department.

Bishop and McFadden had used the half hour between Black's message and their arrival to further explore the area, and now as the four of them stood admiring the reflecting pool, Bishop offered his thoughts on the unorthodox meeting about to convene. "This is a bit clandestine isn't it Harry? Has the Washington espionage bug bitten you?"

Black looked around and gestured to the throng of tourists in the immediate area. "Hardly Leo. We'll be in the background of a hundred selfies and holiday videos by the time we're done. If we were supposed to be doing secret spy business, we'd be put on a performance improvement plan pretty quickly."

"Then why here?" asked Bishop.

"Because this is where you were when I messaged you, simple as that. We wanted to get out of the office for some fresh air, plus we wanted to brief you ahead of time so that you're not caught by surprise again, like with the Cayman Islands matter."

"That's very kind of you," replied Bishop. "Is there an update?"

"I'd say a rather significant one."

"On multiple fronts," added Dekker.

Bishop closed his eyes and breathed deeply – once, twice… three times, in through the nose and out through the mouth as he composed himself for what he assumed was coming. "Please, continue."

Black pulled his phone from his pocket. "Have you by chance seen the news this afternoon?" he asked as he tapped his finger on the news app on his screen.

"Am I going to see Eyebrow in his fucking jocks again?" asked Bishop.

"No, not this time. But it is a pretty serious development."

"More serious than kidnapping a foreign government minister during a fucking military coup?"

"Different category of serious," replied Black as he turned his phone around and handed it to Bishop. A news story titled *Let it Snow! Cancun Chaos* was front and centre on the screen.

"What the fuck is this?" asked Bishop.

"Earlier today, there was a situation in Cancun when a cocaine-laden speedboat crashed onto the main beach," said Black as he retrieved the phone from Bishop. "By the time police arrived, they accounted for approximately fifty-eight kilos of cocaine, however estimates are that the boat was probably carrying a significantly larger amount."

"What happened to the rest?" asked McFadden.

"Indications are that it was looted by the beachgoers in the minutes before the police arrived. I'd say there's a good chance that Cancun will be doing its best impression of Miami in the eighties tonight."

Bishop rubbed his eyes as he posed the next question. "I'm fucking hesitant to ask because I know where it's going, but… what does this have to do with us?"

Black had finished scrolling on the phone and returned it to Bishop. "Here's a video from someone who caught the immediate aftermath of the boat crashing onto the beach."

The video began with the smoking hulk of *The Penetrator* balancing precariously on the beach in the seconds after coming to rest. Moments later, two figures leapt over the edge of the boat and absconded into the distance – each man instantly recognizable to Bishop who handed the phone back to

Black and stooped forward, resting his hands on his thighs. "What the fuck is he doing Harry? I mean, seriously… what the hell is this shit?"

"No idea Leo. The unpredictability he's exhibiting this time around is remarkable, which is why we did what we did the other day."

"What did you do?" asked Bishop.

Dekker took his opportunity to add to the conversation. "Given that Eyebrow has gone international, we've been liaising with Interpol and arranged to have a Red Notice issued for both he and Purple. If they bobbed up anywhere, we were hoping that they could be detained in order to be extradited back here."

"And?" asked Bishop. "Has he poked his head out of the foxhole?"

"Right there in Cancun," replied Dekker.

"Went straight to the US Consular Office within an hour of hitting the beach," added Black.

"So, did you snag him?" asked McFadden.

"No," replied Black. "Both he and Purple skipped out before they could be detained."

"Do you know what they were doing there?" asked Bishop.

"According to the consular officer who was attending to them, they advised that they'd been robbed and had no passports or identification."

"And they just vanished before anyone could hold them?" asked McFadden.

Black nodded his head slowly. "Yep. One moment they were in the waiting area, and by the time security arrived to detain them, they'd disappeared."

"He must have been awake to them," said McFadden.

"Or he was tipped off," added Bishop, who now began to pace as the cogs in his brain ticked over. "They said they'd been robbed, but we know that's bullshit because they only arrived in Cancun not long before when they ran their fucking cocaine boat up onto the sand."

"Whatever bullshit story they concocted, it still sounded like they were trying to get back stateside and needed help in doing so," said Black.

After thinking for a few moments, Bishop made an observation. "Well, they can't fly, and if they weren't able to get help from the Consular Office then there's only one option available to them."

McFadden was already nodding his head as he had quickly worked out where Bishop was headed with his hypothesis. "They're making for the border."

Bishop clicked his fingers in McFadden's direction. "They are indeed headed for the border Mac." Bishop now turned to Black. "What about the phone? Has that been connecting?"

"Just at the Consular Office," replied Black. "After that… nothing."

"Fuck, he's gone dark again. Well even though we can't get a definite location, we at least have a fair idea of the direction he's going."

"We'll be sure to stay on top of it and keep checking for more pings," replied Black. "I'll need to brief Van Pelt and Garrison on this, but before I do, there's another development that I wanted to discuss with you."

"Eyebrow related?" asked Bishop.

"In the broad Eyebrow family. I went back to the beginning and started looking into the Julian Cooper connection a little more. Given that he's still technically missing, I began skulking through ViCAP for missing persons and I stumbled across something curious."

"How so?" asked Bishop.

"I found a further six people who have all been noted as missing within two weeks of each other."

"And that's unusual… why?"

"Ordinarily it might not be. But all six of them, plus Cooper who makes seven, are accountants. So, unless there's some secret accountants' convention that they've all jetted off to without telling anyone, it's a remarkable coincidence wouldn't you say?"

"Where were they located?" asked Bishop. "Did they all live in the same general area as Cooper?"

"No. All over the country."

"Fuck," muttered Bishop to himself before turning to McFadden. "Surely Eyebrow couldn't be behind this, could he? He's a lot of things, but serial killer doesn't seem like one of them."

McFadden nodded in response. "I tend to agree Leo, but then again, he's involved in a lot of shit at the moment that we never saw coming. Our track record on reading him isn't the best."

Black added an observation before Bishop could respond. "On that question, we've already run a check on airline bookings to the areas of interest, and neither Eyebrow nor Purple appear to have travelled anywhere during the period when these guys disappeared. The only record of any flight they've taken was the time they flew to Cedar Falls, where Cooper lives."

"It definitely sounds like something's afoot there Harry," said Bishop. "What's the plan of attack here?"

"Christian and I will need to bring Van Pelt and Garrison into the loop on the Cancun situation, as well as the Red Notice," said Black. "If I send you everything that I have on the missing accountants, could you two have a go at picking at some of those threads?"

"I'll need to let Dennis know what we're doing, but I'm sure it'll be OK," replied Bishop.

"Let's get to it then," said Black enthusiastically. "We've got a reasonable idea about where Eyebrow's headed, so let's see if we can put some sort of plan in place to grab him before he turns to vapour again."

Yet even though the team's deduction as to Eyebrow's intentions was correct, the situation unfolding in Mexico at that moment was dire. The logical assumption that Eyebrow and Purple were making a play for the border *was* accurate. But with Eyebrow's health now deteriorating catastrophically, the taskforce could have very easily been preparing their border plan in anticipation of an arrival that would never eventuate.

CHAPTER 58

The Florence Nightingale Effect

Jimmy Eyebrow's eyelids were heavy as he ever so slowly eased them open, his vision blurred, and the associated brain fog oppressive. He knew not where he was, nor what was happening as his eyes gradually adjusted to the light. Before him he could make out a blurry figure and after several moments of ocular calibration, he recognized that it was a visibly aged Joe Purple, his once dark permed hair now a shock of grey. He had dark circles beneath his eyes and his face looked worn. "Joe?" whispered Eyebrow.

"It's me Eyebrow," rasped Purple. "It's me. Holy shit, I can't believe it."

"What can't you believe Joe?" asked Eyebrow as he tried to rise, before Purple place a gentle hand on him.

"Don't try to move Eyebrow. Just take it easy for now. Oh my God, I can't believe you're awake, after all this time."

"What do you mean Joe?" asked Eyebrow, puzzled. "How long have I been out for?"

Purple paused before answering. "I'm not gonna lube up for this Eyebrow so hold on, because I'm goin' in dry. You've been in a coma for thirty years."

Eyebrow was understandably stunned. "What? Thirty years?" Eyebrow blinked his eyes vigorously and focused again on Purple's hair. "Holy shit, is that why you're grey now? Has it really been that long?"

"I've stayed here all that time Eyebrow, always waiting for you to wake up. It's a miracle!"

"You mean we're old men now?"

"I baked you a birthday cake every year. Ended up eating it by myself each time because you were a fucking vegetable, but I still made one."

"Are we still in Mexico Joe? Did they ever catch us?"

"Never caught us. We're living in a Hacienda in the Mexican countryside. We ended up being pardoned by President Swift, but we stayed here anyway."

"President Swift?" said Eyebrow. "Surely you don't mean…"

"She's still remarkably popular Eyebrow. Has massive support among the middle-aged mother demographic."

"Holy shit, this is crazy," said Eyebrow as he laid flat on his back staring at the ceiling. "I'm an old man."

Purple could no longer keep a straight face. Talcum powder now filled the air as he ran his hands vigorously through his hair. He turned to the side, away from Eyebrow's field of view, where raucous laughter erupted. "I fucking told you that he'd buy it!"

"I must say, you did a good job of selling it Joe," said Alexandra who now walked over beside Purple before looking down upon Eyebrow. "How are you feeling Jimmy?"

Eyebrow didn't respond immediately. "Wait, that was all a lie? I haven't really been asleep for thirty years?"

"No, you haven't been asleep for that long Jimmy," replied Alexandra. "Everything Joe said was made up."

"Except for the bit about him being a vegetable," added Purple. "That part was accurate."

Alexandra now returned to the previous question. "How are you, Jimmy? Are you feeling any better?"

"I feel like I'm hungover," replied Eyebrow as he rubbed his forehead while also noticing an IV tube in his left arm. "I've got a massive headache, but at least I'm not feeling sick." Eyebrow looked around the room. "Where am I? What happened to me?"

Before answering, Alexandra called to Victoria. "Can you please tell Doctor Ralph that Jimmy's awake." Alexandra then refocused on Eyebrow. "You were very sick Jimmy. You had a very bad infection that needed to be treated immediately."

"You were fucking dying Eyebrow," added Purple from the side. "Another hour and you would've probably been past the point of no return."

A bespectacled man now strode toward Eyebrow. "Your friend is correct Señor Eyebrow. If we didn't treat you when we did, this would have almost certainly ended up much different." The man sat Eyebrow up and prodded around his shoulder that was still very tender. "I'm Doctor Ralph. How are you feeling today?"

"Like I said earlier, I feel like I'm hungover. What's happened to me?"

Doctor Ralph laid Eyebrow back down. "First up, we needed to give you a massive dose of antibiotics to fight off the infection that was attacking your body. You're still going to feel the effects of it for some time yet, but you should slowly begin to feel better. Along with that, I tried as best I could to fix your shoulder for you. It's not quite my skill set, but I've managed to clean up most of it. The bullet that was in there was fragmented and I got some of it out, but I'm afraid to say that there's some embedded in the bone that you'll carry with you for all time now. I've cleansed the wound, sutured it shut and applied a fresh sterile dressing. With a little more rest, you should be on your way soon."

"How long was I actually out for?" asked Eyebrow.

"Close to a day and a half now," replied Doctor Ralph.

"I didn't shit myself in that time, did I?" asked Eyebrow sheepishly.

"No, you did not. You may rest easily on that. The antibiotics might make your next few movements somewhat unpleasant however."

"Ugh, OK… I'll keep that in mind."

"Señor Purple, along with your new friends, rushed you here seeking my help. Apparently, you couldn't go to a hospital, the reasons for which are not my business. I am a friend to Alex…" Alexandra interrupted with a cough, causing Doctor Ralph to correct himself. "I am a friend to *Alexandra*… Brandy and Victoria. If you are carrying secrets, so be it. My friends asked for help, I gave it."

"Thank you," said Eyebrow meekly as he looked toward his three new friends.

"They have stayed by your side this whole time," added Doctor Ralph. "The Florence Nightingale effect has been very strong."

"Not the entire time," corrected Purple, who was now using a wet wipe to cleanse his face of the ageing makeup that he had applied earlier. "We did duck out for a quick drink together while you circled the drain Eyebrow. To be honest, I was worried at first that I'd end up with a fucking ball-gag in my mouth, or some sort of freaky shit like that, but these three are actually pretty cool to hang out with."

"Don't give away all our secrets there Joe," said Victoria flamboyantly.

"What happens in the club, stays in the club," added Brandy.

Alexandra edged in closer to Eyebrow and examined his forehead with a flourish of the hand. "We'll give you some guidance on this sweetie. Joe tells us that you have a little trouble sometimes."

"What, my eyebrows?"

"Yes, your fucking eyebrows," said Purple. "You've got the golden opportunity to learn from experts in the field here Eyebrow. I suggest you use it."

"Thanks, that'd be great," said Eyebrow, before pivoting the conversation. "Have you thought of a plan yet for how we're going to get home Joe?"

"Luckily, our new friends are all over this one Eyebrow. I'll let Alex… andra brief you."

"Given that you have issues with Interpol…" began Alexandra before being interrupted by Doctor Ralph.

"Umm, I'm just going to leave right about now," he said as he quickly slipped through the swinging door, the sound of barking dogs briefly seeping into the room.

"He has pets in his office?" asked Eyebrow.

"Not quite," replied Purple. "We couldn't take you to a hospital, so we had to bring you here. Doctor Ralph isn't a people doctor… he's a vet."

"A vet?" screeched Eyebrow. "A vet operated on me?"

"Hey, he fixed you didn't he? We're pretty fucking deficient in the friend department right now, so be grateful for what you get. Anyway, shut up and let Alexandra tell you what's going to happen."

Alexandra continued. "Given your current circumstances, you're going to need specialist help. You won't find that here in Cancun, so you're going to have to get closer to the border."

"That's where the specialist is Eyebrow," added Purple.

"When you say specialist Joe, do you mean…"

"A coyote Eyebrow. We'll have to cross the border with a coyote."

"It is going to cost you," said Alexandra. "Joe said that you have money?"

"I'm getting low. I brought some with us, but I never thought we'd be away for so long and in this much trouble."

"Where are we going?" asked Purple. "Juarez? Tijuana?"

"Oh, good heavens no," replied Victoria. "They're much too far away. It would take us forever to get there overland. We'll be going to Reynosa – it's much closer, but still a long trip."

"Never heard of the place," said Purple. "But given that you're the subject matter experts, I'll defer to your knowledge."

Victoria now added commentary to the discussion. "We know a man there. It's the best option under the circumstances. You need to rest up for a while Jimmy, and then we'll hit the road."

"You're coming with us?" asked Eyebrow with a smile.

"Of course we are Jimmy," replied Alexandra. "You don't think we'd abandon you here, do you?"

"I told you they're pretty cool," said Purple with a wink. "We'll have our own local escort."

"How are we going to get there?" asked Eyebrow.

Alexandra, Brandy and Victoria looked at one another with broad smiles. They nodded knowingly and spoke as one – "El gran plátano."

CHAPTER 59

Nothing so Dark

Secretary of State Myles Garrison rose from his desk and started for the door of his office where he was expecting to see Intelligence Director Van Pelt waiting in his antechamber. It was true that Van Pelt was waiting and ready to brief the Secretary on the developments brought to him by Agent Black earlier in the day. But as Garrison reached for the door, it was flung open by an entirely unexpected visitor – Defense Secretary Ron Irvin.

"Ron, what are you doing here?" asked Garrison, taken aback by the forceful nature of Irvin's entrance.

"What the fuck is going on Myles?" barked Irvin.

"I'm not sure I understand what you mean," replied Garrison.

"What I'm talking about is an employee of one of my biggest, and might I add, top secret, defense contractors travelling to the other side of the planet with some sort of fucking international hitman that you're trying to track down." The veins on Irvin's forehead looked as though they were primed to explode as he spoke. "At what fucking point were you going to tell me?"

"The situation's in flux," said Garrison defensively. "We don't fully understand the connection yet."

"You didn't bring me into the tent because the situation's… *in flux*? I've got a rogue defense contractor on a flight to London with an international hitman who's running a fucking military coup, on their way to see a former

MI6 agent who's under the protection of the goddamn British Home Office, and at no point – no point whatsoever – did you think that maybe you should have looped me in?"

"I'm sorry Ron, it was an oversight on my part."

"You're goddamn right it was an oversight, of monumental fucking proportions." Irvin gestured toward the door. "Is Van Pelt here to see you?"

"He is."

"About this hitman shitshow?"

"Yes."

"Good, then I'm sitting in. I want to know what the fuck's going on."

Garrison walked to the door and eased it open to see Van Pelt dutifully awaiting the call. "Director Van Pelt, come through please." Upon entering, Garrison brought Van Pelt's attention to their guest.

"Mister Secretary," said Van Pelt as he extended his hand in greeting. "I wasn't aware you were joining us."

"Neither was Secretary Garrison," replied Irvin. "But here I am, so tell me, what's going on with the defense contractor from Triochron?" Van Pelt glanced toward Garrison before being snapped to attention by Irvin. "You're talking to me now Director Van Pelt. What's going on with the man from Triochron?"

"Well sir, we've been unpacking a situation involving a hitman who is currently under federal protection..." Van Pelt was quickly cut off by Irvin.

"I'm not interested in any background. I simply want to know what you know about any involvement Triochron Industries may have in this situation. That is my sole point of interest – Triochron."

"We still haven't established a firm connection yet sir," said Van Pelt. "The facts are that Eyebrow and his companion..."

Irvin again interrupted "This Eyebrow character is the hitman?"

"Yes sir," replied Van Pelt before Irvin then gestured for him to continue. "We know that Eyebrow and his associate travelled to London, without advising their handlers, in the company of an engineer from Triochron Industries."

"You're certain that they were travelling together?" asked Irvin.

Van Pelt winced slightly as he delivered his reply. "Not entirely sir. As part of my briefing today for Secretary Garrison, I was going to note that Charles Dunk – the Triochron engineer – was detained for questioning earlier today when he arrived back in the country. As expected, he denies any involvement with anything associated with Eyebrow and argues that it was purely a coincidence that they were seated together."

"Your thoughts on his position?" asked Irvin.

"I'm still fifty-fifty on it," replied Van Pelt.

"That's not very reassuring from an intelligence perspective," added Garrison.

"We are almost certain that Eyebrow visited former MI6 agent Stuart Spaulding whilst in London, however we don't know whether Dunk accompanied them. We have no knowledge of Dunk's movements after landing in the UK. What Dunk did tell us though is that he overheard Eyebrow and his companion discussing an incident that they appear to have had knowledge of in Addis Ababa."

"Ethiopia?" said Garrison as he glared at Van Pelt. "Please, tell me that we haven't been involved in any black ops in Ethiopia."

Van Pelt shifted uncomfortably before answering. "Not recently sir."

"Not... *recently*?"

"There may have been some minor episodes in the past where our presence was... shall I say... a little more hands on."

"Jesus, tell me that Eyebrow wasn't on your books," snapped Garrison.

"He was not sir," replied Van Pelt confidently. "He is not one of our assets."

"Could he be buried so deep that you don't know about him?" pressed Garrison.

Van Pelt leant forward in his chair. "Sir, we may have activities that occur off the books, but I assure you, contrary to portrayals in popular culture, nothing is so dark that it can't be found."

Irvin sought to confirm Van Pelt's position and leant in toward him. "Definitely not yours Mister Director?"

Van Pelt swung his head toward Irvin. "Definitely not sir."

"OK," replied Irvin. "Do you have anything further to brief Secretary Garrison on?"

"Some more operational matters sir," replied Van Pelt.

"Anything related to Triochron, or this Dunk character?"

"No sir."

"Very well. Then my time here is done." Irvin stood and buttoned his jacket. "The moment you hear anything further, and I mean the *moment* that you pick up any new intel related in any way to Triochron, I want to be looped in. Do you understand me?"

"I understand sir," replied Van Pelt, standing as Irvin exited the room.

Over the course of the next fifteen minutes, Van Pelt proceeded to outline the latest Eyebrow development vis-à-vis the Cancun situation. Specifically, he briefed Garrison on the beaching of *The Penetrator* and Eyebrow's attendance at the Consular Office – the same information that Black had relayed to Bishop and McFadden earlier in the day. Ultimately, the discussion also wound its way to the same conclusion. "Do you think he's making a run for the border?" asked Garrison.

"It's likely sir, yes," replied Van Pelt. "There's a very real chance that he has no passport, and with the Red Notice in effect, he can't afford to get flagged in any official systems. He'll be engaging a coyote I suspect, if he hasn't already done so. He's clearly a man of means."

Garrison stood to signal that the briefing had now come to a close. Before Van Pelt departed though, Garrison had one further question. "Has there been any movement on the situation with the missing accountants?"

Van Pelt paused before answering. "Have you spoken to Agent Black or Detective Bishop this afternoon sir?"

"No, not as yet. I've had no need to."

"Very good. No, there's been no updates on that front. Likely a red herring." Van Pelt made for the door. "Will there be anything else sir?"

"Nothing at this stage. Remember what Secretary Irvin said though – if you have any updates that might be of interest to him, please keep him informed. And me also, of course."

"Of course sir," replied Van Pelt with a nod as he took his leave and exited the office.

As had become customary of late, Garrison waited until such time as Van Pelt would be long gone before he also exited and took a short walk to the Vietnam Veterans' Memorial where he could conduct business off-site. Dispersing his security detail in order to have privacy, Garrison pulled out the phone from the inside pocket of his jacket and dialed.

"Yes," came the answer from the other end.

"We have a problem," said Garrison.

"Another one?" enquired the voice.

"I know… I know. Hopefully we can prevent any more. The man we're after, he's on his way the US border in Mexico."

"Any idea where?" asked Garrison's man.

"No. Could be any of the border towns. He'll likely be seeking a coyote. It's suddenly become more imperative that he's removed from the equation as soon as possible."

"Why so?"

"The fucking federal agents went and put a goddamn Red Notice on him, so if he gets detained by any officials of any type, it's going to be harder to get to him. We have to find him in the wild."

"If you don't know where on the border he's likely to cross, undertaking such an operation will be expensive."

"Leave that up to me. Just… I don't know… draw up a shortlist of towns where he's likely to get the help he's looking for and take it from there."

"I will do that. Do we have a timeframe?"

Garrison paused and discreetly assessed his surroundings, ensuring that he was not within earshot of anyone. "Given how little we know as to his whereabouts, I'd say that time is of the utmost essence here. Whatever it takes, I need you to find this prick, and his fucking travelling companion, and fix the problem once and for all."

CHAPTER 60

The Big Banana

Time, as it turned out, was *not* of the essence in the Eyebrow situation. Considering the period that it took for Eyebrow to recuperate from his near-death experience, together with the tediously slow drive across half the length of Mexico, it was several days before Eyebrow, Purple and their three flamboyant companions rolled into Reynosa in Brandy's bright yellow 1972 Volkswagen Kombi – "El Gran Plátano". Or, translated, The Big Banana, which was the name by which Eyebrow and Purple had become accustomed to when referring to Brandy's pride and joy.

It was of course entirely unknown to Eyebrow at that point in time that he was being tracked, and it was therefore equally unknown that he had subsequently remained dark for the duration of the journey north. Concern was mounting back in Washington that the trail may have been lost, with Garrison in particular demanding thrice-daily updates as to whether Eyebrow had resurfaced and if so, where. Garrison's demands though were simply a case of him casting the net as wide as possible, because he was now also using his own backchannels in an effort to pinpoint Eyebrow's mobile phone signal, albeit for far more nefarious purposes.

In reality, the situation was unknowingly playing to Eyebrow's advantage and all he needed to do was avoid poking his head above the parapet again. He had no inkling that the mobile phone he carried was simultaneously his lifeline, and his nemesis. Sitting dead as it was in his pocket at that moment, it was benign. And for so long as it remained that way, the odds would continue to fall in Eyebrow's favour.

Truth be told, the multi-day journey along the coast of Mexico, unhurried as it was, had been a blissful sojourn for Eyebrow and Purple as the troubles that had plagued them drifted away. They knew that they weren't entirely out of danger – there was the issue of the border crossing to come of course. But nonetheless, the friendship they'd struck up with their new companions was something that both of them happily soaked in.

And it wasn't just friendship that was soaking in, as the trip also included more than a few breaks at a forgotten number of cantinas along the way. Eyebrow and Purple had been introduced to a seemingly never-ending selection of Tequila varieties during the past few days and as each day came to its raucous conclusion, the Tequila kept flowing at whatever roadside campsite the five companions had selected for the evening.

Lying on his back one night, gazing at the Milky Way stretching across the moonless sky above him, and with the campfire dwindling nearby, Eyebrow turned his head to Joe Purple. "I could actually get used to this Joe."

"Same here Eyebrow," replied Purple without shifting his eyes from the mesmerizing night sky. "Right about now, the only concern in our lives is whether we're going to die in a flaming Volkswagen accident. But if you can put that to the side, this is pretty fucking special." Purple now turned slightly so that he was facing Eyebrow. "We'll get through this Eyebrow, I know we will. Just a few more days and we'll be back to safety."

"I know Joe," replied Eyebrow softly. "It was great that we hooked up with these three. They're pretty cool."

"You can say that again Eyebrow," replied Purple. "If you said to me on January first, 'happy new year, Joe. This year you're gonna be camping in the Mexican countryside with three cross-dressers that you meet in a bar in Cancun', I'd have told you that you'd finally lost the plot. I mean, I often think that anyway, but every time you still somehow manage to reset the bar. But I'll tell you what Eyebrow, despite every fucking disaster we find ourselves in, thanks to you primarily might I add, we've met some pretty interesting people along the way."

"Very true," sighed Eyebrow. "It's been a wild ride Joe."

A day later, that ride was nearing its conclusion as The Big Banana shuddered to a stop in the car park of *Señor Gabriel's Motel*, with two thousand new kilometres added to its odometer, and a lifetime of memories created within over the course of just a few days. Alexandra turned around and spoke to Eyebrow and Purple. "Here we are. I'll go in and see if they have some rooms for us. Do you want one or two?"

"Seriously, I don't mind anymore," replied Purple. "I've been in this guy's armpit for ages now, so another couple of days won't matter. Just so long as there's two beds. Whatever the fuck he gets up to in there, I do not want to be within touching distance of it."

"Can you find out if they have Wi-Fi?" added Eyebrow as Alexandra stepped out of the Kombi. Turning to Victoria, Eyebrow enquired as to the next steps in the plan to secrete he and Purple over the border.

"We'll stay here tonight," said Victoria. "Tomorrow, a vaquetón will come and collect the two of you and take you to a holding house."

"What the fuck is a vaquetón?" asked Purple.

"The person who collects all of the coyote's clients and gets them ready for the crossing," replied Victoria. "You'll go to a safe house to prepare and when the coyote has determined the best time to cross, he will collect you. I must tell you that the process will be quick once the decision is made. The window of opportunity will be small, so you'll be moved with haste."

"We'll be ready," said Purple. "I assure you of that."

Alexandra soon beckoned the four occupants of El Gran Plátano to the motel's office area where they were advised, thankfully, that there was indeed room for all of them that evening. *Señor Gabriel's* was hardly an upmarket establishment, and it was located on the far outskirts of the town, but at first glance it seemed perfectly serviceable and clean, which was all that was required at that point. And, much to Eyebrow's satisfaction, it also had Wi-Fi.

As Eyebrow and Purple settled into their room, Eyebrow began recharging his once again dead phone thanks to the cable provided by Victoria. As expected, notifications soon began to ring out, signaling that Spaulding had again been trying to raise him, although the queued messages were not as voluminous as the last time Eyebrow's phone rose from its slumber. He checked the first couple of messages. "Looks like he's making progress with that account that I was looking into Joe." Eyebrow continued scrolling. "Holy shit. He says that he might be onto something big."

"Whatever it is Eyebrow, we're not getting involved," snapped Purple. "If I go outside and stand on the roof of this place, I'd literally be able to see the United States across the river. We're not fucking up our chance to get across that border Eyebrow. We're staying put, and God willing, I'll be chowing down at Arby's sometime in the next twenty-four hours. Whatever he's saying, just reply to him in a message. No more phone calls and no more fucking side expeditions. We're almost there Eyebrow, don't fuck it up. I beg of you."

"I won't Joe, I promise," replied Eyebrow. His phone alert sounded again. "Whoa, Joe! I've got an actual signal here. We must be close enough to the border that I can connect to a proper tower."

"Exactly Eyebrow," said Purple. "That's how fucking close we are. This is like being on a plane when the pilot tells the cabin crew to prepare for landing. I need you to not do anything fucking retarded for one day Eyebrow. That's all I ask of you. Do you think you can just sit still and not... I don't know... can you just not be *you* for a day?"

"I should send Esteban a message to let him know that we're OK," said Eyebrow.

"Just be careful," said Purple. "I'd really prefer if you didn't tell him where we are. Go ahead and let him know that you're safe if that helps you sleep, but don't discuss our location or plans. Same goes for your buddy in England." Purple paused in thought as he mulled a suitable metaphor. "Imagine, Eyebrow, that the U.S, just on the other side of that river, is a public park."

"OK," replied Eyebrow, unsure where Purple was headed.

"And you – you're a flasher lurking in the bushes. You need to stay quiet and unseen so that you can leap out when the moment's just right."

Eyebrow repeated his earlier response, nodding as he did so. "OK."

"What's the most important thing for you to do in that situation Eyebrow?"

"Don't draw attention to the bush that you're behind," replied Eyebrow confidently, though probably also far too quickly.

"There you go," scoffed Purple with a wry smile. "I knew that'd paint a picture you'd understand."

A knock at the door interrupted their discussion. Eyebrow eased the door open slightly to find Victoria standing outside the room. "Hi Jimmy. We were thinking that we might get takeout, and we were wondering if you and Joe would like to join us?"

"You hungry Joe?" asked Eyebrow.

"I am actually," replied Purple, sitting up from his prone position on the bed.

Eyebrow turned back to Victoria. "What were you thinking of getting?"

"We're beastly careless," replied Victoria. "Do you have any thoughts?"

Eyebrow again deferred to Purple. "What do you think Joe? Do you feel like pizza?"

"That's not a bad idea Eyebrow," said Purple. "I haven't had pizza since that fucking hipster place, so it might be a nice way to celebrate our last day in Mexico."

"Then pizza it is!" shouted Victoria. "We shall order and then join you for one last night of wild celebration!"

"Not too fucking wild there Vicky," said Purple. "We've got a big day ahead of us tomorrow."

But taking it easy was not in the DNA of Eyebrow and Purple's new friends and as the evening inevitably devolved into raucous mayhem, Señor Gabriel himself paid a visit to the room in an effort to subdue the unruliness that had descended upon his establishment. Eventually, a tick before midnight, the group dispersed, and Eyebrow and Purple finally got the chance to lay their heads on Mexican pillows for what they hoped would be the last time. Tomorrow they would bid farewell to their new friends, though for now, a restful night's sleep was foremost on the agenda.

But after such a chaotic and winding adventure to that point, it should have come as no surprise when an unexpected knock came at the door only a couple of hours after the two men had dozed off. "What the fuck is that?" groaned Purple as he lifted his head from the pillow to address the sudden disturbance. As the knocking persisted, Purple lurched toward the door, kicking at least five pizza boxes out of the way, as well as two empty tequila bottles and a pair of lacy underwear – the original owner unknown. "Jesus Christ, what the fuck did we get up to last night?" he muttered to himself.

"Who is it, Joe?" slurred Eyebrow who had now also been roused from his sleep-state.

Purple inched the curtain open slightly and peered outside. A young man, probably not even twenty years old, stood outside the room. "Who the fuck are you?" said Purple, loudly enough to be heard outside.

"Here to collect you," came the young man's muffled voice from beyond the door.

"What the fuck?" replied Purple as he looked at his watch. "It's not even fucking three in the morning. Come back after breakfast."

"Doesn't work like that sir," replied the man. "I've been told to come and get you now."

Purple turned to Eyebrow. "You didn't fucking tell anyone where we are did you?"

"No, I swear Joe," replied Eyebrow. "I did exactly as you said."

"Fuck," muttered Purple as he rubbed his hands through his hair. "This might be the guy that Victoria said would come for us and take us to the safe house." Purple returned to the window and called out to the man again. "Are you alone?"

"Yes sir," he replied.

Purple again turned to Eyebrow. "Pack your shit up Eyebrow, this might be legit. But if I see a fucking hessian bag in this prick's vehicle, I'm bugging out of there faster than you can blink."

Despite their best intentions, Eyebrow and Purple were not going to be able to say farewell to their new friends as they had planned. Instead, the two of them were to be whisked away anonymously into the night – their motel room destined to be nothing but an empty shell when Alexandra and the Kombi crew swung by later that morning. But both Eyebrow and Purple were, completely understandably of course, on high alert about this new development. They may well be being bundled away under the cover of darkness, but the colossal question now loomed – where to?

CHAPTER 61

Notice to Move

Twelve adults – three of them geriatrics – nine children, four dogs and a chicken. That was the sum total of the clients awaiting the arrival of the coyote at 4140 AJ Bermudez – a nondescript residence in the heart of Reynosa. The single-story house nestled deep within the residential precinct was entirely unremarkable and anonymous, which was precisely its purpose as it served as the staging post for the activities of the coyote who would be overseeing Eyebrow and Purple's leap across the border later that evening.

The house in which they were temporarily sequestered was sparsely appointed, which was to be expected, given its function. Chairs and sofas of various styles were dotted around the rooms, with Eyebrow currently sitting awkwardly in a rainbow-coloured vinyl lawn chair, while Purple was nestled in a tattered La-Z-Boy that must have been at least twenty years old. Interspersed among the furniture was a selection of mattresses, some of which were in use by dozing toddlers, as well as those who had been summoned similarly to Eyebrow and Purple in the dead of night.

The coyote's money man had collected the fees from all present and it was Eyebrow's hope that it was the full payment and not simply a deposit, because he had now officially depleted his cash-on-hand reserves. "That's all I had Joe," he whispered to Purple. "I've got no more cash on me. I'm broke."

"You still have some back at your place though don't you?" asked Purple.

"Yeah, but if we don't get across the border…"

Purple cut Eyebrow off quickly. "We're on the home stretch Eyebrow. Look around you. We're prepped for departure. If we don't get across the border now, we've got bigger issues than no money. Trust the process Eyebrow… just strap in and go with it."

The conversation was interrupted by a buzz from Eyebrow's phone. Pulling the phone from his pocket, he looked at it with a confused expression before answering. "Hello?" There was no response from the other end. "Hello?" he repeated. Again, no response. Eyebrow terminated the call and returned the phone to his pocket. "No idea what that was."

"No-one on the other end?" asked Purple.

"Nothing," replied Eyebrow. "Probably a butt dial."

"Do you know the number?"

"No idea. I've only got a couple of people in my contact list, and it wasn't any of them."

All the occupants were permitted free movement around the house and garden as they awaited their departure that evening and with the clock ticking past midday, Purple rose and made his way to the picnic table in the corner where a basic spread of sandwiches and fruit had been graciously provided for the assembled cohort. Eyebrow's mystery phone call was still bugging him though. "You ever seen that number before?"

Eyebrow stood and joined his colleague. "No, never," he replied as he reached for an egg sandwich.

"Fuck me, you're rolling the dice with that selection Eyebrow," noted Purple, who had performed a risk assessment of the table and instead selected an apple and a plain cheese sandwich. As an occupant on one of the nearby mattresses let out a scorching sleep-fart, Purple turned to Eyebrow and beckoned him outside. "Come on, let's get some fucking air."

Walking into the small garden at the rear of the house, Eyebrow sidestepped a battered tricycle and eased into a deckchair beside the pool that clearly had been devoid of water for an extended period – the only contents being some hardy desert plants that had forced their way through cracks in the parched concrete. "You think we're leaving tonight Joe?"

"Almost certainly," replied Purple. "This place is in a very short notice to move state, so I can pretty much guarantee it. I have no idea where they'll be dropping us though. If you don't have any money left, we might have to bum a ride from someone. Knowing our luck, we'll probably get picked up by some guy with a bunch of chainsaws and masks made out of human skin in his fucking truck."

Joe Purple wasn't wrong with regard to the danger they still faced, even if the form in which that danger would manifest was a little off the mark. As Purple walked to the far end of the pool to retrieve a deck chair for himself, the sound of car tyres crunching to a halt outside the house could be heard, followed soon thereafter by the thud of three doors closing in quick succession. Purple paused in thought momentarily before the reality of Eyebrow's earlier ghost call suddenly dawned on him. He quickly flipped the chair he was dragging and shouted to Eyebrow. "We need to get the fuck out of here right now!"

"What's going on Joe?" asked Eyebrow as he slowly rose from his deckchair far too casually for Purple's liking.

Purple reached over, grabbed Eyebrow by the back of the neck and forcefully ushered him to the fence at the front of the house. "Get the fuck over here now!" he barked. "We've got about three fucking seconds to get out of here." Purple scaled the fence and peered over it to where a black SUV was parked in front of the house. He quickly assessed the situation and, determining that the car appeared to be empty, beckoned Eyebrow to follow him. "Over the fence Eyebrow, let's go!"

As the two men leapt to the ground, Eyebrow again pressed for an explanation. "What's happening Joe?"

Purple didn't respond, instead directing Eyebrow behind a brick fence on the other side of the road. "Get the fuck down Eyebrow. Stay quiet." Purple peered cautiously through one of the ornate bricks in the wall, trying to verify his initial suspicion. As he did so, he whispered to Eyebrow. "It's that fucking phone of yours. That call you got… whoever the fuck this is, they knew we were here, and they used your phone to make sure we were inside." He turned and looked directly at Eyebrow. "Turn it off, NOW!"

Eyebrow quickly obeyed and after returning the now inert phone to his pocket, sought Purple's input on the current state of affairs. "What are we going to do Joe? Who do you think these guys are?"

"No fucking idea, on both counts," replied Purple without taking his eyes off the front of the safe house.

Purple was entirely correct in his theory that Eyebrow's phone had played a pivotal role in identifying their location. What he did not know of course, and it would have been inconceivable even if he'd been told, was that the unknown arrivals were there on the orders of the Secretary of State himself.

Neither man had any inkling that Jimmy Eyebrow, AKA "La Tormenta," was officially destined to be killed in a shootout during an escape attempt after he'd been captured and prepared for extradition. That was going to be the formal line anyway – the truth of the matter being that he, and most likely Purple, were intended to be driven into the desert on the outskirts of town and despatched in a more clinical fashion, after which the fabrication of their demise would begin in earnest.

Joe Purple's astute observation skills from his old life had not let him down in his moment of need and while they had managed to escape the house by the skin of their teeth, the problem now arose as to how they would manage to remain secreted. As Purple identified three men now exiting the house, the situation took a sudden turn for the worse as the words "Oye tú, sal de aquí!" came angrily from behind them.

Purple spun around to see the owner of the property, the garden of which he and Eyebrow were currently crouched in, stalking towards them with a shovel poised for action. Purple tried to placate the man by holding his hands up defensively. "No hablo español. We just need to stay here for a few minutes, that's all."

The homeowner was undeterred and now shouted at them. "Sal de aquí antes de que llame a la policía!"

"What's he saying Joe?" asked Eyebrow.

"I haven't got a fucking clue Eyebrow," replied Purple frantically. "I heard him say 'policia', so it's probably something to do with calling the police." Purple glanced through the brickwork again, seeing that the mystery men had become aware of the commotion coming from behind the wall. Purple turned to the homeowner again, pleading with him for quiet, but this appeared to anger him even more and he lunged at Purple with his shovel.

"Salir! Salir!" he shouted, prodding the makeshift weapon aggressively towards his unwanted guests. Eyebrow and Purple now had little choice but to cede to the man's directions and they rushed through the side gate, into an alleyway that abutted the house, only to immediately come face-to-face with the three men from whom they had been hiding.

Purple reached behind him in an effort to feign moving for a firearm. "Stay the fuck back. I'll start fucking shooting if you don't."

The lead man raised his open palms towards Purple. "There's no need for that friend. We're here to help you. We've been sent to bring you home."

"Who the fuck sent you?" asked Purple skeptically.

"A friend," replied the man.

"Esteban?" asked Eyebrow.

The man smiled. "Yes, Esteban. He sent us to bring you home."

"It's all good Joe," said Eyebrow with a smile. "They're friends of Esteban."

While the front man was all smiles, Purple couldn't help but notice that the other two seemed more sinister and, worryingly, were holding their hands in precisely the same manner as Purple. The lead man spoke again. "It's OK, you can come with us. We'll keep you safe."

Eyebrow began to move before he was halted by Purple. "Stay right where you are Eyebrow," he said as he placed an arm-bar in front of him.

The man now adopted a more menacing tone. "I assure you friend, the easiest way to do this is to come with us right now. Don't make this bigger than it needs to be."

As Eyebrow, Purple and the three men stood in the alley with eyes locked together, a Mexican standoff was underway – not a metaphorical one, but a legitimate standoff in Mexico. It didn't last long though as a sudden roar came from the rear – Eyebrow and Purple pivoting in place to see a yellow blur screech to a halt across the alleyway behind them. A sliding door was flung open and two old friends emerged with fire in their eyes – Alexandra and Victoria.

The head man of the group of three reached behind his back while holding a hand up toward Victoria. "Sir, step back now. This is your only warning."

Alexandra issued a simple command to Eyebrow and Purple – "get down." They did so without hesitation, hitting the dirt at the same time as Alexandra and Victoria produced automatic weapons from behind their flowing gowns.

Victoria in particular was livid, aiming directly for the first man. "Sir? SIR?" A burst from the rifle ensued. "IT'S MA'AM THANK YOU!" Alexandra simultaneously dropped one of the men standing at the rear, while the other quickly turned and fled, clearly understanding that he was significantly outgunned.

Victoria walked over to the first man who was writhing on the ground. Looking up, he spat some blood in Victoria's direction before speaking belligerently. "You fucking bitch," he wheezed.

Victoria stood over him. "You're right, I am a bitch. A BAD one." The final point was rammed home very clearly as Victoria swung the butt of the rifle firmly into the man's face, knocking him unconscious.

The situation resolved, in the short term at least, Alexandra looked down upon Eyebrow and Purple. "You two really thought you could leave without saying goodbye?"

Eyebrow looked up at Alexandra, confused. "What... the fuck is going on?"

"We saw them come to the motel this morning," replied Alexandra. "They clearly had bad intentions for you, so we made sure to follow them. We presumed they'd lead us to wherever you were, so now's the time to thank us for saving your lives." Alexandra flashed a broad smile and held out a hand for Eyebrow.

"Jesus, thanks I guess," replied Eyebrow as he hoisted himself out of the dirt with Alexandra's help.

"Yeah, we owe you one," added Purple, dusting himself off.

They were now joined by Brandy who had emerged from The Big Banana and placed a firm hand on Eyebrow's shoulder. "More than just pretty faces hey?"

"I always knew that," replied Eyebrow with a smile.

Purple interjected. "When you're done flirting, there's a little business that we need to attend to. In case you didn't notice, we just had a fucking shootout in the middle of the street. So... what's the plan of attack here?"

"We should go back and wait to be collected," said Eyebrow as he started walking toward the safe house.

Victoria made to speak but Purple preempted what he knew was going to be said. "Just let him go so that he can work this out for himself. This'll take about five seconds."

Sure enough, as Eyebrow approached the house, several of the coyote's men, who had rushed to see what the commotion was, walked towards Eyebrow, waving their arms. "No, no, no..." they said repeatedly. "Terminado," one of them added. "El peligro," opined another.

Eyebrow turned and sought assistance. "What are they saying?"

"You're too much danger," replied Victoria. "They will not be taking you."

While Eyebrow dejectedly stood rooted to the spot, Purple paced in the middle of the street, hands atop his head. "Fuck! I knew it, I fucking knew it. Right when we were about to get home. Why the fuck did I even entertain the idea that maybe, just maybe, this one time it wouldn't turn into a flaming bag of shit."

"What are we going to do now Joe?" asked Eyebrow.

"Yet again, I have no fucking clue," said Purple as he continued to pace. "Between whoever the fuck that was trying to kill us, and the goddamn Red Notice, I'm almost at the point where Interpol is looking like the fucking preferable option." Purple stopped and looked directly at Eyebrow. "I'm seriously fucking considering just going to the border and walking up to the checkpoint, and I really don't give a shit if I get arrested at this point. We can see if your buddy can help us when we're in the can, and we just clench our balloon knots and ride it out. What do you think?"

Alexandra could sense Purple's frustration boiling to the surface and interrupted before Eyebrow could respond. "Before either of you make any rash choices, I suggest that we get away from here, find somewhere to sit and relax, and begin processing your options. This is not the time or place to be making important decisions."

For Jimmy Eyebrow and Joe Purple, it was once more a case of so near, but still so far. Yet as they were being ushered toward The Big Banana to be whisked away to whatever place of rational reflection their friends had earmarked, neither man knew that their time in Mexico was soon to come to an end. There is an old saying that many people who fail never realized how close they were to success when they gave up. Joe Purple had hit the wall and was preparing to give up, and there was every likelihood that he would drag Eyebrow along with him. What he didn't know was how close they now were to an outcome neither of them saw coming.

CHAPTER 62

Uncle Ron's Cancelled Appointment

The heavens had opened in Washington, but no matter how inclement the weather, Myles Garrison was not willing to run the risk of discussing his off-the-books business within the walls of the State Department. Regardless though, the rain that day was intense, so he forewent his usual walk to the Vietnam Veterans' Memorial in preference to a quick dash across the street to the small, but still suitably private, Triangle Park.

Garrison had been waiting to receive a coded message from his associate in Mexico that would read "Uncle Ron just left for his appointment." Once received, Garrison would sleep soundly, knowing that the Jimmy Eyebrow situation had been resolved. But the message did not come. *A* message came, that much is true, just not *that* message. When the phone buzzed in Garrison's pocket, his pulse elevated in anticipation. But it was only a few seconds after opening the message that he felt as though he'd been struck in the gut by prime Mike Tyson.

Uncle Ron cancelled his appointment.

The word "cancelled" was particularly galling for Garrison because of its meaning in the clandestine nomenclature he and his associate had developed. If Uncle Ron had *missed* his appointment, it would have meant that Eyebrow simply never turned up. But to *cancel* his appointment... cancelling meant that the operation had been initiated but suffered a major setback. As Garrison dialled his phone, the task at hand was now to find out from his associate exactly how major that setback had been.

The call was answered at the other end and Garrison wasted no time cutting to the chase. "What happened?" he asked, without taking a moment for even the most cursory of greetings.

"He got away," came the simple reply.

Garrison was visibly frustrated as the rain cascaded over his umbrella that was putting up a valiant fight against the onslaught from above. "I know he got away," he hissed. "What I want to know now is *how* you lost him."

"He had help," said Garrison's associate.

"Help? From who?"

"They jumped our men in an alley. They weren't expecting your man to have backup."

"What the hell do you mean by backup?" asked Garrison.

"A vehicle pulled up and your man's bodyguards poured out, weapons in hand. It was over in seconds."

"What sort of vehicle? Military?"

"A Kombi van I believe," came the reply.

Confusion spread across Garrison's face. "A Kombi van? Are you sure?"

"That's what was reported."

"So, who were these bodyguards? Paramilitary? Mercenaries?" There was a pause of significant length from the other end of the line, causing Garrison to enquire if the call had been dropped. "Hello? Are you still there?"

"Yes, I'm here," came the soft reply.

Garrison pressed again. "Who were the bodyguards?"

The response was a mix of defeat and shame. "Mexican transvestites."

This time the silence came from Garrison's end of the line as he stood immobile, the only sound being the rain pounding atop his umbrella. It lingered, but the man on the other end was not going to interject. Eventually Garrison spoke haltingly. "Mexican... *transvestites?*"

"Yes," came the simple reply.

Frustration began to break across Garrison's face. "You mean to tell me, that your trained men, who I pay you a LOT of goddamn money to keep on the payroll, were taken out by a squad of fucking cross-dressers?"

"Two."

"What do you mean two?"

"It was two of them."

"TWO???" bellowed Garrison. "There was only two of them?"

"They seemed very well trained, and apparently very angry."

Garrison closed his eyes and firmly pinched the bridge of his nose. "Jesus Christ! I need you to do what you're fucking paid to do and FIND THIS PRICK!" There would be no formalities as Garrison angrily terminated the call and immediately began typing a message to Gustavo Torres.

Barbary ASAP. On my way there now.

The Secretary of State was already fuming when he walked into *The Barbary Kitchen*, and his foul mood was exacerbated when no-one was there to meet with him. To be fair to Torres, Garrison did arrive within ten minutes of dashing off his text message, so maybe a little understanding could be in order. But as the time ticked by, Garrison soon began to take on the look of a man who had been stood up by a blind date after she sent her friend into the bar for a reconnaissance mission.

Each time the door swung open, Garrison expected Torres to enter, but he did not. Instead, another man approached the table and sat, eliciting a response from Garrison. "I'm sorry, but this table's taken. I'm waiting for a guest."

The man was unmoved by Garrison's words. "I'm sorry Mister Secretary, but I've been sent to let you know that Mister Torres will not be joining you today. He wishes me to convey to you that his business with you has come to an end."

"Bullshit," snapped Garrison. "Who the fuck are you? Where's Torres?"

"As I said Mister Secretary, Mister Torres no longer wishes to meet with you."

The man made to stand up, but Garrison grabbed his arm and dragged him back down into his seat. "Don't you fucking walk away from me. Tell me what the hell's going on here."

The man glanced at his arm, indicating non-verbally that it would be wise for Garrison to remove his hand, which he promptly did. "The situation in Venezuela has not played out as expected Mister Secretary. Popular support is crumbling, due in large part to you not being able to control the narrative on this La Tormenta character of yours."

"He's not ours for Christ sake," snarled Garrison through gritted teeth. "He's a fucking anomaly – something outside our control."

"Be that as it may Mister Secretary, the flow-on effect has been significant. The coup *will* fail, it is a certainty from this point. Mister Torres's situation is now untenable."

Garrison angrily pounded the table, drawing stares from some of the other customers. "I'm fixing it!"

The man stood again, this time with more certainty than before. "I'm sorry Mister Secretary. The moment has been lost." And with that final statement, the man turned and departed, leaving a devastated Garrison alone with his thoughts.

His back-channel partnership with Torres had been a gamble of the highest order and as his roulette wheel slowly came to a halt, the ball was about to settle far from the number where he had placed his entire stack of chips. In the evolution of roulette science, it was determined very early that an understanding of basic physics could swing the pendulum in the player's favour, hence why later iterations of roulette apparatus introduced what are termed "hazards" around the wheel to add randomness to the spinning ball. On Garrison's wheel, Jimmy Eyebrow was a hazard that hadn't been accounted for, and his presence had caused the entire Venezuela operation to veer so far off course that it was now unsalvageable.

With the coup going to hell in a handbasket and Torres cashing out before he lost his entire bankroll, Garrison was now faced with a fight for his own political survival. His anger toward Eyebrow – this man he had never even met – was now at boiling point. In his own mind, the plan that he and Torres had hatched was a masterpiece, yet all it took was an oiled-up Jimmy Eyebrow and his star-spangled jocks to bring it all crashing down. Garrison's resolve was now doubled – he would find Eyebrow and make him pay.

CHAPTER 63

The Crossing

A handful of miles outside Reynosa sits an elegant hacienda that is the home of Javier Calderon, arguably the most powerful and well-connected human trafficker in the Mexican North-East. On this day he was sitting poolside, his turquoise shirt spread open and exposing his deeply tanned chest to the sun, while he dragged on the final remnants of a cigar that some time earlier in the day, would no doubt have been significantly larger.

Calderon remained silent, digesting the information that had just been given to him, along with the request that had accompanied it. He took in the sight standing before him – three significantly makeup-challenged drag-queens, alongside Jimmy Eyebrow and Joe Purple, both of them grimy, haggard and showing the obvious effects of their prolonged time on the run. Calderon was likely to be Eyebrow and Purple's final option for a clandestine border crossing, and he was far higher in the pecking order than the coyote to whom they had originally been assigned. Fortunately for Eyebrow, Victoria had been able to arrange a meeting, and it was a small win to be even granted an audience.

As Calderon assessed Eyebrow and Purple, he offered his thoughts. "You must understand that I am not your garden variety coyote. My business model is much more sophisticated, and I am the one you call upon when you have, shall I say, *special needs*."

Purple glanced sideways at Eyebrow before responding to Calderon. "Well, we tick the special needs box, that's for sure."

Calderon stood and walked a few feet before turning. "Moving the infamous La Tormenta and his assistant across the border will be a challenge. With Interpol on the lookout as well… resources will be required. And, my friends, resources such as those required to get you two safely across will cost."

"How much?" asked Eyebrow. Calderon returned to the table, scribbled a number on a slip of paper and handed it to Eyebrow, who quickly turned to Joe Purple. "Jesus Joe, I don't have this on me. I'm broke."

"Do you have it back at your place?" asked Purple.

"Yeah, at least twice that much," replied Eyebrow.

Purple turned to Calderon. "We don't have that money on us at the moment. Can we pay you once we're over?"

"That's not how it works my friend," replied Calderon. "I get you across the border and you disappear, how am I to be sure that I will be paid?"

Eyebrow paused in thought before reaching for Calderon's pen. "May I?" Calderon shrugged his shoulders and handed Eyebrow the pen, at which point he scribbled out Calderon's figure and replaced it with his own, higher amount. "This is how much I can give you if you'll let me pay you at the other end."

"What the fuck are you doing Eyebrow?" whispered Purple. "Is that all your money?"

"That's all of it Joe. We're in trouble, and I'm trying to fix it."

Calderon perused the slip of paper and raised his eyebrows. "You'll pay this much if I'll extend you credit?"

"Yes," replied Eyebrow. "I'll get it for you on the other side. Extra for you taking on the risk."

"Excuse us for a moment," said Purple as he dragged Eyebrow away and lowered his voice. "How the fuck do you plan on getting that money? He's not going to drive us to fucking Coffee Pond."

"I hadn't thought that far ahead Joe," replied Eyebrow.

"Oh, there's a fucking surprise!" hissed Purple. "You're promising this guy a bag load of cash and you have no way to actually get it. Jesus, I wonder how that'll end up playing out?"

Eyebrow turned to Calderon. "If I can get you this money on delivery, will you take us?" Calderon stayed silent, thinking his way through the proposal. Eyebrow was no longer prepared to wait though and pushed forcefully, bordering on insolence. "Answer me! Is this enough?"

Victoria quickly stepped in. "Jimmy, don't speak to Mister Calderon like that."

But instead of responding with offence, Calderon waved off Victoria's words. "It's OK," he said. "Señor Eyebrow is a businessman, like myself. Sometimes, you have to be firm, I understand that." Calderon walked toward Eyebrow and stood directly in front of him. He nodded gently as he spoke. "I am taking a risk, but that risk is factored into your offer. I'm thinking… I'm thinking that we may have an agreement."

Calderon extended his hand, which Eyebrow grasped firmly in return. "Thanks Mister Calderon. I won't let you down."

"We are friendly at the moment," cautioned Calderon. "But if you are lying to me, I will not hesitate to extract payment from your friends here that you leave behind." He turned and waved his hand toward Alexandra, Brandy and Victoria. "Have I made myself clear?"

"Crystal," replied Joe Purple. "Can we have a few moments please?"

"Be my guests," replied Calderon, before he added an observation. "Well, technically you *are* my guests, so feel free to take as many moments as you need."

Eyebrow and Purple walked a short distance away onto the lawn before Purple spoke. "So, what's the plan Eyebrow? How are you going to get this money?"

"I don't know Joe. I need your help to think of an idea."

"Fuck, I don't know Eyebrow," replied Purple as he began to pace. "We don't even know where they're going to drop us."

"What if we *did* know? Maybe if we can find out exactly where we're going to be delivered, I can arrange for someone to meet us with the money."

Purple bit his lip as he considered Eyebrow's suggestion. "Not the worst idea you've had Eyebrow. That might work." Purple turned to Calderon. "Mister Calderon, can we agree on a location to be dropped before we leave? We want to ensure the money's at the agreed spot."

"We can do that, yes," replied Calderon.

Purple turned back to Eyebrow. "OK, how are you going to get the money to where you need it?"

"I'm working on that," replied Eyebrow. Silence descended on the two of them as Eyebrow's thought processes worked overtime. After close to a minute of pacing and muttering to himself, he spoke. "I need to make a couple of calls."

"Not fucking here you're not!" snapped Purple immediately. "That phone of yours will get us all killed."

Eyebrow turned and spoke to Calderon. "Am I allowed to leave Mister Calderon?"

"Any time you wish," replied Calderon. "You're not my prisoner. You being here, or not, is entirely inconsequential to me."

Eyebrow was in full understanding that the moment a tower picked up his phone's signal, the people who had earlier confronted he and Purple would be on their way again, and probably in greater numbers. If Calderon was going to help him, it would be poor form to lead them directly to his estate. "I'll go somewhere else Joe."

"Where are you going?" asked Purple.

"I need to be near a tower so I can get a signal. I'll have to be as close to the river as I can."

Purple mulled over Eyebrow's plan before he offered his thoughts. He too had come to the same conclusion that the phone signal would start a ticking clock, and as such, Eyebrow would have to be on a tight leash. "I'm coming with you. You're going to have to get your business done quickly so that we can be out of there before you're located. And can you do me a favour when you're done Eyebrow?"

"What's that Joe?"

"Throw that fucking thing into the river. Take care of all your business and then get rid of it. Once you're done with whatever it is that you're doing, we need to stay as low as a snake's nutsack until we're over the border. Got it?"

"Got it Joe," replied Eyebrow.

And with that, the endgame had begun. Less than an hour later, Eyebrow, Purple and Victoria descended a small rubbish-strewn hill toward the Rio Grande in a vehicle graciously loaned to them by Calderon – The Big Banana being far too conspicuous for this mission. The chosen location served two purposes, the first being proximity to a stateside tower, while the second was a tactical decision as the layout would allow Purple and Victoria to take the slightly higher ground in their role as lookouts, while Eyebrow attended to his business.

"You got everything?" asked Purple as Eyebrow prepared to walk as close to the river as he could.

Eyebrow did a quick check of his inventory. "Pen, notebook, and exact location where Mister Calderon told me we'll be dropped off. I've got everything I need Joe."

"And what's happening to the phone when you're done?" asked Purple, to which Eyebrow responded with a simple flick of his hand toward the river. "We'll be right up here," said Purple, pointing a short distance up the road. "If we spot any danger, I'll come get you. Try to be quick Eyebrow. There's fucking danger everywhere here."

"Got it Joe," said Eyebrow as he began to walk off. "I'll be back shortly," he added, looking over his shoulder.

But Eyebrow wasn't back shortly. As Victoria and Purple watched over him from slightly higher, Purple was getting anxious. "What the fuck is he doing? He's been on that phone for fucking ages." Both Purple and Victoria stayed on high alert as they observed the surrounding roads for incoming danger, all the while Eyebrow's ear remained glued to the phone, save for occasions where he appeared to terminate a call before starting a new one. It also appeared that notes of some significance were frenetically being recorded in the notebook that Purple had astutely encouraged him to take with him.

"Come on Eyebrow…" whispered Purple. "Hurry up." Eyebrow's version of "shortly" soon ticked past twenty-five minutes and as each subsequent minute elapsed, Purple's anxiety increased proportionally. "I've gotta go get him," he said with panic in his voice before Victoria sought to allay his concerns with a steadying hand on the arm.

"Just give him a little longer Joe." But no sooner had the words fallen from Victoria's mouth than Purple's fear of the inevitable became reality. "Actually, let's not give him any longer Joe," added Victoria, quickly rising and drawing Purple's attention to a convoy of vehicles approaching in the distance.

"That's gotta be them," said Purple as he rushed down the hill, arms flailing and screaming for Eyebrow's attention. "Come on! We gotta go NOW!" he yelled. Eyebrow immediately terminated the call and began running back up the hill before Purple intervened. "The phone! Get rid of the fucking phone!"

"Shit!" replied Eyebrow as he quickly turned on his heels and made back toward the river before heaving the phone into the water like a trebuchet hurling a smallpox infected corpse over the wall of a medieval castle. Turning again, he sprinted up the hill to where Purple was frantically beckoning him.

"Quick Eyebrow!" he yelled as Victoria started the vehicle and swung the door open. Both men dove inside as Victoria peeled away from the scene and departed with haste, Purple staring intently through the rear window in the hope that they weren't followed. Thankfully, they were not.

Purple had been correct about the phone signal being their Achilles heel and with the phone now out of the picture, he could begin to breathe a little easier. Hopefully they were now on the home stretch. "So, fill me in Eyebrow," he said. "Is your guy going to be there tonight?"

"No," replied Eyebrow. "It's a long way for him to come and he needs to organize a few things, so it's going to be around two days until we can leave."

"Ahh, fuck me, are you serious?" moaned Purple.

"I am, but trust me Joe, it's gonna work," said Eyebrow. "It's complex. I was on the phone for a while…"

"Yeah, we saw that," interrupted Purple.

"I had to be Joe," replied Eyebrow, now looking Purple directly in the eye. "I had a million messages from Spaulding, so I called him first. He's managed to pull the whole thing apart. And Joe, this is fucking way bigger than you could ever imagine." Eyebrow waved his notebook triumphantly. "What's in here Joe, is our golden ticket. If we can get this information to where it needs to be, we'll be fucking untouchable."

CHAPTER 64

Agent of Chaos

Myles Garrison was none too pleased to be summoned to a briefing with Deputy Director of Intelligence Operations Van Pelt, especially as it involved a dash across the open courtyard to a different conference room than the one that the Eyebrow taskforce had been using to that point.

As he walked into the room, he let his displeasure be known. "What's going on?" he asked brusquely.

Leo Bishop slipped in alongside Garrison. "Can I take your overcoat sir?"

Garrison didn't reply but eased out of his coat and handed it to Bishop who promptly hooked it onto the coat rack. Van Pelt stood and beckoned Garrison to join him. "We've had a development of sorts sir," said Van Pelt.

"Eyebrow?" asked Garrison. "Have you located him?"

"It's in the broad Eyebrow sphere of influence sir. Not specifically about him, but a situation around the edges."

"Go on."

"If you recall sir, among the many briefing points, we discussed a missing accountant by the name of Julian Cooper."

Garrison sat forward in his chair ever so slightly. "I do recall that. Please continue."

Van Pelt continued. "Well, we did some further background work, and it turns out that Cooper is just one of at least seven accountants who were all reported missing within a very short space of time."

"Six of whom have not reappeared anywhere," added Bishop.

"Seven? Really?" asked Garrison, hoping that his feigned surprise would pass muster, especially in the face of the Deputy Director of Intelligence. "And you say that you couldn't find six of them... what about the seventh?"

"He walked into a field office earlier today sir. We've arranged for Agents Black and Dekker to interview him..." Van Pelt glanced at his watch. "Probably about now actually."

"Very well," said Garrison as he stood. "This is probably not something for me to get involved with, as interesting as it may sound. Please keep me informed if you hear anything of substance."

"Let me get your coat for you sir," said Bishop as he held Garrison's overcoat open for him to slide into.

"Thank you, sir," said Van Pelt as Garrison departed as briskly and devoid of fanfare as he had arrived.

Van Pelt's revelation that one of the missing accountants had resurfaced was a disaster for Garrison. He quickly and rudely dismissed his security detail in the courtyard while he made an urgent phone call – the criticality of the situation overriding any established protocol of visiting a nearby park. The call was quickly picked up at the other end and Garrison wasted no time in cutting to the chase. "What the fuck have you done? You told me it was all done clean."

"What are we talking about?" came the reply.

"The goddamn accountants," snapped Garrison. "You told me that you got them all. They've done the background on it and pulled the threads. They fucking know about all of them."

"We did get them all," said the man on the other end. "What have you heard otherwise?"

"What have I heard?" growled Garrison. "I've got the fucking Deputy Director of Intelligence telling me that one of them has wandered into a field office and they've sent a couple of federal agents to interview him!"

"When?"

"Right fucking now! You fucking left one of them alive!"

"We did not."

"Then how the fuck do they have one? You need to fix this, NOW!"

There was silence from the other end for a few moments before the unknown voice responded. "I'm sorry, but there's too much heat on this now. We're out."

"YOU'RE OUT?" bellowed Garrison, drawing attention from one of his security men before waving him away. He lowered his voice and repeated himself. "You're *out*? You're not out. You work for me. *I'm* the one who decides when you're out."

For the second time recently, Garrison's bravado was again shut down. "You seem to misunderstand the dynamic of our relationship Mister Secretary. We have been paid generously, I understand and appreciate that. But now the time has come when our business is concluded. Whatever heat's coming down, it's yours and yours alone to deal with." And with that, the call ended, and Garrison was left alone while his world burned around him. Abandoned by Torres and now without the protective umbrella of his hit squad, Garrison painted a sad and sorry picture as he trudged forlornly back inside the State Department.

As Garrison entered the small foyer off the courtyard, Van Pelt was descending the stairs inside. "Sir, there's been a development. Could you come back up to the conference room?"

Garrison was hardly in the mood for a meeting of any sort. "Now isn't the best time, Robert. Whatever the development, I trust you to manage it."

"We really need you sir," pushed Van Pelt. "I wouldn't ask if it wasn't absolutely necessary."

Garrison sighed audibly and accompanied Van Pelt back up one flight of stairs where Van Pelt ushered him into the conference room. Expecting the same contingent as the one he'd left only a short time before, he was understandably surprised and more than a little confused to see agents Black and Dekker in the room when he was of the belief that they were in the field. Even more astounding was the presence of a man he knew very well in his professional capacity – Attorney General Dick Salveson.

"Dick, what are you doing here?" asked Garrison, extending his hand in greeting – a greeting that was not returned as Salveson stood and walked toward the window. "What have you done Myles?" he said glumly.

"I don't understand what you mean," replied Garrison, before pausing. "What the hell is that?" he added as he walked towards the desk to see a mobile phone sitting there. He spoke once more. "What's this?" His face fell as he heard his own words coming from the speaker.

Salveson turned and looked at Garrison with a subtle tinge of sadness in his eyes – clearly a man torn between friendship and duty. He repeated his earlier question as Garrison rummaged furiously through the pockets of his overcoat. "Myles, what have you done?"

Garrison had found what he was looking for and brandished the small GSM listening device angrily. "What the fuck is this? Who put this in my goddamn pocket? I'll have you arrested!" Garrison was by now beginning to lose all composure. "I'm the fucking Secretary of State of the goddamn United States of America! Who the fuck put this in my pocket? This is treason!" He turned angrily to Van Pelt. "Was it you, you prick?"

Van Pelt raised his hands defensively. "Sir, you know that our charter prevents us from conducting operations domestically."

"Bullshit!" thundered Garrison, his forehead giving every indication that a massive cardiac event may be imminent. "This has your fucking fingerprints all over it. You may as well have gone down to the Archives, taken the Constitution out of its case and wiped your arse with it. You're fucking finished, I'll see to it."

"It wasn't him sir, it was me," said Bishop, entering the conversation. "This has nothing to do with the Deputy Director."

Garrison in his heightened state was not going to be placated. "I don't give a flying fuck. You're finished too…. every single one of you." Garrison pointed furiously at every law enforcement officer and intelligence official in the room. "I'm going to go and see the President right now."

As Garrison began to move toward the door, Attorney General Salveson intervened. "You'll do nothing of the sort Myles. Come back here please."

"This is a bullshit setup Dick, you know that," raged Garrison as he half-complied with Salveson's direction by at least halting his departure, though not returning to take a seat.

"It's not a setup sir," said Van Pelt from the side. "This has come about because of your own carelessness."

"What are you talking about?" snapped Garrison.

"When you and I were talking recently, you enquired about whether we'd had any breakthrough with regards to the missing accountants. Something that struck me as curious at the time was a small point, but interesting nonetheless. You mentioned accountants, plural, yet we'd never briefed you about the fact that multiple accountants had disappeared. I asked around the team, and no-one had disclosed that fact to you at that point. Now, unfortunately, we have *not* in fact discovered one of the missing accountants. But, as suspected, your belief that Agents Black and Dekker were questioning one allowed us to sit ringside for that enlightening conversation you just had." Van Pelt punctuated his point by tapping the phone on the table for emphasis.

"Proves nothing," replied Garrison dismissively.

"Myles, please," said Salveson. "I listened to the entire conversation."

"Completely inadmissible in court," countered Garrison confidently.

"I agree," replied Salveson, eliciting a smug smile from Garrison. "A court of law that is. But the court of public opinion… well, that's a different matter."

Garrison now paced, as if he were a defense attorney questioning a witness. "I'm curious. What's the end game here? I mean, all you've got is one half of a conversation that you've listened to, illegally might I add, and some pure speculation based on a single comment that I made." Garrison spun on his heels theatrically to continue pressing his point. "And, if I may note, a comment that could easily have been misconstrued by our esteemed, soon to be former, Deputy Director of Intelligence. Tell me Dick, is that really all you have in your arsenal?"

"Interesting you should say that Myles," replied Salveson. "Because no, it isn't. I think that in the bigger scheme of things, you organizing the murder of enough accountants to shock even the most ardent anti-capitalist is probably the least of your concerns right now." Salveson now waved for Bishop to open the door to a side room. "Bring them in please detective."

"What the fuck is going on?" asked Garrison frantically as Bishop returned with Jimmy Eyebrow, Joe Purple and one other man. Garrison squinted and took a few moments before ultimately recognizing the infamous "La Tormenta" who had derailed his entire operation, instantly exploding with rage and gesticulating wildly toward Eyebrow. "It's YOU! What is this prick doing here? Fucking arrest him!"

Salveson paid no heed to Garrison's outburst and instead walked toward the three, extending his hand to the man accompanying Eyebrow and Purple. "Robert, it's great to see you again. I caught your lecture at Georgetown last year. I must say, I was quite surprised to see you getting involved in this. I thought you were done with practicing."

"Just this once," replied the man as he shook Salveson's hand warmly. "I owed an old friend a favour."

Joe Purple leant over and whispered in Eyebrow's ear. "I can't fucking believe that you actually got OJ Simpson's old lawyer on your case. You never cease to surprise me Eyebrow."

"Esteban organized it Joe," whispered Eyebrow in return. "I had nothing to do with it."

Garrison was flummoxed. "Anyone care to explain what the hell's going on here?"

***

What was going on had its genesis several days earlier as Jimmy Eyebrow stood on the bank of the Rio Grande organizing his and Purple's escape from Mexico. He had made four phone calls that day, the first of which was to Esteban Gutierrez to advise that he was safe and that he expected to return home imminently. Eyebrow briefed Gutierrez on the failure of his mission to recover Santiago's money, to which Gutierrez responded that he was simply grateful that Eyebrow appeared to be safe after such a torrid experience.

At that stage, Eyebrow had only two more calls to make, and he pondered in which order he should approach them. He quickly chose to call Spaulding first, given that the plethora of messages popping up on the newly connected phone indicated that there had been a development of some importance. As it turned out, Spaulding had been on a crusade to unravel the money trail, and his findings were definitely in the bombshell category.

Eyebrow furiously scrawled down notes in his notebook as Spaulding relayed detail after shocking detail, and by the time he was done, even he knew that the information he now held was a double-edged sword. While it was likely that this revelation explained the hit squad that had been stalking he and Purple, it was also a massive bargaining chip for his return home.

It was fortuitous that of the calls he needed to make following his call to Gutierrez, he had chosen to speak with Spaulding first. Without Spaulding's extraordinary information, his next call would likely have turned out much differently than it ultimately did.

An apoplectic Leo Bishop answered Eyebrow's incoming call with a near one-minute uninterrupted diatribe that felt like Bishop's fist was about to erupt from the phone and punch Eyebrow in the face. Eyebrow's request of Bishop was ambitious to say the least – to not only fly two thousand kilometres to collect he and Purple from a roadside diner in rural Texas, but also swing past Coffee Pond beforehand to retrieve a duffel bag of cash hidden in Eyebrow's kitchen. If Eyebrow did not have Spaulding's findings immediately at hand, the chances were high that his request would have been met with a refusal of the "go to fucking hell" kind.

But armed with an information cache of blockbuster proportions, Eyebrow eventually, through considerable effort, talked Bishop onside and secured his assistance for the events to come in the following seventy-two hours. The reluctance on Bishop's part still simmered close to the surface though, and he couldn't help but wonder if he was being played, and if he was simply a pawn in a broader game being played by Eyebrow.

But if what had been relayed to him was in fact true, Eyebrow and Purple had uncovered one of the greatest scandals to ever envelop the Executive Branch of the country. Bishop was understandably intrigued and cautiously agreed to the plan, albeit with the caveat that if he detected that he was being taken advantage of, he would find the nearest Texas town that still had a resident "Boss" and leave Eyebrow and Purple there for safekeeping while awaiting their day in court. Given the nature of the intelligence that Eyebrow had relayed, Bishop advised no-one, not even McFadden, of the true intentions of his journey south, simply that he was departing for a short time for "personal reasons".

Javier Calderon's high-end coyote operation was a well-oiled machine, with Eyebrow and Purple being delivered to the precise location relayed by Eyebrow within a twenty-minute window of when Calderon had promised. Ultimately though, the entire process had been somewhat anti-climactic for Eyebrow and Purple. They had images of being whisked across the border crammed into a false fuel tank or secreted in a barrel of chicken fat with a snorkel. But in the end, they just rode as normal passengers in the back seat of a car.

Calderon had spent many years cultivating a network of compliant border agents and his entire operation revolved around ensuring that he used the intelligence available to him to choose the right night to cross. His associates on the US side would inspect the manifest with a flick of the flashlight into the back of the car and in turn assess the appropriate import duty – the hotter the cargo, the higher the payment required. And the infamous La Tormenta was indeed hot cargo.

Thankfully, Bishop had successfully retrieved the bag of cash – something that Eyebrow had fretted about given that once he had thrown his phone into the river, he had no further means of communicating with the outside world. With the exchange complete, Eyebrow and Purple were left in the care of Bishop for in-flight briefings on the way to DC that would be far more comprehensive than the few minutes of frantic intelligence dumping of a couple of days prior.

Due to the sudden turn of events as he stood on the bank of the river, Eyebrow needed to make a fourth and final phone call, again to Gutierrez, to update him on the rapidly evolving situation that had suddenly developed in the mere minutes since their previous discussion. As he'd done with Bishop, Eyebrow this time relayed an abridged version of the intelligence he had on hand, as well as the plan that he and Bishop had settled on. Gutierrez, understanding the significant nature of Eyebrow's situation, assured him that he'd arrange for legal counsel of the highest order to shield both he and Purple during the events that would undoubtedly soon be unfolding.

And those events were now unfolding with ferocity in the conference room of the State Department where Garrison was raging. "Tell me what's going on!" he demanded as he fumbled through the bar fridge on a side table for a bottle of water, the gravity of the evolving situation now beginning to have its effect on him.

Attorney General Salveson spoke deliberately, firmly and devoid of emotion. "The JP Mears Foundation."

Garrison took a sip of water, his hand shaking as he did so. "Means nothing to me," he said, although the colour draining from his face told a completely different story.

Salveson turned to Bishop. "Maybe you could brief the room detective, given that you're the one who brought this whole affair to our attention."

"Happy to sir," replied Bishop as he opened a folder and began laying out the matter for everyone in the room. "Mister Eyebrow, whom we were working on the assumption was involved in a military coup in Venezuela, was in fact on nothing more than a fact-finding mission tracking some missing money when he was unexpectedly caught up in the rapidly unfolding events in Caracas."

"Oh, come on!" interrupted Garrison. "He's fooled you before and you're falling for it again. He's a fucking conman."

"I concede the fact Mister Secretary that Eyebrow is, shall we say, somewhat less than reliable at times," noted Bishop. "However, on this occasion, I've had the information he provided verified and what we have is…" Bishop screwed up his face slightly while considering the appropriate words. "What we have is… problematic for you sir." Garrison did not respond, possibly beginning to realize the inevitable outcome, and deciding that standing mute might now be the best course of action.

Bishop continued with his briefing. "Mister Eyebrow was on the trail of a cryptocurrency account where he believed the money belonging to his associate Mister Rafael Santiago had been transferred. Another associate of Mister Eyebrow's – he has many apparently – managed to breach the account and determined that a number of incoming transfers had in fact occurred, not only from Santiago's money man, but from another six different sources."

Harry Black added some commentary from nearby Bishop. "Seven different sources, and seven missing accountants. With the assistance of Mister Eyebrow's associate, we were able to trace every incoming transfer back to every one of those missing men."

Bishop seamlessly picked up where Black had left off. "The *outgoing* transfers from the crypto account, however, went to a bank account in Venezuela that, much to our surprise, is held in the name of one of the key figures involved in what has now become the failed coup."

Garrison shrugged his shoulders nonchalantly and took another sip of water. "I know nothing about that, and you could never prove that I do."

"Possibly sir, possibly," countered Bishop. "But for the fact that two months ago, the outbound transfers from the crypto account ceased, at least to the original Venezuelan account, at which time outgoing transfers began to occur to a new account – The JP Mears Foundation, which is a bank account held at the First National Bank of the Caymans." Bishop himself now took a sip of water from the glass in front of him and composed himself.

Dennis Burnett sidled up beside him and whispered. "You're doing great Leo, keep it up."

Bishop flipped a page on his notes and continued. "It appears that the flow of funds changed and now occurred from the money men, into the crypto account and out to the JP Mears account before being funneled to Venezuela – the JP Mears Foundation now being the go-between. The thing is though sir, the money going to the Mears Foundation was considerably less than the money coming *into* the crypto account. It's almost as if the owner of the crypto account was using the diversion through the Mears Foundation to skim what appears be a considerable amount from the top before filtering the money to Venezuela."

Bishop looked to Garrison for a flicker of recognition as to where the matter was headed, but Garrison remained stoic and silent. As such, Bishop pushed forward. "A little digging on the JP Mears Foundation reveals that it's registered as a charitable body, however there's no record of any activity, nor is there any online presence for the organization. In effect, there's no public footprint for it at all. The Foundation was registered by a company named Thirteen-Ten Global which, surprise surprise, is an empty shell, again with no public activities or online presence." Bishop now turned to Black and beckoned him to bring the matter home. "I'll defer to Agent Black to put the finishing touches on this matter."

"Thanks Leo," said Black as he shuffled some papers in front of him. "We were able to identify the sole director of Thirteen-Ten Global. It was quite easy in fact… it's not a very sophisticated setup." Black passed a piece of paper to Salveson. "The record indicates that the sole director is one Roger Bourke, currently residing in Parrot Key, Florida."

Salveson briefly perused the report that had been handed to him, closed his eyes and rubbed the bridge of his nose. "Jesus Christ Myles," he muttered.

Black now continued. "Clearly the Attorney General now knows where this is headed, and I suspect you do too Mister Secretary. You've been married to your wife for, what is it… fifteen years now?"

"She's got nothing to do with this!" snapped Garrison. "Keep her out of it."

"I'm sure she's got no knowledge of it sir," replied Black. "But this isn't her first marriage, is it. Before she became Jennifer Garrison, she was Jennifer Bourke for over twenty years. Married to…"

"Roger Bourke," muttered Salveson with a tinge of disgust. He stood and faced Garrison directly. "You got your wife's ex-husband involved in your deception? Without any thought about the blowback that it might have on Jennifer? What were you thinking Myles?"

Oftentimes when a rumbling volcano is on the verge of erupting, the tremors will briefly cease, and an eerie silence will descend as the pressure for the imminent explosion quickly builds. Such was the feeling that now pervaded the conference room at the State Department as everyone braced in uncomfortable silence while Garrison fought a losing battle to maintain his composure.

"It was fucking drug money for Christ sake!" he yelled furiously. "All of it! Every goddamn dollar. Who gives a shit what happened to it!" Garrison now paced and ranted. "These people make millions and sit happily in their mansions, all from selling drugs, but somehow *I'm* the bad guy here?"

"Myles, please…" began Salveson before being cut off.

"No Dick! You had your say, now it's my turn. You have no goddamn idea what I was trying to achieve here."

Salveson stood and countered firmly. "Whatever you were hoping to achieve Myles, there are ways to go about things, and this was not the way."

"Spare me," snapped Garrison. "You can live in a world of goddamn academia and rules, but I operate in the real world, where real problems exist. Sometimes a solution might not be PG rated, and things might get messy, but you know what? That's the fucking world we live in Dick – THAT'S the world we live in."

Garrison turned and stalked toward Jimmy Eyebrow, his finger outstretched like a spear at the vanguard of a Roman wedge. "And as for you... Jesus Christ, everything was in place, everything was in order, everything was running like clockwork." Garrison's eyes became wild with frustration. "But no, you had to waltz in like some goddamn hero, with your oiled-up body and fucking star-spangled jocks and screw it all up. The worst part is that you didn't even need to fucking do anything. You just... turned up and everything went to shit. You're not some big shot international hitman like they all make you out to be... you're a fucking agent of chaos, that's what you are. You're nothing... you're just like one of those goddamn monkeys that sometimes pushes the right button and gets a reward."

Eyebrow's lawyer stepped between his client and Garrison. "That'll be enough thank you Mister Secretary."

"Indeed, it will," added Salveson. "Myles, you've had your time to vent, and now I'm going to tell you what's going to happen."

"I'll never set foot in a courtroom, that's what's going to happen," Garrison retorted. "None of this would stand up to legal challenge... none of it. It's just an endless parade of illegal and warrantless cowboy policing, using this fucking idiot as a star witness and relaying the hearsay of a goddamn foreign operative that's been deemed too dangerous for his own country's intelligence service. And as for your covert listening device... good God, if that doesn't have constitutional violation written all over it in giant red letters, then I don't know what does."

"Unfortunately, Myles, you are correct on all counts," replied Salveson. "But, as we noted earlier, there is a difference between a court of law, and the court of public opinion. If this becomes public knowledge, then not only will you be hung out to dry, but it will unleash a tsunami of scrutiny onto the President and the entire administration as well. I have to assume that the President is entirely unaware of this ill-conceived escapade of yours?"

"He knows nothing," replied Garrison softly.

"He's going to have to be briefed at some stage," noted Salveson. "However, what will happen now is that your time as Secretary of State will cease as at today. Sometime in the next hour, you will advise the President that you are stepping down due to health reasons... personal reasons... to spend more time with your family... it doesn't really matter. But whatever you choose, it happens today. I'm taking it upon myself to ensure that the President is protected, so if one word of this shitshow of yours leaks, I will ensure that you get paraded in front of the pitchfork-waving mob and plastered with full responsibility."

Salveson now walked toward Eyebrow and Purple and continued addressing Garrison. "No matter how unorthodox you feel Mister Eyebrow and his assistant's methods were, there is to be no retribution on your part against them."

Joe Purple winced at yet again being perceived as Eyebrow's "assistant" but nonetheless allowed Salveson the opportunity to continue without interruption. "It should be abundantly clear that Mister Eyebrow has legal representation of the highest caliber, and any move against him I'm certain will be met with a swift and forceful counter. I don't wish for it to ever get to that point Myles, do we understand each other?"

Garrison slumped in a chair, defeated. His will and ability to fight back was exhausted. He had no leg left to stand on – the day of his reckoning had arrived with ferocious intensity. Garrison did not need to answer verbally, his pathetic wave to clear the room and leave him to his thoughts was enough to convey his concession to Salveson's demands.

As those assembled in the conference room began to file out, Joe Purple broke from the pack and sauntered over to Garrison. Leaning down to look him directly in the eye, Purple spoke quietly and menacingly. "Don't ever talk to my friend like that again. You might think he's an idiot, and you might have convinced yourself that he's not a competent hitman, but dare I point out that he managed to walk right into the State Department and get within a few feet of the Secretary of State, without anyone batting even so much as an eyelid." Garrison looked up in a way that signaled to Purple that his words had delivered the desired effect. Purple smiled deviously and tapped Garrison's bottle of water. "Enjoy the rest of your drink there buddy."

As Purple hurried to rejoin the group, Eyebrow shuffled over to him. "What did you say to him Joe?"

Purple smiled contentedly. "Nothing that you have to concern yourself with Eyebrow." Purple then slung his arm across Eyebrow's shoulders. "Let's go home."

CHAPTER 65

Gone Viral

Going home wasn't immediate for Jimmy Eyebrow and Joe Purple, as there was no conceivable way that they would be released from Washington without a complete debrief on their entire journey. The Julian Cooper affair, London, Gabriel Longchamp, Venezuela, Mexico – the intelligence community wanted it all. Van Pelt, who unsurprisingly remained the Deputy Director of Intelligence despite Garrison's empty threats, was determined to pull on every thread in order to convince himself that Eyebrow was little more than a hapless passenger as events unfolded. Van Pelt had scolded Bishop and McFadden, as well as Black and Dekker, for accepting Eyebrow's version of multiple events at face value, and even after a debrief that extended into a second day, he still had difficulty accepting that there wasn't more to Jimmy Eyebrow than met the eye.

In time though, they were returned to Coffee Pond, along with a stern message from Van Pelt that both men were firmly on the intelligence radar from that point forth. Returning home, Joe Purple was aggrieved that he had been forced to abandon his fledgling business for such an extended period, unannounced at that. What had initially been expected to be a two-day flying visit to London had turned into a much longer absence and he dreaded the thought of not only the lost momentum, but also the food wastage that he was going to walk into the following morning. Notwithstanding the monetary loss, the place was going to stink of rotten cheese, smallgoods and anchovies, and would probably take a week to deep clean.

It was ten o'clock the next morning when Purple finally found the motivation to tackle the matter at hand. As much as he found comfort in the fact that he was safely home, he had nonetheless been replaying his and Eyebrow's adventure in his head, especially the wild array of different characters they had met along the way. In particular, he was happy that they'd been able to hook up once more with Alexandra, Brandy and Victoria and farewell them properly when they made their final push for the border with Calderon – leaving nothing but an empty room at the motel would not have been a fitting farewell for such loyal travelling companions.

As Purple gingerly approached the front of *Turd's Pizza*, apprehensive about the abomination waiting within, he saw, much to his confusion, three people sitting on the pavement outside. Purple looked at his watch. "We're not open until three," he said as he slid the key into the door.

"We know," said one of the people sitting on the ground. "We just want to be at the front of the queue."

Queue? What the fuck are they talking about? thought Purple to himself as he slipped through the door and locked it behind him. He looked around the interior of the shop, expecting the worst, only to be surprised by its cleanliness. He sniffed the air – no stench of rotten food. Purple had fully expected that he'd need to hit the place with bleach from ceiling to floor. But as he opened the cool room, he saw no indication that it was going to be necessary. In fact, it was... pristine. He walked to the preparation area and examined the trays – full and, at first sniff at least, fresh.

"What the hell is going on here?" he muttered to himself as he pulled out a bag of flour. With the expected cleaning tasks not necessary, the shop appeared to be in a position to resume trading immediately. Purple surmised that getting back into a routine might be good for him, so if everything was ready to go, why not reopen? As Purple began making the dough for that day, he gazed out the window and saw two more people join the three already encamped on the sidewalk. By the time it came to the point of beginning the dough's proving process, the line outside had swelled to at least twelve, with several of them brandishing mobile phones and excitedly taking selfies outside the shop.

With a steady stream of people now arriving and the area outside the shop beginning to take on a carnival-like atmosphere, Purple noticed Sam, the young man he'd taken on board as an assistant, approaching the shop.

"Fuck, I'd forgotten about him," muttered Purple as he made his way to the door. He expected to uneventfully usher Sam into the shop, but instead, Sam halted outside, accosted by the assembled masses and manhandled for selfie after selfie.

Purple opened the door to hear Sam bellowing at the throng. "Fuck off, the lot of you!"

"Whoa, Jesus Christ, what are you doing pal?" asked Purple incredulously.

But much to Purple's surprise, there was no offence taken by the crowd. Instead, there was a cheer and further rounds of selfies, after which a loud "chicken apocalypse!" from Sam drew screams and more applause from the swarm that had gathered on the sidewalk.

Purple grabbed Sam and pushed him into the shop. "What the fuck's going on here?"

"Turd, you're back!" said Sam, beaming with joy and throwing an unreturned hug around Purple. "*Jism!* – where have you been?"

"Long fucking story," replied Purple. "What I want to know is what the hell's going on outside my shop. Who are all these people?"

"They just started coming all the time when I began running the shop. There'll be heaps more of them later."

"Wait... what the fuck did you say? You've been running the shop?"

"Yeah. When you didn't turn up, I thought I'd run the shop for you. I don't know how to use the card machine, so I've been telling people that we only take cash." Sam beckoned Purple to the storeroom. "I've been keeping it in here – *skidmarks!* – because I don't know which bank you use."

Sam retrieved a bag from behind some boxes and opened it. Every cubic inch of air appeared to burst from Purple's lungs as he fixed his eyes on the contents, clutching his chest as he did so. "What's the fuck is that?" he rasped in shock.

"That's part of the takings," replied Sam.

"Wait... *part* of the takings?" said Purple incredulously.

Sam reached behind the boxes. "Yeah, there's a couple more bags back here. I'm glad you're back, because I was starting to run out of room."

Purple could do nothing but stand rooted to the spot, speechless. Due to his extended absence, he was of course completely oblivious to the fact that Sam's Tourette's, coupled with the rise of social media, had created the perfect conditions for Sam and *Turd's Pizza* to become an online sensation.

People were being drawn from all corners of the country to have crude insults hurled at them by the pizza cook and they reveled in the experience, filming thousands of hours of social media content that was subsequently streamed onto devices around the world. *Turd's* had, unexpectedly and by a sheer stroke of luck, become the hottest pizza shop on the planet.

Purple walked out of the storeroom to see that even in the short time he'd been out back, the crowd outside had swelled even further. Glancing toward the road, his jaw dropped, and he turned to Sam. "Is that a fucking… tour bus?"

"Yeah, there's a few of them that come by each day – *gaping rectum!* There'll be a couple more that'll stop once we open. They always buy stuff."

Joe Purple turned away and inhaled deeply. If one were observing closely, a small tear of joy would have been evident as it pooled and tried desperately to escape down his cheek. Purple quickly wiped it away – there would be no overt show of emotion this day. But inside, he was feeling overwhelmed. His pizza shop was a success. Not due to any plan that he'd put in place, that much was true, but a success nonetheless. Henceforth he could transition into an oversight role and just let Sam do whatever the hell it was that he did, at least until the social media consumers moved onto the next big thing. But for now, he was happy – finally, something had gone right for him.

Meanwhile, on the other side of town, Jimmy Eyebrow was preparing to farewell Leo Bishop and Ike McFadden from Coffee Pond, introducing them to the joy of wings from *The Sundancer Inn* before they departed. But as both detectives indulged heartily, there was another matter at hand as neither Bishop nor McFadden could shift their gaze from Eyebrow's forehead and his new razor-sharp eyebrows.

Bishop was the first to broach the subject. "I have to ask, what the hell is going on up there? You look like a fucking Thunderbird."

"I got some lessons while I was in Mexico. They look awesome right?"

Bishop paused while finding the right words. "Well… it's an improvement, we can agree on that."

"The bar was set pretty low initially though," noted McFadden.

Bishop was keen to move on from the subject of makeup lessons. "Got to hand it to you Eyebrow, you know your wings."

Eyebrow turned and pointed to the bar behind him. "Right there is where I got my first job when we moved here."

Bishop dropped a now meatless bone in the basket. "We need to talk about that Eyebrow. This whole idea of you starting a murder for hire business has to stop. It's not happening, you got it?"

"I don't understand what you were thinking," added McFadden. "You can't be receiving the support you're getting and then decide to become a criminal. It doesn't work that way."

"I get it," replied Eyebrow. "I made a promise to myself that I'd walk away if I could just get myself out of that jam I was in. I'm out, I swear."

"Good to hear," said Bishop as he began on another Buffalo sauce-lathered wing. "Now, on that subject. You'll be glad to know that the conspiracy charges have been dropped." Bishop now leant across the table and pointed his half-eaten wing directly at Eyebrow. "But I cannot stress enough that if there's even a hint of trouble from you going forward, all hell will break loose."

"You have my word detective, no problems from now on. How did you manage to get the charges dropped?"

Bishop finished his wing, the twenty-third of his stack, and burped quietly before continuing. "The whole thing hinged on that fucking business card of yours."

"I don't know what possessed you to think it was a good idea," added McFadden. "It's basically a portable smoking gun."

"I know... I know," replied Eyebrow. "So what happened?"

"It was Black and Dekker who came up with the idea," said Bishop. "They convinced the local police that you're an author just doing research for a novel you were writing about some hapless budget hitman. You got the business cards printed as a marketing gimmick."

"Black arranged for one of his colleagues to quickly ghost-write a book for you to complete the façade," added McFadden.

"There's a book?" said Eyebrow with excitement. "Will I get paid for it?"

Bishop had to pause momentarily while he coughed in response to Eyebrow's question. "Paid? As in, actual royalties? For fuck sake Eyebrow, get a grip. Who'd want to buy a fucking book about a budget hitman? It's probably crap anyway."

"So, I'm off the hook?"

"You are very fortunate pal. Just remember going forward though that your intelligence file has suddenly become a whole lot bigger after this last fiasco and the filing cabinet where it's sitting is shaking like a Fukushima power station, just waiting to burst open. You need to be fucking careful from this point on."

"What about Garrison?" asked Eyebrow. "Is he likely to come after me?"

"You've got some pretty heavy cover there Eyebrow. I wouldn't worry about it," replied Bishop.

Eyebrow wasn't entirely satisfied with the reply. "What about the guys he was working with? Who were they?"

"No idea about the guys who tried to hit you in Mexico. We never did work that out. What we *did* discover though is that Garrison was working with a high level former Venezuelan official named Gustavo Torres who was supposed to be the new Vice President if the coup succeeded."

"Is he going to come for me?" pressed Eyebrow.

"Van Pelt was tracking him," said McFadden. "I'd say you're going to be fine there. Turns out he fled as far away as possible to get away from the heat."

"Australia," added Bishop. "Apparently he's started a whole new life and opened up a kebab shop, or something like that."

"Kebabs?" asked Eyebrow, confused. "But he's South American."

"Doesn't matter in Australia," replied Bishop. "Over there, they think anyone with slightly tanned skin is Lebanese."

"That's why they have ten kebab places on every block," added McFadden. "Give it a few weeks and Torres will have been absorbed into the place. He won't be coming back. You've got nothing to worry about there."

Bishop wiped his mouth and stood. "Come on Eyebrow, it's time for us to go. I'll give you a ride back to your place." Bishop turned to McFadden. "Are you OK to get back to the motel and check us out Mac?"

"All good Leo, I'll see you back there," replied McFadden as Bishop and Eyebrow began to make their way to the door.

"Let's go Eyebrow," said Bishop with a smile. "One more stop and then I'm on my way home. Do you have any idea how happy I am today? I might even shake your hand when I drop you off." Bishop had endured much over recent times, so for him to openly acknowledge that he was happy was a reasonably significant event. But there is a difference between long-term joy and fleeting happiness, with the term "fleeting" meaning just that. The problem with fleeting happiness is that it isn't built to last.

CHAPTER 66

Nitimur in Vetitum

Following the short drive to Coffee Pond, Leo Bishop eased the car along the dirt road to Eyebrow's cabin, only to be surprised to find another vehicle already parked outside – a gleaming blue late model Audi sedan. "You expecting visitors Eyebrow?"

"Uhh, no," replied Eyebrow. "Were you sure when you said earlier that no-one's coming after me?"

Bishop gazed warily out of the car window. "As sure as I could be Eyebrow." There had been no requirement for Bishop to be carrying a firearm during his current duties so as such, the two men were somewhat exposed if things were to go south. "We need to be alert here Eyebrow," he said as they began to exit the vehicle. Walking up to the front of the cabin, Bishop peered cautiously through the window where he could see a figure moving slowly inside. He whispered to Eyebrow. "Someone's inside. You sure you weren't expecting anyone?"

"No, no-one," said Eyebrow softly in response.

"Very well," said Bishop. "We need to make an entrance then." He beckoned Eyebrow toward the door where he burst through confidently, with Eyebrow in tow. "You! Stop right where you are!" yelled Bishop with authority.

The man did as directed, held up his hands and turned slowly toward them. A huge smile broke out across Eyebrow's face. "Esteban!" he yelled as he rushed forward to greet his friend. "What are you doing here?"

Gutierrez didn't get a chance to respond before his minder, who had been in the bathroom, rushed into the room having heard Bishop burst through the door moments earlier. Gutierrez immediately threw up a hand. "It's OK, Jakob. Nothing to be concerned about. These are friends."

Bishop shot Gutierrez a look of disdain at that proclamation. "I'm not your friend pal," he snarled. "I should arrest you right here."

Gutierrez slowly edged closer to Bishop. "For what, detective? What have I done?"

"Take your pick. Maybe we start at industrial-level drug trafficking and work our way out from that point. Bringing you in would be a career bonanza for me."

Jakob the bodyguard edged closer to Bishop, but he was waved off by Gutierrez who spoke calmly. "Come now detective. What would that achieve? I'm here to welcome home my friend Jimmy, nothing more. You will find no business being transacted here today."

Bishop was unmoved. "Don't come at me with the line that you're some benevolent businessman. You… you, and everyone like you are parasites. You feed yourself off human misery."

"And you do not?" asked Gutierrez matter-of-factly.

"Jesus Christ, you're not going to give me one of those fucking 'we're not so different' speeches, are you?" snapped Bishop.

"All I am saying is that you get satisfaction from your job, yes? You feel fulfilled as a homicide detective?"

"Of course I do, especially when I catch the pricks who murder people."

Gutierrez moved closer to Bishop as he spoke. "Yet in order for that to happen… for you to have personal fulfillment… someone must die first. An innocent family somewhere must have their whole world destroyed, for you to have a job to do. All that pain, just so you can have some meaning to your daily existence. Tell me, would you get as much satisfaction writing parking tickets every day? An entirely victimless crime?" Bishop remained silent, prompting Gutierrez to continue. "I thought as much."

Bishop finally interjected. "The difference is Gutierrez, I don't create the mess. People like you do. I just clean it up. You pour your drugs onto the street and everyone else suffers. It's unconscionable."

Gutierrez shook his head. "You don't understand the human condition detective. Human beings, by our nature, will always seek out something to numb the reality of our tragic lives. For some it's caffeine, others alcohol…"

"Cocaine?" interrupted Bishop, smugly.

"Indeed, detective Bishop. Cocaine. Ban something, and people will still seek it out." Gutierrez paced, assuming the air of a lecturer. "Consider the terrible drugs that have been flooding the streets of late. You have seen the consequences, I am sure. The complete and utter waste of human life. These modern drugs are an abomination. They are not the drug of a civilized society. May I ask detective, what would you rather see on the street? Cocaine, or the horrors that are befalling the cities right now?"

"I'd like to see none of the above," snapped Bishop.

"But that's where you don't understand," countered Gutierrez. "People will always desire the forbidden – it has been in our nature since Eve plucked the apple from the tree. That desire, that need, it will always be there, whether you like it or not. I provide a service for those who seek it. If I, and my associates, do not provide the people what they desire, they will still seek it, but the alternatives will instead lead them down a dark path, where terrible deeds are perpetrated." Gutierrez now edged to within mere feet of Bishop's face and lowered his voice. "The one who sits in the jail cell… the one you watch with vengeance in your eyes. It was not cocaine in his body that night, was it."

Bishop glared at Gutierrez with a look that could melt steel. "Don't you fucking dare." Bishop fought to find the right words to continue, failing to do so and instead simply waving his finger at Gutierrez before offering a parting comment. "You're a piece of shit to even go there." Bishop then turned to Eyebrow and waved an open hand toward Gutierrez. "See Eyebrow, it's *this* that gives me no confidence that you won't fuck up again. You assure me that you've reformed, yet this is the company you keep."

"I'm sorry, but Esteban's been good to me," replied Eyebrow.

Bishop stormed to the door and offered a farewell of the most fleeting kind, devoid of any warmth. "Our business is done Eyebrow." It was not the parting that Eyebrow had envisaged and as Bishop slammed the door behind him, Eyebrow felt a sense of emptiness. He had developed a feeling in recent times that he and Bishop were in some ways becoming closer, but this episode seemed to have driven a significant wedge back between them.

"Jimmy, come and sit down," said Gutierrez, breaking the silence. "We have some things to discuss."

"What was that about?" asked Eyebrow.

Gutierrez patted the cushion on the lounge. "Nothing for you to worry about Jimmy. First things first, it's wonderful to see you and your friend back home safe. You did a remarkable job under great stress."

"Well, you helped out a lot Esteban. We would've ended up in Colombia otherwise."

"Yes, on that subject Jimmy. Mister Santiago wishes for me to pass on the sincerest of appreciation for your efforts, even though it was not the result that he and Mister Ortiz were hoping for. They both understand that you tried your best, and Mister Ortiz wishes to apologise for any distress that he may have caused you. He was… unaware at the time of the complexities of the matter and there were some significant miscommunications. He knows that now."

"That's good to know," said Eyebrow. "We got lucky that Yuri turned up at Coronado to help fight off his men. If he didn't, then we were probably finished."

Gutierrez now placed a gentle hand on Eyebrow's leg. "Which brings me to my most important business today Jimmy. Your bravery on this journey did not go unnoticed. The stories of your efforts not only protecting my friend Rudy, but also at Coronado protecting my dear mother travelled fast. There is no question that she owes you her life, and you put your own on the line to protect her." Gutierrez reached for Eyebrow's hand and grasped it firmly. "I am forever indebted to you Jimmy Eyebrow. From this day forward, whatever you need from me, you shall have."

"I didn't even think Esteban. It wasn't bravery, it was just… I don't know… acting on impulse."

"You doubt yourself Jimmy, but what you did when faced with that split-second decision is the mark of a true hero. You didn't think – you *did*. It will not be forgotten. The name Jimmy Eyebrow has been written into the annals of Coronado for all time." Gutierrez patted Eyebrow's thigh and stood. "It is time for me to go now Jimmy."

"You can't stay for a drink?" asked Eyebrow.

Gutierrez smiled. "I'm afraid not Jimmy. I must be moving on. Plus, you never know, detective Bishop may have a change of heart and decide to come back for me, with reinforcements this time." Gutierrez paused momentarily before continuing. "You should prepare yourself Jimmy. I believe that one day, detective Bishop may come to you seeking help."

"I'd never roll over on you Esteban, I hope you know that."

Gutierrez placed a hand on Eyebrow's arm. "I know that Jimmy. That is not what I meant though." Gutierrez let his words hang in the air for a few moments. "Anyway, I must be going. Please pass on my regards to Señor Purple when you next see him."

"He'd be very appreciative of your help Esteban," said Eyebrow. "I'll be sure to let him know that you were here." Eyebrow walked Gutierrez to the door where the two shook hands heartily. "Thank you Esteban, your friendship means a lot to me."

"Until next time Jimmy," said Gutierrez as he made his way to the car where Jakob was holding the door open for him. A final wave, and Esteban Gutierrez was gone once more. Whether they would cross paths again, Eyebrow did not know. But it was comforting to know that whatever path Eyebrow might find himself on in the future, he had Gutierrez firmly in his corner.

For now though, it was time to reintegrate into a normal lifestyle, or at least try to. Eyebrow of course had never been what one would term a conventional member of society, so his future still remained significantly blurred before him – there was little chance that he would be seeking a career as a librarian or a data analyst for example. One thing he did know though was that his cache of money was gone, having blown it all on extricating he and Joe Purple from the situation in Mexico.

Almost all of it anyway – he'd had enough squirreled away in a wallet at home to purchase a new phone, which now buzzed in his pocket. It was a message from a number that appeared to originate in London.

Good afternoon, Mr. St. Claire. Mr. Spaulding would like you to install the secure communications application on your phone, pending an incoming call.

Even now, as he sat in his own loungeroom, it appeared that Spaulding may have had one final surprise in the chamber for Eyebrow.

CHAPTER 67

Shadows

With Joe Purple's assistance, Eyebrow had successfully installed and configured the secure communications application on his phone and sent a message to Spaulding advising him of such. Now the two of them sat on Eyebrow's sofa awaiting Spaulding's return call, that didn't come until forty-five minutes later.

"Hello?" said Eyebrow as he answered.

"St. Claire, great to hear that you're alive!" said Spaulding from the other end. "Is your associate Mister Ferguson with you?"

"Yes, he's here."

"Good, put me on speaker please. What I have is probably of interest to you both."

Eyebrow fumbled with the phone momentarily before replying. "OK, you're on speaker."

How are you both? Happy to be home?

"Very happy," replied Eyebrow.

"Absolutely," added Purple.

OK, listen up please. I need you to grab a pen and paper. Let me know when you've got it ready.

Purple stood and moved toward the kitchen. "Where?" he asked Eyebrow as he searched.

"Top drawer there probably," replied Eyebrow.

Purple rummaged for a few moments before locating both items requested by Spaulding. "Got 'em," he said as he sat back down.

Splendid. Now I want you to copy the following down and read it back to me. Spaulding proceeded to recite a nonsensical string of characters that Eyebrow soon recognized.

"It's another key," he whispered to Purple, who was still furiously writing.

Purple repeated the two sequences he had been given back to Spaulding, who in turn confirmed them as correct. Purple then added an observation. "Listen pal, we think we know what this is, and if you think that we're going to be jetting off on another fucking expedition for lost money, I can tell you, it ain't happening."

I assure you, I'm doing nothing of the sort Mister Ferguson. This is a small gift for Mister St. Claire. Or should I say… Jimmy Eyebrow.

Eyebrow looked at Purple wide-eyed. "Umm, how did you work that out?" asked Eyebrow.

You have to understand my field of work Eyebrow. Part of what I do is look for shadows.

"Shadows?" asked Eyebrow curiously.

People get erased all the time. Their identities at least. It happens every day somewhere. But you can never really fully erase someone. Their old life may be gone, but they leave shadows behind. Shadows in the form of aliases when a Red Notice is issued for example. Sometimes that shadow is faint, but it's there.

"Then you know that this is Joe too?" asked Eyebrow.

I do. Pleased to meet you, Joe Purple.

"Likewise," replied Purple. "So, what's this gift?"

As you've worked out already, it's a crypto account. Except this one is yours. If you log into it, you might find a little surprise in there.

"Where did the money come from?" asked Eyebrow.

Does it matter?

Purple's brain was ticking over as he assessed the development. "Wait a minute. When we were in the Cayman Islands and you told Eyebrow that the crypto account we were trying to access was empty, did you mean that it was empty when you found it? Or empty by the time you'd spoken to Eyebrow?"

There was a pause from the other end. *I think you have your answer Mister Purple. And I have my payment for services rendered.*

"Wait, how do I get into this thing?" asked Eyebrow.

That, my friend, is not my hay to bale. You've proven yourself to be very resourceful Jimmy Eyebrow. I'm sure you'll work it out. It's over to you now. I'll be sure to look you up if I'm in town for another poker tournament. We must do it again some time.

"Absolutely," replied Eyebrow. "Thank you for all your help. We couldn't have done any of what we did without you."

A pleasure, said Spaulding, after which the call was over, and Eyebrow and Purple sat in silence, pondering their next step.

"What the fuck do we do with this Eyebrow?" asked Purple.

Eyebrow was doing what Spaulding had encouraged him to do – work it out. "I think I know what we need to do Joe."

***

The following day, Eyebrow and Purple had come full circle as they stood outside *Zander's* in Cedar Falls. "I cannot fucking believe that we're back here Eyebrow," said Purple. "If I'm being honest, I'm a bit fucking nervous. Last time, things didn't work out that well."

"Different time now Joe," replied Eyebrow without a care in the world. "We're not on any job… this is all about us." As they walked inside, Eyebrow spotted the three young men who had given them their original lesson in crypto accounts – Jed, Ryan and Ethan. "Hey guys," said Eyebrow with a smile. Eyebrow had called *Zander's* the previous day to organize a meeting with the three and now, as they sat together in a booth, Purple enquired as to the state of pizzas in the time since they'd left.

"Better actually," replied Ryan. "He's got the crust thing happening now."

"And they come out of the oven faster," added Ethan.

Purple turned towards the counter. "Hey Alex! Can we get a couple of Margheritas over here?"

"It's Alixzander, for God's sake," came the unamused reply.

"No, no it's not. Why can't you just be normal?" said Purple as he turned back to the booth crew. "We need your help on something."

"What's that?" asked Ryan.

Eyebrow slid the piece of paper with the crypto keys across the table. "We've got a crypto account, but we don't know how to access it."

Ryan looked at the paper. "You have both keys for this one. Who does it belong to?"

"It's mine," replied Eyebrow. "I've just never used a crypto account before."

All three looked skeptical. "He's not bullshitting this time," said Purple. "This is actually his. But when it comes to computers, he's like one of those chimpanzees trying to put shapes through the holes."

"Let's have a look," said Ryan as he opened an application and typed in the private key. After a few seconds, a look of shock came across the faces of Jed, Ryan and Ethan. "Holy shit," muttered Ryan.

"This is really yours?" asked Ethan, looking at Eyebrow.

"Yeah, it's mine," replied Eyebrow. "How much is in there?"

"You genuinely don't know?" asked Jed.

"Not a clue," replied Eyebrow. "If there's money in there, it'll come in handy, because I'm broke."

Ryan inhaled deeply and looked directly at Eyebrow. "That's not going to be a problem you'll have again." He flipped the screen around for Eyebrow and Purple to view.

"HOLY FUCKING SHIT!" screamed Purple. "Surely there's a fucking mistake there. That can't be right."

"There's no mistake," replied Ethan.

Eyebrow was catatonic, the colour drained from his face. Purple clicked his fingers toward him. "Eyebrow! Snap out of it." There was no movement. "Eyebrow!" he yelled again, before slapping him forcefully across the back of the head. "Get back here with us."

Eyebrow shook his head, blinked several times and turned to Purple. "This can't be real Joe, can it?"

"I'd say that the original account had a shit ton of money in there Eyebrow. Spaulding's probably cleaned it out and then kicked your cut over to you. That's what this looks like."

"How can I ever spend that much Joe?"

"I don't know Eyebrow. But you can have fun trying."

Eyebrow rubbed his chin in thought. "I'm going to need someone to manage this for me. I wouldn't know the first thing about how to move this around." Eyebrow looked at Jed, Ryan and Ethan. "Could you do it for me?"

"Ahh, hold up there Eyebrow," said Purple. "Can I see you for a moment?" Purple led Eyebrow away from the booth, out of earshot. "What the fuck are you doing? You don't even know these pricks."

"I know, but I don't know what I'm doing Joe. These guys obviously do."

"And what if they steal the whole lot? You see that shit on the news all the time – people embezzling massive sums of money."

Eyebrow considered Purple's words of caution. He called towards the booth. "Hey, if I get you guys to manage my account, you won't steal the whole lot, will you?" All three instantly responded in the negative and Eyebrow turned back toward Purple. "See Joe. They won't steal it."

"Fuck me Eyebrow," said Purple as he rubbed his eyes. "Every time I see a glimmer of hope, you go and do something fucking stupid like this." Purple threw his hands up. "You do what you want to Eyebrow, but I'm not responsible if everything goes to shit."

Eyebrow returned to the booth and spoke with the three men. "Will you manage this for me?"

"Uhh, sure... I guess," replied Ryan. "What do you want us to do?"

"Just send me money any time that I need it. I'll call you, and you send it to me. That's it." He paused for a moment. "Oh, and keep it safe."

"That's it?" asked Ryan. "So, we're like... your money men?"

"That's it," said Eyebrow. "How much do I pay you to do this?"

The three looked at each other. "No idea," replied Ryan. "We've never done something like this before."

Eyebrow considered the hastily developed employment agreement currently being negotiated. "Pay yourselves what you think is fair. I trust you." Off to the side, Joe Purple closed his eyes and shook his head but otherwise remained mute.

In a short space of time, Jimmy Eyebrow had banked a life debt from a powerful Latin American drug lord, solidified his relationship with a former MI6 agent, secured his financial future for multiple lifetimes, and employed three money men. Joe Purple's accomplishments by comparison were relatively insignificant – he had only become the pizza king of the United States. There was only one more administrative matter to come, and that was awaiting both men back at Coffee Pond.

Later that evening, Eyebrow and Purple were sitting with Harry Black in Purple's cabin – his partner Christian Dekker having departed the previous day. "Well, we're back where we started gentlemen," he said as he shuffled two large envelopes in his hands. "We've managed to reprint all your documentation that was destroyed in Venezuela." He paused, as if he wanted to avoid what was coming next, a mannerism that wasn't lost on Purple.

"What's going on Harry?" he asked. "Is there something you need to tell us?"

Black looked uncomfortable as he began sliding his finger nervously along the edge of one of the envelopes. "Well... yes there is. As you'd understand, these exercises are complex. And, as you'd remember Marcus, I previously told you that there's no do-overs."

"I do remember that you prick," replied Purple gruffly. "So, what's the issue here?"

"Well... there was a mix-up with the government printer that oversees these documents. It seems..." Black paused briefly before continuing. "It seems as though the files got swapped during the process." He handed Purple his envelope, which he swiftly tore open.

Purple leapt to his feet. "YES!" he screamed at the top of his lungs. He flipped the passport around to show Eyebrow. Emblazoned next to Purple's photo was the name Max Von Steel. "Oh, fuck yes! Tell me that you're not messing with me Harry. Tell me this isn't some elaborate prank."

"I'm not messing with you Marcus," replied Black. "I have no idea how it happened, but... it did."

Eyebrow tore open his envelope and, as expected, found that he was now Turd Ferguson. "That's OK Joe, I don't mind."

"Oh hell yes!" shouted Purple as he danced with glee. "Ever since we got back, I'm finally getting shit go my way. Look at this Eyebrow!" He triumphantly brandished his new passport aloft once more. "Finally, some justice! Yes, yes, YES! Now *I'm* Max Von Steel! This is how it was always supposed to be."

Purple paced the room in triumph. "You see this shit Eyebrow? Finally, things are working out for me. This is the Universe's way of rewarding me for everything I've had to endure with you." He held the passport high above his head one more time, as if he'd just won the World Cup. He bellowed at the top of his lungs. "I am Max Von Steel!"

EPILOGUE

A cigar smoldered in the poolside ashtray of a rented villa in Mexico. The owner of the cigar, Angel Rodriguez was, up until recently at least, a senior officer in the Venezuelan army but now carried the word "disgraced" alongside his former title. Rodriguez had been the principal plotter behind what was now the spectacular failure that was the Venezuelan military coup attempt.

Everything had been planned diligently, and he had worked tirelessly for over a year to secure in-principle support from influential pockets of the broader Venezuelan population. The only impediment was the lack of funds to support a protracted campaign, and it was there where Secretary of State Myles Garrison became his primary benefactor. Naturally there would be a quid pro quo of significant proportions upon ascending to power, but Rodriguez was willing to cross that bridge when he came to it. Such was the necessity for Garrison's sponsorship that the two made an almost inconceivable alliance through an intermediary – Gustavo Torres.

Of course, any United States participation in the coup, even the slightest fingerprint, had the potential to bring the whole delicately balanced plan crashing down. The United States was less than respected in that part of the world, having left the entire region a smoking ruin on more than one occasion in the past. For the coup to succeed, the involvement of the United States, known only to Garrison, Rodriguez and Torres at the time, had to remain cloaked.

Rodriguez came from an established military family and was a career soldier, eventually rising to a rank where he could infiltrate the halls of power and initiate the coup that had, unfortunately for him, just been quashed. While his father had shunned a military career, Rodriguez's grandfather had been a highly feared general in his time, maintaining order in the outer regions of the country with skill, cunning, and more than a little Machiavellian authority.

Rodriguez aspired to be as feared as his late grandfather, and this public humiliation, especially after such diligent planning, was something that he vowed to avenge, even if it cost him his last breath. The coup had experienced a cataclysmic and irretrievable shift in public sentiment when Charles de Klerk's photograph of the mercenary La Tormenta was beamed around the world and with the perception of United States involvement gaining more traction by the day, the collapse of the coup became inevitable.

Rodriguez's rage was focused on the mysterious La Tormenta, but he had little intelligence to go on up to that point. However, on this day, one of his underlings accompanied a man to where Rodriguez sat beside the pool – a man who carried with him something of interest. From his satchel he retrieved two charred documents that Rodriguez identified instantly as United States passports. The fire at Rudy Ventura's house had all but destroyed the documents, but among a handful of pages, the document numbers were still visible. Rodriguez flipped what was left of the pages between his fingers.

"These numbers, they are sequential," he said to his minion. "The odds of finding two random passports with consecutive numbers is beyond measure. There is only one explanation for this – they were issued together. The owners of these passports were United States government assets, I'm certain of it."

"What do you want me to do sir?" asked his underling.

Rodriguez stood and walked a short distance before turning – a giant United States flag fluttering in the distance behind him, such was the proximity of the villa to the border. He examined the personal details pages of each passport. One was completely destroyed by fire and useless. The other had the photograph melted off, but a name could still be made out.

Rodriguez waved the passport angrily. "*This* man – I want him located, and I want him to pay for what he has done." Rodriguez took another puff of his cigar before reinforcing his point.

"Find Max Von Steel and bring him to me."

FROM LOU POWERS

Well, it looks like you pushed through to the end of the third Jimmy Eyebrow book. If this is in fact your third trip on Eyebrow's bullet train of chaos and idiocy, then I have to think that I've done something right. So, if that's the case, and you enjoyed *The Full Package*, please do Big Lou a favour and tell someone about it.

As always, it would be great to hear about your experience with Jimmy Eyebrow so please, leave a review where you purchased the book, or jump onto the Jimmy Eyebrow website and drop me a note – I'd love to hear from you.

Jimmy Eyebrow will return again soon with an all new adventure. In the meantime, if you'd like to stay up to date with all the news from Eyebrow's world, swing by the website and subscribe to The World of Jimmy Eyebrow newsletter.

Thank you again for your support of Jimmy Eyebrow – Budget Hitman.

Big Lou.

jimmyeyebrow.com

ABOUT THE AUTHOR

Ex soldier, sports coach, former IT professional, previously unemployed bum and one-time pizza delivery driver who once fell agonizingly short of the one-night delivery record at the shop that served as inspiration for one of the settings in this book, Lou Powers weaves aspects of his entire life into his stories, often drawing on real-life experiences for inspiration.

In full understanding that his works are as likely to win a literary award as he is of being appointed the Archbishop of Canterbury, he instead hopes simply that you get enjoyment out of his stories and read them through the same ridiculous lens with which they were written.

www.ingramcontent.com/pod-product-compliance
Lightning Source LLC
Chambersburg PA
CBHW031422270326
41930CB00007B/540